To the Corner of the Province

To the Corner of the Province:

The 1780 Ugarte-Rocha Sonoran Reconnaissance and Implications for Environmental and Cultural Change

Deni J. Seymour
and
Oscar Rodríguez

The University of Utah Press
Salt Lake City

The Defiance House Man colophon is a registered trademark of The University of Utah Press. It is based on a four-foot-tall Ancient Puebloan pictograph (late PIII) near Glen Canyon, Utah.

LIBRARY OF CONGRESS CATALOGING IN PUBLICATION DATA

Names: Seymour, Deni J., author. | Rodriguez, Oscar (Oscar S.), author. | Ugarte y Loyola, Jacobo, -1798, author.
Title: To the corner of the province : the 1780 Ugarte-Rocha Sonoran reconnaissance and implications for environmental and cultural change / Deni J. Seymour and Oscar Rodriguez.
Description: Salt Lake City : University of Utah Press, [2018] | Includes bibliographical references and index. | Contains appendix with transcriptions of original Spanish documents, as well as annotated, English translations of those documents. All extended discussion of the documents is in English. |
Identifiers: LCCN 2018005492 (print) | LCCN 2018007083 (ebook) | ISBN 9781607816218 () | ISBN 9781607816201 (cloth)
Subjects: LCSH: New Spain—Discovery and exploration—18th century—Sources. | New Spain—Social life and customs—18th century—Sources. | Sonora (Mexico : State)—Discovery and exploration—Sources. | Sonora (Mexico : State)—Social life and customs—Sources. | Indians of North America—Mexico—Sonora (State)—18th century—Sources. | Apache Indians—Mexico—Sonora (State)—History—18th century—Sources. | Fortification—New Spain—History—18th century—Sources.
Classification: LCC F1231 (ebook) | LCC F1231 .S49 2018 (print) | DDC 972/.02—dc23
LC record available at https://lccn.loc.gov/2018005492

Printed and bound in the United States of America.

This book and the years of research that went into it
is dedicated to:

The late Dr. Mark Edward Harlan,
who honored his wife and her work in so many ways,
but especially in support, insights, and critical assessment.
Mark had an astounding mind for historical fact
and analytical process. He had a passion for knowledge
and was consumed by curiosity until his end.

The late Launa Barbara Patton Seymour
whose abiding interest in history, historical landscapes,
and all things historical inspired passion in others.
This book would have been her delight.

Contents

Figures

Acknowledgments

As in any completed endeavor there are many people to recognize. Among these is the late Norm "Mick" Meader, whose love for and knowledge of the San Pedro River brought us to intimate crossings, remote high places, and private stretches of the river where we both learned about its secrets. Phil Halpenny graciously shared knowledge of and field time in the Sonoita and Santa Cruz Valleys and provided the color Rocha map used in this book. David Tenario, Tony Burrell, Felicia Nunez, and many others in the Wa:k O'odham community ardently shared knowledge and together we have been uncovering the O'odham past, ethnographically, archaeologically, linguistically, and ethnohistorically; some of this knowledge has contributed to this book, including some of the place name translations. Jacob Daukei of Mescalero and Willem de Reuse provided valuable input into some of the Chiricahua Apachean names for landscape features. David Snow was consulted on various eighteenth-century Spanish word usages and engaged in the argument for their variations. Deni Seymour wrote the text for the book and transcribed and translated the documents, while Oscar Rodríguez reviewed the translations. Appreciation is also extended to the many volunteers, too many to name, who have assisted with this research through the years. Yet among these there are a few who stand out for their persistence: Chris Sugnet, Mary Dahl, and Nancy Daunton. Jean Gilberto provided useful guidance in locating the libraries in which the original Gerónimo de la Rocha y Figueroa journal and maps were located. A special thanks to Diana Nash of Circle Z Ranch, Andy Smallhouse, Brent Musslewhite and the others at BHP, and the many other private landowners, managers, and cowboys who allowed access.

CHAPTER 1

The 1780 Ugarte-Rocha Reconnaissance for the New Presidial Line

There is something enchanting about a document, artifact, or place that transports one back in time, to a bygone era that differed so substantially from our own. Through a variety of means we can reach back a century or more, interfacing with the past in a way that allows us to engage with the actors, understand their realities, and grasp elements of the timelessness of the common human experience. Part of the attraction of history and archaeology is that these areas of study allow us to establish this interface in as genuine and authentic a way as possible, using the written word and material culture as props in a theater of conceptual time travel. We cannot be there, but we can nonetheless experience their world through snippets that have survived the ages. We understand that each new data point—whether it is a newly translated document or an unexpected find on a desert hilltop—has the potential to touch the soul and bring an entirely different perspective to light.

So it is with documents resulting from a 1780 reconnaissance of the northwestern frontier of New Spain. This three-month tour of the tattered edges of the Spanish empire is embedded deeply in the events of the day. The often richly detailed accounts provide insights into the region at a critical point in military, colonial, and indigenous histories. The frontier defenses were failing, overrun at will by marauding enemies, and administrators and principals in old and New Spain, and especially in Sonora, were seeking solutions. The king, Carlos III,[1] set priorities that were embedded in international politics, and that were often neglectful of, if not at odds with, policies that would have been most effective on the Sonoran frontier (Figure 1.1). Commandant-General Teodoro de Croix and those beneath him, Military Governor Don Jacobo de Ugarte y Loyola and Lieutenant of the Infantry and Engineer of the Royal Armies Don Gerónimo de la Rocha y Figueroa, were worthy of the task and steadfastly willing to fulfill their duties (Figures 1.2 and 1.3). The men on the front lines, the common soldiers and settlers, however, were worn ragged, starved, wounded, fearful, and beaten. Even the consideration of a monthly ten pesos per family given to the settlers to colonize the latest settlement beyond the frontier (Moorhead 1968:58; Thomas 1941: 220) was, in hindsight, insufficient to equal the threats they faced.

In April 1780 Ugarte and Rocha embarked on a 92-day journey through the northern frontier of Sonora, which was documented with Chief Engineer Rocha's 110-day journal (Figure 1.4).[2] Rocha's words provide an in-depth environmental and cultural view of this region, which now includes the modern state of Sonora and southern Arizona. This book presents his diary and supporting documents, which resulted from this 1780 reconnaissance, along with summaries of the trip by both Ugarte and Rocha. This book, however, is more than a simple transcription, translation, and annotation of these documents. The senior author has visited and is familiar with

FIGURE 1.1. King Carlos III, King of Spain and the Spanish Indies at the time of this reconnaissance. Portrait by Anton Raphael Mengs.

FIGURE 1.2. Commandant-General Teodoro de Croix.

FIGURE 1.3. Military Governor Don Jacobo de Ugarte y Loyola.

many of the places and routes discussed, and we share this information from over thirty years of colonial period research in this specific region, which is intended to add depth to, and increase the value of, these historical documents.

Ugarte, Rocha, and their troops[3] undertook this three-month journey in the spring and summer of 1780. This trip brought them from Arizpe in modern-day Sonora to the confluence of the San Pedro and Gila (HEE-lah) Rivers in central Arizona and back (Figures 1.5 and 1.6). They went to the corner of the province (*se halla en un rincón de la Provincia*), as Ugarte referred to Tucson, and from there they looked toward what they perceived as a vast wilderness that separated them from the new and distant settlements in the Californias. They also anticipated the value of proposed settlements in the Yuma area.

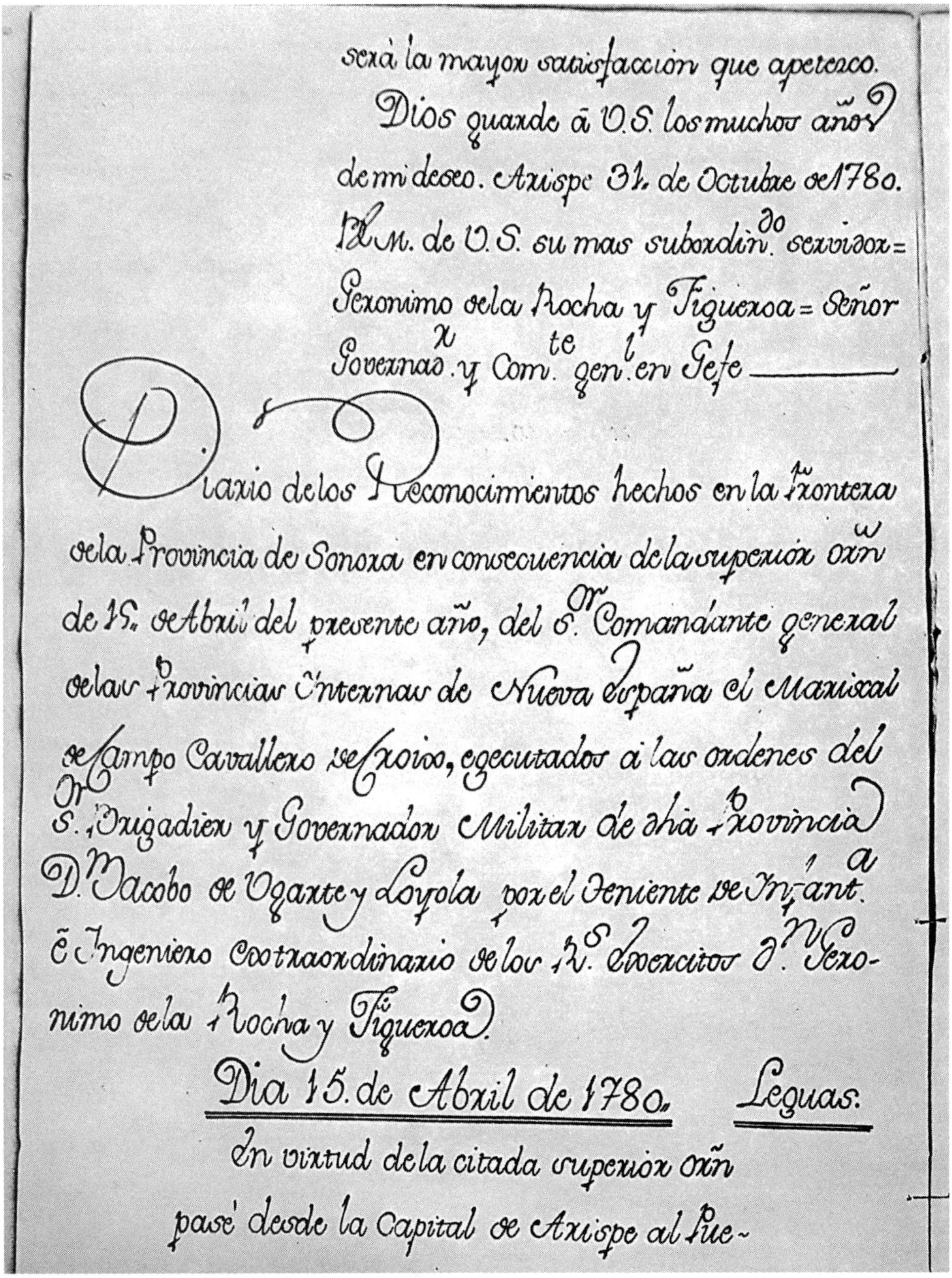
será la mayor satisfacción que apetezco.
Dios guarde á V.S. los muchos años
de mi deseo. Arispe 31. de Octubre de 1780.
B.L.M. de V.S. su mas subordin.do servidor=
Geronimo de la Rocha y Figueroa= Señor
Governad.r y Com.te gen.l en Gefe
Diario de los Reconocimientos hechos en la Frontera
de la Provincia de Sonora en consecuencia de la superior ord.n
de 15. de Abril del presente año, del S.or Comandante general
de las Provincias Internas de Nueva España el Mariscal
de Campo Cavallero de Croix, egecutados á las ordenes del
S.or Brigadier y Governador Militar de dha Provincia
D. Jacobo de Ugarte y Loyola por el Teniente de Infant.a
é Ingeniero Extraordinario de los R.s Exercitos D.n Gero-
nimo de la Rocha y Figueroa.
Dia 15. de Abril de 1780. Leguas.
En virtud de la citada superior ord.n
pasé desde la Capital de Arispe al Pue-

FIGURE 1.4. The opening page of the original manuscript of Chief Engineer Rocha's journal.

FIGURE 1.5. The area covered by this reconnaissance and discussed in this journal, including what is now northern Sonora, Mexico, and southern Arizona in the United States.

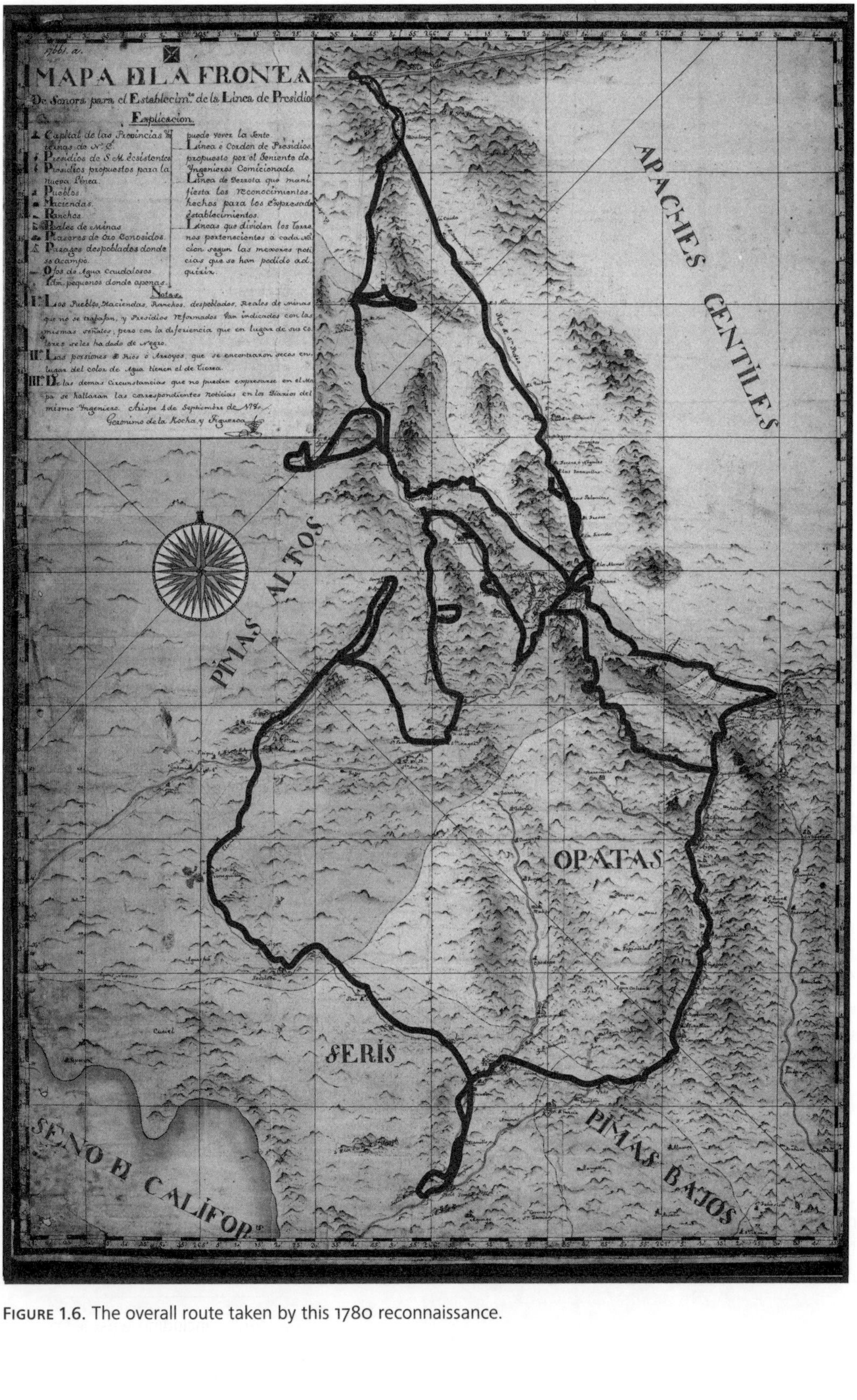

FIGURE 1.6. The overall route taken by this 1780 reconnaissance.

At the time, this region they traversed was known as Sonora and was referred to as the *Provincias Internas del Norte* ("Interior Provinces of the North") or simply the *frontera* ("frontier" or "border"). Ugarte and Rocha were charged with examining proposed changes to the line of presidios that guarded the northern edge of the Interior Provinces and with evaluating the current and proposed placements of presidios. Presidios of the Interior Provinces, those at the ragged, rugged edge of the Apache frontier, were most often garrisoned fortifications (Moorhead 1975: xiii). This meant the investment of considerable treasure in seeking suitable places for their positions, in their construction and maintenance, in their removal, and their reinstatement and removal once again. This, of course, is not to mention the blood and sweat involved in their defense. Yet, from a larger perspective, investment in this frontier region was minimal relative to the more permanent and substantial fortified presidios to the south and in Europe, both because of materials used and effort invested, and because they were frequently moved, and so often were not completed (Moorhead 1975:161–177, passim; Williams 1992:35).

Here in the north, adobe rather than stone was used to construct the walls, and many outside perimeter walls were either not part of the original defensive plan or, later, were not completed and so were not in compliance with the 1772 regulation. Nonetheless, despite its architecturally antiquated features and often incomplete construction, the frontier presidio was secure enough against the types of forces encountered (Moorhead 1975:177). The men who defended the frontier, either in fortified presidios or as militia, were required to sustain themselves and their families by tending crops and herding livestock, a requirement necessitated by long, dangerous, and unreliable supply lines. Moreover, this was still a relatively unknown land, which meant that administrators felt the need to obtain new and useful information from this border region to guide the costly and sometimes deadly consequences of their decisions. Decisions made on high involved considerable risk by those who garrisoned these presidios and those who settled nearby, facts that were not lost on, though sometimes ignored by, those in positions powerful enough to have some influence. Ugarte and Rocha were tasked with gathering this information and their travels led them along the major rivers and to the key pueblos, missions, and presidios in the area. Many of these known places they visited had been recently abandoned, owing to intensive Apache depredations. Others were hanging on, but few other than Tucson were thriving. Tucson was in many ways positioned too far north to aid in the protective efforts of the line, but its success and the benefit of its placement in conveying goods and communicating with the Californias could not be denied.

In 1780, Governor Ugarte and Lieutenant Rocha and their men were directed to carry out this exploratory campaign under orders from Teodoro de Croix, commandant-general of the *comandancia general* of the Interior Provinces of New Spain. These orders are included, translated, and transcribed in the following pages (Chapter 2 and Appendix), as are the summary reports by Ugarte and Rocha (Chapter 3). Most important in this series is a map (Figure 1.7; also see Chapter 4) and the journal (Chapter 5) prepared by Rocha (Rocha 1780a, 1780b). The documents are annotated throughout, while the most important content is discussed and placed in context in individual chapters.

In his journal Rocha described the places he encountered, some in considerable detail, consistent with his orders (Chapters 2 and 5). In the process Ugarte and Rocha were evaluating the suitability for settlement and for the new placement of a presidio at the junction of the San Pedro and Gila Rivers, a placement Adjutant Inspector Don Antonio Bonilla had suggested in 1774. Of a presidio at the junction of the San Pedro and Gila Rivers, Bonilla had surmised that

> this is the real frontier which we must cover in Sonora to defend it from all its enemies. Thus it supposes that there is established a new presidio at the junction of the Colorado and Gila to sustain the missions of the heathen who may wish to be reduced, and to

open communication with those of Monterey. I propose that another presidio be placed at the junction of the rivers of San Pedro and Gila, as this spot, being the beginning of the Apache frontier, will impede the entrance of these Indians (Thomas 1941:173).

This presidio and one at Yuma would have been manned by the transfer of the garrisons of Horcasitas and Buenavista, although this transfer never occurred owing to an ill-timed Seri (Comcaac (phonemically /kom'ka:k/, phonetically [koŋ'ka:k]) uprising (Moorhead 1968:49, 54, 55, 57; Thomas 1941:52). The expected establishment of the Yuma (Colorado and Gila area) settlements later in the same year (and then their destruction in the following July [1781]), in the absence of the sustaining troops, meant that the logic of this northern alignment would have to be reconsidered.

At the end of the same year at Bonilla's suggestion (1774) and after reconnoitering the frontier, Sonoran governor Colonel Don Francisco Crespo again promoted this notion of a presidio at the San Pedro–Gila junction, stating,

> I believe that attention should be directed from the said junction to San Bernardino.... Accordingly, locating the three presidios in San Bernardino, or Coaguionoc, Santa Cruz, and the junction of the rivers, or their neighborhoods, this line will be protected as is provided for in the royal regulations (Thomas 1940:175).

Crespo's reasons for this are founded on an inaccurate understanding of Apache distributions in general and travel routes relative to water sources and landscape features (see Chapter 8), and in his conclusion he even qualified his recommendations by stating that they should be carried out "assuming this is true" (e.g., "accordingly" and "supposing this"). In the meantime, the Seri uprising of 1777 meant that it was not advisable to move presidios that guarded the Seri area, with Anza warning in 1779 that they were still restless and could easily align themselves with the Gileño Apache from the north (Thomas 1941:47).

Nonetheless, had this string of presidios been established, keeping Santa Cruz and San Bernardino in the alignment, their efforts at a cordon might have been more successful, for as Crespo noted, in all, the line would not have exceeded 70 or 80 leagues guarded by three presidios, and "all passable without the necessity of crossing any sierra" (Thomas 1941:175; Figures 1.8 and 1.9). Yet many more troops and a greater number of fortified settlements would have been required to make this plan a success, issues not lost on Croix and his staff. But by the time of this 1780 Ugarte-Rocha reconnaissance, Spain had gone to war with England (1779–1783; Moorhead 1968:57–58, 120–123, 1975: 84–85; Thomas 1941:43–44), so funds were short and focus was elsewhere. Good administrators were looking for savings while effective ones were looking for innovative ways to shift use of the money at hand and to create new sources to meet pressing needs. Earlier the same year Santa Cruz Presidio had failed, its garrison moved back south to Las Nutrias, and the previous year San Bernardino's garrison had also been pulled back to Fronteras (Thomas 1941:226). In an effort to salvage this concept of a leading edge of presidios to guard the route to California and settlements to the south of the line, the notion of a presidio at the San Pedro–Gila junction was again raised and addressed in 1780, but by then the beleaguered and terrorized Santa Cruz troops were stark evidence of the ruthlessness of the northern frontier and the grave miscalculation of extending the line too far north with too great a distance between presidios and too few men to guard it. The Seri uprising tethered soldiers to the interior, rather than allowing these troops to redeploy to the north, and the ultimate destruction of the Yuma settlements shattered plans of colonizing the Yuma area and establishing a presidio along the Gila.

The presidio was never moved to this location at the San Pedro and Gila confluence, largely because of the negative reports Ugarte and Rocha prepared of the dry, barren, and rugged nature of the terrain in this area. In their view, the river valley was unsuitable for settlement and the junction was not appropriate

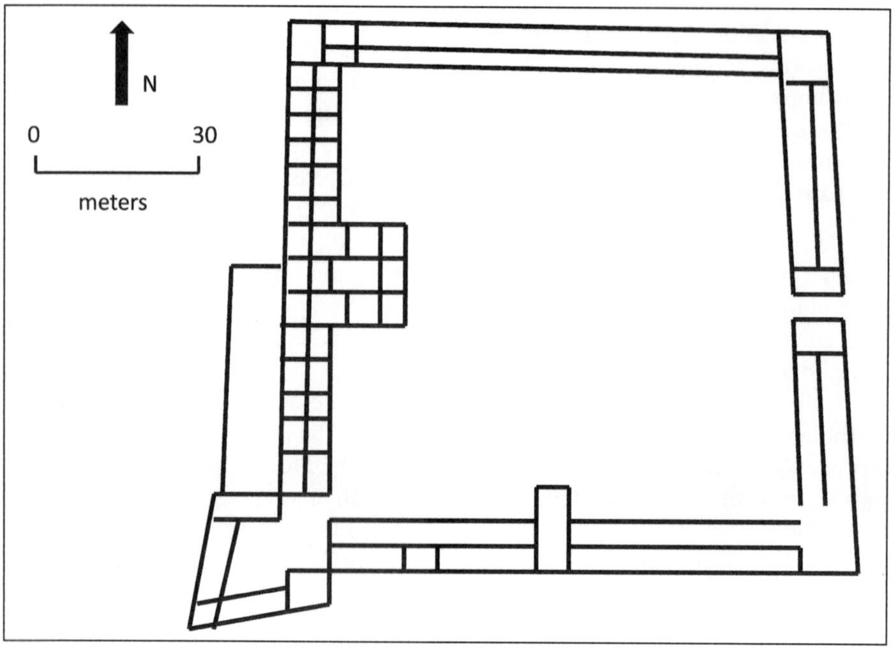

FIGURE 1.8. Plan drawing of Santa Cruz de Terrenate Presidio.

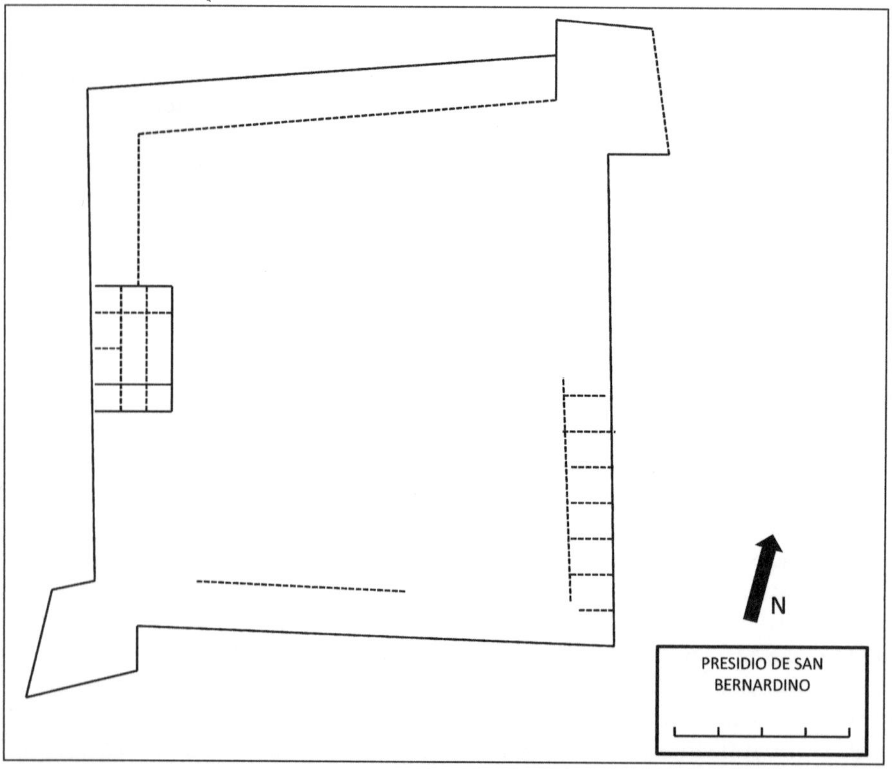

FIGURE 1.9. Plan drawing of San Bernardino Presidio.

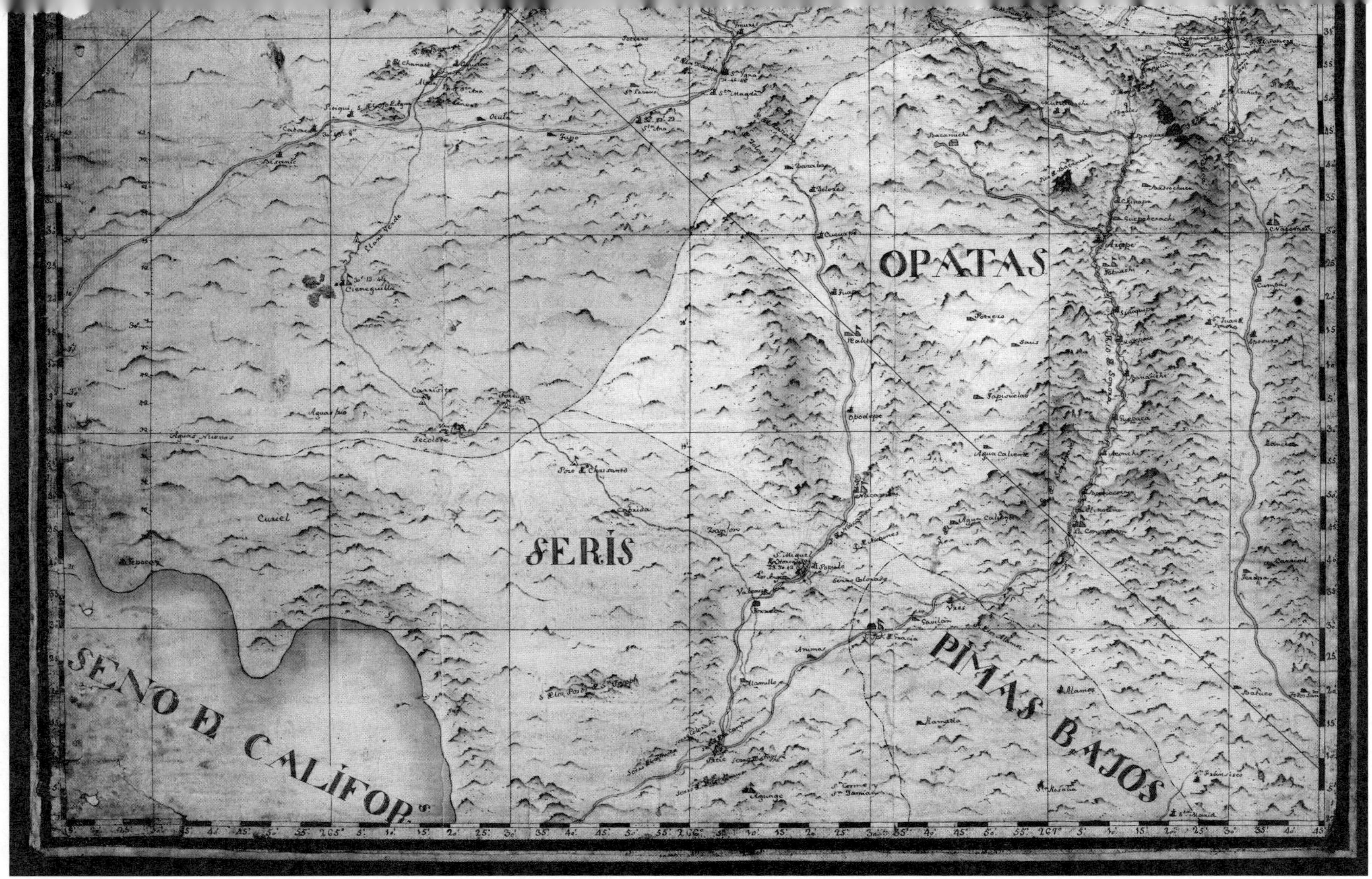

FIGURE 1.7. Rocha prepared a map of the province, as directed by Croix. As shown here the figure shows the route taken and key geographic and political features of the landscape. *Mapa de la Frontera de Sonora para el establecimiento de la linea de presidios*, Sept. 4, 1780, on a scale of eight inches to a degree. Courtesy of the British Library; Shelfmark: Cartographic Items Additional MS. 17,661.a.

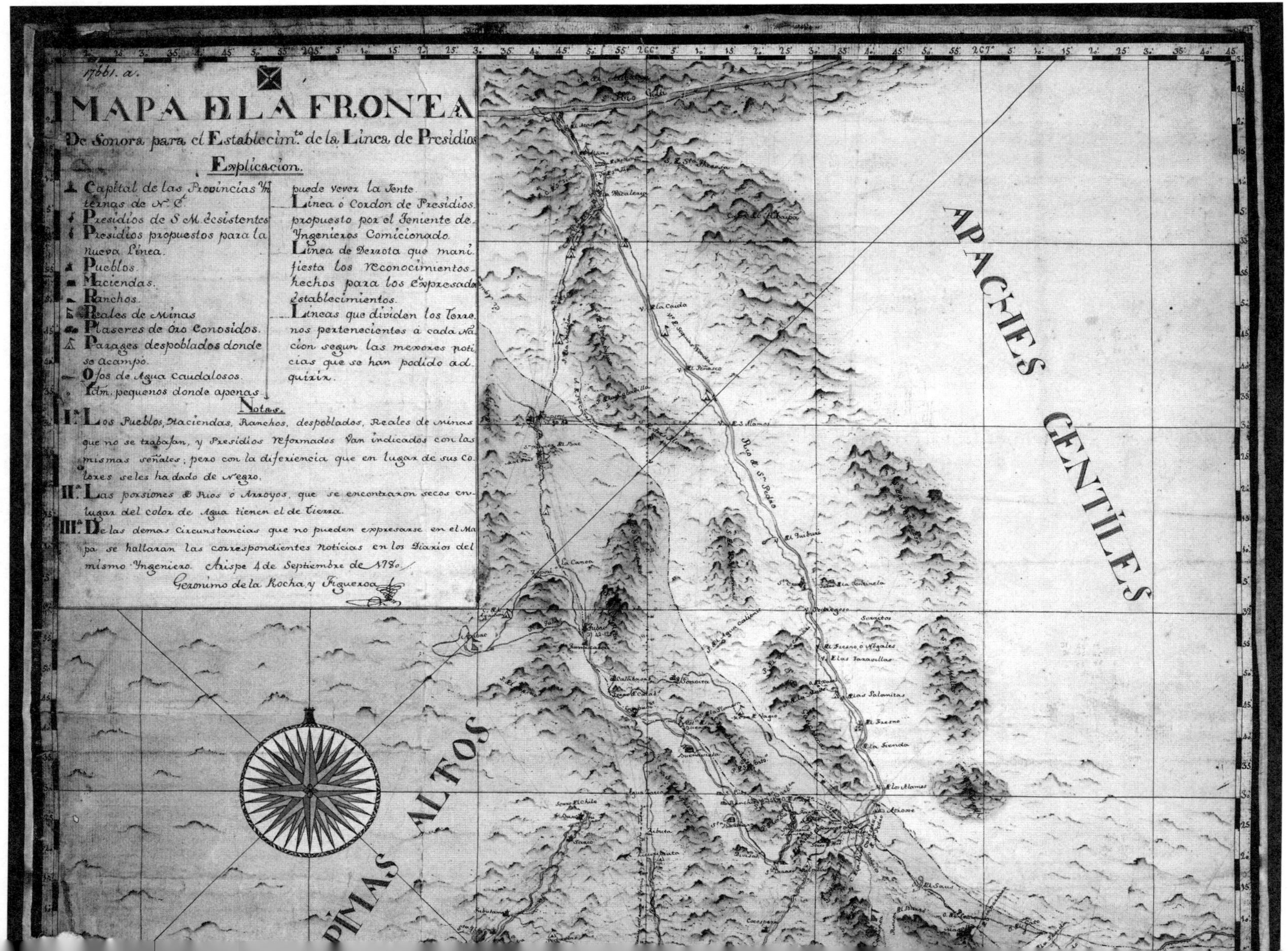
17661. a.
MAPA DE LA FRONTERA
De Sonora para el Establecim.to de la Linea de Presidios
Explicacion.
Capital de las Provincias Internas de N. E.
Presidios de S. M. ecsistentes
Presidios propuestos para la nueva Linea.
Pueblos.
Haciendas.
Ranchos.
Reales de Minas
Plaseres de Oro Conosidos.
Parages despoblados donde se acampo.
Ojos de Agua caudalosos.
Idm. pequenos donde apenas puede verer la Gente.
Linea o Cordon de Presidios propuesto por el Teniente de Ingenieros Comicionado.
Linea de Derrota que manifiesta los Reconocimientos hechos para los Expresados establecimientos.
Lineas que dividen los Terrenos pertenecientes a cada Nacion segun las mexores noticias que se han podido adquirir.
Notas.
I.a Los Pueblos, Haciendas, Ranchos, despoblados, Reales de Minas que no se trabajan, y Presidios reformados van indicados con las mismas señales; pero con la diferiencia que en lugar de sus Colores se les ha dado de Negro.
II.a Las porsiones de Rios o Arroyos, que se encontraron secos en lugar del color de Agua tienen el de Tierra.
III.a De las demas Circunstancias que no pueden expresarse en el Mapa se hallaran las correspondientes Noticias en los Diarios del mismo Ingeniero. Arispe 4 de Septiembre de 1780.
Geronimo de la Rocha y Figueroa
APACHES GENTILES
PIMAS ALTOS
Rio de S.n Pedro
La Canoa
El Terrenate
Arizpe
Los Alamos
El Fresno
Las Salomitas
Sonoitos
El Saus

FIGURE 1.10. The San Pedro near its confluence with the Gila River today, which, as the proposed location of a new presidio, was inspected by Ugarte and Rocha during this expedition.

for a presidio (Figure 1.10). It was also too far from the support of neighboring presidios. From these descriptions in Rocha's diary and the accompanying summaries one can see either a desolate and pitiable land devastated by previous occupants, including those of the now abandoned Santa Cruz de Terrenate Presidio, or an effort by Ugarte and Rocha to downplay the qualities of the San Pedro River Valley so as to provide a suitable basis for not placing a presidio in this far northern position. Either way, Rocha in particular presents an accurate assessment of many of the characteristics of this river, its discontinuous flow, its entrenched channel, and its sometimes-rugged margins. We can also see changes brought to the landscape from overuse of key resources by the Santa Cruz de Terrenate soldiers and settlers in the increasingly dense and concentrated pockets of settlement in what is now the northern portion of Sonora and southern Arizona. The fragility of the landscape is apparent in Rocha's assessments, though he did not view the degrading environment in the same way we do now. Changes are evident also in the increasing vigor with which the Apache made entrance to settled areas, either avoiding the routine presidial patrols along predictable routes while on their way to a raid or anticipating the arrival of patrols and setting repeated and successful ambushes. Military formality clearly worked against the Spanish in this instance. The northern regions were too thinly settled for their populations to serve as militia in a protective role in support of the presidios, so ranchos retracted toward the protection of presidios and defensible settlements. Rather than serving as a point of expansion, presidios provided havens for settlers huddled within their partially constructed walls, or within settlements without curtain walls that maintained somewhat fortified structures. This process of calculated Apache incursions continued and accelerated through time, for as Bartlett (1965:II: 295) mentioned in the mid-1800s, the lands around Tucson had once been extensively cultivated but "the Apaches compelled the people to abandon their ranchos and seek safety within the town. The miserable population, confined to such narrow limits, barely gains a subsistence, and could not exist a year but for the protection from the troops."

Ugarte and Rocha initiated their trip in mid-April and Rocha's journal concludes on August 3. Rocha's commission ended (as he notes on

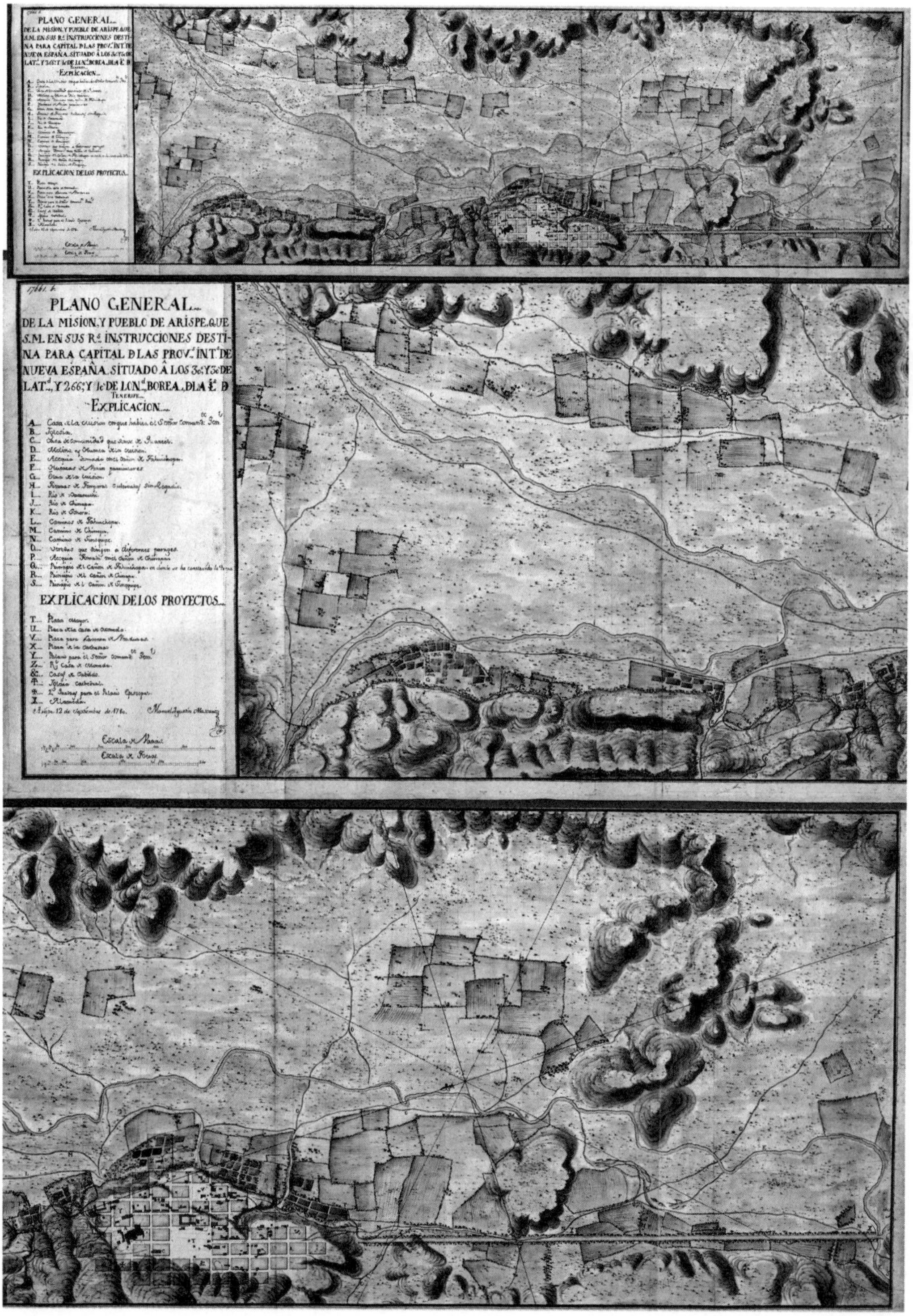

FIGURE 1.11. Manuel Agustín Mascaro's map of the mission and pueblo of Arizpe, [*Plano general de la mision y pueblo de Arispe*], 1780. Courtesy of the British Library Shelfmark: Cartographic Items Additional MS. 17,661.b.

July 23) at Pitic Presidio, but since he did not have the wherewithal to work on his maps and papers there, he claimed (but see Chapter 2), he then traveled on, escorting a party to Arizpe, and arrived at the capital on August 3, ending his journey and his journal account (Figure 1.11). In his 1781 summary report Croix (Thomas 1941: 151) placed the end date for the reconnaissance as July 16. Croix's orders specified Pitic as the concluding point of their work, and while July 16 is not the date they arrived at Pitic Presidio (they arrived on July 12), it is the date at which they stopped reconnoitering the surrounding terrain.

Setting the Stage

Teodoro de Croix was commandant-general of the *Comandancia General* of the Interior Provinces of New Spain. The *Comandancia General* was a recently founded (1776) military government which separated the northern provinces from viceregal control, which at this time was under consummate bureaucrat Viceroy Antonio María de Bucareli y Ursúa (Figure 1.12; Moorhead 1968:45; Thomas 1941:17; Weber 1992:249). As executive officer of the new and more powerful *Comandancia General*, Croix succeeded Commandant-Inspector Hugo O'Conor, who had been transferred to Guatemala (Moorhead 1968:45; Santiago 1994:75–76; Thomas 1941:21).[4]

FIGURE 1.12. Viceroy Antonio María de Bucareli y Ursúa.

Whether it was a consequence of the movement of the Presidial Line (and the resulting greater distance between presidios) or just a normal ebb and flow of hostilities, the frontier was in worse condition when Croix took office than before. After O'Conor's move of presidios, Viceroy Bucareli had reported that conditions were in a promising state: "Indisputably, the condition of the frontier, the quality and the discipline of the troops of the presidios have been ameliorated. The injuries that the citizens suffer are fewer and much less frequent" (Thomas 1941:22). Perhaps this was nothing more than whitewash or blind incompetence, as was later implied (Thomas 1941:21–23). From a distance of over two centuries it seems that, in addition to an invested opinion, a change in placement or strategy were themselves likely effective in temporarily interrupting Apache aggressions, an advantage that soon was overridden by Apache adaptability.

Croix, Ugarte, and others were in agreement that additional troops were needed, the line was too far north, and presidios were too far apart and too far from settlements to provide aid. All of these factors were responsible for the increase in Apache attacks over the previous five years (Moorhead 1968:46). This sentiment is conveyed in Rocha's summary of the reconnaissance:

> Since the presidios were inserted into the enemy's country, they withdrew from the populations that they were supposed to protect and defend, and consequently they took on a greater portion of advanced land [terrain in front of the line]. It turned out that by necessity a greater circumference of the line had to be formed and occupied, and the distance at which one [presidio] was placed from another became greater, and the difficulty that their small garrisons had to prevent the entry of the enemy because of how open and exposed their flanks became (see Chapter 3).

The reconnaissance included in this book was another effort to obtain more information about the frontier region so as to determine where the best placement for presidios might be. The movement to the north of some fortified positions meant, in their estimation, that the intervening distance was too great, so presidios were moved back. Then inappropriate locations were selected so they were shifted again. New reconnaissance was needed to identify the ideal spots as attacks were increasing, assuming as they did that the perfect location would represent the relevant factor in turning the tide in their favor. The Apache and others in rebellion (actually at war) probably viewed these shifts as successes in pushing the Europeans back, emboldening them in their offensive tactics. The willingness of Spaniards to negotiate and seek peaceful solutions likely meant weakness in the mind of the Apaches (Moorhead 1968:46–48, 50; Thomas 1941:23). If only more information could be had, the Spaniards thought, they would solve these problems and find the ideal locations for presidio placements. Yet, if they had understood the Apache way of life and the strategies the various Apachean bands employed, they might have been more successful (see Chapter 8).

Presidio Placement

Initially, in the 1500s, presidios in northern New Spain were strategically placed along travel routes, at mines, and in communities (Moorhead 1968:11, 1975:5, 7). The idea of a cordon of presidios to guard the main trails or invasion routes into the interior was presented as early as 1667 by the governor of Nueva Vizcaya (Moorhead 1975:18–19; Powell 1982). Through systematic placement of a cordon of watch towers the defense of towns, ranchos, missions, and mines could be coordinated with the goal of sealing off the heart from hostilities, thereby protecting settlements and commerce. But this concept of sealing out the hostile tribes was not immediately feasible, owing to an unwieldy chain of command and fragmented authority, so this approach was not adopted until the third quarter of the 1700s. The implementation of a cordon of presidios was formalized in the royal regulations of 1772 (*Reglamento e Instrucción para los Presidios que se han de Formar en la Línea de Frontera de la Nueva España*).

The regulations of 1772 resulted in part from a three-year inspection (1766–1768) of the Interior Provinces and twenty-three of its twenty-four presidios and posts on the northern frontier by the Marqués de Rubí (Kinnaird 1958; Moorhead 1968:16; Weber 1992:212). The portion of Rubí's inspection that is relevant to this Ugarte-Rocha reconnaissance is shown in a map prepared by cartographer Joseph Ramon de Urrutia in 1768, with versions from 1769 and 1771 (Figures 1.13 and 1.14). This first part shows the first of four separately numbered maps and includes an area that extends from the Gulf of California to Texas. Engineer Captain Nicolás de Lafora and Ensign Urrutia prepared several maps, including this overview of the region and some twenty-two presidio and town plans visited during this 1766–1768 trip (see Kinnaird 1958). Lafora also prepared a journal of this inspection trip, which provides a glimpse into frontier conditions just over a decade before the Ugarte-Rocha entry. Many of these conditions observed during this trip and recorded by Lafora are included as annotations to the journal in Chapter 5 to supplement information not included by Rocha, who did not always describe the places he visited.

This was a critical time because Rubí's inspection circuit overlapped with the Jesuit expulsion, though Rubí makes no mention of it and was already within Franciscan domain by the date of the notice. On June 25, 1767, by decree of King Carlos III (*Real Pragmática Sanción*; Royal Pragmatic Penalty of 1767) the Society of Jesus was suppressed in New Spain, just as it had been expelled from Portugal in 1758 and from France in 1764 (Baegert 1952:208n47; Ilaronie 2000:219n29,30; Roehner 1997:167). The order was signed by Carlos III on February 27, 1767, but was kept sealed and secret until June 25 so that it could reach all government representatives and be enacted simultaneously and immediately. This was a critical event for this period because the expulsion led to rebellions and unrest throughout the province. Because of the

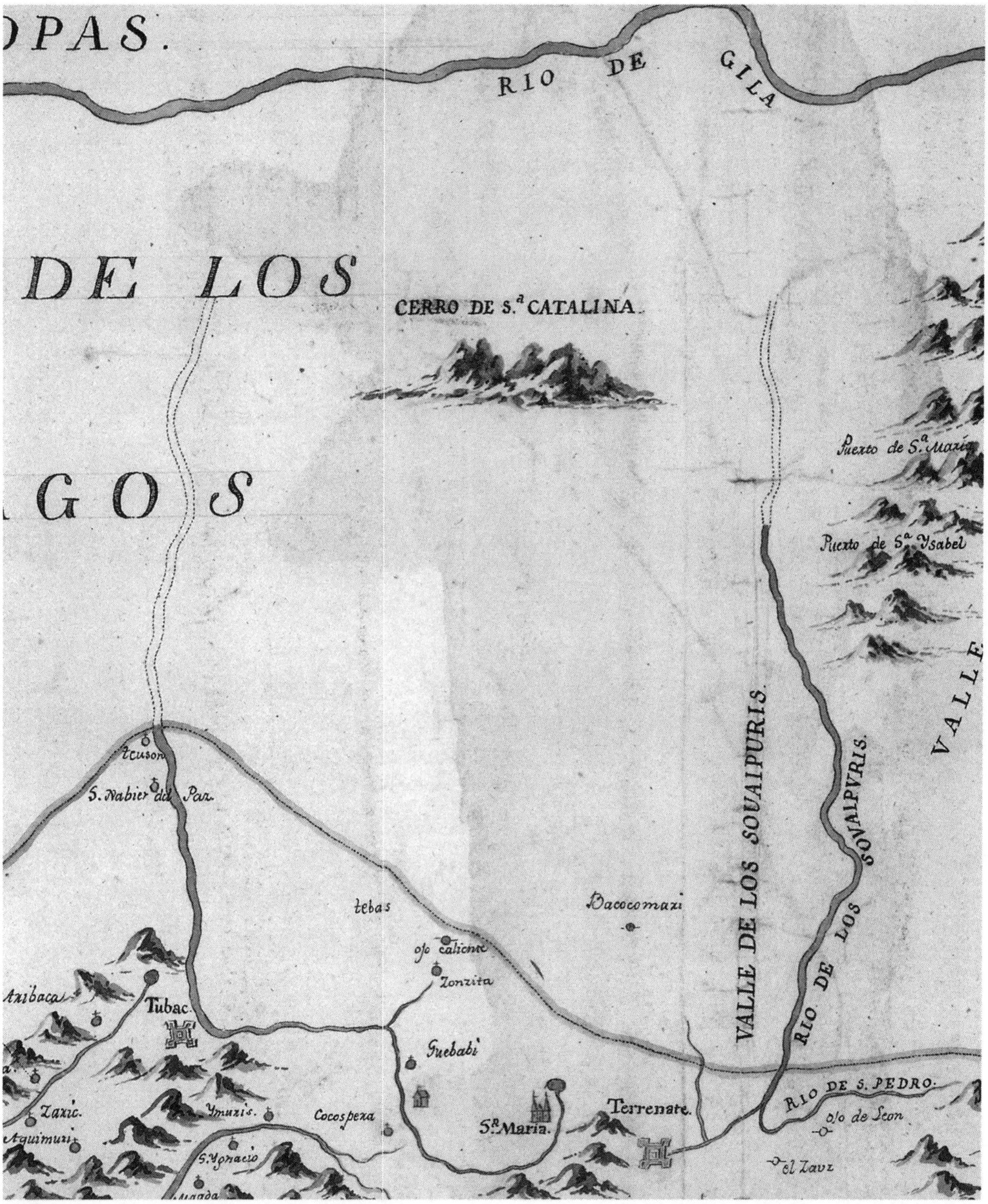

FIGURE 1.13. Relevant section of map prepared by cartographer Joseph Ramon de Urrutia in 1768, dated 1769 [*Mapa, que comprende la Frontera, de los Dominios del Rey, en la America Septentrional*, 1769]. Courtesy of the Library of Congress; https://www.loc.gov/item/00556406/.

unrest that followed the expulsion it is possible that many of the missions and *visitas* ("visiting stations") experienced the reduced populations at levels noted by Rocha that were below what was viewed by members of the Rubí inspection. It was also during this time that the presidio eclipsed the mission as the dominant frontier institution (Weber 1992:212).

José de Gálvez was immediately sent by Viceroy Marqués de Croix (uncle of Teodoro de

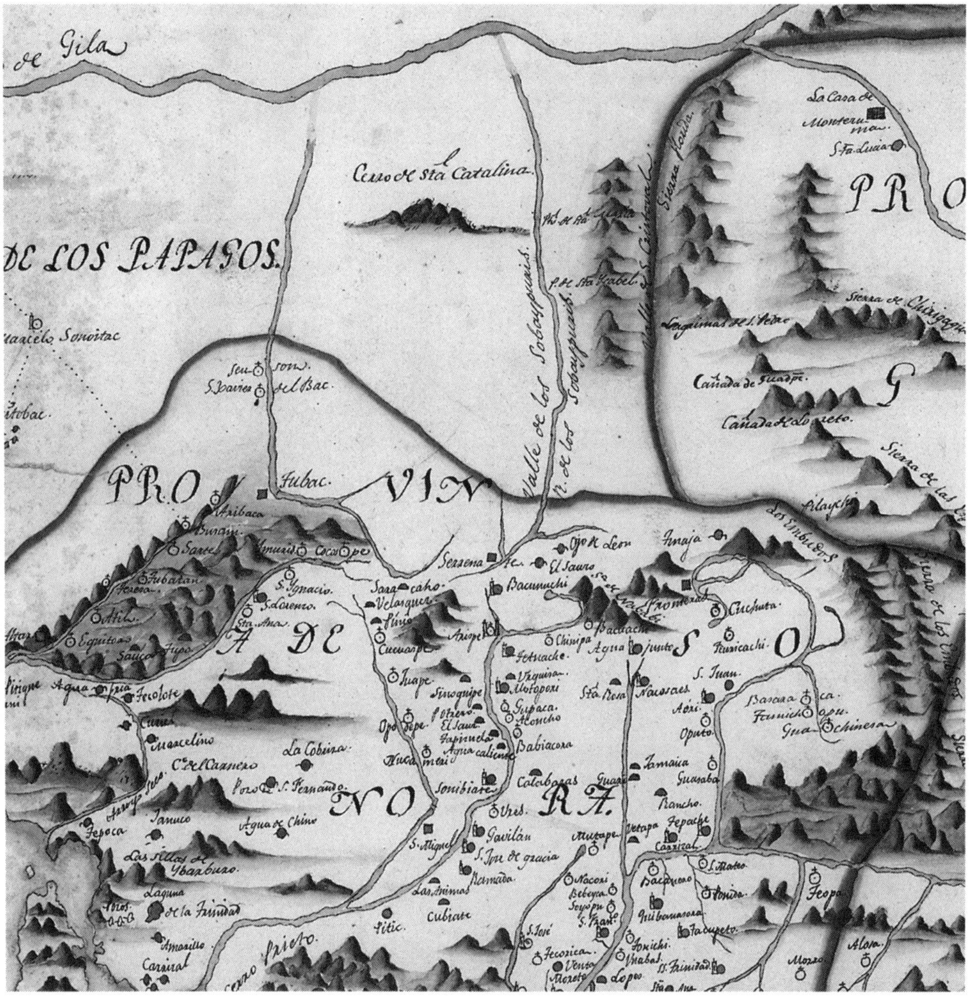

FIGURE 1.14. One of the two maps in Figures 1.13–1.14, prepared by cartographer and engineer Joseph Ramon de Urrutia while on a reconnaissance with the Marqués de Rubí, was probably the map provided to Ugarte and Rocha as preparation before they began their reconnaissance. [*Mapa de toda la frontera de los dominios del rey en la America septentrional*, 1771.] Courtesy of the Library of Congress; https://www.loc.gov/item/2001622423/.

Croix) to curtail this expulsion-related unrest and bring perpetrators to justice with considerable brutality (see Priestley 1916:213–224). Gálvez's expedition began after the completion of Rubí's trip but before his official report, nonetheless Gálvez made recommendations regarding reorganization of the frontier that were consistent with those of Rubí.

Rubí had recommended a single outer line of defense consisting of presidios spaced at regular intervals (forty leagues or 120 miles apart), which also included six new presidios (Gerald 1968:7; Moorhead 1975:59). The line of presidios was intended to cordon off the frontier, prohibiting incursions from the Apache and other hostile tribes. The effectiveness of the stationary fortresses would be reinforced with regular patrols, with the soldiers from one presidio responsible for the defensive of the zone half way to the next presidio (Moorhead 1975:59).

Well timed to reinforce the findings of the Rubí expedition, in 1768 José de Gálvez, serving as visitor general, laid out parallel but distinct plans for reorganizing the frontier. Among the many goals were straightening the alignment of presidios and reducing their number (to reduce costs) along with establishing new frontier towns of armed colonists who were to form a provincial militia that could subsist on its own frontier resources (Priestley 1916:241). With the intent of reorganizing the Interior Provinces, Gálvez was authorized to establish a town in Sonora that would form the seat of a new *comandancia general*, independent of the viceroyalty (Priestley 1916:242). This seat was placed in Arizpe in 1780 and Caballero Croix (Teodoro de Croix) was the first to occupy this position.

The royal regulations of 1772 codified some of Rubí's and Gálvez's recommendations, including the cordon of presidios, providing guidance for the relocation of existing presidios, the suppression of others, and the construction of new ones. The royal regulations also prescribed construction of uniform plans for the layout of presidios and changes relating to the governing of military personnel and treatment of Indians. These new policies were implemented in January of the following year (Brinkerhoff and Fault 1965; Gerald 1968:7; Moorhead 1968, 1975).

Beginning in February 1772, as the newly appointed commander-inspector of the military forces in the frontier provinces, Hugo O'Conor was made responsible for implementing the 1772 regulations by Viceroy Bucareli. His responsibilities included realigning the nearly 1,800-mile Presidial Line and establishing, suppressing, and moving presidios (Figures 1.15 a and b; Gerald 1968:7–8; Thomas 1932:5). Between 1773 and 1775 O'Conor relocated twelve presidios and added two more, consistent with the overall plan. The presidio alignment after 1775, from west to east, included Santa Gertrudis del Altar, San Agustín del Tucson (Tuquison), Santa Cruz (de Terrenate), San Bernardino, San Felipe y Santiago de Janos, San Buenaventura (Velarde), San Fernando del Carrizal, San Elizario (El Porvenir), El Príncipe (Pilares), Junta de Los Ríos (El Norte), San Carlos, San Sabá (San Vicente), San Antonio Bucareli de la Bahía (or Babia), Santa Rosa (Agua Verde), Monclova, San Juan Bautista, and Bahía del Espíritu Santo (Cutter 1994: 74–78; Gerald 1968:8) (Figure 1.16 a).[5]

Part of the plan was for a more concerted offensive to break the enemy into submission. Yet the royal order of February 20, 1779, demanded that offensive operations cease and efforts be made to forge peace, owing to a shortage of funds as a consequence of the war with England, placing Spain in a de facto alliance with the American revolutionaries (1779–1783; Moorhead 1968: 57–58, 120–123, 1975:84–85; Thomas 1941:43–44). Moreover, earlier policies designed to establish peace had proven successful, for a while at least. For example, the aid-for-peace program initiated with the Chichimeca in the late 1500s and the policies of peaceful persuasion in the regulations of 1729 were effective in subduing many hostilities on the frontier (Moorhead 1968:12–13, 16).[6] Yet, as peace was established with one group, raiding and warring would continue in the adjacent province (Moorhead 1968:15), owing in part to Apache conceptions of alliance formation and political relations. They did not view their agreements with the Spanish government in general as encompassing all Spanish settlements, mines, missions, and presidios. Instead, they made agreements with each specific settlement or establishment, while at the same time they felt free to pillage the remainder at will. Their perceptions were based on their own organization, wherein each band was its own governing body. Consequently, the Spaniards would institute new instructions and regulations requiring active and incessant war against declared enemies, at least until it became apparent that this approach was not working, and then the Spaniards would once again revert to efforts of peace and conciliation (Moorhead 1968:17; Powell 1982:137).

By 1780 numerous changes to this Presidial Line had already occurred. The line had stretched too far north, with too much distance between presidios to stay the tide of enemy raids. The enemy thrusted southward, including into Sonora, at will. Consequently, just prior to the 1780 reconnaissance, those presidios along the northern line in Sonora, together with those south of the northern boundary, included

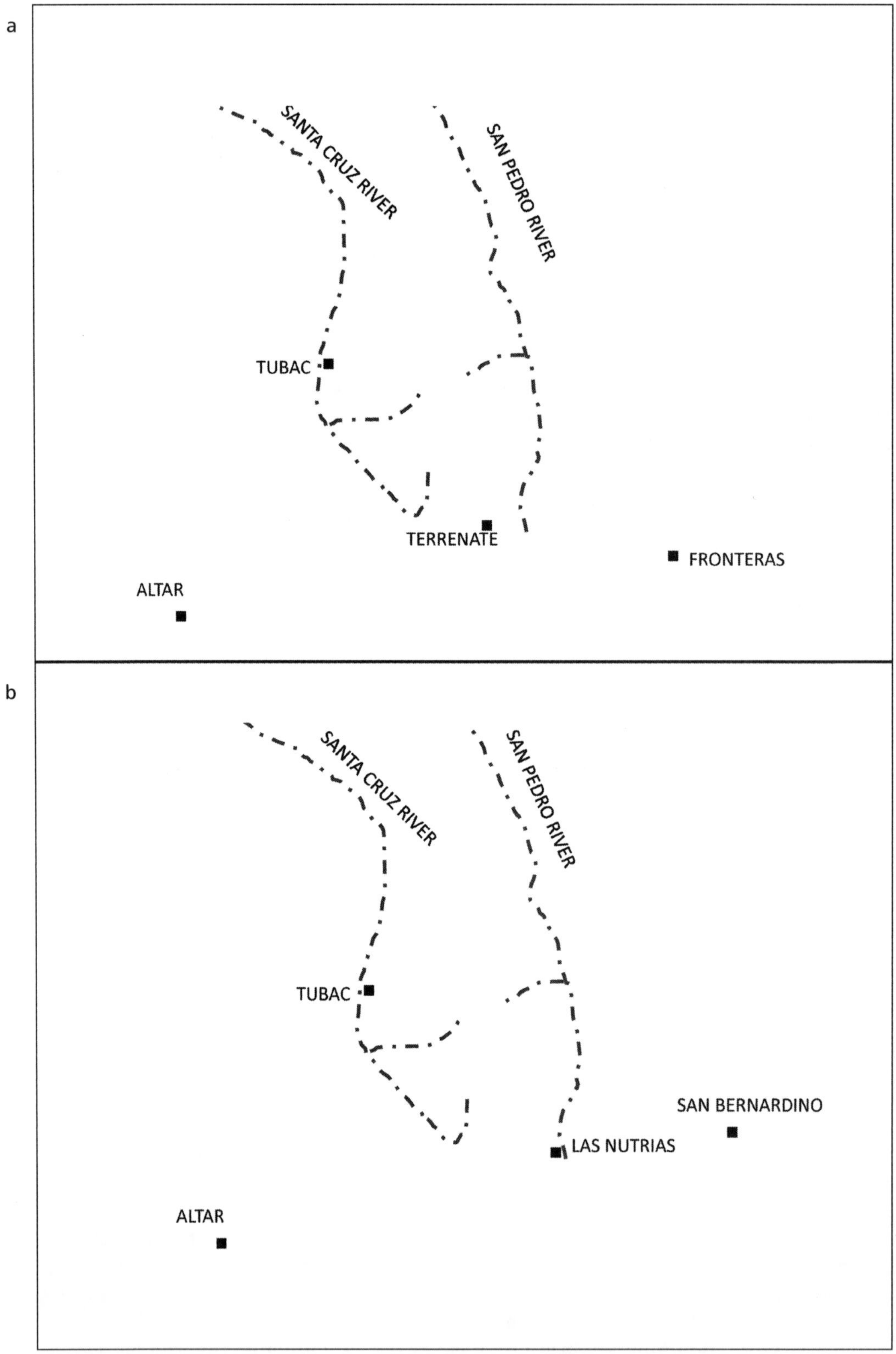

FIGURE 1.15. The Presidial Line in Sonora as it changed through time. (*a*) The original set of presidios is shown here with Tubac the furthest north, established after the 1751 Pima Revolt. Altar protected the western flank. (*b*) Presidio positions were not much improved with the move of Terrenate to Las Nutrias and Fronteras to San Bernardino.

a

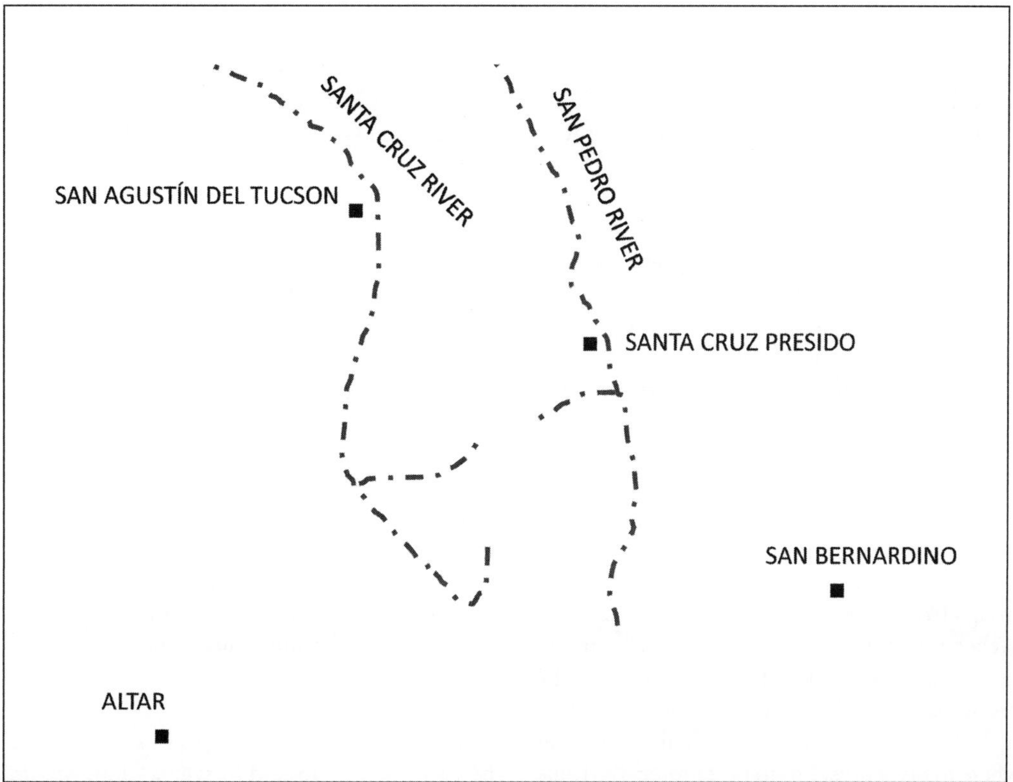

b

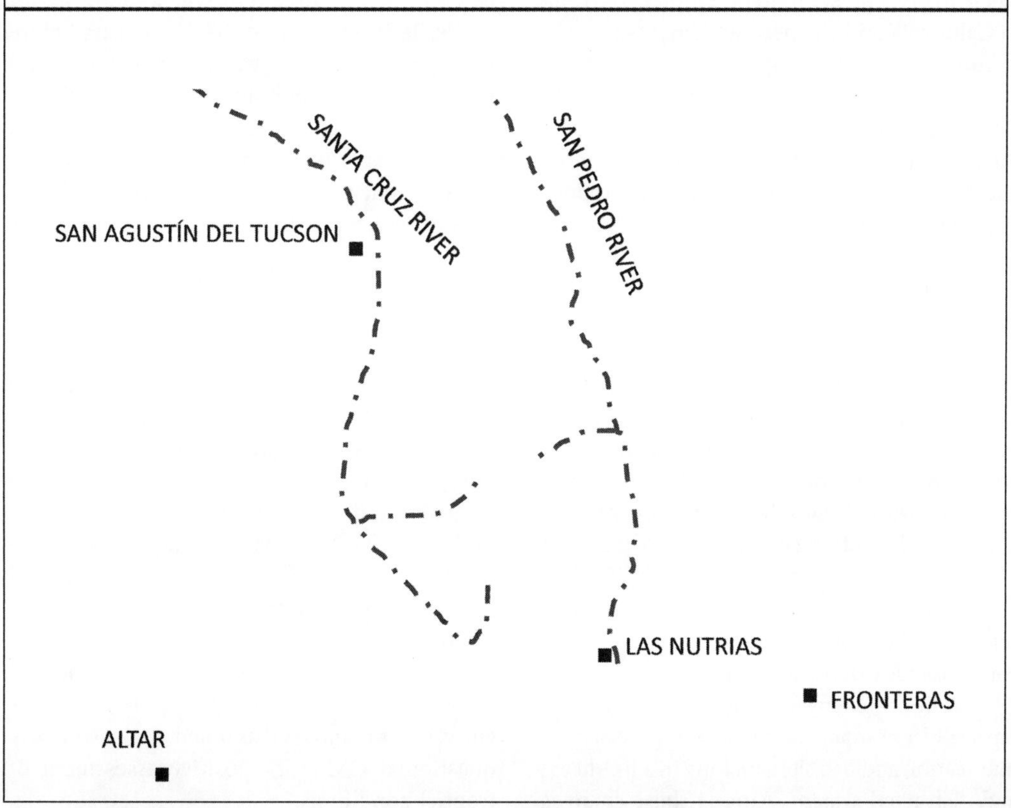

FIGURE 1.16. (*a*) Soon, in late 1775, Las Nutrias was moved to Santa Cruz and Tubac to Tucson. (*b*) In March 1880 the Santa Cruz garrison moved south, returning to Las Nutrias, and San Bernardino retreated to Fronteras.

Buenavista on the Yaqui River, Altar on the Altar River, Tucson and Tubac on the Santa Cruz River, Las Nutrias on the San Pedro, Fronteras on the Fronteras River,[7] and Pitic (Figure 1.16b).[8] These reflected the recent abandonment of Santa Cruz and San Bernardino and the withdrawal of troops south to their previous locations (Las Nutrias and Fronteras).

Croix's plan involved shortening the presidio cordon with more manageable distances by separating posts, reinforcing existing garrisons with new *tropa ligera*,[9] establishing towns garrisoned with militias behind the Presidial Line as a second line of defense, and using the mobile force of *compañías volantes* as a backup for enemy incursions into the interior of Sonora (Moorhead 1975:85). He also increased the number of troops from 1,900 to 2,840 (Moorhead 1975:91; Weber 1992:226). Now Croix was interested in reassessing the most suitable locations for the presidios along the northern line. Consistent with the king's wishes, he also had to consider where to place presidios to best protect the route to California and the new settlements planned at Yuma.

In carrying out their orders, Ugarte and Rocha's assessments were guided by those of their predecessors (O'Conor, Crespo, Bonilla, and Díaz), all of whom had written reports that were forwarded to both of them in preparation for the journey. Adjutant Inspector Don Antonio Bonilla was commissioned by O'Conor to establish the line in 1774 (Thomas 1941:168). At the end of the same year Colonel Don Francisco Crespo reconnoitered the Sonoran frontier (Thomas 1941:174–175). In early 1775 Father Fray Juan Díaz sent a report authored by himself and Father Fray Francisco Garcés to Bucareli (Bolton 1930:276–290; Thomas 1941:175–178). Croix noted that these reports along with a map of the province, a copy of the regulation of the presidios, and various instructive papers were sent to Rocha to study prior to initiating the reconnaissance (Thomas 1941:150).[10]

Conditions changed rapidly on the frontier, especially in comparison to the slow pace of communication and decision-making in a top-heavy and distracted system. Among these changes, just a month or two before Rocha left Arizpe to meet up with Ugarte, the garrison and all the families and settlers at Santa Cruz de Terrenate had moved south to Las Nutrias.[11] Rocha had been in charge of this evacuation in March of 1780 (Fireman 1977:146; Rocha 1780c).[12] San Bernardino had also been abandoned; its garrison had moved back south to Fronteras in 1779 (Thomas 1941:226).

Although two presidios had already moved, Croix had tasked Ugarte with moving the other presidios back to the locations they had occupied before the O'Conor revisions recommended by Rubí. Ugarte oversaw Rocha in evaluating the new and old sites and supervising the presidio transfers (Fireman 1977:146; Thomas 1941:148–149). The goal was to maintain presidios that were spaced between 20 and 30 leagues (60 to 90 miles) apart (Thomas 1941:215).

Ugarte and Rocha

Don Jacobo de Ugarte y Loyola was assigned his first frontier command in 1767 and arrived in Coahuila in 1769, more than two years before the regulation of 1772 was in force (Moorhead 1968:18, 23). Throughout his term as political and military governor of Coahuila he suffered from illness. During the last full year of his term in that province, in 1776, the northernmost provinces had been separated from viceregal control, forming the *comandancia general de las Provincias Internas del Norte*. In 1777 the commander-general Croix appointed Ugarte as the military governor of Sonora.

By the time of the 1780 reconnaissance Ugarte was in his thirty-ninth year of service, which meant he was in his late fifties or early sixties.[13] The preceding year he had been promoted to brigadier and is repeatedly referenced as such in the journal.[14] His extensive experience (both prior to and after arriving in New Spain) and his age likely contributed to his resentment of O'Conor, which in turn created friction between him and the Viceroy Bucareli (Moorhead 1968:34). In Sonora, however, Ugarte was under Croix's command, and as noted, Croix similarly questioned O'Conor's positive assessment of frontier conditions.

It was widely known that Governor Ugarte exhibited "an independence of judgment and an initiative in action that sometimes bordered on outright insubordination" (Moorhead 1968:19), which resulted in the "repeated provocation of immediate superiors" (Moorhead 1968:20). This knowledge and an effort to check the reliability of Ugarte may have been the reason Croix requested a secret version of the report of the reconnaissance from Rocha (see Chapter 2).

Don Gerónimo de la Rocha y Figueroa had not been in Sonora long when he embarked on this reconnaissance. He had arrived in Sonora from Cadiz in November 1779, less than six months before leaving for Fronteras. This did not mean he was inexperienced, but rather simply unfamiliar with Sonora. Rocha was born in 1750 in the North African Spanish fortification colony of Orán (Fireman 1977:145). In Barcelona he entered the corps of engineers in 1771 and served as second lieutenant and assistant engineer at the fortification of San Fernando de Figueras until 1777, when he was transferred to the Interior Provinces of New Spain (Fireman 1977:146). Before leaving Spain he was promoted to lieutenant and "extraordinary engineer," the title indicated on the reconnaissance diary (Chapter 5). On arriving in America he served as Ugarte's engineer.

Following the reconnaissance, in March 1781, Rocha was appointed interim captain of Fronteras presidio and commander of its cavalry company (Croix 1781; Fireman 1977:147). While there he supervised the construction of new facilities, including walls around the forts, at both Fronteras and Las Nutrias.[15] The lack of labor, both craftsmen and workers, as well as the absence of building materials prohibited him from fulfilling the objectives, particularly since, as he stated, he was faced with bad water, unhealthy climate, and the ever-present threat from Apaches. His failing health was also a factor, though he was promoted to captain in February 1782, as he was recuperating in Arizpe. There he continued with duties until relocating to New Mexico in 1785. Earlier he had designed the Santa Fe presidio, sending the plan and accompanying building instructions from Arizpe, and then he left for Spain in August of 1787 (Fireman 1977:145–150; Moorhead 1974:132).

After leaving Fronteras, Rocha prepared another map of northern Sonora dated 1784 (Rocha y Figueroa 1784; Figure 1.17). This map incorporated existing knowledge and was prepared for a projected expedition against the Gila Apaches (Fireman 1977:149). It is titled: "Map of the terrain to search for the expedition to be executed against the Gileño Apaches,[16] arranged by Brigadier Don Felipe de Neve, commander-general of the province in five divisions" (*Mapa del terreno que ha de vatir la expedición que deve ejecutarse contra los apaches gileños dispuesta por el Brigadier Don Felipe de Neve, Comandante General de la Provincia en cinco divisiones. Arizpe, 18 de marzo de 1784.*) Much of this information derives from the 1780 reconnaissance, although it is not presented in anything near the detail of his 1780 map.

Content

The 1780 map prepared by Rocha as a companion to his journal is described by Garcia (1964: 456) and also Fireman (1977:149; also see Reinhartz in Reinhartz and Saxon 2005:72–73) as the most detailed map of the area produced during the Spanish period. It is called: "Map of the frontier of Sonora for the establishment of the line of presidios" (*Mapa de la Frontera de Sonora para el Establecimiento de la Linea de Presidios*), as shown in Figure 1.7 and Chapter 4.

Rocha's journal, translated in Chapter 5, is equally useful, providing information found in no other sources.[17] The summaries by Ugarte and Rocha supplement this more extensive and detailed treatment. We discuss the specific route taken in Chapter 4, where the map key and map are presented. The implications of the content of these documents for our understanding of the environmental history of the area are discussed in Chapter 6. Rocha's journal is particularly informative with respect to issues relating to environmental history of the San Pedro and Santa Cruz Rivers and their tributaries in southern Arizona. He described the condition of the lands they traveled through, noting the presence of timber, firewood, permanent water, pasture,

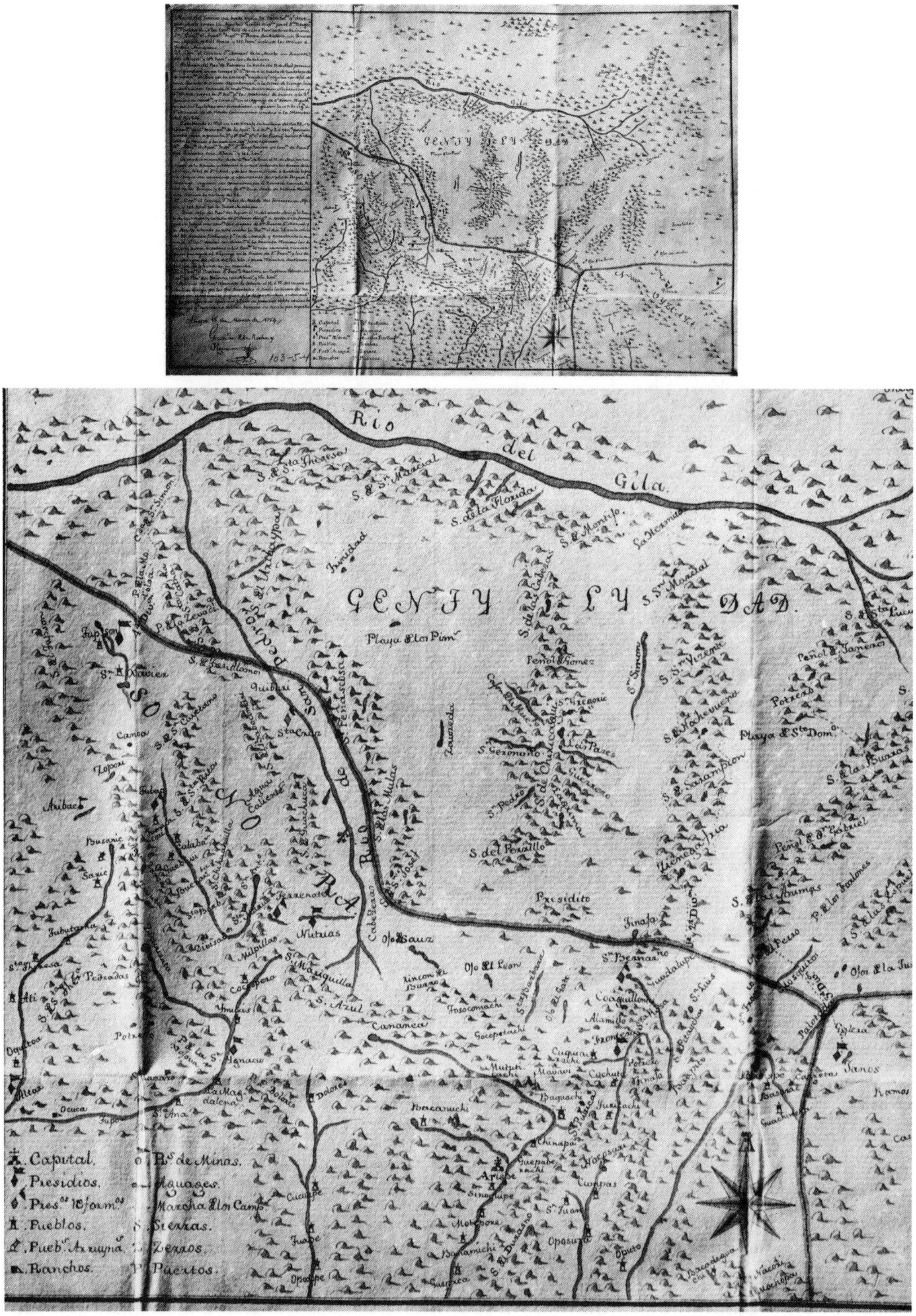

FIGURE 1.17. Rocha's 1784 map with a close up of much of the area covered by this reconnaissance [*Mapa del Terreno que ha de vatir la Expedición que deve executarse contra los Apaches Gileños*, March 18, 1784]. Courtesy of The Newberry Library, Chicago. Call # Map Photo Spain, AGI, 103-5-4, Vol. 1.

and fields suitable for agriculture. Many misconceptions have arisen through the years, which convey the notion that it is only recently that the San Pedro and Santa Cruz Rivers have taken on certain characteristics. Rocha's and Ugarte's observations provide greater time depth with which to explore these issues, revealing that arroyo cutting and devegetation occurred earlier than often thought and are likely related to the intensive settlement at these presidios. Rocha's map also provides certain details in this regard that are not included in his journal (see figures in Chapter 4).

Most noteworthy are Rocha's descriptions of native settlements or missions and the presidios along with details of their layouts, lands, and populations. Chapter 7 provides a discussion of indigenous practices and customs at the time, as conveyed in this journal, providing a glimpse into how things had changed since Kino's time in the 1680s through 1710s, and some of the changes that had occurred even more recently. Details provided in the journal are indispensable for understanding colonial processes underway, especially at the northern edge of the frontier. Rocha provided details of interest to frontier defense and the viability of establishing new settlements and presidios, and at the same time he provided a view of an important transitional period in regional history. These descriptions provide a hint of the increasing levels of violence and mounting tensions on the frontier as well as the indigenous response of allied peoples in the form of settlement layout, village placement, relocation, and aggregation. Rocha also provided insights into variations in agricultural practices throughout the region and included details of the nature of the *acequia* system in Tucson. All of these are discussed in the context of the maps and on-the-ground observations today. An added benefit is provided by comparing journal and summary content to what we have learned from archaeological investigations and what can be learned from understanding the geography of the region.

If Rocha's map is the most detailed, Thomas (1941:ix) has argued that Croix's general report of 1781 (Croix 1781) is "for its time the most comprehensive survey ever written of conditions in the area of our present Southwest and northern Mexico." Croix's 1781 general report references the summary documents by Ugarte and Rocha that resulted from the 1780 reconnaissance as are found in this book, and included excerpts from these summary reports. These documents therefore contribute an important basis for the thoroughness of the content of Croix's 1781 report. In fact, while Croix's general report covers a broader area than Ugarte and Rocha's, and so is more geographically inclusive, it may be said that Ugarte and Rocha's reports provide the most comprehensive accounts written of conditions in southern Arizona and northern Sonora during a specific year of the Spanish colonial period.

Secondary Sources

Numerous secondary sources are referenced in the discussions and endnotes in an effort to provide context for the reader and in an effort to understand inferences drawn by other researchers. This is especially important given the multiple shifts in locations, changes in the names of some places, and the retention of names in other cases despite places moving. A significant amount of change occurred over a five-year period during this era, as settlements moved, places were attacked and residents killed, or settlers were relocated to a new presidio. Rapid changes occurred as a result of the Jesuit expulsion, shifts in policy and leadership, and so on. The sources included offer details not otherwise provided by Ugarte and Rocha's records alone. For example, Ugarte and Rocha did not supply population estimates for pueblos, other than to note that a place was occupied or depopulated. Therefore, we draw this information from other sources as close to the time of the reconnaissance as possible, as well as from earlier and later texts to document changes through time. For example, the Lafora diary and Urrutia's maps provide information from before the unrest and resettlement associated with the Jesuit expulsion. Another account, resulting from Father Fray Thomas Eixarch's visitation at Tumacácori during the first decade of the Franciscan administration in the Pimería Alta, provides population information for 1775 (Kessell 1965), information lacking in the Ugarte and Rocha documents. By combining information from many sources, a more comprehensive understanding of this period and the importance of these Ugarte and Rocha documents is possible.

Transcriptions and Translations

The documents contained in this book represent an important perspective into the northern frontier province of Sonora toward the end of the eighteenth century. Although pieces of these documents have been widely cited, including in the senior author's work, the diary had not been previously published. The orders and summary reports that precede the diary provide context and establish a basis for evaluating diary content, while the map is indispensable for understanding the route taken. Because these documents are so important in the interpretation of late–eighteenth-century frontier history, we have included the transcriptions and translations of the orders, summaries, and diary.

The transcriptions of these documents are included in the appendix. The orders, summaries, and journal were obtained from the Harvard College Library, Sparks Collection, MS 98, Vol. VII. The map is from the British Library; the color version was graciously provided by Philip Halpenny. We worked from a direct copy of the microfilm, which is a complete and very clear copy of the manuscripts. The handwritten version of these documents represents a copy of the original made by Antonio Bonilla on December 31, 1781. We have also included five documents that precede the diary, the orders and summary reports, which provide context for and a synopsis of the journey. In the transcription we prepared an exact as possible replica of the handwritten document.

Most of the document is very clear, with legible handwriting and clearly written text that often includes some explanation (see Figure 1.4). This means that while it was sometimes necessary to interpret what Ugarte and Rocha were saying or the meaning they were conveying, most of the document does not require much clarification. Throughout the documents we have not embellished. We have tried to convey what is written, nothing more. As noted in the preceding section, Seymour's familiarity with much of the region has provided assistance in understanding what the documents are saying in many instances. Understanding the geographical layout and the nature of the terrain proved indispensable in clarifying what particular sentences meant.

Endnotes provide clarification and elaboration on points, indicating where there is some uncertainty, providing the basis for our interpretations, and also sometimes providing background information to clarify meaning. Much additional historical information is included in the endnotes.

Fortuitous Outcomes

History is always fragmentary, something that is easy to forget, given the illusion of completeness often provided by subsequently constructed narratives. The subset of historical documents preserved, and an even smaller subset made available, provide a narrow window into conditions in the past. Yet in the instance of this 504-league reconnaissance we are especially fortunate to have the diary, given an event that occurred toward the end of Rocha's trip. On July 31, 1780, Rocha's mule tumbled down the slope to the river, and, as he said, "it was necessary to stop for having rolled a mule of mine down a slope or cliff to the river, and made entirely useless my papers, books, tools, clothes, and the rest that I was bringing." He stopped for the rest of the day and most of the next, delaying his plans to finish the trip so as to salvage these materials. Such are the accidents of history. In this case his journal survived and we are particularly fortunate for his consideration during those hot, humid July days.

Notes

1. Carlos III was king of Spain and the Spanish Indies from 1759 to 1788. He was intent on dispensing with the inquisitors, who were supported by the Jesuits, and supported the Enlightenment. Consequently, his policies focused on weakening the church, promoting science and university research, trade and commerce, modernizing agriculture, and avoiding wars. This was instigated by a letter forged by the prime ministers of Spain and France purported to have been written by Fr. General Ricci that questioned his legitimacy. This forged letter was shown to the king, who acted accordingly.
2. April 15 through July 16 were the official dates given by Croix in this report of 1781 (Thomas 1941:150–161), although they did not reach their starting point until April 18. They reached the endpoint, Pitic presidio, on July 12, and Rocha does not conclude the journal until August 3, so Croix uses a different means to determine the duration of the trip.
3. On June 11 in his diary Rocha commented that he had forty men, along with some officers, including retired Captain Don Juan de Oliva, Lieutenant Don Pablo Romero, and Captain Pedro de Allande y Saavedra (then captain of Tucson presidio), who accompanied him to Guevavi. Ugarte had taken a different route south, probably with an escort, to Imuris, where the two officers were to meet.
4. Santiago (1994:75–76) says O'Conor was transferred to Yucatan, and likely means the Yucatan Peninsula rather than the Mexican state, while Moorhead (1968:45) says Guatemala, which is part of the Yucatan Peninsula.
5. In addition, there were the presidios that were beyond the line, including Santa Fe and San Antonio de Béxar, and also detachments at the Arroyo de Cíbolo, and perhaps Robledo (Moorhead 1975:64–65; also see Weber 1992: 216). These garrisons and detachments were necessary to protect sizable Hispanic and Hispanized Indian populations located north of the line, and they also protected the more prosperous provinces to the south.
6. Bernardo de Galvez's 1786 *Instrucción* resulted in the establishment of peace camps in the later part of the 1780s and 1790s that would operate until the 1820s.
7. Note that Santa Cruz and San Bernardino had already moved, contrary to the discussion provided by Morehead (1968:54).
8. Note that Moorhead (1975:62–63) shows the accurate location of El Pitic whereas Thomas (1941:figure between pages 82 and 83) plots it inappropriately near Altar, which is where Pitiqui is located.
9. Light troop, lightly armed to be effective specifically against the Apache. Although a *tropa ligera* soldier wore the presidial uniform (pattern coat, breeches, leggings, shoes, and hat), he went without the leather armor, shield, and lance. He carried a carbine and sling, a belly box, and a sword.
10. Excerpts from these reports can be found in Thomas (1941).
11. As Jackson (1982:139) points out, it was hoped that garrisons would eventually be relocated and defensive responsibilities transferred to retired soldiers and settlers organized into militia companies. The 1772 regulations stipulated that settlers living at the relocated presidios receive house lots and arable lands. Settlers did remain at Tubac Presidio, formed a militia, and continued to farm land, even though this journal indicates that they were not faring well against the Apache and were asking to be allowed to resettle. This problem was solved seven years later with the reinforcement and reactivation of the post with the assignment of Piman/O'odham troops and Spanish officers. Yet, with regard to Santa Cruz de Terrenate, there is a question as to whether everyone left or whether some settlers or soldiers remained behind. Brinkerhoff and Faulk (1965:94) state that a few soldiers remained at Santa Cruz until 1788. In the citations provided, it appears that this notion derives from Di Peso (and perhaps Almada), but upon examination of the statement by Di Peso it becomes clear that this is a misinterpretation found in Hammond's translation and annotation of Zuniga's journal. Rocha's (1980c) journal from the closing of the presidio indicates that soldiers were not left behind.
12. Fireman (1977:146) states that the shift was only about twelve miles between Santa Cruz de Terrenate and Las Nutrias. In fact, as Moorhead (1975:88) notes, the distance is actually about forty miles.
13. Ugarte died in 1798 (Moorhead 1968:23).

14. Throughout these documents Ugarte is referenced by Rocha as *señor brigadier*, a title that has been shorted herein to "brigadier." While according to an ethnohistorian reviewer, *señor brigadier* "is more typically translated as simply 'The General' or, if the name is provided, General John Doe," this title is not appropriate for the time. In some countries, as in New Spain at this time, the title *brigadier* was not considered to be a general officer rank, but rather the title of one commanding a brigade in the field, a brigade being uniform in composition, such as cavalry. The rank of brigadier was established in 1702 by Felipe V and was intermediate between colonel and general. As a military rank, seniority depended on the country and changed through time. In Spain brigadiers came to be full generals in 1871, and in 1889 they were renamed *general de brigada* (Cañete Paez 2009). In further support of this interpretation, an early-eighteenth-century dictionary provides the following definition of brigadier: "*El official que manda una Brigada de Caballeria, o Infanteria, y a Los Coroneles de los Regimientos que las componen, inferiór en grado al Mariscal de Campo. En voz nuevamente introducida del Francés, en cuyo idióma significa esto mismo*" ("The official who commands a brigade of cavalry, or infantry, and the colonels of the regiments that comprise them, lower in rank to the field marshal. Newly introduced term from French, in which language this means the same") Real Academia Española (1990 [1726–1739]:1:682).
15. Fireman (1977:147) says he built walls at Terrenate but it would have to have been at Las Nutrias (see Kessell 1966:38).
16. Many consider that Gila Apaches, or *Gileños*, was an overarching label applied to Apacheans who resided north of the Gila River, groups who were later differentiated or who were already distinctive in the colonial period, but were not distinguished by the Spanish. Alternatively, De Reuse (2012) linguistically documents possible evidence of Gileño and Mimbreños Apaches as distinctive tribes who eventually lost their identity as discrete groups. Linguistic evidence suggests that these Athabascan speakers were neither Western Apache nor Chiricahua speakers but spoke a variety of Athabascan that was linguistically intermediate between the later recorded Western Apache and Chiricahua languages. This suggests that some Apache groups disappeared from history, leaving only a slight linguistic trace, a process that occurred as a result of a variety of processes, including intermixing with other Apachean and non-Apachean groups (Seymour 2012).
17. Throughout these documents the spelling, capitalizations, and punctuations from the original documents are largely maintained, except where needed for clarification. This system has created some awkward translations, but will hopefully help to remove a layer of mediation between the English-only reader and the Spanish documents.

CHAPTER 2

Instructions and Justifications

The documents in this chapter are the instructions given by Croix to both Ugarte and Rocha regarding their upcoming reconnaissance. As is made clear in the first paragraph—in the first sentence—of Croix's instruction, the goal of this reconnaissance was to fulfill the charter of the royal instructions that were inserted in the *Reglamento de Presidios* of 1772 to realign the presidios.

Preceding Note

A note preceding the orders identifies the succeeding documents, as follows:

> Copies of the orders dispatched to the military governor, Don Jacobo Ugarte y Loyola, and the engineer Don Gerónimo de la Rocha for the reconnaissance of the frontier of Sonora and the repositioning of its presidios, and reports of the head and his officer.

Instructive Order to the Military Governor: Croix to Ugarte

To begin, the first sentence of Croix's instruction to Ugarte quotes the royal instructions that are inserted in the *Reglamento de Presidios* for guidance on the purpose of this expedition. The articles Croix cites—2, 3, 4, and 5—are included here. The entire *Reglamento* document is long because it pertains to the entire northern frontier of New Spain, including neighboring provinces. This boundary stretched for about 1,800 miles from La Bahía on the east to Altar on the west. Along the Sonoran province alone there was a 300-mile-long boundary to defend (Anza in Polzer and Sheridan 1997:307; see Figure 2.1). When taking into account the adjacent Nueva Vizcaya and New Mexico, the distance was substantially increased, as demarcated by the placement of the Presidial Line.[1] Yet this conception of the line provides a false sense of the territorial boundaries because various bands of Apache permeated the areas behind (south of) the lines and made their homes in the mountains that bordered the valleys where Spanish settlements were located. Further to the east there were Apache, Comanche, and other groups who were opponents, so the demarcated line did not represent actual territorial boundaries.

Only those portions of the *Reglamento de Presidios* relating to Sonora and the places mentioned in Rocha's document are addressed here because the others are not especially relevant to this topic. While the *Reglamento de Presidios* has been translated elsewhere (Brinkerhoff and Faulk 1965), our original translation and transcription are from a different exemplar (Carlos III 1772).

Articles 1 and 2 of Title 10 relate to the treatment of Indians, and the rest pertain to the Presidial Line. These are cited here for the reader's convenience.

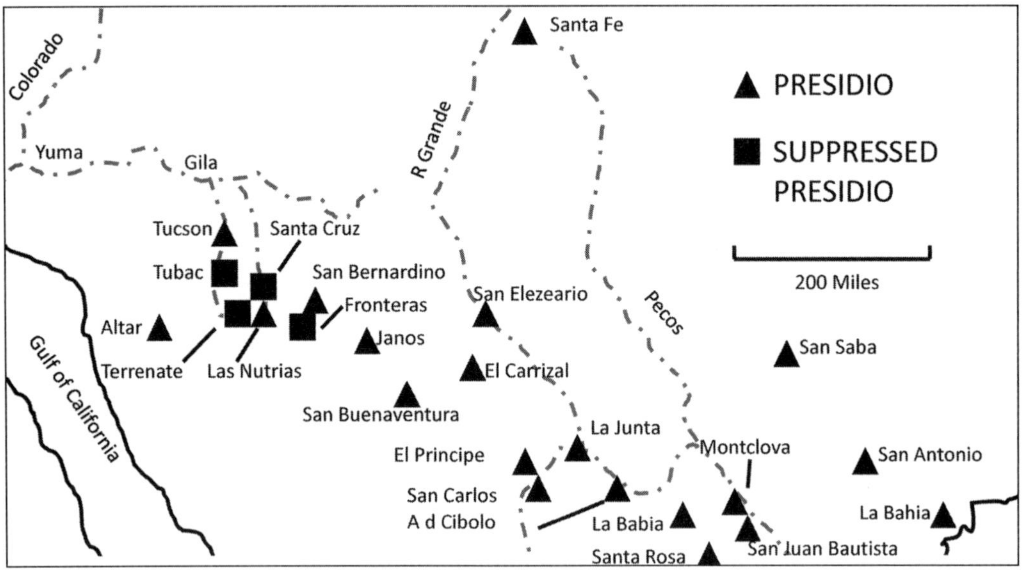

FIGURE 2.1. Distribution of presidios along the Presidial Line.

Regulations

Title 10, Articles 1 and 2

[Article] 1. As the object of war should be peace, and as my main goal is the welfare and conversion of the gentile Indians and the tranquility of the frontier lands, the commandant-inspector, the captains, and the presidial troops will always keep in mind that the most effective measures for attaining these useful and pious ends are vigor and activity in war, and good faith and gentle treatment of those who surrender peacefully, or the prisoners. Therefore, the primary attention of all should be directed to waging active and incessant war against the Indians who are declared enemies, wherever possible attack them in their own villages and lands; but with the prisoners that are taken in war, I prohibit all bad treatment and impose the penalty of death upon those who kill them in cold blood; they shall be sent to the vicinity of Mexico City where my viceroy may dispose of them as shall be convenient. I order that prisoners be provided with the same daily food ration as are given Indian auxiliaries; and the women and children that are apprehended will be treated equally and assisted, in order to procure their conversion and instruction.

[Article] 2. But having been shown by experience that gentleness and good treatment are as useful when dealing with the entire nation, as are pernicious both complaisance when dealing with the entire nation and readiness to concede safe passes and peace treaties which are not stable or secure, especially with the Apaches, who under different names ravage the frontiers. When their forces are inferior, or they are overwhelmed by our victories, they profess a desire for peace; afterwards, they abuse our clemency at the first opportunity, interpreting as weakness the clemency with which they have been treated and received. I prohibit the commandant-inspector and the captains of presidios from granting them peace; in case they ask for it with assurances and with indications that their request is genuine and that they will submit to my authority, the captain will concede them only a truce, or suspension of fighting (with hostages), for the number of days necessary to seek confirmation from the commandant-inspector; and he is not to extend it any longer than the time necessary for obtaining the approval of my viceroy and for formalizing the terms

Figure 2.2 Enlargement of Urrutia's map of the settlement area at Altar presidio, [*Plano del Presidio del Altar, en la provincia de Sonora*], 1767. Courtesy of the British Library; Shelfmark: Cartographic Items Additional MS. 17,662.e.

and conditions, demanding always during the aforesaid truce the total cessation of hostilities and, if possible, the restitution of Spanish and friendly Indian prisoners.

Regulations: Location and Cordon of Presidios

In the first line of Croix's instructions he references articles 2, 3, 4, 5, and 29 of the royal instruction inserted in the royal regulations for presidios (*Reglamento e Instruccion para los Presidios que se han de formar en la Linea de Frontera de la Nueva España*). Specifically, he is referring to instructions for the new locations and cordon of presidios in Sonora (now southern Arizona and Sonora) and California. These articles are included here for clarity.

Cordon of Presidios

Altar

[Article] 2. The first of the frontier presidios is Altar, currently situated thirty leagues from Vizani and Pitiqui—towns belonging to the old mission of Caborca, which was destroyed by the Apaches—should be removed and relocated at another site closer to the coast of the Gulf of California, making sure to place it on level terrain where there is adequate water and fodder for the horse herds such that it will not be difficult for their detachments to survey and reconnoiter the areas which are to the right and left of this presidio, and the edge of the sea, and between it and the next presidio in the line, in order to prevent the enemies from the northwest from intruding and raiding in the province [see Figure 2.2].

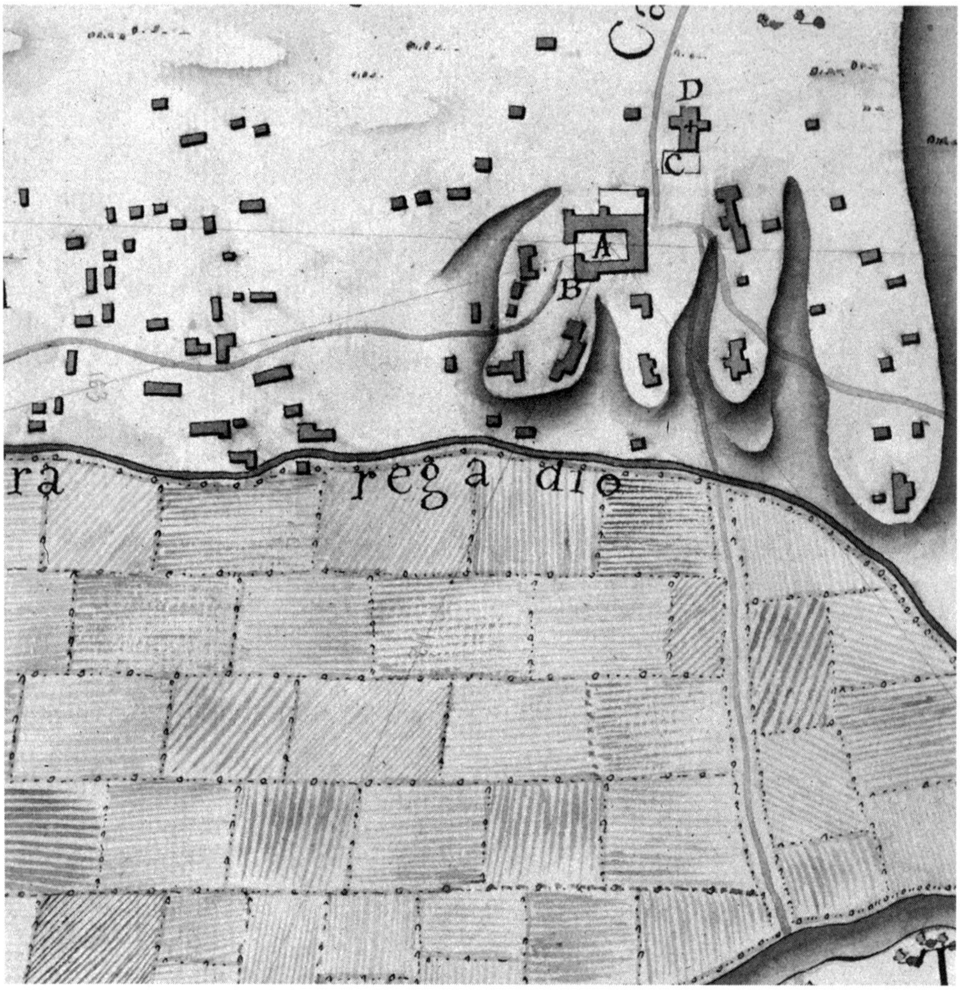

FIGURE 2.3. Enlargement of Urrutia's map of the settlement area at Tubac Presidio, [*Plano del Presidio de Tubac en la provincia de Sonora*], 1766. Courtesy of the British Library; Shelfmark: Cartographic Items Additional MS. 17,662.h.

Tubac

[Article] 3. At a distance of less than forty leagues from the aforementioned presidio is found that of Tubac, with a considerable number of civilians in the vicinity who have congregated there in the shade of its garrison; the civilians can subsist in that place with the company having moved to another nearby where the land offers the indispensable necessities, one situated precisely the exact distance of forty leagues from Altar, getting as far west as possible while assuring reciprocal communication, constantly cutting paths through the intervening terrain, and hindering the raids of the enemies to the interior country [see Figure 2.3].

Terrenate

[Article] 4. This presidio is closer to Tubac than the forty leagues required of all presidios of the line with minimal differences between one another, and for this reason should be removed and situated following an individualized reconnaissance

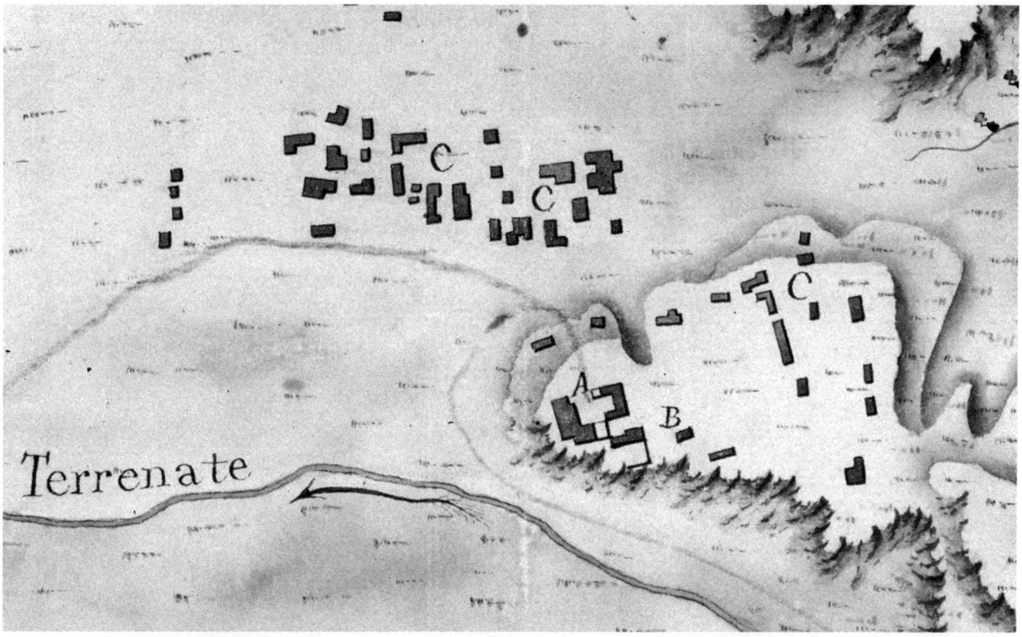

FIGURE 2.4. Enlargement of Urrutia's map of the settlement area at Terrenate Presidio, [*Plano del Presidio de Terrenate, dependiente de la governacion de Sonora*], 1766. Courtesy of the British Library; Shelfmark: Cartographic Items Additional MS. 17,662.g.

of the terrain in one of the many valleys bathed by the rivers San Pedro, Las Nutrias, Guachuca, Terrenate, and others, making sure to keep close to your back the mountain ranges of Magallanes and Mababe, and closer to the presidio of Fronteras, so in this way they can impede the invasions of the Apaches and the detachments from the two sides can render mutual assistance to one another [see Figure 2.4].

Fronteras

[Article] 5. Given that this presidio, where there is a medium-sized group of civilians, is poorly situated at a distance of sixty leagues from Janos, consequently leaving uncovered a large part of the frontier that is most exposed to the incursions of the Gileño Apaches, it should be moved with all possible haste to the valley of San Bernardino, or some adjacent site if there is a more advantageous one, with the precise purpose of its detachment crossing paths with and joining forces with those of Janos and Terrenate in order to contain the penetrations of the barbarians frequently coming down on their camps or rancherías [see Figures 2.5a and b and 2.6].

[Article] 6. It should be left to the four referenced presidios to relocate from the locations whey they are presently found, occupied by the civilians they had and augmented by other Spanish settlers and Ópata Indians, parceling out to everyone lands and houses, or lots to build them, with the specific conditions that they keep them occupied and keep themselves equipped and prepared to defend their respective districts, and help the detachment of troops that should guard the frontier. To this end the Spaniards shall be provided the arms they need for what they cost my own treasury, and the Ópata Indians shall be given from my budget arquebuses and carbines for their noteworthy valor, and for the loyalty they have proven since they voluntarily came under my dominion.

a

b

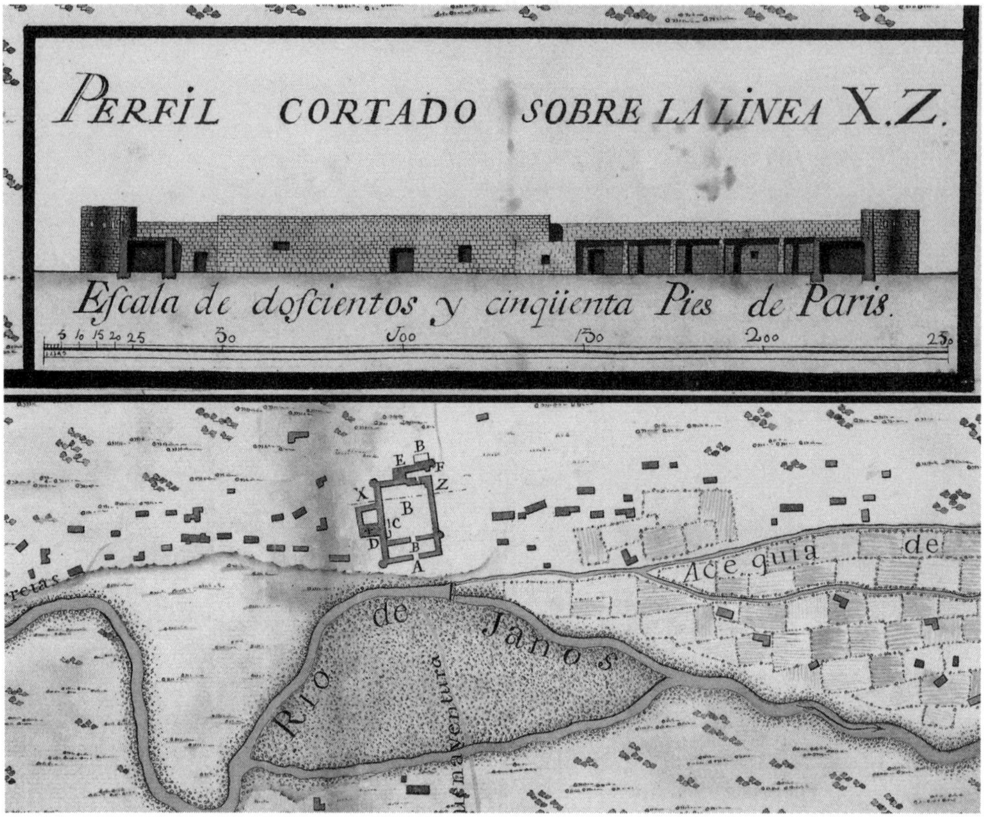

FIGURE 2.5. (*a*) Enlargement of Urrutia's map of the settlement area and (*b*) Enlargement of the cross section drawn by Urrutia at Janos Presidio, [*Plano del Presidio de San Felipe y Santiago de Tanos*, sic], 1766. Courtesy of the British Library; Shelfmark: Cartographic Items Additional MS. 17,662.l.

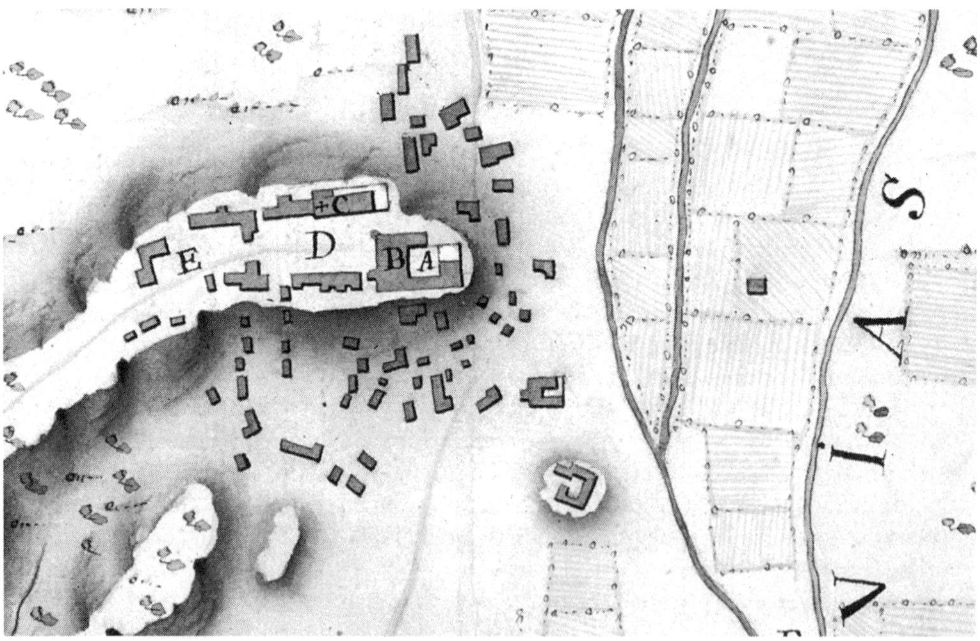

FIGURE 2.6. Enlargement of Urrutia's map of the settlement area at Fronteras Presidio showing some of the fields under cultivation, [*Plano del Presidio de Fronteras, dependiente de la governacion de Sonora*], 1766. Courtesy of the British Library; Shelfmark(s): Cartographic Items Additional MS. 17,662.f.

The Californias

[Article] 29. Having straightened out the presidios of the mainland and their annual appropriations—the two interior presidios of Sonora will be kept as they are so long as the submissive Indians are being gathered into towns; in the meantime they are subject to all that is in this regulation—I declare that the presidios of the Californias are to continue on the same footing that they now have, confirming to the decrees given by my viceroy, until the conquest and settlement of the Indians has been completed as far as the port of Monterey; and understanding that the quantity of 33,000 pesos has been provisionally appropriated annually for the care and security of that peninsula, I order and command that this sum continue to be paid at the end of each year at the royal treasury of Guadalajara, as has been the practice in the past, and that my viceroy support and aid by every possible means the old and new settlements in the said province. He is to inform me of all measures he takes conducive and useful to the development, colonization, and extension of new settlements for gentile Indians.

Letter

Instructive Order of the Military Governor [Croix to Ugarte]

In the 2nd, 3rd, 4th, and 5th articles of the royal instruction inserted in the regulations for presidios, His Majesty deigned to resolve the movement of Santa Gertrudis del Altar, Tubac, Terrenate, and Fronteras to the new line proposed by the Lord Señor Marqués de Rubí. And in article 29 from the same instruction, the suppression of those of San Miguel de Orcasitas, and San Carlos de Buenavista [see Figure 2.7 a and b].

The completion of these sovereign resolutions having been delegated to the deceased Commandant-Inspector Don Hugo O'Conor,[2] this chief carried out the required errands resulting from their partial change to the predetermined direction of the line of the frontier, namely the transfer of the presidio of this name [Fronteras] to the valley of San Bernardino, Terrenate to the ruined pueblo of Santa Cruz, and Tubac to Tucson with Altar kept in its position, and the reforms of those in Orcasitas and Buenavista suspended.

Beyond all these measures, and the successive ones that were thought up to improve them and ensure the defense of this province, the aforementioned commandant-inspector and Governor Don Francisco Antonio Crespo[3] issued their recommendations, but nothing could go forward because of the restlessness of the Seris and the hostilities of the Apache.

Some of these and others obliged Lieutenant Colonel Don Juan Bautista de Anza, being *Comandante de las Armas* [commandant of arms] of the province, to represent to me the need to return the presidios (that had been moved) to their former lands. And I acceding to his request, determined that he should proceed as things presented themselves to him, and with the precise responsibility which, of course, led him to these proposals.

I gave an account of them to His Majesty, and although in the royal order of December 30, [17]77, His Honor deigned to approve my resolution, it could not be established until now what commission this conferred to Your Lordship for the reconnaissance of the frontier, I hope that its results be the happy fulfillment of the sovereign resolutions of the king.

To provide it [the desired result], it is indispensable that Your Lordship carry out the most scrupulous and thorough examination, not only of the lands that are currently occupied by the presidios of the province, but also of those that they formerly covered [protected], prior to the royal instruction for the new line, and those that

a

b

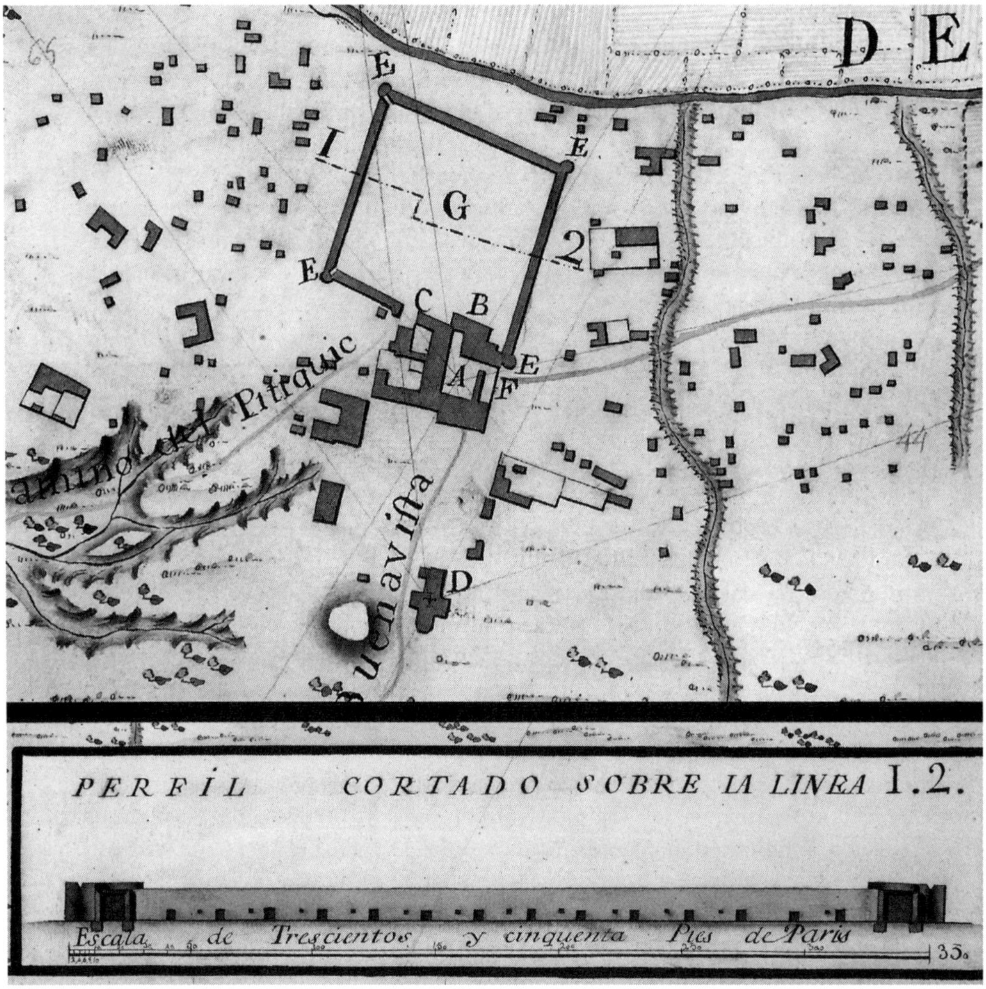

FIGURE 2.7. (*a*) Enlargement of Urrutia's map of the settlement area, and (*b*) enlargement of the cross section drawn by Urrutia at Horcasitas Presidio, [*Plano della villa de S. Miguel de Horcasitas*], 1767. Courtesy of the British Library; Shelfmark: Cartographic Items Additional MS. 17,662.d.

could be advantageous to link up with the new settlements of the Colorado River and open communication with northern California, because the importance and seriousness of the goals for which the royal resolutions are contracted require these aforementioned indispensable surveys.

Take Your Lordship's orders to help the engineer Don Gerónimo de la Rocha, and devoting Your Lordship, begin your commission at the presidio of Fronteras. After you take hold of the situation, resources, and advantages of the said presidio, Your Lordship will continue your march along the straight road, or route parallel to the place where the San Pedro River starts to flow without interruption [to flow continuously], from there examining the arroyos of Guachuca, Las Nutrias, and Terrenate, and the source of the river.[4] Afterward, Your Lordship will go by its margins to the place where it joins with the Gila, and withdrawing to the presidio of San Agustín del Tucson, Your Lordship will reconnoiter the old one at Tubac, returning to that of Terrenate.

Having concluded this examination, Your Lordship can move to Pitic by way of the presidio of Santa Gertrudis del Altar, reconnoitering on this return trip the valley of Arivac, Busanic, Saric, Tubutama, and other missions along this route, and send me, with the corresponding plan or survey drawing that the engineer Don Gerónimo de la Rocha will prepare, a clear and very detailed report of the distances, mountains, passes, canyons, rivers, springs, arroyos that maintain water all year, and those that lack it [water] in the dry season, conditions of the San Pedro River, number and names of its fordable crossings, the qualities of the lands at its margins, possibility or impossibility of making them fruitful.

Following this thorough description of the country, Your Lordship will expound to me on whatever else he should come across or think of the places that ought to be occupied on the line that truly is the border for the defense of the province, bearing in mind the specific circumstances, that under the shelter[5] of the presidios respectable populations may be established that with time may not require the aid of the troops.[6]

In the same report or a separate one, Your Lordship will give to me your recommendation regarding the erection of the presidio that the Ópatas have requested, and finally, however it is that Your Lordship acquaints himself through experience the territories of the frontier, I hope to find in your reports all that may be desired and conducive to the benefit of this province, compliance with the royal resolutions of His Majesty, and execution of my supporting orders.

Near the arroyo of Las Nutrias Your Lordship will find the relocated presidio of Santa Cruz and Captain Don Joseph Vildosola[7] with the order to raise some barracks for the interim accommodation of the troops until Your Lordship informs me whether it is suitable to situate the presidio there.

In this way, the aforementioned captain, like the one at San Agustín del Tucson, Don Pedro de Allande, will accompany Your Lordship if you consider it necessary, and Your Lordship may entrust to them the surveys that you may have ready because, although I have detailed all that must be executed with the guidance of the engineer Don Gerónimo de la Rocha, I leave to Your Lordship the discretion to do this on your own, or through officers who deserve your trust for the most speedy conclusion of these important orders, which I undertake according to Your Lordship's known zeal.

God bless Your Lordship for many years, Arizpe, April 15, 1780. El Caballero de Croix to Señor Don Jacobo Ugarte y Loyola

Another One with Accompanying Documents and Advising of the Commission for the Engineer Don Gerónimo de la Rocha [Croix to Ugarte]

My dearest Lord: I am able to send to Your Lordship the attached copies of reports that were made by the late Commandant-Inspector Don Hugo O'Conor, Colonel Don Francisco Crespo, Adjutant-Inspector Don Antonio Bonilla, and the Reverend Father Friar Juan Díaz regarding the establishment of the line of presidios of this province so Your Lordship will have them before you during the commission that I have conferred upon you, and return them to me once you have finished it, making sure that Your Lordship give said documents to the engineer Don Gerónimo de la Rocha.

God grant that Your Lordship have many years,
Arispe, Abril 16, 1780
I, your most attentive and reliable servant, El Caballero de Croix, kiss the hand of Your Stewardship,
Don Jacobo Ugarte y Loyola

Order to the Engineer Rocha from Croix

This confidential letter from Croix to Rocha is of interest because Ugarte is not included, suggesting that this request for a secret report is more than an effort to obtain candid information (e.g., shielded from the king and other authorities) about the frontier and presidio placements themselves. In the third paragraph Croix instructs Rocha to send the requisite report and maps to Ugarte, but also to provide copies to Croix confidentially. The eighteenth century is famous for its intrigue at court, and this particular statement seems to convey a concern for duplicity. By requesting a blind copy, Croix was protecting Rocha while at the same time he seems to have been testing the dependability of Ugarte and forestalling the consequences of any potential treachery. This is perhaps not surprising given that Ugarte had a reputation for insubordination (Moorhead 1968:19, 20, 23, 34, 36). Croix's objective may have been to determine how effectively Ugarte followed his directives in order to evaluate his field performance and the content of the journal and summary reports. This order and the journal content itself demonstrate that these are the secret documents, not the official ones that would be forwarded to the king and made available to Ugarte. Places within the summary reports and diary that convey this are flagged in endnotes.

Ugarte may have been aware of Croix's strategy, as Croix had made a similar request for a secret report from Ugarte after convening with the temporary military governor of Sonora Pedro de Tueros and (civil) Intendant-Governor Pedro de Corbalan in 1779 (Moorhead 1968:49). Also, in Ugarte's summary (Chapter 3) he states that Rocha's "diary, clear and detailed... with the corresponding drawing [map] will have already passed into the hands of Your Lordship." This suggests that Rocha played this safe and complied with Croix's request, and at the same time told Ugarte about this order and gave him an idea of contents, while still hinting at the differences of opinion between them.

Croix was thinking big, consistent with the grandiose size of the Interior Provinces. Just a few years before Anza had discovered a route to Alta California, traveling to the newly established presidio of Monterey, and then in 1776 he led colonists to Monterey, exploring San Francisco. From this instruction it is clear that Croix is conveying the king's desire to link the northern portion of the Sonoran province to California with a presidio placed far to the north, at the confluence of the San Pedro and Gila Rivers.

This letter conveys that the directive to place a presidio at the confluence of the San Pedro and Gila Rivers comes from the king himself, and his fulfillment of a much larger plan relies on the success of this placement. This directive explains the amount of text Ugarte and Rocha commit to explaining how inappropriate that specific location was for the placement of a presidio and how unsuitable the San Pedro was in general for settlement. This also partially accounts for why Rocha takes such care to explain in his journal and in the official record the circuitous route by which they checked the confluence for suitability, on the one hand, and the need for a more thorough survey of the margins of the Gila, on the other. The rivalry between Rocha and Ugarte (and the value to Croix of the secrecy of this report) is also apparent: "I cannot say if there will be on the banks of the river [a suitable place] following the current, or ascending against it [upstream, against the current], for Brigadier Loyola did not allow me to stop to reconnoiter them with the scrupulous care that I wanted, for which I asked him in several instances to give me an escort and permission, and he did not see fit to grant it to me" (Chapter 3).

Order to the Engineer [Croix to Rocha]

By verbal order I have prepared for Your Mercy that under Brigadier Don Jacobo Ugarte y Loyola, you should execute the most extensive reconnaissance of the frontier of this province.

You should start at the Fronteras Presidio, repeating those that Your Mercy has just done for the relocation of the one at Santa Cruz to the origin of the San Pedro River[8] and from there continue along the banks of the river to the place where it meets the Gila, continuing this scrupulous examination with one of the land where is presently found the presidio of San Agustín del Tucson, which a long time ago used to be in Tubac, and that of Terrenate.

Having concluded these essential surveys, and Your Mercy having moved to the pueblo of Pitic through the plains of Arivac, Busanic, Saric, Tubutama, and the other missions, presidio of Altar, and the *real* of the Cieneguilla, create a plan [map] of all the lands examined, delivering it to the brigadier cited, so that it can be routed to me with the corresponding reports, Your Mercy confidentially sending me yours.

So that Your Mercy develops them with the refinement I desire, you will receive from the secretary of the command a copy of the regulations of the presidios, a general map of these provinces, and other documents needed to illustrate the information that I want,[9] and shall focus into a clear presentation of the entire country to be examined. To show its condition, and the means to contain the hostilities that are suffered from the Apaches and Seris, knowing that, the [Presidio] Line provided for in the royal instruction inserted in the regulation for presidios being not yet established, it is necessary that Your Mercy tell me the places you consider suitable to place it, bearing in mind that the king has resolved the erection of a presidio at the junction of the San Pedro River and Gila so that collaboration with the new pueblos of the Colorado will open the road and lines of communication between this province and California.

And, as I have repeatedly said verbally to Your Mercy, the ideas I put forth to bring to fruition: the sovereign resolutions of His Majesty intend that the presidios be established on land able to maintain respectable populations that, over time, will not require the aid of troops for their own defense. I hope that the reports of Your Mercy achieve the desired outcomes, and the just purposes to which I aspire to the best service of the king.

God bless Your Mercy with many years.[11] Arizpe, April 15, 1780. El Caballero de Croix to Señor Don Gerónimo de la Rocha.

Summary Statement

These orders and the documents resulting from the reconnaissance convey the impression that these three men had met prior to the trip to decide upon their approach and the character of their conclusions, within the confines of the king's directives. With every intention of fulfilling the king's charter they were also aware of the conditions on the frontier and each had their own views on the futility of extending the line even farther north.

Notes

1. After Rubí's inspection, the new line of fortifications was to be composed of fifteen presidios situated at about forty leagues (or 120 miles) apart, and although they were not in a straight line, this represents something like an 1,800-mile-long perimeter that had to be defended. In reality, there were differing numbers of presidios, and they were moved more than once, but this establishes an idea of how the Spanish were conceiving of the frontier perimeter at this time.
2. Don Hugo O'Conor, then Brigadier, died on March 9, 1779, at the age of forty-four (Santiago 1994:79).

3. Kessell (1976:Chapter 5) describes Don Francisco Antonio Crespo, career officer of the infantry regiment of Granada, as energetic and Spanish-born, and suggests he was bidding to upstage Anza in an expedition to California.
4. He is concerned with the source of the San Pedro River, not specifically the tributaries.
5. *Al abrigo*: "shelter" or "protection," rather than "shadow" as in Thomas (1941:149).
6. This references the Crown's desire for the troops to be self-sufficient, growing their own crops and raising their own livestock.
7. Captain Don Joseph Antonio Vildosola served as interim governor of Sinaloa in the 1740s and then captain of the Terrenate Presidio. Vildosola commanded an expedition between November 7 and December 16, 1780, against the Apaches and prepared a diary.
8. Rocha had just overseen the transfer of Santa Cruz de Terrenate's residents south to Las Nutrias and at the same time had inspected areas along the route; consequently there would be some overlap.
9. It is likely that he was given Urrutia's map of the province to take with him. This would have been the most recent, the most comprehensive map available at the time. The regulations of the presidios were in the 1772 regulations.
10. One translation of *Vuestra Merced* is "Your Mercy." *Vuestra Merced* is the origin of the second person singular form of address, *Usted*, and in modern usage is usually translated as "you." Your Mercy is both precious and inaccurate in modern usage. Yet, at the time and in that context, *Vuestra Merced* is best translated as Your Mercy or Your Worship, and during this specific period and earlier was used in this way (see Sanz-Sánchez 2016).

CHAPTER 3

Summary Reports Regarding the Corner of the Province

Both Ugarte and Rocha prepared summary reports of their findings. These summary reports are more than simple condensations of the diary. Ugarte gave his own opinion that is not recorded elsewhere. Rocha provided details and explanations not included in his journal, such as when he discussed the presence of acorns and forage that would be suitable for pigs and goats. Rocha also reiterated the order to discreetly send a map to Croix, separately from the one given to Ugarte, exposing an important aspect of Croix's management strategy for this reconnaissance.

These documents show the authority of their words, and how these field men were really the decision-makers, laying the foundation for assessments through their arguments and presentation of their observations. As a result of the ways they described what they found and what they did not find, they were able to sway the king, convincing him not to shift the Presidial Line to the north with the placement of a post at the confluence of the San Pedro and Gila Rivers. These documents provide an insight into the substantial influence these two officers had in shaping the northern frontier, and consequently, the modern American Southwest, specifically southern Arizona. Rocha, in particular, was adamant that Tucson was the most useful location for a presidio, and he convincingly and repeatedly argued that the lower San Pedro and the junction of the two rivers was not an appropriate location for a presidio. We see his vision of the region, like ripples sent through time, shaping the settlement and defensive terrain of the area to this day in the persistence of population centers established and maintained then. This is consistent with Bolton's (1917:42) concept that a mere handful of Spaniards took possession and expanded the boundaries of this New World empire while most of Spain's blood and treasure were committed to European wars (also see Dobyns 1980:6).

Ugarte's Summary Report to Croix

Once the expedition was completed, Ugarte wrote this report to Croix, summarizing the results of the trip based on the orders presented to him, which are found in the previous chapter. It is clear from his first paragraph that Rocha bypassed Ugarte and sent the map and journal directly to Croix, as ordered, but this act was clearly known to Ugarte, even though it was not specifically out in the open. This exposes the difficult position Ugarte was placed in as a superior of Rocha, but with his authority being circumvented by Croix's request and Rocha's compliance. Rocha seems to have played his role exceeding well from a political standpoint by letting Ugarte in on his orders but still complying with those of Croix. This was a shrewd play by Rocha because Ugarte remained powerful in the region long after this reconnaissance.

Report of the Military Governor [Ugarte to Croix]

My dearest sir: Having carried out the reconnaissance of this frontier accompanied by the Lieutenant of Engineers Don Gerónimo de la Rocha in accordance with what Your Lordship ordered me to do in your superior order of last April 15, I began this mission at the presidio of Fronteras, as is denoted in the thorough diary, clear, and detailed, that with the corresponding survey drawing [map] will have already passed into the hands of Your Lordship, the aforementioned engineer, describing with great precision the mountains, passes, canyons, rivers, springs, arroyos that kept water all year, and those that lack it in the dry season, places providing support for population, crops, livestock pens, and the other details that, in the aforementioned, Your Lordship ordered me to communicate.[1]

From the aforementioned Fronteras [Presidio], Your Lordship, I made Your Lordship's presence known on the said date of April 29, having gone to reconnoiter the beautiful valley of Cochuta, which I judged to be more appropriate for the location of the presidio of Fronteras due to its large open space in which there are an abundance of pastures and sufficient farmland, and it is very easy to convey the necessary supplies from Fronteras [Presidio],[2] even when the waters of the valley should not be enough to give the necessary fruit. I add, in my communiqué of the sixth of this month, that I had acquired new knowledge from subjects who seemed truthful and knowledgeable and who assured me that with only the seasonal rainfall (even without the use of the waters of the valley for irrigation), the harvests that the Indian settlers left behind were most abundant, the same ones [Indian settlers], concluding that water was more abundant here than in Badeguachi.

To these reasons must be added the following advantages that I explained above and repeat briefly:

1. Families will live without the continual fear of being surprised by the enemy as they have done several times due to the proximity of the hill.[3]
2. It leaves the territory covered to the extent possible and impedes the continuous transit of the enemies that by Teras Pass and those that form the Sierra Purica intrude into the interior of the province.
3. That reconnaissance from here by a captain of conduct and resolution—the running springs of this mountain, and of the narrows (where in these parts is found Batepito Pass) and the box canyons that form in its ruggedness, where for a long time, and in safety they tend to gather together[4]—[would] take away this hideout[5] and remove them from the vicinity, with the consequence that their interruptions will be less frequent.
4. Those who devote themselves to the useful work of working the many placers, which, according to the report by residents of Bacuachi, are found right next to the Sierra Purica from Turisachi Pass, near that of Mabavi, will be able to be supported.

And lastly, once the envisioned presidio of Ópata is placed in the valley of Bapispe (I deem it advantageous as I explain to Your Lordship in a separate study), they will be able to help each other mutually this way with the aforementioned patrols,[6] others that may be carried out in the Sierras de las Espuelas ["Spurs"] and in San Luis, and others nearby.

Placed on this site, or (if that does not seem suitable to Your Lordship) in Fronteras or Badeguachi, [should be] the first presidio of this line; I will explain my opinion simply, and with candor about the others that must complete it, using the information

FIGURE 3.1. San José de Tumacácori Mission, Courtesy of the Library of Congress, https://www.loc.gov/item/az0129/; Historic American Buildings Survey John P. O'Neill, Photographer, March 3, 1937, View from North in Courtyard Showing Mortuary Chapel.

I have acquired through experience in the thorough reconnaissance that I have just completed, setting for myself the sole purpose of obeying Your Lordship and informing you about what was achieved that is most conducive to the royal service, happiness of the province, and punishment of its enemies.

Under this assumption, the second presidio should be placed in the spot of Las Nutrias, where currently the company of the abandoned presidio of Santa Cruz is camping. The reasons which support the preference for this site I put forth to Your Lordship in my official minutes of May 7, adding now only that this place is removed from that of Cochuta[7] by the *Camino de Magallanes* ["Magellan Road"] by twenty-five to twenty-six leagues, and from the *Ojo del Gato* ["Cat Spring"] (which is better terrain) by twenty-eight to twenty-nine [leagues].

On the spacious and well-proportioned mesa of Buenavista I judge suitable to place the third: It is located on the banks of the San Antonio River with all the resources[8] for a good population,[9] and is a league and a half distant from the deserted hacienda of Buenavista, thirty-five from the presidio of Altar, twenty-six from that of Tucson, and twenty-one from the site of Las Nutrias. The location of a presidio on this site would encourage people, and over time it may be possible to populate the advantageous places of Santa María Suanca, San Antonio, Rancho del Torreón, Valle de San Lázaro, Hacienda de Santa Bárbara, Rancho de San Luis, Buenavista, Pueblo de Guevavi, all located at a regular[10] distance from the proposed presidio, which, once carried out, will serve the province, as the engineer's diary indicated, most usefully for planting and livestock breeding.

Moreover, in this way the missions and pueblos of Calabazas, Tumacácori, and Tubac that form a line from Buenavista to Tucson are protected, and their residents will be able to cooperate with the troops of the presidios for mutual defense (Figure 3.1).

The three presidios of which I have spoken so far I consider advantageous to form a new line that truly is the border for the defense of the province, without losing sight

FIGURE 3.2. Casa Grande near the Gila River, Courtesy of the Library of Congress, cph 3g05612 //hdl.loc.gov/loc.pnp/cph.3g05612; Ancient Halls of the Montezumas, ca 1870, Carlo Gentile, photographer.

FIGURE 3.3. The confluence of the San Pedro and Gila Rivers today.

of the precise circumstances that under their protection respectable populations may be established, that with time may not need the aid of the troops, but Your Lordship, serving himself to advise me on the cited point, put forth my recommendation on those that could be advantageous to continue it [the line] until it joins hands with the new settlements of the Colorado River, and open communication with northern California; I have to say in obedience to this superior order,[11] that for these purposes, I maintain that the present presidio of Tucson is very necessary and advantageous.

Although this presidio, which is located in a corner of the province, can serve very little for its [the province's] defense, with the exception of the missions of San Xavier del Bac and Tucson that are nearby, it is, however, the most appropriate to follow the above mentioned line, sending it through Casas Grandes of Moctezuma,[12] where hitherto have traveled, and will travel, the religious and others that pass through to the Colorado River, on which site or in its vicinity a good presidio can be established (Figure 3.2). I am not able to speak about this site, nor of the subsequent ones, with the certainty of the previous ones for not having surveyed them.

What is certain is that I am not of the opinion that we should route the line along the banks of the San Pedro River, or Terrenate, or place any presidio at the junction of this river and the Gila (Figure 3.3). The presidio that would be positioned here would be too forward [far north of the other presidios in the line] and distant from the interior country and could not offer any defense of the province. It would need to be supported by a large detachment, and it would be necessary to convey from Tucson

Figure 3.4. Area along the San Pedro that was once referenced as *Acequias Hondas* or "Deep Ditches," because of the arable land and water available for irrigation.

everything essential because that place does not have any land for planting, much less for new populations that should be established under its protection in the future.[13]

And although in the Santa Teresa Valley,[14] about a league and a half distant from this site, some crop plantings can be confirmed, they will always be so limited that the scarcity of supplies in the presidio would not be avoided, nor will it attract people to settle in a place that offers them so little by way of resources and convenience.

The only advantage that can be found here is that this routing of the line connects it with the new settlements of the Colorado River, but I have already said to Your Lordship that through Tucson it may be continued with greater ease, and more directly [with respect to the existing line].[15]

I think the same must be said of the San Pedro River, or Terrenate, that it does not serve the purpose of continuing the frontier line, because although on its banks there are several places where it seems presidios could be placed, as at El Quiburi, Tres Alamos, Cequias Jondas,[16] (Figure 3.4) and others, this line would always be of no advantage and very detrimental. In the first place, because these places do not have enough land except for small populations that will never be able to sustain themselves without the aid of troops.

Second, because they would inevitably be placed at a significant distance one from the other unless you add more of them, resulting in considerable expense to the royal treasury.

Third, because the province would be left helpless, and the interior pueblos without defense, because the presidios would be advanced at such a great distance from which neither could they aid each other nor could they hold the border towns in the event of an invasion.

And lastly, it would be essential that in these (as I have said of the junction of the rivers), a large detachment be placed, or they will otherwise be useless to wage war against the enemy, defending only the walls[17] of the presidio.[18]

In contrast to all of the disadvantages expressed before, the biggest advantages and opportunities are present with the line I have detailed, which covers [protects] the interior pueblos as far as possible; with more ease, citizens [*vecinos*], friendly Indians, and soldiers can mutually aid one another; the presidios are positioned at regular distances; the transits from one to the other are less risky; respectable populations can settle under its protection that, besides not needing the help of the troops, will be useful to the province, cultivating the fertile lands that are now depopulated. And finally, it will unite them by the shortest route toward the above-mentioned new settlements, according to the reports with which I find myself.

And although, as I conceive it, the hostility of the Apache will never be entirely avoided, wherever you may put the line; nonetheless, realigning it where I propose, we must persuade ourselves it will be less frequent, especially if what becomes practice is the providence that Your Lordship communicated to me in your superior [order] of May 16, indicating two assembly posts on the border to make war on the enemy in accordance with the scant forces with which we find ourselves, meanwhile, His Majesty provides the aid needed to do it under the terms that his Royal Piety advises in Articles 1 and 2 of Title 10 of the *Real Reglamento de Presidios.*

In regard to this border of the Seri I have nothing to add to what several times I have presented to Your Lordship, who knows that the forces of Pitic, Altar, and Buenavista are indispensable for the possible containment of these rebels and of the Tiburones, and Tepocas,[19] and in my opinion, even engaging them in the most active war possible will not achieve their true subjugation or extermination without the approval of their overseas deportation, which I proposed in my confidential recommendation last January 15 to Your Lordship in response to your superior [order] of December 31, 1779.

This is my recommendation related to the lands that I have surveyed, the totality of which I subject to your superior and most prudent Lordship.

I ask that Our Lord conserve the life of Your Lordship for many years.

Pitic Presidio
August 14, 1780
Señor Commandante General,
Your most attentive and recognized servant, Jacobo Ugarte y Loyola, kisses the hand of Your Lordship,
Señor Commandante General, Cabballero de Croix

Dear Sir: obeying the superior [order] of Your Lordship of last August 28, I include with the documents that Your Lordship asks me in the aforementioned, and these are the reports of the late Commandant-Inspector Don Hugo O'Conor; of the governor who was of this province Don Francisco Crespo; of the Assistant-Inspector Don Antonio Bonillo; and of the R.P.F. [*Reverendo Padre Fray*] Juan Díaz.[20]

Our Lord, I ask that the life of Your Lordship has many years as I have wished.

Pitic, September 1, 1780

Your most attentive and recognized Señor Jacobo Ugarte y Loyola kisses the hand of Your Lordship,

Señor Commandante General, Caballero de Croix

Rocha's Summary Report to Croix

Some of the differences in perception and intent between Rocha and Ugarte become clear in Rocha's summary and his diary. One specific difference in the journal is the clear indication Rocha provided as to his desire to push forward and explore further when at the confluence of the San Pedro and Gila. Ugarte, on the other hand, was satisfied to have fulfilled the orders of the mission to evaluate the confluence for the new placement of a presidio (that is, the repositioning of the Santa Cruz garrison that was now relocated once again to Las Nutrias), which had already been judged unsuitable, a judgment this expedition would reaffirm. Below, Rocha also comments that his instructions from Croix were in conflict with the direct orders given him in the field by Ugarte and so he was unable to comply. Specifically, he begins by outlining Croix's desire to have them go up the San Pedro first and then over to the Santa Cruz but then notes that he was not free to comply with these instructions because he was under Ugarte's orders and instead they completed the mission in the reverse order. These examples provide an indication of the tension between the two travelers set in motion both by Croix's behind-the-scenes orders and by Ugarte's character and reputation.

Report of Engineer Don Gerónimo de la Rocha

My very dear Sir: In the order of April 15 of this year Your Lordship took it upon himself to direct me under the orders of Brigadier Don Jacobo Ugarte y Loyola to undertake the most extensive reconnaissance of the border of the province, beginning it at the presidio of Fronteras, continuing by way of those that had just been executed for the movement of Santa Cruz up to the source of the San Pedro River, and by its margins until its junction with the Gila, and from there to that of the terrain that San Agustín del Tucson currently occupies, that of Tubac, where it was formerly, and that of Terrenate. Once I had left these, I was to return to Pitic Pueblo via the plains of Aribac, Busanic, Saric, Tubutama, and the rest of the missions, the presidio of Altar, and *real de la Cieneguilla*, drawing up a survey of everything and handed it over to Brigadier Loyola so that it would be routed to Your Lordship with his reports, and that I should pass mine on confidentially; that the information I was supposed to give in them, and Your Lordship desired should come together as a clear presentation of the whole country examined, and to make known their status, and the means to contain the hostilities that are suffered from the Apaches and Seris, in the knowledge that not having established in this province the line that was anticipated in the royal instruction, inserted in the *Reglamento*, which would have been handed to me in ministry, it was necessary to indicate the places I considered appropriate to place it, bearing in mind that His Majesty has resolved to erect a presidio at the junction of the San Pedro and Gila Rivers, so that uniting with the new pueblos of the Colorado, the road and communications can be opened between this province and that of the Californias. And finally, guided by Your Lordship's ideas, in compliance with the sovereign resolutions from His Majesty for the establishment of presidios on land capable of maintaining respectable population centers that with time will not need the assistance of troops for their own defense, I hoped that my reports complete the achievement of these just purposes to which you had aspired.

On the same day I received this order I undertook my march to the pueblo of San Joseph de Chinapa, where I found and presented myself to Brigadier Don Jacobo Ugarte y Loyola, and had to carry out under his [orders] the aforementioned surveys. To obey [his orders] the sequence was reversed from how they were mandated to be executed, as Your Lordship will notice in the accompanying diary, as well as the fact that it was not possible for me to avoid [prevent] it, not having the discretion to not comply with that [order] of Your Lordship, which directed me to be under those [orders] of that officer in command to whom I did not deliver the map of the surveyed areas which nonetheless got to the hands of Your Lordship. Not having been able to construct it during our extensive march, I had neither the opportunity nor time to carry it out in the short time that I stayed in the presidio of Pitic, from where I returned immediately to this capital.[21]

FIGURE 3.5. Aerial image of San Ignacio, Sonora, with irrigated fields below and house gardens among the trees, from Google Earth.

Of the lands that I have surveyed, the ones suitable for populations are the valleys of Fronteras, Badeguachi, Caveceras de San Pedro, Nutrias, Guachuca, and Terrenate, Santa María Suanca, San Lázaro, Santa Bárbara, San Luis, Buenavista and its estancia, Guevavi, Calavazas, Tucson, Zicurizuta, and Busanic, for having abundant permanent waters, much fertile land, which when improved with irrigation and cultivation will produce copious harvests, pastures, stone, firewood, and timber with the exception of the headwaters of the San Pedro, where the last two items are scarce, and it would be necessary to search for them in the mountains of Guachuca, Las Mulas, and San Joseph, distant two or three leagues. Among these, very useful ranchos could be established for breeding all species of livestock in the places called Nogales, Capulin, the valleys of Cochuta and Turicachi, the springs of León del Saus, and of Los Alamos Largos, Sonoyta, San Antonio, Torreón, and El Quiburi, which all produce abundant pastures, adding in some the fruit of the acorn that, with the hackberry tree[22] of its oak forests, would promote the breeding of pigs and goats,[23] extremely necessary for the supply of butter, tallow, and hides which are so familiar for consumption, because of the shortages experienced in the province. All have permanent water but not enough for settlement, it is enough for watering places for a multitude of livestock, for the consumption of their shepherds, cowboys, and other people who regularly live in similar estancias, and it could even be enough for someone to water their gardens and make small agricultural fields that provide them with fruits, vegetables, and seeds for their consumption (Figure 3.5 through 3.7). And as in the journal, I expound in minute detail the position and course [bearing] of all, and the average distance from one to another, which I excuse myself from repeating in this report.

The margins of the San Pedro River do not have any appropriate site, not even in terms of resources[24] necessary to found communities, up to its junction with the Gila, and it is the same for this one whose terrain is extremely broken and rough in the short space that we managed a view to examine it. I cannot say if there will be on the banks of the river [a suitable place] following the current, or ascending against

FIGURE 3.6. (*above*) Multi-cropping and multi-story plantings make the most of moisture by shading the ground and breaking the force during periods of high river flow. (*below*) Extensive vegetable fields, positioned along the river, take advantage of river flow for irrigation.

FIGURE 3.7. Local resident discussing his fruit trees adjacent to his porch.

it [upstream, against the current], for [Brigadier] Loyola did not allow me to stop to reconnoiter them with the scrupulous care that I wanted, for which I asked him in several instances to give me an escort and permission,[25] and he did not see fit to grant it to me,[26] and although the precincts of both rivers have several very opportune places for livestock estancias, you cannot think about establishing them without destroying or subduing the Gileño Apache that prevents them, and annihilate them as he has done with others located in the interior of the province which because of it enjoyed greater protection and defense.

This nation, with its continuous thefts and killings, has managed to destroy the small ancient pueblos of Cohuta, Turicachi, Sonoita, Santa María Suanca, Guevavi, El Busanic, Cananea, and Aribac, so that only the vestiges of their ruins remain, and has diminished considerably those of Chinapa, Bacuachi, Cuquiarachi, Fronteras, and others adjacent to the line, and has entirely depopulated the haciendas, and the ranchos of San Pedro, Terrenate, Torreón, San Lázaro, Santa Bárbara, Ranchito, San Luis, Buenavista, San Lázaro de la Magdalena, and several others that are deserted and forsaken and could be restored or repopulated if it would not be prevented by the aggressions that reoccur frequently, which have in the same way delayed the progress of the missions and other pueblos that I have examined and find themselves in a quite decadent state, and especially in regard to the breeding of livestock of which is greatly lacking, for they are the object that has always primed the ambition of the enemy.

The situation of Tubac Presidio, moved to Tucson, lacks resouces for a community because, although it has some useful land for cultivation and planting, they lack the benefit of irrigation, without which crops are meager or lost (Figure 3.8). And being very near the foothills of the Santa Rita Mountains where its slopes extend, they form

FIGURE 3.8. Historical photograph of the commander's quarters at Tubac Presidio, represented as a fortified house (*casa fuerte*). Photograph courtesy of Tubac Presidio.

many breaks and ravines that allow the enemy to enter clandestinely right up to the houses, from which they have pierced with arrows, and killed a few *vecinos*, reducing them to such a small number that no more than nine[27] remained by the time of my transit through that pueblo. And even of these [nine remaining residents], I learned the news that the day following my departure the enemy had killed two. Because of these irremediable disadvantages I do not consider the site appropriate, neither for a presidio, nor for settlement, and as I have put forth to Your Lordship previously, it would be of known usefulness and benefit to the unfortunate persons who have stayed to have them move to Tucson, or San Xavier del Bac, where there is sufficient land and water to give them opportunities, and to provide them with better and safer settlement.[28]

The terrain to which Tucson moved, and where the presidio[29] of Tubac is, is among the more useful and suitable for the support of the company and a place that under its [the company's] protection fosters a good population that over time can defend itself and even provide aid to prevent the entry of the enemy by its flanks and especially via the south, which is the most frequented point of entry, and needs the most guarding because there are located the populations of San Xavier del Bac, Tumacácori, and Calabazas. And because it is in the same direction as the uninhabited [places]of Sonoita, the passes of Agua Caliente, Babocomari, and other places where the enemy penetrates, launching from the mountains of Guachuca, Santa Rita, Babocomari ["Mustang" and "Whetstone"], Peñascosa ["Dragoon"], and other places [mountain ranges] that lie at their backs, which is why I consider it very useful to keep it [Tucson Presidio] in the place where it is located, and I have not seen another [place] where it would be better.

Persuading myself that with the foregoing I have given Your Lordship all the news I was able to acquire relative to the condition of the terrain I have surveyed, and of the resources that each one enjoys to encourage populations or new settlements, I consider it necessary to establish that their subsistence cannot be assured, nor will they make the progress expected if the enemy is not punished and removed,[30] whose hostility has been and will be, while it lasts, the main cause of the ruin of so many populations, haciendas, and ranchos, and of the delay and decline in which others are found. Since the presidios were inserted into the enemy's country they withdrew from the populations that they were supposed to protect and defend, and consequently they took on a greater portion of advanced land [terrain in front of the line]. It turned out that by necessity a greater circumference of the line had to be formed and occupied, and the distance at which one [presidio] was placed from another became greater, and the difficulty that their small garrisons had to prevent the entry of the enemy because of how open and exposed their flanks became, and added to this, it [the garrison] is not able to use all the force in this precise and basic objective because having no supplies in the new locations to provide for the troops and their families it has been and is still necessary to go out and search for them at a distance from where the people who harvest them are, and use large allotments [of troops; parties] in leading and escorting them, without being able to do any other service, nor to be used for defense, or offense. And because of this has come, in my opinion, the ease and frequency with which they [enemies] have repeated their aggressions because they are finding unrestrained entry to the open area between presidios; they come in without obstruction to the interior of the country. And they do damage without encountering any resistance, for not being [numerous] enough, the settlements cannot do it themselves, and without the protection of the troops of whom they are deprived because they have been advanced.

When it happens that sufficient troops are garrisoned at the frontier to address this harm, it seems essential that they have no other duty or function than to defend it, keep the enemy out, pursue him, and punish him, [by] making active and incessant war and attacking them as much as possible in their very rancherías and lands as provided for in Article 1, Title 10 of the *reglamento*, because if a great part of the force is used, as has happened so far, in searching for and escorting remounts, and supplies, it will necessarily fail in the first objective of its institution, and the occasion will never come when it [the objective] can be fulfilled as demanded by the condition of the province. And this idea not being attainable without placing the presidios on land capable of producing crops for their supply and consumption, and without fomenting within them, and within what is under its protection, agriculture and livestock breeding, I go under this principle to indicate those that I have found with these qualities, and that seem to me to be most appropriate to form the new line.

In my previous reports of April 29 and the 25th of the present [month], I presented to Your Lordship the bad situation of Fronteras Presidio, that it is the first of it [the line], and the advantages that would be achieved by moving it to the site of Badeguachi, distant only a league south of its current location, and referring to them [the reports] I have nothing to add about this establishment. The same goes for that of Santa Cruz de Terrenate which is the second post, and relocated to campo de Las Nutrias, as I have also informed Your Lordship, will reduce to twenty-five leagues the distance of nearly fifty leagues it currently is from its adjacent Fronteras [presidio]. It will facilitate the communication of both, and the joining of their forces for defense and offense. They will cover better the passes and *cañadas* ["narrow valleys" or "canyons"] most frequented by enemies. Protected by both, and with the benefit of the extensive fertile lands and abundant waters nearby, two good communities can be fostered that provide them with what is necessary and assemble as auxiliary troops if necessary. And it has to still be expected that under the protection of the first, the destroyed ones of Cochuta, Turicachi, and Real de Nacosari, will be revived. Those of Cuguiarachi, Baquachi, San Joseph de Chinapa, Bacanuchi Hacienda, Cumpas, and others more internal [within the province] can be improved. And finally, that with defense, and under the protection of the two [presidios], the gold placers of Bacuachi, La Cananea, and various others can be worked with freedom and determination, while today they only provide constant evidence of their prodigious wealth and do not allow the search and acquisition of it, owing to the risk and fear that the aggressions of the enemy have infused.

I also have informed Your Lordship [that] the current location of Tucson Presidio is very advantageous, that it enjoys all the opportunities that can be desired for a good population and to promote the shelter and defense of those found close to it, for these reasons I conceive it cannot, nor should it be removed. But having discovered the long intervening space of forty-five leagues that is between it and the one at Campo de Las Nutrias, and since it is not possible for the force to prevent both the entrance and exits of the enemy of which it has many and much frequented ones in the intermediate terrain, I think it is necessary to realize the placement of another presidio in the center, or midway of that distance, and having not found or surveyed another place more appropriate to locate it than the estancia of Buenavista, in this it seems to me the new erection would be very suitable because, on top of being beautifully proportioned for a medium-sized population and for many ranchos and haciendas, it divides equally a short difference in the said distance from Las Nutrias to Tucson, leaving twenty-six leagues to one and twenty-one to the other, with the advantage of covering the passes of La Plomosa, Chihuahuilla, Divisaderos, and San Antonio, defending the pueblos of Calabazas and Tumacácori, facilitating their return to their old state the ones that were destroyed, of Guevavi, Sonoita, and Santa María Suanaca, to cover with livestock the beautiful valleys and ruined haciendas and ranchos of Buenavista, San Luis, Ranchito, Santa Bárbara, and San Lázaro; and finally, it also provides the best communication of the line, and the joining of its forces with those of its two neighbors, and even if necessary with the presidio of Altar, located outside the line it comes to be at a distance of thirty-five leagues to the southwest.

I have already presented to Your Lordship that along the margins of the San Pedro River I have not found any site at all appropriate to establish a presidio, let alone for founding a population, and the same applies in its junction with the Gila, which is why I cannot indicate which one will be appropriate for a new construction decided by the piety of His Majesty and to do so with knowledge and certainty I consider it indispensable to proceed with a new and more thorough survey of the margins of the Gila to its junction with the Colorado, since in addition to the examination of those lands it will inform so as to choose one that is most advantageous, it will also lead to the selection of the one over the others that offers resources to better facilitate communication, and joining of their forces with those intended to cover in the same way the new pueblos of the Colorado.

The line formed by the sites that are proposed, the current presidio of Fronteras will remain placed in Badeguachi at 30°57'52" latitude, free from the floods that those valleys have suffered, in [a] very open [unobstructed] site, and with enough land for a good population at the point where the valleys of Fronteras, Cuguiarachi, and Cochuta meet and they come together along the road from Potrero Pass by which the pueblo of Babispe communicates with the line of Vizcaya, and it will have the pueblo of Fronteras a distance of one league to the north, two to the west, that of Cuguiarachi, three to the south, the abandoned pueblo of Cochuta, and about eight hundred *varas* ["rods," one *vara* is approximately a yard] to the east,[31] the Fronteras River, that lacking any ford whatsoever in the space of more than a half a league, it is very valuable to protect, and safeguard that entire front against the enemy, and moreover there is a high narrow ridge where if a small tower or lookout were put in place, one can control and expose the extent of the three valleys, whose fields can be supported; and also the placers of Bacuachi encouraged, making frequent crossovers [shortcuts, cut offs][32] from the Sierra Purica, up to the slopes of the Mavavi, to impede the entry of the enemy, to which end it would be very conducive to place a detachment in the abandoned pueblo of Cochuta, which three leagues to the south is Turicachi, three to the southwest quarter to the south to Turicachi Pass, five to the west southwest of Mababi, and four to the east that of Teras that are the places where he [the enemy] enters from.

That of Santa Cruz, moved to campo de Las Nutrias, will remain at 31°24'10" latitude distant from the previous twenty-five leagues to the west northwest by the road that they call Magallanes, located on fertile terrain, abundant and open; it will have the valleys of Guachuca two leagues to the northwest, the headwaters of the San Pedro and its fields two and a half to the east, the pueblo or old Terrenate Presidio, two to the west northwest, eight to the south, la Abra[33] that is formed between the old Cananea, and the Rincón del Burro ["Burro Corner"], where the enemies enter and leave for most of their robberies,[34] and it will be easy to track them, going out to engage them at any warning that the populations may give, which they could very well give, as they are at a distance of twenty five leagues; and finally, in the case of making campaigns to search for them and attack them in their own rancherías, it would be the most important point for the joining of the troops, so, for the ease of being able to quarter them, and provisioning them, as well as being closest to the mountains where they huddle,[35] and more quickly will come the encounter [fight, skirmish].

The new and third presidio placed in the estancia of Buenavista, will be at 31°40'25" of latitude, on a large mesa, whose skirt irrigates[36] the Santa María Suanca River which has its origin in the San Antonio Spring, and although it is not very voluminous it never loses its flow even in the dry season; it will have a beautiful and pleasant valley in which a league to the south, once stood the abandoned hacienda of Buenavista, which was the most abundant in fruits and livestock, three [leagues] west quarter northwest to the ruined pueblo of Guevavi, four to the northeast, the Sierra de la Chihuahuilla [Patagonia Mountains], it is prolific[37] in rich and well-known minerals, it will be within distance of twenty-one leagues northwest quarter west of Las Nutrias and in the best position to cover the passes of Plomosa, Chihuahuilla, Divisaderos, and San Antonio; to defend the pueblos of Calabazas and Tumacácori, and promote the repopulation of the ruined Sonoita, and the pleasant valleys of Buenavista, San Luis Ranchito, Santa Bárbara, San Lázaro, Santa María Suanca, Torreón, San Antonio, and others deeper in the Province, I should advise, that although the site of Guevavi better divides the distance between Las Nutrias and Tucson I choose with preference that of the estancia [Buenavista] because it has more abundant pastures and is closer to Altar Presidio.

The fourth and final [presidio], San Agustín del Tucson, lies at 32°31'50"[38] of latitude on very clear terrain, plenty of water and farmland with a pasture isolated by two irrigation canals where with a small garrison the drove of horses is well protected, it defends and supports the missions or pueblos of Tucson and San Xavier del Bac, which have made well-known progress under its protection, and they will decline entirely if they [troops] were lacking; and finally it is necessary to point out that it is precisely at this point, that the Gila River opens and facilitates the communication of this province with Colorado and California; It has the place of Tres Alamos at a distance of seventeen leagues to the east, the Cebadilla pass nine east-northeast, that of La Mololoa, four north quarter northeast, El Aquitune, sixteen to the northwest, the Sierra del Tucson three to the west, El Ojo Grande or the source of its waters a quarter of a league to the south-southeast, and twenty-six leagues to the south-southeast to the presidio of Las Nutrias, having another twenty-nine to the north the junction of the San Pedro and Gila Rivers.

It [the junction of the San Pedro and Gila Rivers] is at 32°21' latitude in a closed canyon formed by the rough mountain range that they call Aribaipa, and for the flow of the Gila being so copious, and the channel [*caja*] of its current being so shallow, in any rise of waters [freshet][39] the immediate terrain is flooded, that which as far as the eye can see and discern proved to be very broken, and whenever there is a new survey that must be undertaken along the margins of the Gila, the opportune place to locate the presidio ordered by His Majesty will be found well to the west, it will be too far from its adjoining one of Tucson, and perhaps it may not be able to establish communication between them by the road they call Aquitune, (which now is taken to the Colorado River) because of not having permanent *aguajes* ["waterholes"], it will be forced to open it [a route] through the Cañadas del Oro, and the Virgen del Consuelo, or by the San Simon to come out at the San Pedro River, and the Santa Teresa Valley, and then follow the margins of the Gila to the new settlement, in which case to defend this excessively long transit,[40] I conceive it necessary to form a new post, with a strong detachment in the Santa Teresa Valley, which although it does not have the best resources, is the most appropriate of those that I have surveyed in those lands.

The location of Santa Gertrudis del Altar Presidio is 30°53'25"[41] of latitude on sufficiently unobstructed land but scarce in pastures and water, especially in the dry season which cuts off the river, but it has never lacked that which is needed for the consumption of the troops and local inhabitants, which on some occasions they search for and convey from quite some distance, as was the case when I was examined it; it has various gardens[42] that abound in fruits because of that very fertile soil, and to the west southwest this mission of Caborca (Figure 3.9)[43] with its *Pueblos de Visita* ["pueblo visiting stations"], El Pitiqui and Bisanic; the Sierra de Santa Teresa, twelve leagues to the northeast; the Cerro del Bamuri one and a half northwest quarter north; the Chanate Pass one and a half northwest quarter west; La Sierra del Ojo de Agua three to the south-southwest; the Cerro del Carnero ["Ram Hill"] one to the southeast quarter south; and another to the east-southeast of the Santa Ana Pass; and although this presidio is internal to [within] the province and outside of the Line of the Frontier, I think it is essential as well to contain and punish the uprisings of the Seris and Tiburones ["Sharks"], and keep free the road of the Real de la Cieneguilla, and to maintain the proper respect and obedience of the Upper Pimas and other nations of the pueblos of its perimeter whose loyalty is very suspect, and it would not be surprising for all of them to rise up [in rebellion] if they were lacking the bridle of force that compels them to remain in a calmness that is more feigned and apparent than real and true.

The presidio of Pitic is 29°11' latitude in a very spacious location, with abundant lands and waters that are quite exposed to flooding, as experienced last year, 1770, in which it was necessary to take refuge on the Cerro de la Campana ["Bell Hill"], a risk that would be avoided by locating them where the Seri currently have their jacals ["huts"]: Santa Gertrudis del Altar Presidio is more than sixty leagues to the north-northwest, the Cerro del Tonuco four to the west, the Colorado two to the northwest quarter north, to the *pozos* of San Joseph ten to the northwest, and to Santa Teresa three to the east quarter southeast; to Palos Blancos two to the south southwest, and very little to [Cerro de] La Campana which is to the north; and combining or uniting their forces with those of Altar [Presidio] they may be used to punish the rebel Seri, and their friends and allies, the Tiburones; whose damages I conceive will not

FIGURE 3.9. Caborca Mission, Sonora.

cease,[44] until those that are called reduced remain in the pueblo because according to what I have been able to observe, they are only so in appearance; maintaining communication and dealings with those who harass us, and it will not be strange if they serve them as faithful spies. To let them do so without risk, and in order to avoid these known evils that each day will be greater, because of the rising number of those that desert and return to the sierra; I cannot find a more opportune means than of transplanting them all at quite long distances,[45] and to places where they will not even have the hope of returning to their homeland or soil.

With the foregoing I have given Your Lordship all the intelligence I was able to acquire of the lands that I have surveyed, of those I have found to be more appropriate for the establishment of the new Line, and of the means that according to my limited knowledge, and experience, may be conducive to the best defense of the interior of the province; and so that Your Lordship can learn with greater ease the places in which the presidios are and must remain, and the designated location for those that must be removed, and augmented, accompanied by a drawing [plat] of each,[46] and another of the junction of the San Pedro and Gila Rivers, in which work I have had no other objective than the best service of the King, and the intense desires that they assist me in figuring out how to carry out the Superior Orders of Your Lordship that if I have obtained it, as I hope, it will be the greatest satisfaction that I long for.

I hope that God may bless your Lordship for many years. Arizpe, October 31 1780. Your Lordship's most subordinate servant, Gerónimo de la Rocha y Figueroa, kisses the hand of Your Lordship,
Señor Governor and General Commander-in-Chief.

Notes

1. Many Spanish words (sierras, passes, arroyos, etc.) are in common use today throughout the region and so are maintained in these documents.
2. He could be saying to conduct the necessary supplies from the border, but the sentence construction suggests he means the presidio of Fronteras.
3. He is referring to the hill at the current Fronteras Presidio.
4. Translated from *arrancharse*, meaning "to congregate," but it is unclear whether he recognizes that they gathered or came together in these locations, or whether he is saying they settle in there. The former provides a more accurate description of their behavior.
5. *Rocela*, perhaps *rochela*: a place frequented by some animals, a den, hiding place, hideout.
6. He is suggesting that a new presidio be placed at Bavispe.
7. The original text clearly states Cochuta, but Thomas (1941:184) states Fronteras.

   The minutes of May 7 referenced here have not been identified and were not with the other pages relating to his reconaissance.
8. *Proporciones*: this can mean a variety of things and is used in different ways throughout the text. Thomas (1941) consistently translates this word as "resources." In many instances "resources" is appropriate, while in other instances "land" or "opportunities" is more appropriate. Ugarte and Rocha are using the term in a different way.
9. *Población*: this can mean settlement (town, city, pueblo), the act of settlement, population or populating, or community. Rocha and Ugarte seem to be using this term to reference population, as in populating and so on, as they use different words for settlements (*establecimientos*).
10. *A una regular distancia*: Thomas (1941:185) states "a fair distance."
11. *Superior orden, decreto*: documents of the *Superior Gobierno* (legislation, edicts etc., originating from the Central Government).
12. He is referring to Casa Grande near the Gila.
13. The soldiers who would serve in this location would have been both a fighting force and responsible for producing their own crops and livestock to sustain their families (Carlos III 1772, Title 11, Article 1, Title 12, Item 3). Consequently, Ugarte and Rocha both stressed the viability of an area for supporting troops and a settled population, noting the unsuitability of the confluence. Reference to the large detachment required to convey supplies from Tucson acknowledges the considerable danger involved in transporting large mule trains of supplies long distances into this remote location.
14. The Santa Teresa Mountains converge with the Gila on the north and are located to the east of the Galiuro Mountains that border the east side of the San Pedro River Valley. He is probably referring to the Klondyke area. Rocha's map shows the valley of Santa Theresa in a location that would be consistent with Aravaipa Creek. The valley between mountains in which Aravaipa Creek is situated extends from the Klondyke area to the San Pedro, and so this interpretation makes the most sense.
15. This sentence is not included in the document translated by Thomas (1941:186) that was included as part of Croix's General Report.
16. This is the first and only mention of this in the documents related to this reconnaissance. This place is indicated on Rocha's map and is referred to as *Ve [Valle] de Sequias Hondas* or Valley of Deep Ditches. It is the valley just north of the Peñasco Crossing at modern-day Redington where substantial and distinctive crags pinch the river channel before the valley widens out into an expansive and verdant valley downstream to the north. The deep ditches probably relate to indigenous canals in the area that would have originated at the narrows taking water down-valley to water fields in the floodplain. Settlement patterns indicate that this was the first best place north of Tres Alamos where the river was sufficient to support major irrigation systems. Today it represents one of the most verdant and productive sections of the river. Rocha referred to the area from Santa Cruz [de Terrenate] up to the Gila River as *piélagos*, asserting that the San Pedro had excessive dryness in many parts. There is a dry stretch indicated on Rocha's map to the north of this, as is consistent with the valley characteristics where the river flow probably went underground.
17. *Cascos*: inner part or edge of the populated area, meaning in effect, defending the walls of the presidio. Thomas (1941:187) translates this as "skulls," e.g., "defending only the skulls of the presidio." This may have been a typo and he may have meant "walls."

18. He is not saying so directly but is probably implying that this is essentially what became of the presidio of Santa Cruz de Terrenate. They were only able to defend the presidio itself and not make an offensive war against the enemy.
19. The Tiburones and Tepocas were bands of the group referred to as Seris.
20. In 1779 Father Fray Juan Díaz and Father Fray Francisco Garcés established two missions on the lower Colorado River at Yuma Crossing. Díaz, Garcés, and their fellow friars were among those killed in a civil uprising (Yuma [Quechan] Uprising or Yuma Revolt) at Misión San Pedro y San Pablo de Bicuñer in 1781.
21. This convoluted explanation of his passing of the map to Croix, and therefore not having the copy completed, reminds Croix of his orders to pass the map along secretly. From some of the contents it seems clear that the report and map included in this volume represent the secret ones rather than the official one that passed through Ugarte.
22. The *ramón* or "hackberry tree" produced fruits, and also the top branches were cut off for feed in snowy weather.
23. The acorn would have been valuable pig and goat food, as apparently would the hackberry. Here Rocha is referring to free-ranging pigs and goats. Goats tend to be adapted to rugged terrain, are resilient, and are able to subsist on an array of resources, including grass, brush, scrub, and brambles, and can thrive on sparsely vegetated slopes. They produce meat, milk, hair fibers, and skins (Gade in Kiple and Ornelas 2000:531–536).

    Pigs are especially prolific and fast growing, resulting in a high return for energy invested. As omnivores they consume a wide range of foods and thrive on mast or nuts from the forest floor. Rocha's discussion indicates that these would have been free-ranging pigs, which would have foraged both on and beneath the forest floor for plant and animal foods. They eat nuts, fruits, and other plants as well as eggs, snakes, birds, mice, and rabbits. The practice of pasturing pigs in a forest or pannage is ancient, and is still practiced in Spain (Parsons 1962).

    Spaniards have a special affinity for pork, which in part may have resulted from its role as a symbol of cultural identity. Moors and Jews did not eat pork, so for Christians this became an outward proclamation of their devotion to Christianity, which was especially important during the Inquisition (Anderson 2002:191–192; Gade in Kiple and Ornelas 2000:536–542).

    In late autumn semiferal animals were slaughtered, and their flesh was salted and stored and their fat rendered into lard and soap, and as Rocha mentions herein, pigs and goats provided a supply of butter, tallow, and hides.
24. *Proporciones*: proportions, proper or equal share, portion, apportion, allotment, resources, land, supplies.
25. Here we see why Croix wanted a secret summary that did not first go to Ugarte. This sentence suggests that this summary is the confidential report that bypassed Ugarte. This also may explain the discrepancies between Thomas' translation of Croix's 1781 report and ours where some of the text is missing or different in his.
26. There is no doubt that Ugarte was in charge. It was he who was tasked to undertake this reconnaissance but it was Rocha who was given responsibility of preparing a journal and map, and so Rocha's version of history prevails. Not only is this statement indicative of the secrecy of this summary (see preceding note), but it also may reveal Rocha's knowledge of Ugarte's reputation as someone who demonstrated "an independence of judgment and an initiative in action that sometimes bordered on outright insubordination" (Moorhead 1968:19, 20). His statement would feed into this flaw in his reputation, reinforcing Rocha's efforts to follow orders while his superior would not allow its full execution, presumably lending to favorable impressions of Rocha's service and loyalty. Rocha could not have known that Ugarte would eventually be promoted to commandant-general.
27. He means that there were nine heads of households, which would total many more people when including their families and servants.
28. It was not for another seven years that these residents were relieved. In 1787 the viceroy reactivated the presidio as the Royal Fort of St. Rafael at Tubac with eighty Pima Indian troops and four Spanish officers.
29. Here he means garrison or troops rather than the physical place.
30. Throughout this, mention is made of removing the troublesome tribes. In one sense he is suggesting the routing of the enemy, but in a second sense he is suggesting the expatriation

of the problematic peoples to an area far away. This is apparent in Captain Don Pedro de Tueros' 1778 letter to Croix, wherein he concludes that they will never behave themselves and therefore must be expatriated (Thomas 1941:142). This solution is also mentioned in Rocha's reference to the Seri in his summary statement below. As Moorhead (1975:86; also see Moorhead 1968:49–51) points out, this solution had been proposed by almost every ranking officer who had faced the problem in the past, including Croix. After his 1698 inspection of the frontier the Marqués de Rubí also suggested this option: an all-out war of extermination or exile of the Apaches (Moorhead 1968:16). This resulted in the regulation of 1772, by which captured enemy were to be interned near the presidios or sent far into the interior (Brinkerhoff and Faulk 1965:31–35; Moorhead 1968:17). This view toward a solution was also held by some of the religious, for example Padre Visitor Juan Antonio Balthasar noted that in the time of Viceroy Juan Antonio de Vizarrón y Equinreta (viceroy from 1734 to 1740) that an order was given to exile such troublemakers to the *obrajes*, or "workhouses," of Mexico City (Dunne 1957:79, 115–116n67). Ugarte was of an opinion similar to Rocha's on this matter, believing it best to send the Seris away and to wage unrelenting war on the rebellious Tiburón and Tepoca until they were exterminated or reduced to obedience (Moorhead 1968:50–51).

31. The river is clearly drawn east of Fronteras Presidio on Rocha's map, and the text does say east. Thomas (1941:191) says west.
32. *Cortadas*: Thomas (1941:191) says sallies.
33. *Abra*: between mountains, mountain pass, gorge, valley, cove, or opening, open area. It is unclear if this is a named place or simply a description of the space/valley between the mountains, between old Cananea and the corner of the Burro Mountains. Rocha's map does not name this place but shows a clear break in mountains. This suggests that this is simply a description of the area through which the Apaches raided.
34. Another divergence from Croix's summary report that suggests a difference was included in that report or a different exemplar was used for it (e.g., Thomas 1941:192).
35. *Arrochelarse*: *Rochela* is pejorative of a group, e.g., gang, mob. *Arrochellar* means huddle, as a gang or group of people up to no good. Thomas (1941:192) states: "where the enemies are ranching."
36. Here he uses the word *riega*, which means "irrigates," but he may really mean "waters," because this seems to be referencing a natural process rather than irrigation ditches. On the other hand, he may be indicating that local residents irrigate using ditches that collect the water originating in the mountains as well as the spring.
37. *Fecunda en ricos y conocidos minerales*: Thomas (1041:192) reads *fecunda* as *Segundo*, or "second in riches and known minerals."
38. Thomas (1941:193) says thirty seconds.
39. *Avenida*: sudden rise of water in a river, onrush of waters, freshet. Thomas (1941:193) translates this as "in all directions" rather than as a freshet. Rocha's journal also references the rise in waters on July 30 along the Sonora River.
40. Thomas (1941:194) says "line" rather than "transit."
41. Thomas (1941:194) has 35°3'.
42. *Huertas*: Thomas (1941:194) says irrigated lands.
43. In 1688 Jesuit missionary Francisco Eusebio Kino established an Upper Pima mission at what is now called Caborca Viejo (Old Caborca), and in 1790 it was moved to the place it now occupies on the right (east) bank of the Asunción River. The name comes from the O'odham word "Kawulk" which means "hill."
44. Late in 1779 the Seri had revolted again, this after having risen up in 1749, the late-mid 1760s, and 1777 (Moorhead 1975:51, 61, 86).
45. See note above regarding removal or expatriation of troublesome groups. Here there is no question as to the meaning, relating to the exile or deportation of these peoples to where they would not cause trouble.
46. If he is referring to drawings he made, these drawings have not been located. It is possible that he is referencing Urrutia's drawings.

CHAPTER 4

Map and Route of the Sonoran Frontier

Rocha prepared a map to accompany his journal, as ordered by Croix. Garcia (1964:456; also see Fireman 1977:149; Reinhartz in Reinhartz and Saxon 2005:72–73) described this as the most detailed map of the area produced during the Spanish period (see Figure 1.6). Despite this, in the notes following the journal, Rocha provided numerous hedges and qualifications for its inaccuracies, perhaps attesting to his proclivity for precision as a consequence of his engineering nature and background (see Chapter 5). Given the scale of the map, the routes depicted are especially accurate, particularly as compared to any previously prepared maps of the region. Despite this, throughout we discuss deviations and inaccuracies as are known today, almost 240 years later.

In this chapter we provide a translation and an illustration of the map key itself (Figure 4.1). This key can be used to interpret portions of the map we have reproduced throughout this volume that illustrate specific points raised in or by the content of the journal. The map key provides insights into the environmental characteristics Rocha observed, the organization of Sonoran settlements, and a clear conception of the line of presidios. Rocha's signature is also included, providing a somewhat personalized connection with the engineer (Figure 4.2).

Rocha used a consistent set of symbols to depict various places and geographic characteristics. He also used color coding to convey information, including colors that distinguish existing, suppressed, and proposed presidios. In addition, differences in shading green or tan (darkness or lightness) correlate to journal content or known characteristics of the region, including river flow characteristics (see Chapter 6). The direction of flow for rivers is indicated by arrows.

In addition to the relevant information provided in the key, the map itself is an important source of information about the region that further informs on mountain ranges, water sources, settlements, route traveled relative to landforms, and more. It provides details not included in Rocha's journal or in the summaries and so is an important information source in itself. The map has been described by Fireman (1977:149) as follows:

> It locates Apache strongholds south of the Gila River and east of the San Pedro within Spanish occupied territories, and shows the location of other local Indian groups. Relocated presidio sites are distinguished from the old places by color. Rocha's own suggestion for location of the presidio cordon is also included. Mountains and river courses are stylized, but an attempt was made to indicate gradations of height and true flow" (Fireman 1977:149).

Some of the assessments Fireman notes that were made by Rocha are not altogether

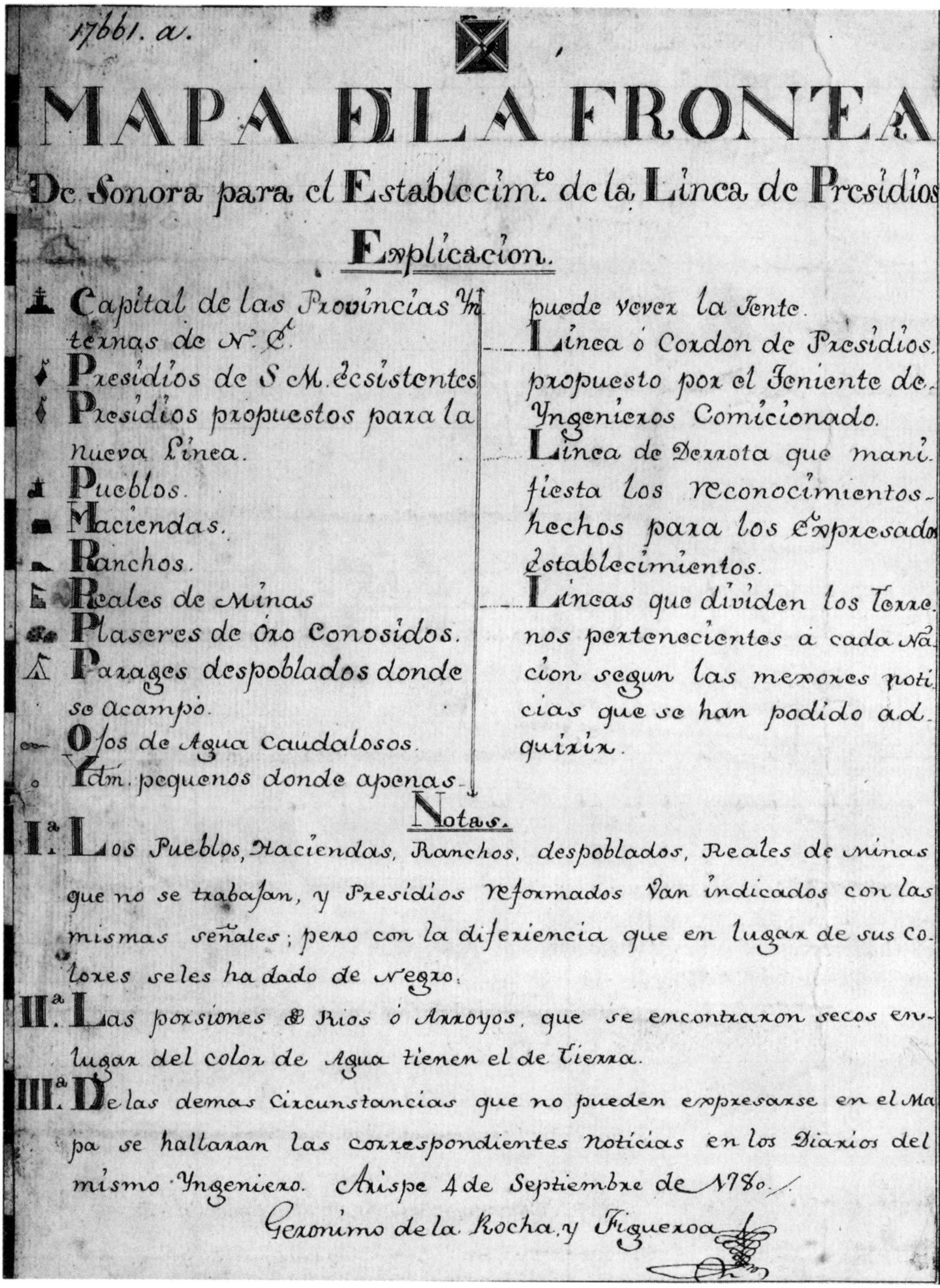

17661. a.

MAPA DE LA FRONTERA

De Sonora para el Establecim.to de la Linea de Presidios

Explicacion.

Capital de las Provincias Ynternas de N.E.
Presidios de S. M. ecsistentes
Presidios propuestos para la nueva Linea.
Pueblos.
Haciendas.
Ranchos.
Reales de Minas
Plaseres de Oro Conosidos.
Parages despoblados donde se acampo.
Ojos de Agua caudalosos.
Ydm. pequenos donde apenas puede vever la Jente.
Linea ó Cordon de Presidios propuesto por el Teniente de Yngenieros Comicionado.
Linea de Derrota que manifiesta los reconocimientos hechos para los expresados establecimientos.
Lineas que dividen los Terrenos pertenecientes á cada Nacion segun las mexores noticias que se han podido adquirir.

Notas.

I.a Los Pueblos, Haciendas, Ranchos, despoblados, Reales de minas que no se trabajan, y Presidios reformados van indicados con las mismas señales; pero con la diferiencia que en lugar de sus colores seles ha dado de negro.

II.a Las porsiones de Rios ó Arroyos, que se encontraron secos en lugar del color de Agua tienen el de Tierra.

III.a De las demas Circunstancias que no pueden expresarse en el Mapa se hallaran las correspondientes noticias en los Diarios del mismo Yngeniero. Arispe 4 de Septiembre de 1780.

Geronimo de la Rocha, y Figueroa

FIGURE 4.1. Illustration of Rocha's map key. From *Mapa de la Frontera de Sonora para el establecimiento de la linea de presidios.* Courtesy of the British Library; Shelfmark: Cartographic Items Additional MS. 17,661.a.

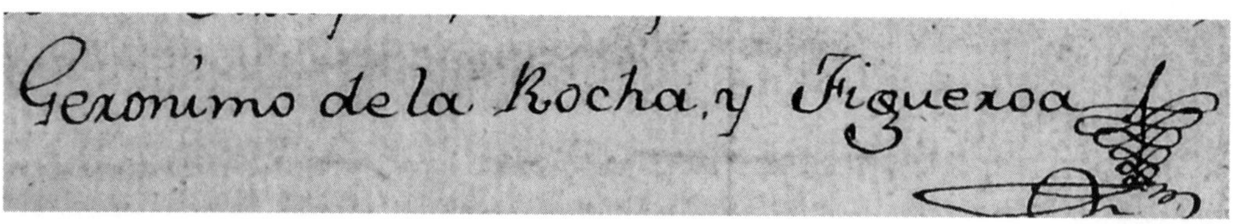

FIGURE 4.2. Rocha's signature from his 1870 map. Courtesy of the British Library; Shelfmark: Cartographic Items Additional MS. 17,661.a.

accurate based on what we know now from archaeological investigations, but they do depict understandings at the time. For example, Rocha depicted a line demarcating the boundary of the Apache *Gentiles* ["heathen"] running west of the San Pedro Valley. Apache territory as conveyed on the map (and noted in the journal) included the mountains west of the river, including the Whetstones, Huachucas, Catalinas, Rincons, and Mica Mountain and all but the uppermost reaches of that river. This Apache area he differentiated from that of the *Pimas Altos* (e.g., including that of the Sobaipuri O'odham), which encompassed the entire northwest (upper left) portion of the map. While this depiction is consistent with the official Spanish position that the San Pedro had been abandoned to the Apache in 1762, the area was still within the domain of the Sobaipuri O'odham (Seymour 2011b). Moreover, this map presents indigenous distributions as if these were exclusive use zones, which may simply be an artifact of transcribing distributions to paper and of mapping itself. Nonetheless, the distributions seem oddly mischaracterized, which may explain why the Spaniards were so ineffective in combating the Apache. As noted, the Sobaipuri O'odham were still in the San Pedro Valley, an area they had held for centuries, and for an equally long period the Apache and their mobile allies had utilized the mountain zones that bordered the river valleys, using the basins as part of their territorial round. It is no wonder, however, that the much more widely distributed Apache slipped through Spanish defenses as if they did not exist. A somewhat more accurate map might have incorporated overlapping use zones, with highland oases demarcated for the Apache and lowlands reserved largely for the Sobaipuri O'odham.

Additionally, the map and the key indicate that presidios proposed for the new line (*Presidios propuestos para la nueva Linea*) are differentiated from His Majesty's existing presidios (*Presidios de SM de esistentes*), but in some instances presidios in use (such as Tucson and Fronteras) were indicated by the same color as abandoned ones (such as Santa Cruz). The proposed presidios indicated by distinct coloration on the map are Buenavista, the mouth of the San Pedro at the Gila River, and one south of Fronteras at Badeguachi. Despite these differences in interpretation (probably just errors), the map is clearly an invaluable resource for understanding Spanish perception of the Sonoran frontier.

Translation of the Map Key

The following is a translation of the map key. The symbols indicated to the left of the entries can be seen in Figure 4.1.

Map of the Frontier of Sonora for the Establishment of the Line of Presidios
Explanation
[Key]

Capital of the Interior Provinces of New Spain

His Majesty's existing presidios

Presidios proposed for the new line

Pueblos
[Village or town; Indian town which would be the lowest level of municipal administration.]

Haciendas
[Land grants or landed properties to privileged members of Spanish society involved in livestock production, usually including smaller properties and employing many families in raising crops or livestock.]

Ranch, stock farm
[Small, privately owned farm for raising crops, livestock, or both; a subsistence-type farm.]

Mining district
[A mining district consisting of a principal community, its lesser settlements, and the surrounding environs.]

Known placers of gold

Unpopulated places where [the expedition] camped
[Places the expedition camped that were not in occupied towns, missions, or presidios. They also camped in named places, but these tended to be populated, though not all were, and those in which they stayed, overnight or for a midday rest, were indicated.

Strong flowing springs

and small ones where people can scarcely drink

Line or cordon of presidios. Proposed by the commissioned lieutenant of engineers .

Route that shows the reconnaissance made for the delineated settlements

Lines that divide the land belonging to each nation, according to the best information we have been able to obtain.

Notes
I. The towns, haciendas, ranchos, abandoned areas, mining towns that were not worked, and reformed [suppressed, such as Santa Cruz and also Terrenate] presidios are indicated with the same signs, but instead of in color they are indicated in black.
II. The portions of rivers or arroyos that are dry [and] rather than the color of water have that of earth.
III. Other relevant circumstances that cannot be expressed on the map will be found in the relevant entries of the daily account of the same engineer.

Arispe, September 4, 1780
Gerónimo de la Rocha y Figueroa

Redrafted Segment Maps

To supplement this original map prepared by Rocha, we have schematically redrafted portions of the map that correspond to segments of the trip and reproduced enlarged sections of the map with dates appended. These segment maps are intended to clarify the location of places mentioned in the journal, to show the route along with the dates they encamped in specific locations that correspond to dates in the journal, and to facilitate dialogue and understanding of places discussed in the summary reports and journal.

Enlargements of relevant portions of the map are included in this chapter, and drafted segment maps have been included in the next chapter to accompany the journal. Each set is keyed to the original map, with segment numbers providing guidance as to where on the overall original map the segment is located. When these segment maps are used along with the regional map, and the image of the original map provided in Chapter 1 and in the foldout map, important areas discussed throughout this volume can be located. To keep the drafted segment maps clear and readable we have not included symbolic representation of mountain ranges, but we have included most of them by reference to their names. We also have not differentiated between types of settlements, using a single symbol instead of the many used by Rocha himself. The original symbols can be seen on the reproductions of portions of the original map provided in this chapter (Figures 4.3–4.13).

Differences between the Map and Texts

As part of each day's entry Rocha often mentioned the distances and directions to known places, such as mountain ranges or passes, but some of these places are not indicated on the map. Mountain ranges provided important features of the landscape if for no other reason than they were impediments to and landmarks for travel as well as hiding places for the enemy. Many of these are referenced in the journal or in the summary reports and are labeled on the map.

There are a few places indicated on Rocha's map that are not mentioned in the journal or summaries. Some of these are without formal names, such as a small range labeled "Serritos" which almost certainly corresponds to the Tombstone Hills. Other places were probably so well known that their identities were assumed or presence expected. This is probably the case with the "Serro de la Sentenela" across from Santa Cruz de Terrenate Presidio. Vado de Santa Teresa on the lower San Pedro is not mentioned in any text but is shown on the map. A place labeled *A troxe* (*a troje*, "granary" or "barn") is illustrated near Las Nutrias, with a rectangle drawn (probably the barn being depicted) near the symbol that represents their encampment location.[1] On June 7, Rocha stated that they ended the day's journey at the San Pedro agricultural fields, so the name makes sense. Here a split in the channel is indicated, consistent with the floodplain widening at the San Pedro fields. Lafora (1958:107) noted that the storehouse there had been repeatedly burned by the enemy.

Rocha's map sometimes illustrates a deviation from the river margin route that is not discussed in the journal, such as on the lower San Pedro in the vicinity of Aravaipa Creek and on the middle San Pedro between Quiburi and Santa Cruz de Terrenate Presidio. In the latter case the senior author's efforts to follow this portion of the trail indicate that these demarcated bows, both outward from the terrace edge and back inward, seem to correspond to washes, river bends, and other terrain characteristics and obstructions. This, of course, assumes that the arroyos were obstacles historically, an issue that will be discussed in Chapter 6. The journal also does not mention an apparent double-back shown in the area between Las Palomitas and La Tienda Crossings, but without taking this into account the leagues traveled for the day and between known locations do not make sense (see Chapter 5, June 7 note). By incorporating this double-back into the leagues traveled that day the overall leagues between known places make more sense. This is where a hut or ranchería was identified and, by inference, this may be where prisoners were captured during this or (more likely) a different campaign (see note for June 6 of the journal).

Rocha indicated his camping locations with a tipi symbol. These are not depicted at pueblos and other named places they stayed, suggesting that these symbols represent unimproved camps, places they stayed along the trail. While most of these uninhabited camping places are identified by the tipi symbol, an overnight camping location near Ojo del Gato (to the east of Las Nutrias) specified by Rocha in the journal is not depicted by a tent symbol. This is probably just an oversight on an already complicated and detailed map.

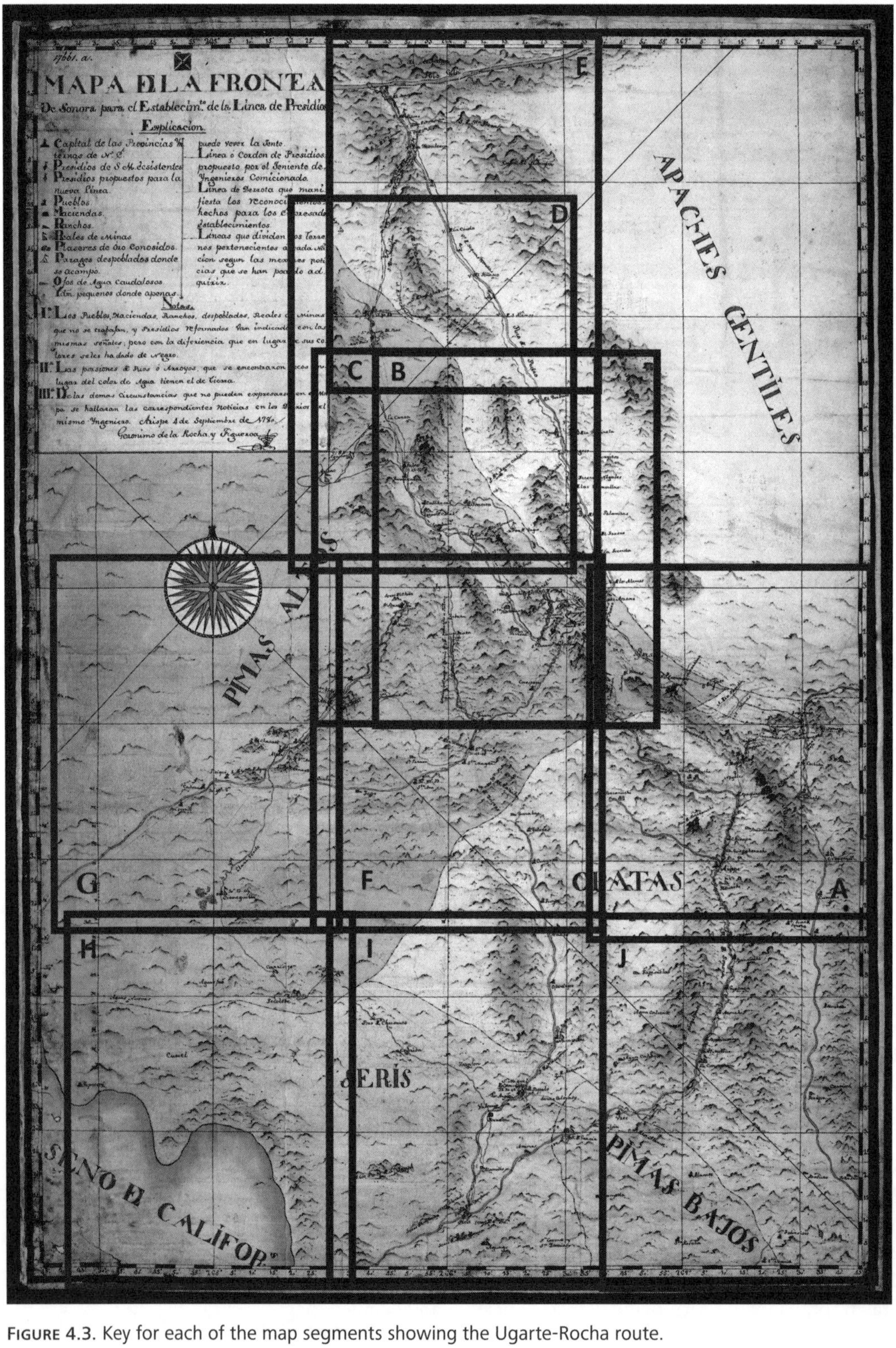

Figure 4.3. Key for each of the map segments showing the Ugarte-Rocha route.

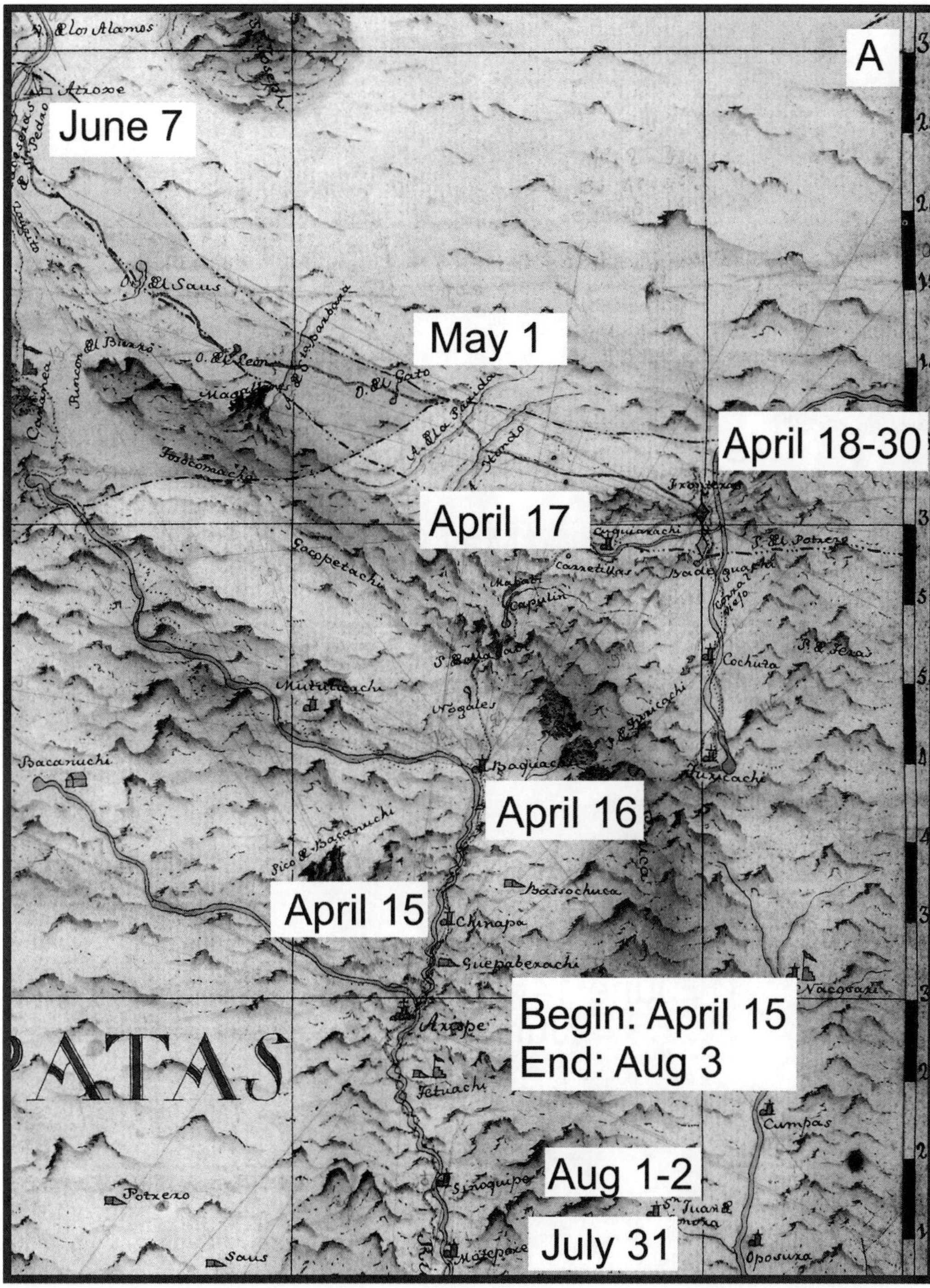

FIGURE 4.4. Map Segment A: The beginning (April 15) and ending (August 3) of the reconnaissance.

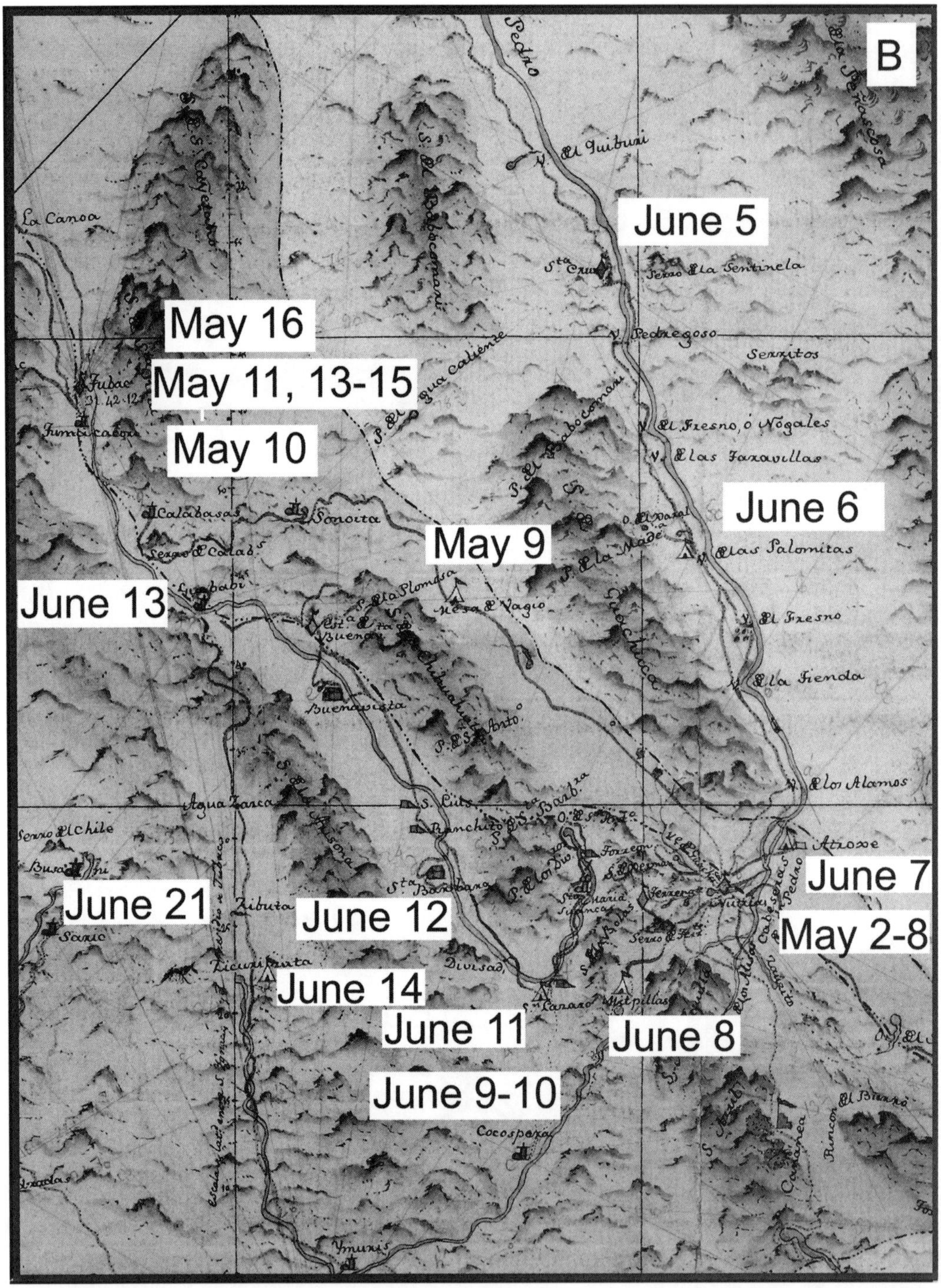

FIGURE 4.5. Map Segment B: May 2 through June 21.

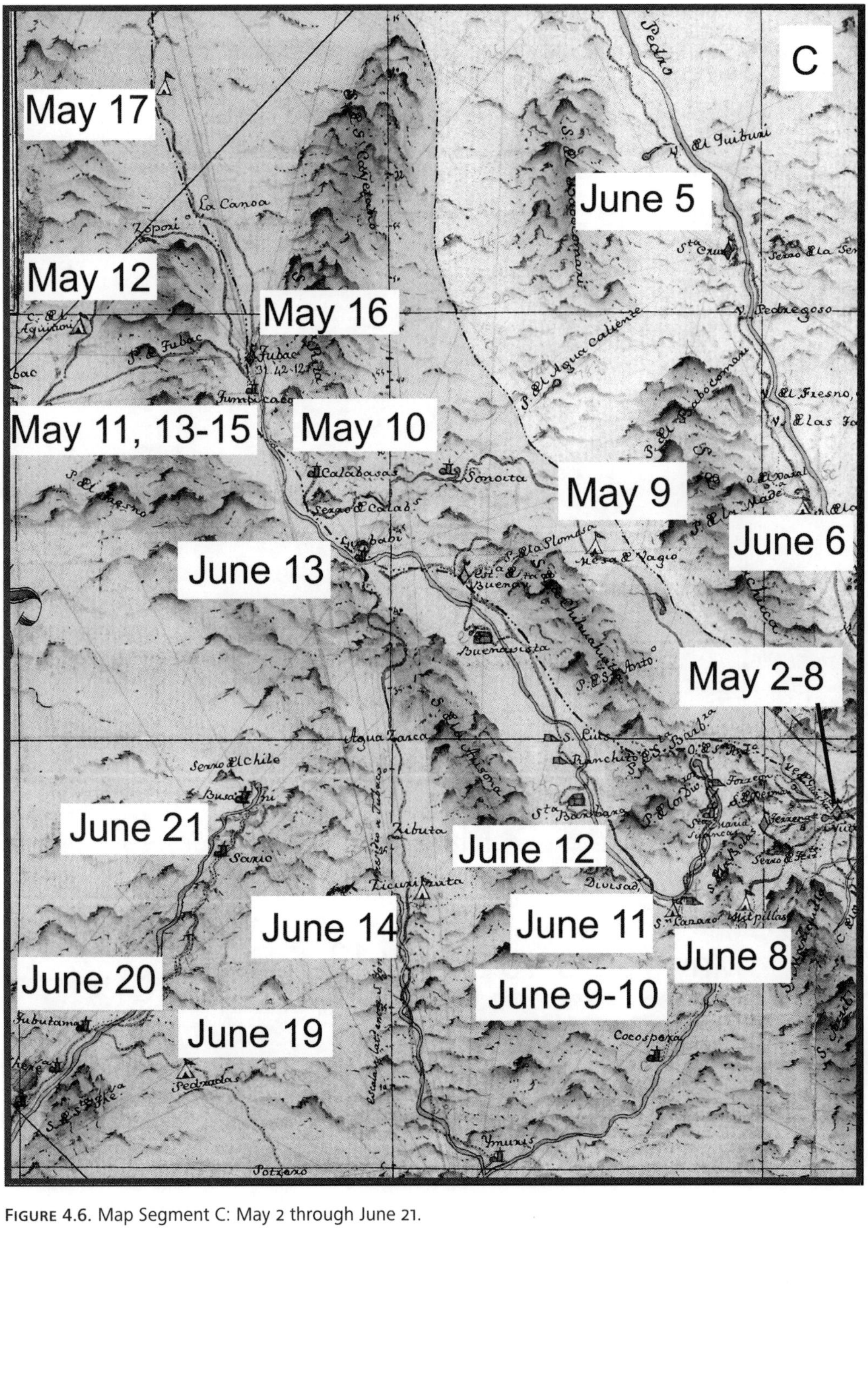

FIGURE 4.6. Map Segment C: May 2 through June 21.

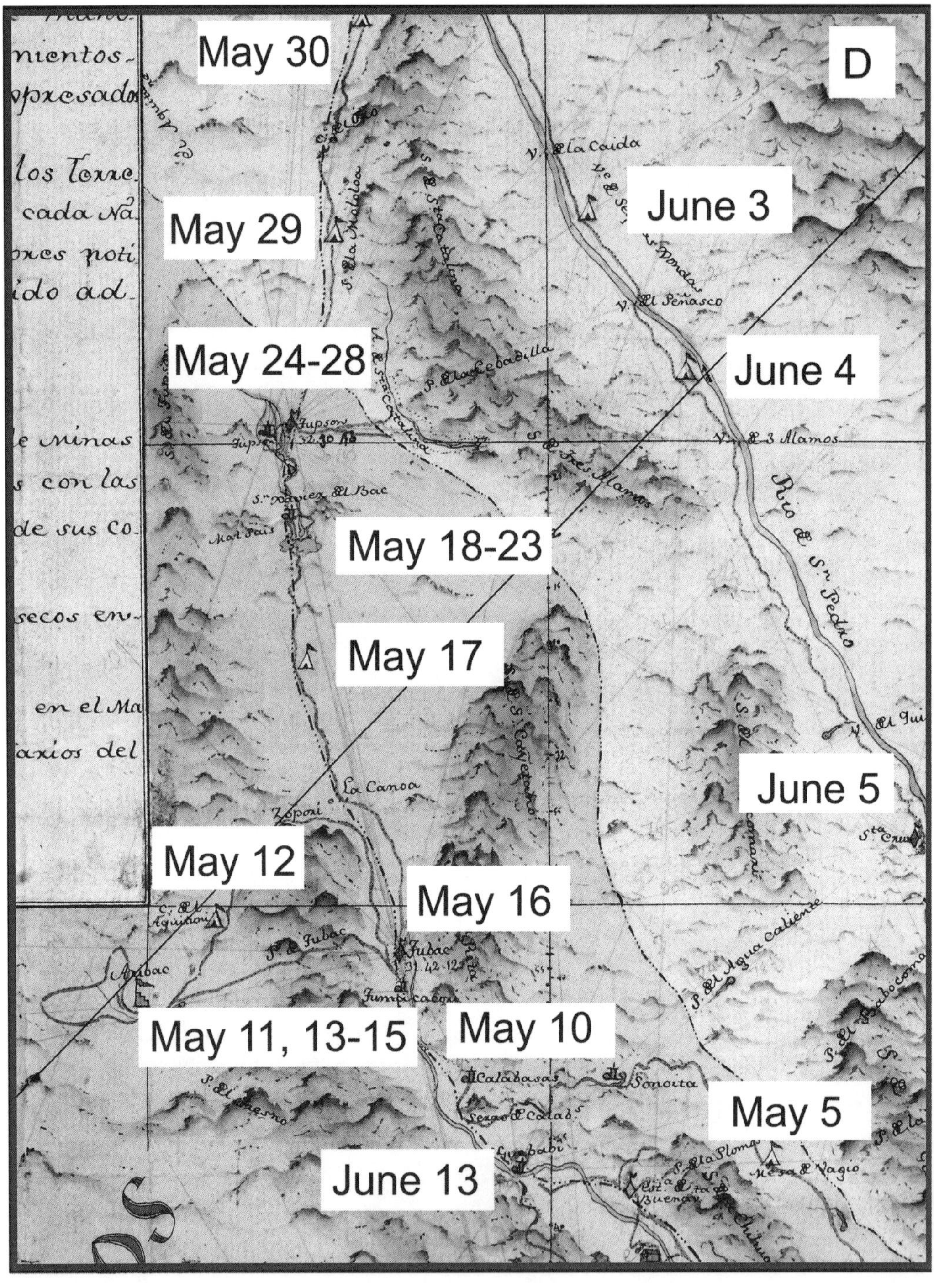

FIGURE 4.7. Map Segment D: May 9 through June 13.

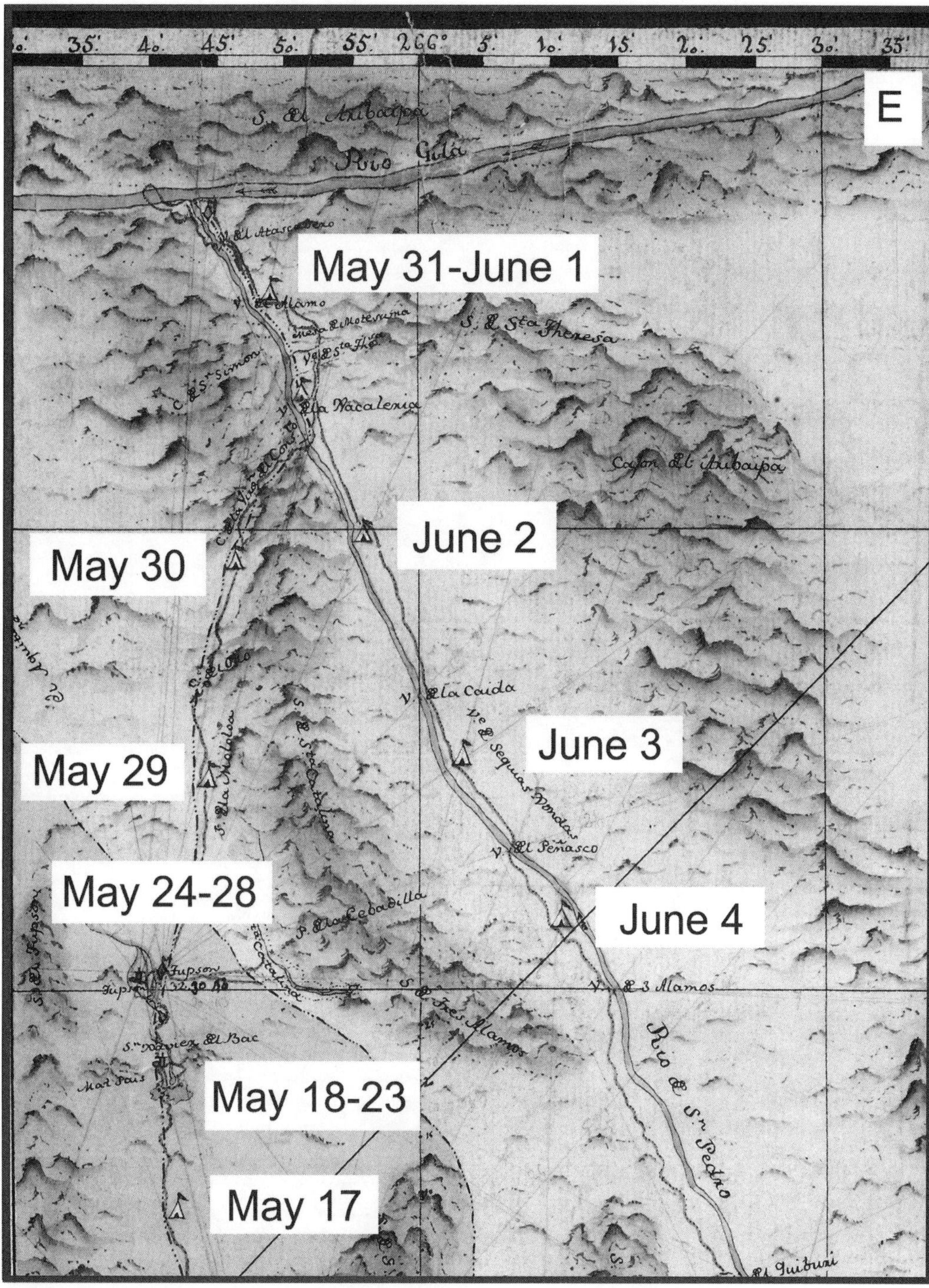

FIGURE 4.8. Map Segment E: May 17 through June 4.

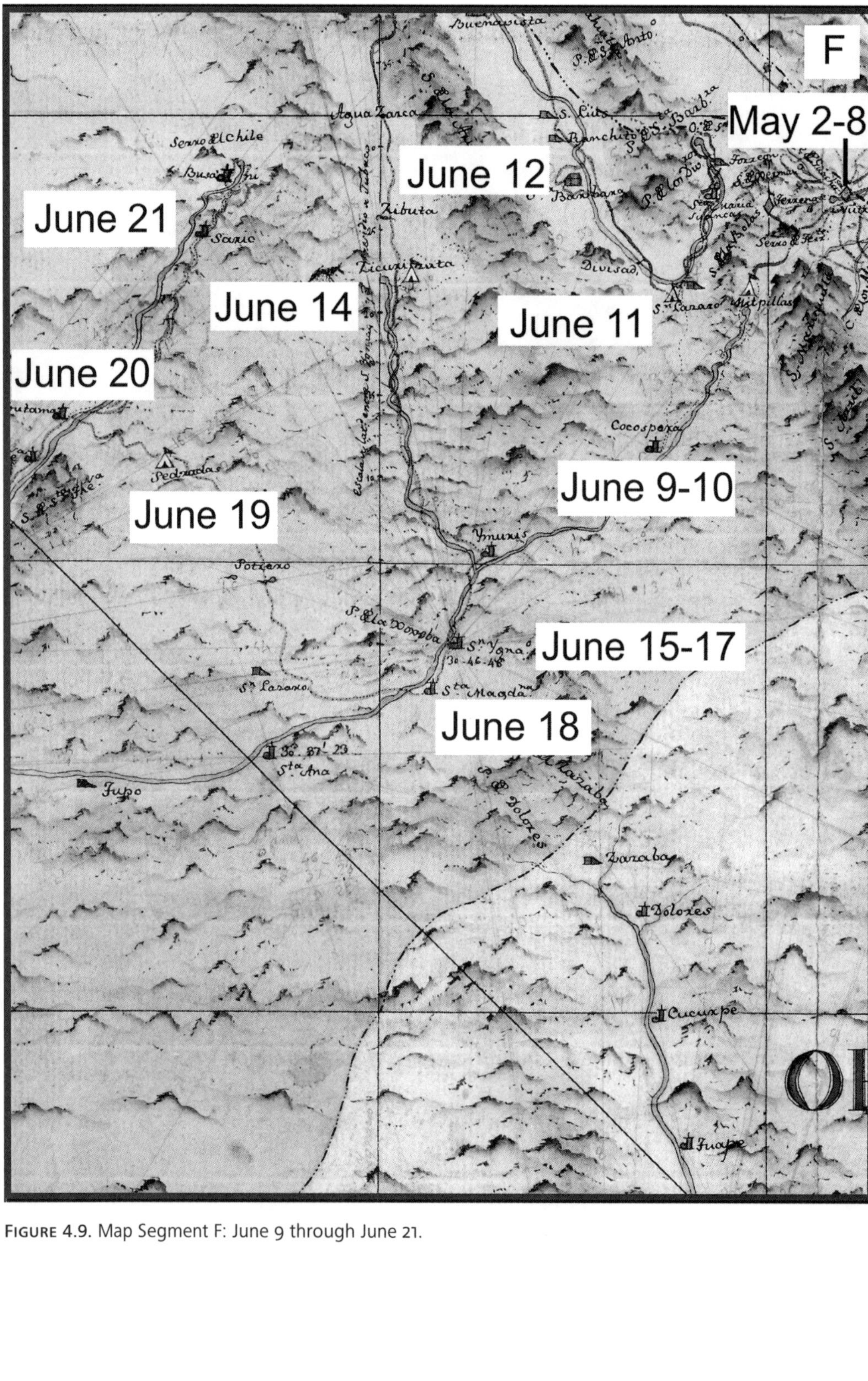

FIGURE 4.9. Map Segment F: June 9 through June 21.

FIGURE 4.10. Map Segment G: June 22 through July 4.

FIGURE 4.11. Map Segment H: July 5 through July 6.

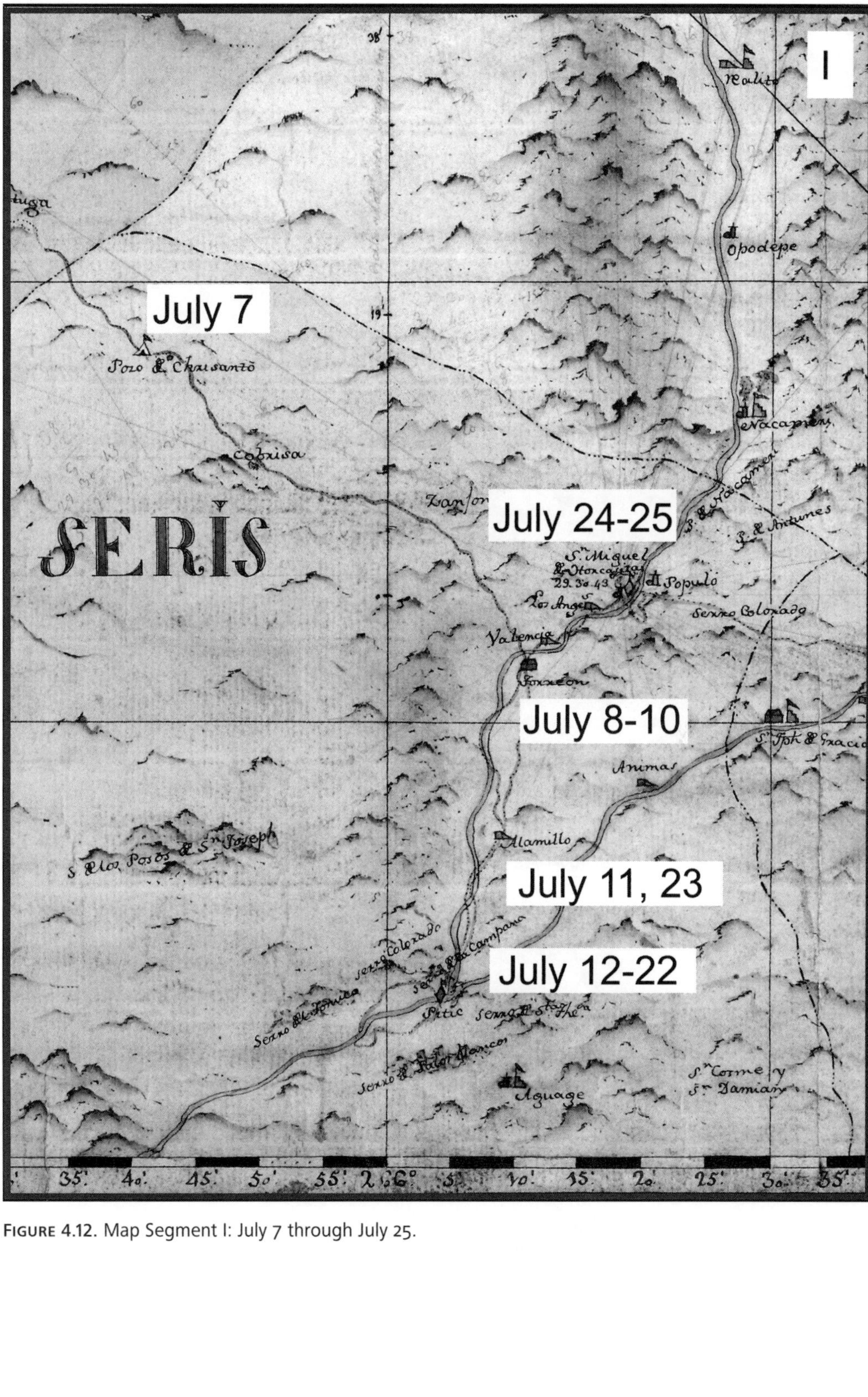

FIGURE 4.12. Map Segment I: July 7 through July 25.

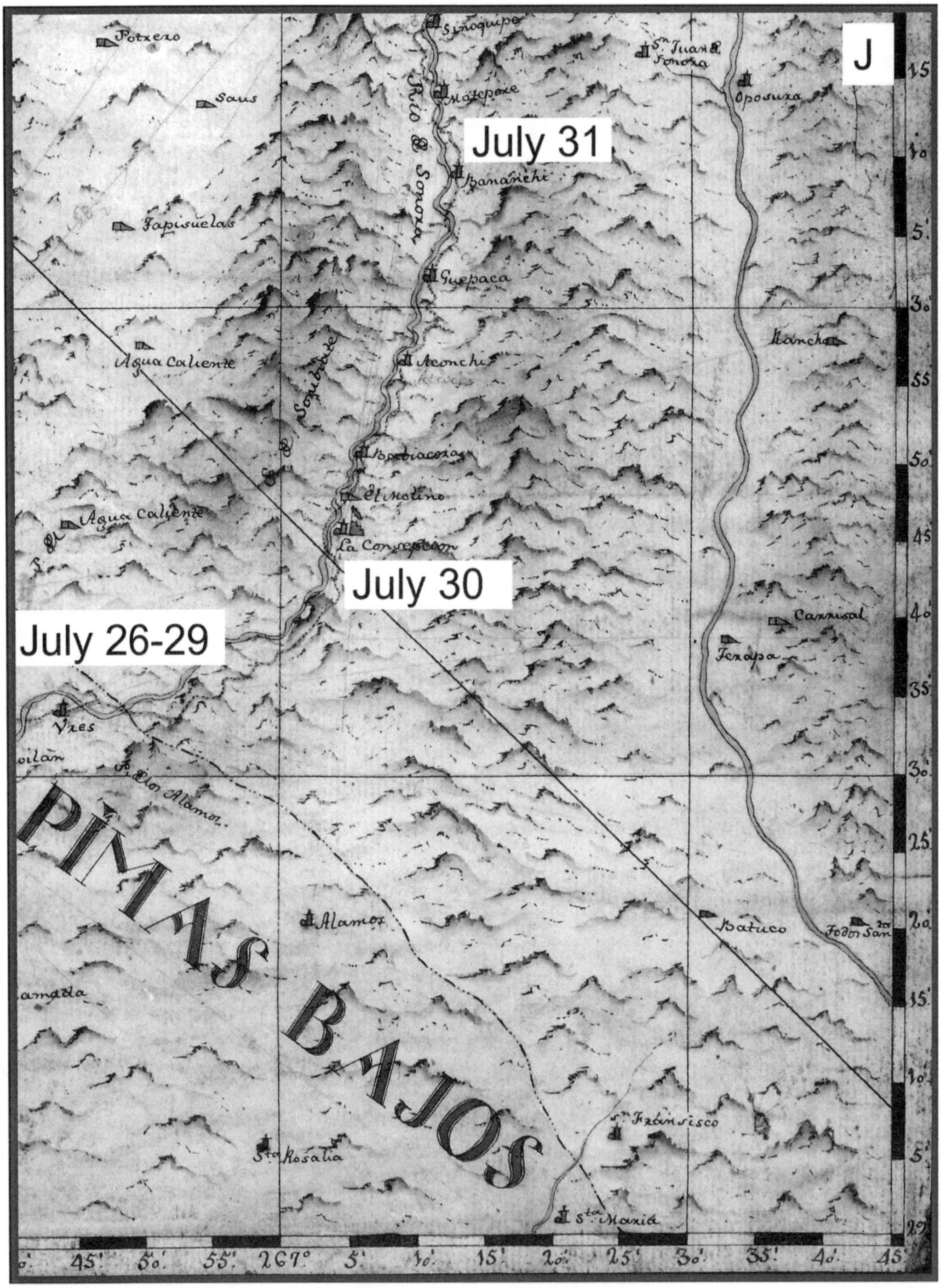

FIGURE 4.13. Map Segment J: July 26 through July 31.

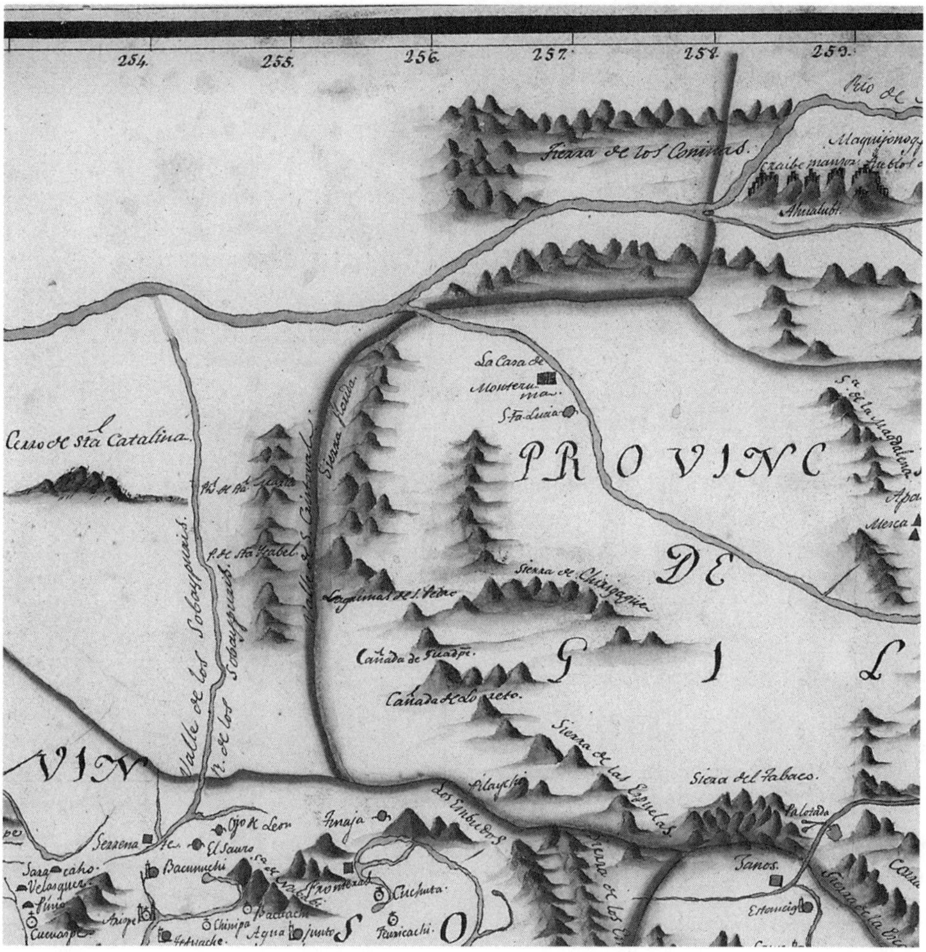

FIGURE 4.14. Close up of Urrutia's 1769 map showing the San Pedro as the Río and Valle del Sobaipuri and also showing Montesuma along the Gila River. [*Mapa, que comprende la Frontera, de los Dominios del Rey, en la America Septentrional*, 1769]. Courtesy of the Library of Congress; https://www.loc.gov/item/00556406/.

Another instance where Rocha depicted a place on the map which was not mentioned in the journal is the "Mesa de Motesuma" located just south of the confluence of the San Pedro and Gila Rivers (and south of Alamo Crossing). This is likely a large pueblo known in this area near the mouth of Aravaipa Creek or perhaps another of the late-occupied Western Pueblo villages known from this area. It is probably relevant that Urrutia also indicated the location of a place he referenced as "La Casa de Montezuma" on his 1771 map of the region. Urrutia's "La Casa de Montezuma" is located further east, along the west side of the Gila River (Figure 4.14). One suspects that as explorers happened along an especially large or well-preserved pueblo they referenced it as a "House of Montezuma," owing to the pervasiveness of the legend of Montezuma. Much of this history is lost, but in 1694 Jesuit Father Eusebio Kino was told that Casa Grande near the Gila River was built by Montezuma (Bolton 1948:128; Lumholtz 1912:341; Wilson 1999:16). Captain Juan Mateo Manje in 1697 (Karns 1954:287–288) and Jesuit Father Luis Velarde in 1716 also discussed this connection (Wyllys 1931). In 1865, Davidson (1865:131) recorded an origin story involving Montezuma as told by Con Quien, a leader of the "central Papagos." Although at this time all peoples of the south were referred to by outsiders as Papagos, clarification is provided by Underhill (1936), who noted that Chona, the daughter of Con Quien, grew up in Mesquite Root ("Kui Tatk" or "Kvitatk"), which is northwest of Sells in Tohono O'odham ("Desert People") territory.

Montezuma was also important in a revitalization movement documented in 1737, where Agustín Ascuchul proclaimed that Montezuma had appeared to him and named him his prophet. Over five thousand indigenous Sonorans fled their settlements hoping to expel the Spaniards and follow this new inspiration. Montezuma was said to have returned to reinstate traditional conditions. This nativistic movement, described by Segesser, was suppressed in 1737 by Juan Bautista de Anza the elder (see Seymour 2007; Treutlein 1945). While much of this history has been forgotten or revised, the concept of Montezuma seems clearly tied to resistance to Spanish colonialism and, perhaps earlier, resistance to intrusions by others, the Apache specifically being mentioned in the 1690s, connecting places on the landscape to mythology (Karns 1954:287).

Routes and Context of Travel

The route of travel during this operation is clearly indicated in the text of Rocha's journal and also by a dotted line on the map. Despite this, some scholars have misrepresented the route of travel, probably because the map has not been widely available. For example, Moorhead (1968:52–53) states: "The group began in Fronteras Presidio on the west slope of the Sierra Madre. They then proceeded to the north to the far upper reaches of the San Pedro." This error is also based on the content of Croix's orders, which outline the intended route. Yet, in contrast to Croix's orders and the summary of this reconnaissance provided by Moorhead, Ugarte and Rocha did not continue down the San Pedro. As Rocha stated in his summary report: "the sequence was reversed from how the reconaissances were mandated to be executed, as Your Lordship will notice in the accompanying diary, as well as the fact that it was not possible for me to avoid [prevent] it, not having the discretion to not comply with that [order] of Your Lordship" (see Chapters 3 and 5). Instead, they embarked from Las Nutrias on a cross-country trek through the San Rafael Valley, intersecting with Sonoita Creek, which they followed downstream until its junction with the Santa Cruz. They then turned north, encountering Calabasas, Tumacácori, and Tubac before sidetracking to Arivaca. Intersecting the Santa Cruz River again, they headed downstream, to the north, through La Canoa, San Xavier, and Tucson, where they stayed before marching north along the west side of the Santa Catalina Mountains. It is only via this route that they intersected with the lower San Pedro, probably in the area of Mammoth, and then ventured north to the confluence of the San Pedro and Gila Rivers, which was one of the key objectives of their journey. After inspecting this area for a future presidio, they headed south along the San Pedro, again resting at Terrenate/Las Nutrias before splitting up so that Rocha could explore another area. Rocha headed west through the Santa María Suanca Valley (the upper Santa Cruz in the modern San Rafael Valley) and on along the Santa María River (Santa Cruz River) as it ran south through modern Sonora. They went to San Lázaro where the river bends, flowing to the north. They followed the route of the river north to the Santa Barbara hacienda, and the ruined pueblo and mission of Guevavi, before releasing those members of the party who returned to Tucson. Rocha and the remaining thirty men turned south to rejoin Ugarte at San Ignacio on June 15. Together they then traveled south to Pitic, where the commission ended, and then on to Arizpe, where Rocha presumably met up with Croix to hand over the secret copies of his journal and map.

Rocha often used the term *caminamos*, which is easily interpreted, as it has been in the past, as "walked." Yet in all likelihood Rocha and his men did not walk but rather rode horses, an inference that is reinforced by references to horses in the text. A mule is mentioned once as a pack animal, but then only incidentally, with reference to the ill fate of his documents and equipment. These were facts that were understood and so would not have been mentioned in a more consequential way.

Latitude and longitude tick marks occur at the map margins, and triangulation lines cross various portions of the map. Yet when considering the current latitude of known places and converting from the Greenwich to the Tenerife meridian, it is apparent that there is some variation. There is about a 20' difference relative to the latitude of Santa Cruz de Terrenate Presidio, San Xavier del Bac, and Guevavi Mission, a 17' difference at Tucson Presidio, and this difference decreases to about 6' for Tubac. Distortion of the map image, enlarged place symbols, and exceedingly large map scale size contribute to some inaccuracy, as does the approximate nature of the minute-to-mile conversion, although for Tucson (lat 32°30'40") and Tubac (lat 31°42'12") and some other key places Rocha actually wrote the latitude on the map near each presidio. Despite minor differences, the latitudes provided by Rocha are relatively precise, sufficiently to locate a place within a mile and to distinguish between possible locations for places that have been "lost," such as Sonoita and Calabasas, and to discern when moves of certain settlements occurred, such as at San Xavier del Bac (as is discussed in Chapter 7). With respect to Calabasas, the latitude confirms that at this time it was north of Sonoita Creek, as Rocha's map plot indicates. The locations of Calabasas, Sonoita, and their encampment in the San Rafael Valley were triangulated from Guevavi, which in turn was pegged to Altar Presidio. Latitude derived from Rocha's plot of Sonoita indicated it was south of modern-day Patagonia. This location has been archaeologically identified in the field, representing the only Sobaipuri settlement to the north (or west) of the Sonoita Creek drainage in this area (see Chapter 7).

The text of the journal indicates the number of leagues traveled each day and the distance in leagues to designated places. The value of the league has varied through time, but tends to correspond to about 2.6 miles (or 4.2 kilometers) per league for this period.[2] During the missionary period (1690s) Father Kino and his military escort Captain Manje sometimes presented different league distances between the same two closely spaced settlements, for example between the Sobaipuri O'odham villages of Quiburi and Santa Cruz. Even short distances between places varied between these two men, which suggests either greater attention paid by one, different methods used to measure or estimate, differences in distance equations, or perhaps slightly different routes taken between two settlements. It is also likely that these two were measuring from different locations, as Seymour (2003) has noted previously, and as Rivera noted: "Although the Spanish planning precepts for town layout and physical design were followed loosely—adapted to local conditions and resources—the upstream boundary of each village was usually designated according to the place where the stream source was diverted and a diversion dam installed" (Rivera 2006:3). This and other factors would certainly account for the difference in league distances between known communities, such as was noted for Kino and Manje, where one may have been using the official village boundary at the canal head, while the other might have been using the center or edge of the housing or fields. This type of measurement would also likely decrease differences between Rocha's latitude and those measured today at the village or presidio center.

One of the more important factors contributing to variations, if not inaccuracies, in measured or estimated distances traveled involves the ways in which they traversed the landscape. For example, the distance given between two known places may vary depending on whether straight-line miles along a river were being indicated or whether they were following all the curves and turns of the river. If travelers followed along the river's edge, the distance would be longer than if they followed a relatively straight line with the river at a distance but within view. There is a substantial difference in distance between these two approaches and, in all likelihood, both procedures were used. The considerable variation in distances traveled based on these many factors is probably one reason Rocha repeatedly qualified his results in his notes at the end of his journal. He clarified that his estimated distances were not exact. In fact, true to his engineering training, he repeatedly commented on this lack of precision, suggesting that it bothered him deeply. This is probably no surprise, given he was extraordinary engineer of the royal armies (as conveyed in his introductory paragraph to the journal).

Ugarte and Rocha followed rivers and established *caminos* for much of their route. One reason to follow existing trails is that in some areas the terrain was rough and rocky, and in others the landscape was incised by arroyos and gullies requiring major effort to bypass, and many areas were excessively brushy, with not only thick but thorny vegetation. Known routes often followed the river courses because these were major thoroughfares for indigenous residents. Most of the time Ugarte and Rocha were on indefinite and generalized trails, though at obstructions or constructions the route was likely more clearly defined. About a century earlier Kino and Manje had followed established trails in their journeys and, as Manje noted in 1697, the Sobaipuri O'odham guided them along a "clear beaten track" as they veered away from the San Pedro to find a way around a bog (Karns 1954:285).

In all likelihood Ugarte and Rocha stayed as close to the river as possible, consistent with Croix's orders regarding the San Pedro, which required them to follow the banks of the river (Instructive Order of the Military Governor, Chapter 2). Their goal was to note the presence of water, firewood, timber, and pasture as well as the suitability of the terrain for settlement and agriculture. Military protocol, as conveyed in Bernardo de Vargas Machuca's *Milicia y Descripción de las Indias*, established that a lookout should be left on the trail within sight of a watering hole or stream and that when establishing a camp they should take care that there was a watercourse nearby (Machuca 1892 [1599]). Their route of travel along rivers likely followed the terrace edge overlooking the floodplain. If this assumption is incorporated into distance assessments when reconstructing the route on Google Earth and topographic maps, the most accurate league distances are obtained. This routing would have allowed them to avoid the dense vegetation of the floodplain, which would have obscured visibility and made them vulnerable to ambush (Machuca 1892 [1599]). Yet, near the end of the trip Rocha said they veered far around their intended route, going through rough high country because of the flooding from recent rains (Diary, July 30). A veering from the river's edge is visible in a couple of other places not mentioned in the text but depicted on the map, including at Calabasas on the Santa Cruz River and those already noted at the far northern end of the lower San Pedro (between Alamo and Hacaleria fords) and on the upper San Pedro (between Las Palomitas and La Tienda fords).

There were many places where Ugarte and Rocha intentionally left the river margin, traveling across grassy plains or through mountain passes. One such location was the route from Las Nutrias on the San Pedro up through La Mesa del Bajío ("Highland Mesa"), to the deserted village of Sonoita along Sonoita Creek, and then on to Calabasas on the Santa Cruz. The route through the Bajío took them up through the San Rafael Valley, in the opposite direction taken by John Russell Bartlett in 1851 as part of the United States Boundary Commission's project to map the international boundary established as a result of the Treaty of Guadalupe Hidalgo of 1848. Ugarte and Rocha took what was perhaps part of the same route as Marcos de Niza or Coronado, who many local residents believe traveled up this valley. Kino almost certainly crossed this valley on his way from Dolores, down the Babocomari River and on to its San Joachín settlement, and then on to Santa Cruz de Gaybanipitea and Quiburi on the middle San Pedro near modern-day Fairbank. The San Rafael Valley, Rocha's Bajío, is one of the few places in southern Arizona where the luxuriant grass still chafes one's thighs and forms an expansive golden quilt, gently folded over on itself, woven of brilliant threads, etched with dark squiggles, and decorated with green

FIGURE 4.15. The landscape today San Rafael Valley, Rocha's La Mesa del Bajío.

lines of cottonwoods and oak (Figure 4.15). All of these travelers passed through this valley far too early to appreciate the impressionistic quality of this pastel landscape.

When going cross-country Ugarte and Rocha went from waterhole to waterhole. Mostly they stopped at an *ojo de agua* ("spring") or *aguate* ("flowing spring"), generally following water courses to their source. As much as possible, however, they traveled along rivers, which in the Basin and Range Province of southern Arizona are south–north trending, but north flowing. This leapfrogging to waterholes is not surprising given the time of year during which they traveled. They made their trip in mid-April and continued through the hottest and driest part of the year (May and June), and well into the rainy season of July and early August. At first consideration, it seems foolhardy to have traveled during a drought year into some sectors that were still unknown during the hottest and driest part of the year. Yet, spring would have provided sufficient pasture for the horses, which would have been one of the primary concerns for these men, as it had been for expeditions since the 1500s. Ugarte and Rocha's intent was to evaluate the reliability and distribution of water for future use, settlement, and travel. By traveling at the driest part of the year they would be able to determine which water sources were truly perennial, providing valuable and reliable information for future campaigns and for settlement. Because 1780 was an especially dry year, the water sources they found were those which were most reliable. Despite the dryness, the rainy season or monsoons had begun in earnest by the time they were headed south. Rocha's journal records the incredible rains, the floods, the required adjustments to the route, and the inconvenience caused by high waters and incessant rains. The occurrence of a drought was simply a coincidence, as plans for the reconnaissance had been finalized previously. There was a sense of urgency because the Santa Cruz garrison was temporarily encamped, awaiting a more permanent presidio, and because the king wanted to expand the Presidial Line to encourage settlement so as to increase communication, strengthen the supply line, and connect a string of settlements between the Gila-San Pedro confluence and the Colorado River and northern California.

FIGURE 4.16. Los Alamos Crossing today showing boulders and cobbles deposited in the San Pedro from the tributary flow from the mountains.

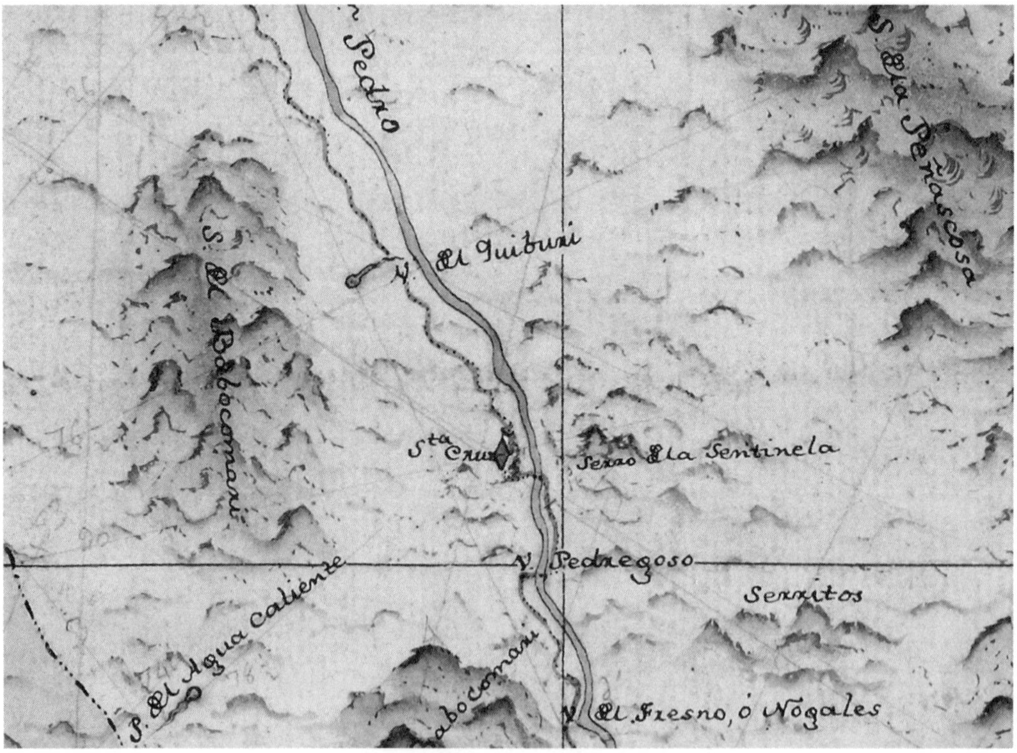

FIGURE 4.17. Close-up of Rocha's 1780 map. The dotted line suggests that at least four times at various points along the segment north of Santa Cruz de Terrenate presidio they moved in toward and out away from the terrace edge and floodplain, possibly because of down-cutting of tributary channels. Courtesy of the British Library; Shelfmark: Cartographic Items Additional MS. 17,661.a.

Field Visits

Rocha's words are infused with special significance in many instances, as becomes clear when knowledge derived from decades of field work and familiarity with the local terrain assists in interpretation. An apparent unimportant passage takes on new meaning when placed in historical, cultural, archaeological, and geographic context. The senior author has revisited many of these places mentioned in Rocha's diary, assessed what he meant and the specific routes he seems to have taken, and photographed relevant aspects of the terrain: a pass, a mission, or a presidio. This has allowed a more thorough analysis of the specific route than would otherwise be possible. For example, when Ugarte and Rocha approached the San Pedro, traveling north from Tucson Presidio, they skirted the western edge of the Santa Catalina Mountains all the way to the general area around Oracle. Here several arroyos cut to the north and northeast. The Spaniards could have taken any of these, but most join to form a single well-entrenched arroyo called Tucson Wash (Rocha's *Cañada de la Virgen del Consuelo*) that directs travel toward and empties into the San Pedro at Mammoth. Knowledge of this, obtained both from local residents and our tracing of the route, allowed us to determine that it was in the Mammoth area where Ugarte and Rocha likely intersected with the San Pedro, not further south as originally thought. As just noted, some of the discrepancies in league distances are likely accounted for by an outcurve in their trail that is shown on their map, but has little meaning until this entry point is understood.

The expedition's stay was so short in any one place that little evidence of their passing is expected, yet they describe certain places they visited, such as crossings, and so considerable effort was made to identify these specific crossings, which most likely lasted through the ages. One such crossing or *vado* is at the confluence of Tres Alamos wash and the San Pedro, where a clear boundary is visible in cobbles that would have provided a suitable substrate for crossing (Figure 4.16). Many identified crossings occur where a tributary wash empties into the San Pedro, because the arroyo empties out as the current slows to intersect with the San Pedro channel. This knowledge of the consistent nature of many of the more definitive crossings allowed us to build inferences as to where the other, less obvious crossings were located, including one near Palominas on the San Pedro that served as the crossing point on the route between Santa Cruz de Terrenate and San Bernardino.

Little cultural evidence of these crossings exists, owing to the limited nature of their use and reuse through the years and the flooding events of the rivers. The most substantial evidence is at the crossing associated with the recently abandoned Santa Cruz de Terrenate Presidio. The trail indicated by a dotted line on Rocha's map crosses over from the west to the east side just south of the presidio at an unnamed ford (referenced as the Santa Cruz Crossing, Diary, June 7) and then back over to the west side at Pedregoso Ford (Figures 4.17 and 4.18). Here evidence of repeated use of the ford is present, found during the senior author's 2007–2010 archaeological work at the Santa Cruz Presidio, in the form of period-specific artifacts and some probable burials that are likely related to the indigenous scouts residing at the presidio (Seymour 2011a, b, c).

Effort was also made to identify Rocha's encampments, even though they stayed but a single night in most locations along the trail. Military manuals provide a hint of what modifications might have occurred, what types of landforms they might have chosen as camps, and how the encampments might have been arranged (Machuca 1892 [1599]). None have been identified to date, but much was learned from this exercise. So much of the land is privately held that systematic coverage of the area is not possible, although many generous land owners allowed us access.

Images from a variety of sources are included throughout this book for reference because they clarify the intent or meaning of the text, including both images from today that illustrate places and many historic images that provide insights into the places closer in time to 1780. Some of

FIGURE 4.18. The Santa Cruz Ford today, just south or upstream from Santa Cruz de Terrenate Presidio.

these places the senior author has spent the better part of her professional career working and studying. In some instances the meaning of the text is clear only because of this familiarity. In some instances historians have misinterpreted the route and aspects of the texts because of their lack of familiarity with the specific region or because they have not spent the time with the texts and maps as we have for this book. These differences in interpretation are indicated throughout the text and endnotes.

In other cases, the texts of past military men, explorers, and missionaries provide important links to on-the-ground places. For example, Urrutia's maps show passes and mountain ranges mentioned but not illustrated by Rocha, and while names of places change through time and are often transferred to new locations, in these instances the locations fit with the journal text and route. Other sources provide links between these Spaniards' conceptions of the landscape as these names persist or change through time. For example, Nicholas de Lafora referenced San Antonio Pass just south of the modern-day Patagonia Mountains and north of the San Antonio Mountains in 1766, as does Rocha's map, establishing and extending this familiarity of place though time. They were building a working knowledge of landscape, with their new "conquest landscape" overlaid on that of the indigenous peoples', including many places that maintained the names given them by the O'odham, Tarahumara (Rarámuris), and Ópata (Joyl-ra-ua, village people). Many other places were named for the activities of the enemy, including *La Tienda* ("tent" or "tipi"), *La Hacaleria* ("jacal" or "hut"), and *La Abra* ("a pass between mountains"). Others were named for the characteristics of the place, such as *Tres Alamos* ("three cottonwood trees"), *Atascadero* ("bog"), and so on (see Chapter 9).

The map provides an indispensible com-

Figure 4.19 Historic photograph of Guevavi mission 160 years after Rocha's observation that the mission and settlement had been abandoned, although as recent archaeological work has shown, the mission area was reoccupied several times after this. Even abandoned, Guevavi would have been much grander then than today. This 1940 image shows still-standing walls. Today few walls stand, while mostly low mounds indicate the locations of former buildings. San Gabriel de Guevavi, Santa Cruz County, Arizona. Historic American Buildings Survey AZ-1 (HABS), Courtesy of the Library of Congress, Delos H. Smith, February 1940.

panion document to the diary and summary reports. Experience shows that many different interpretations of text passages are possible in the absence of a map to guide descriptions. The land is vast and presents numerous possibilities for interpretation of specific routes taken. The map narrows the specifics of the route sufficiently that most of the trail can be reconstructed.

Notes

1. Rocha's 1784 map also shows a rectangle in the general area, perhaps also denoting this granary (see Figure 1.18).
2. Several references are available that discuss the relationship of the league to the mile (among these, Chardon 1980). These types of analyses as well as on-the-ground and Google Earth calculations of distances between known places indicate that the mile equivalent varied depending on the particular chronicler, the day, and the particular way chosen between two points; it also likely changed through time. For 1780 it most closely corresponds to 2.6 miles per league, but like earlier, is sometimes three miles per league.

CHAPTER 5

Gerónimo de la Rocha y Figueroa's Diary

This chapter includes the translation of the full text of Rocha's diary. As with preceding chapters the places mentioned are cross-referenced to the maps, yet for this chapter a special set of maps is included that track the day-to-day journey (Figures 5.1–5.14). These are keyed to the larger map as well (with a map key, Figures 1.5, 4.3–4.13, and 5.1) so that their location can be identified relative to the journey as a whole. Information in parentheses is included in the original document, while we have added the information provided in brackets and in endnotes. Throughout we have mostly kept the Spanish terms for those used commonly in the region (e.g., pueblo, arroyo, sierra, vecinos, presidio, ciénega, cañada, estancia, rancho, hacienda, aguaje, ojo, etc.).

Rocha's Diary

Diary of the reconnaissance made on the frontier of the Province of Sonora as a consequence of the superior order of April 15 of the present year, from the commandant-general of the Interior Provinces of New Spain, the field marshal Caballero[1] de Croix, executed under the orders of brigadier and military governor of said province, Don[2] Jacobo de Ugarte y Loyola, by the lieutenant of infantry and extraordinary engineer of the royal armies, Don Gerónimo de la Rocha y Figueroa.

Day 15 of April, 1780

Under the aforementioned higher order, I went from the capitol of Arispe (see Figure 1.10) ["large cave" (Treutlein 1949:236)][3] to the pueblo of San Joseph de Chinapa,[4] where I presented myself to Brigadier Jacobo de Ugarte y Loyola to continue my trip under his orders. I made five leagues toward the northeast quarter-north: 5 [leagues]

Day 16 [of April]

Continuing along the same canyon of the Sonora River, we traveled eight leagues north quarter-northeast to the pueblo of Bacuachi: 8 [leagues]

Some eighteen leagues to the northwest is the deserted Real de Minas ["Mining Camp"][5] de la Cananea ["Canaanite Woman" (Treutlein 1949:236)]. Two leagues

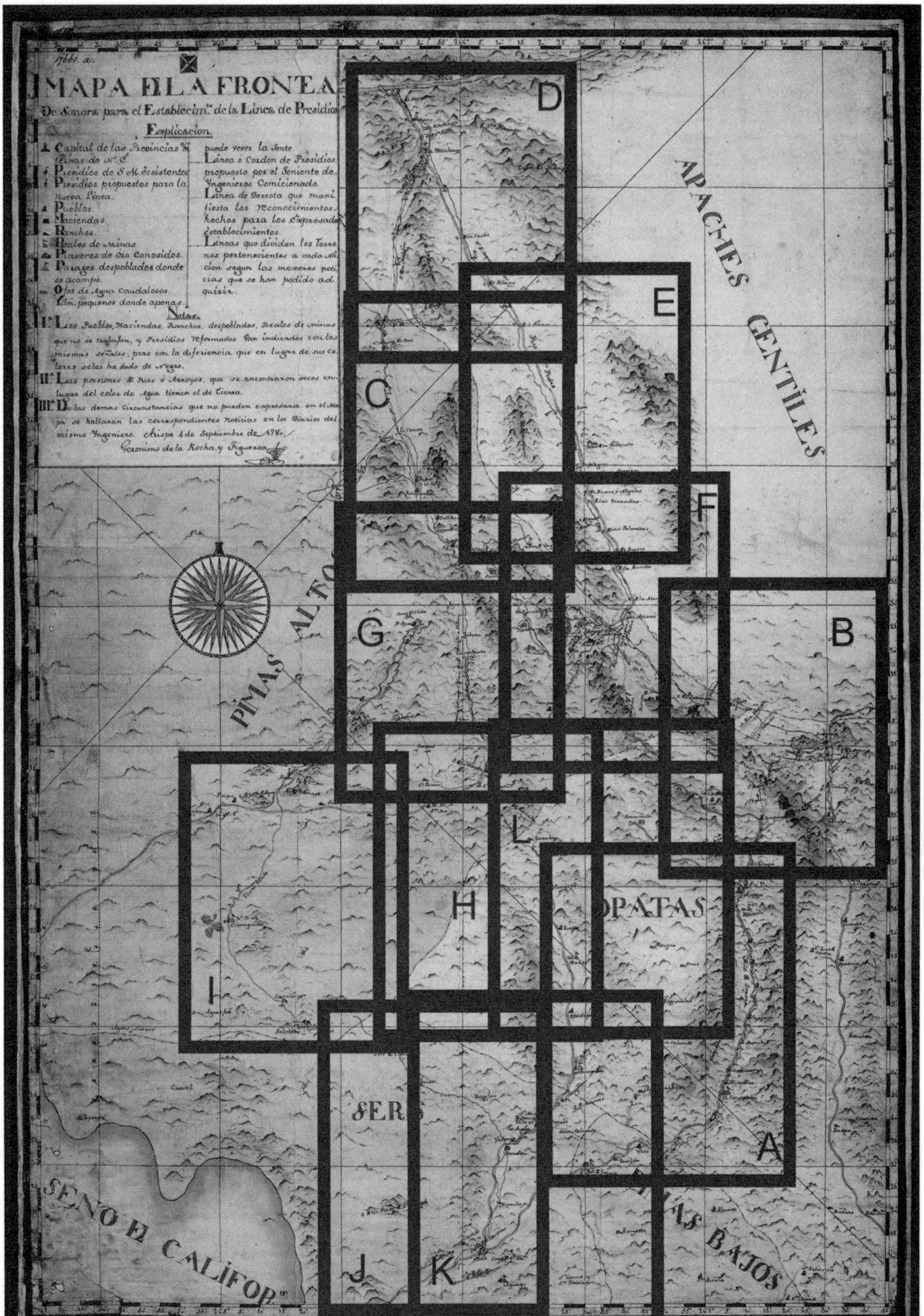

FIGURE 5.1. Key for each map segment showing the Ugarte-Rocha route.

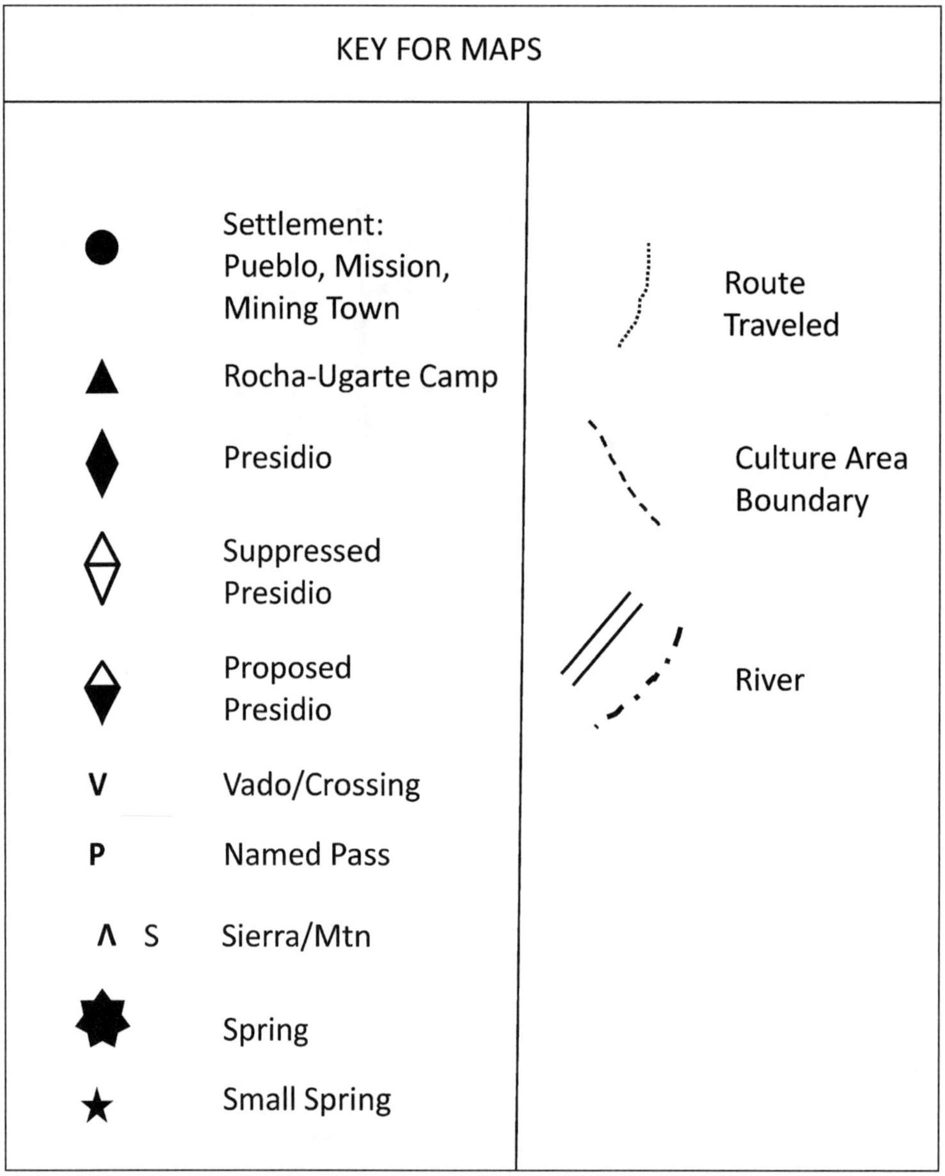

FIGURE 5.2. Map key.

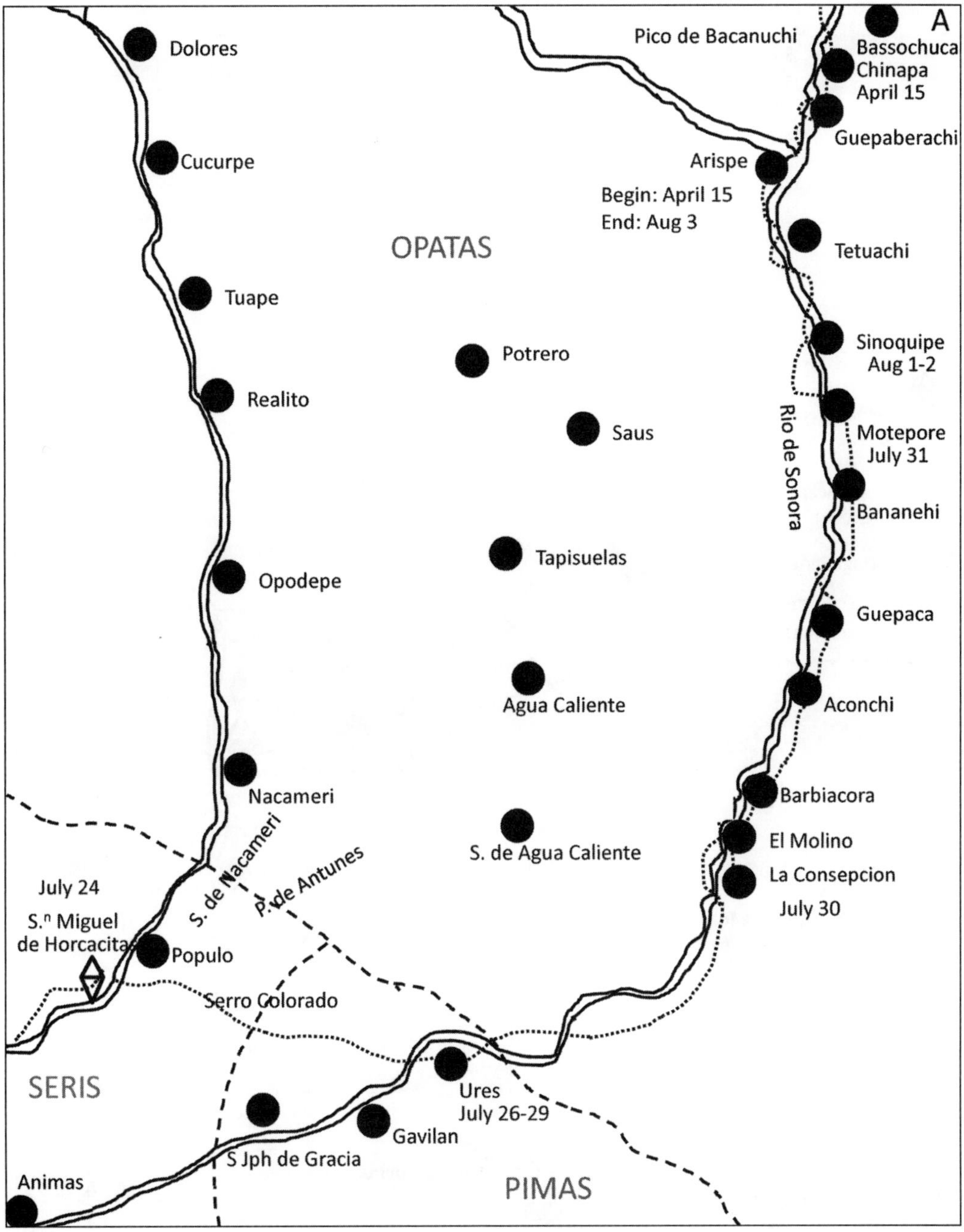

FIGURE 5.3. Map A.

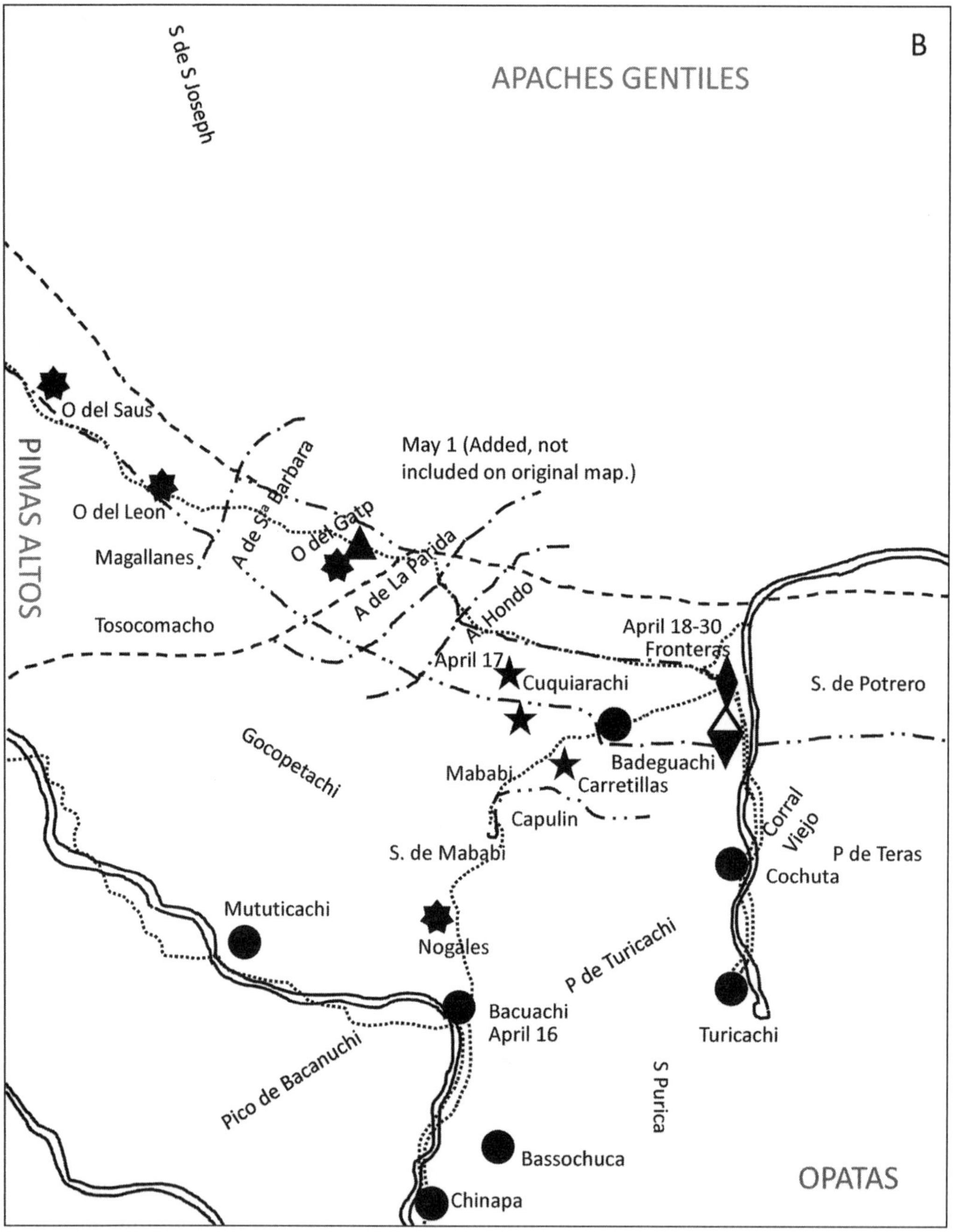

FIGURE 5.4. Map B.

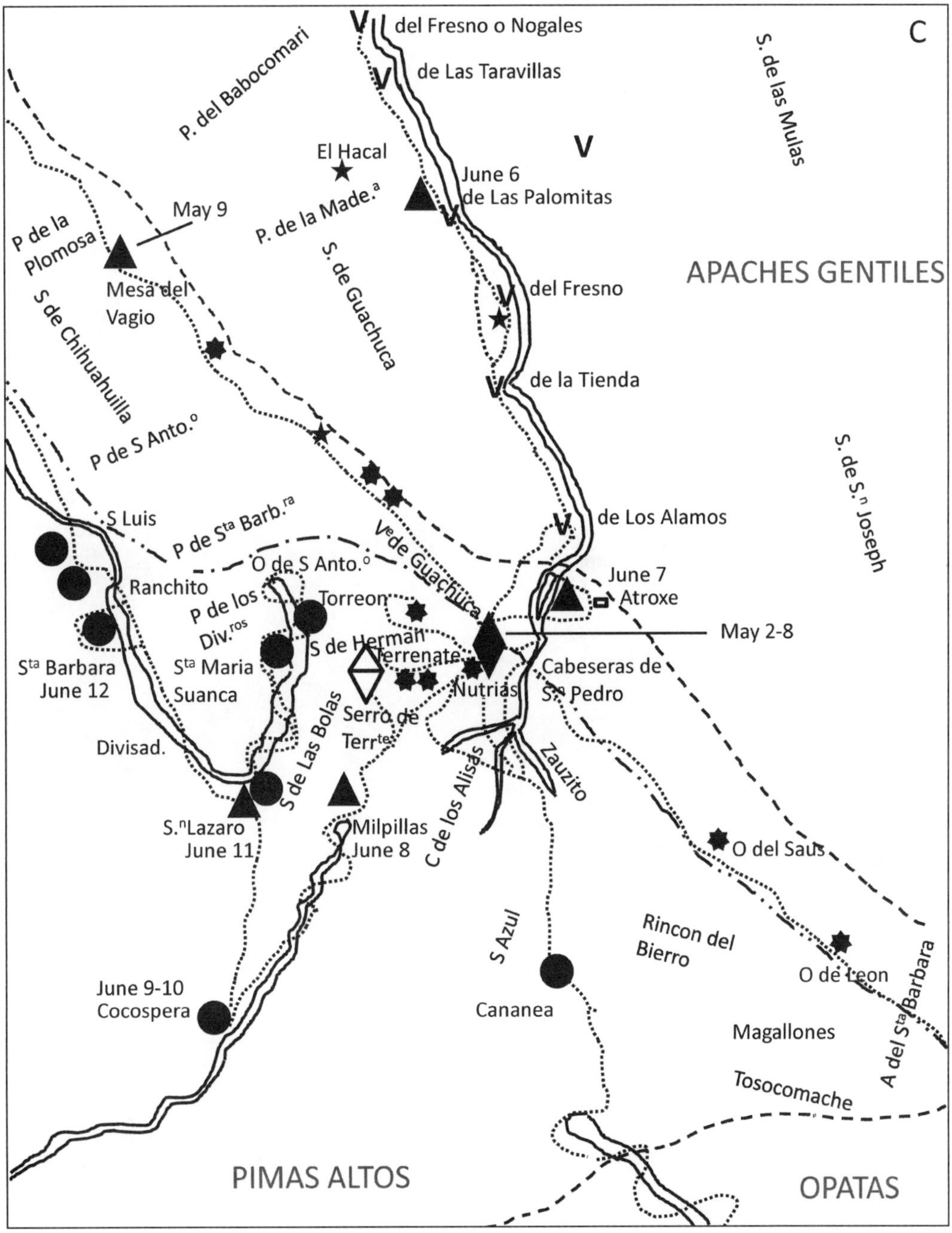

FIGURE 5.5. Map C.

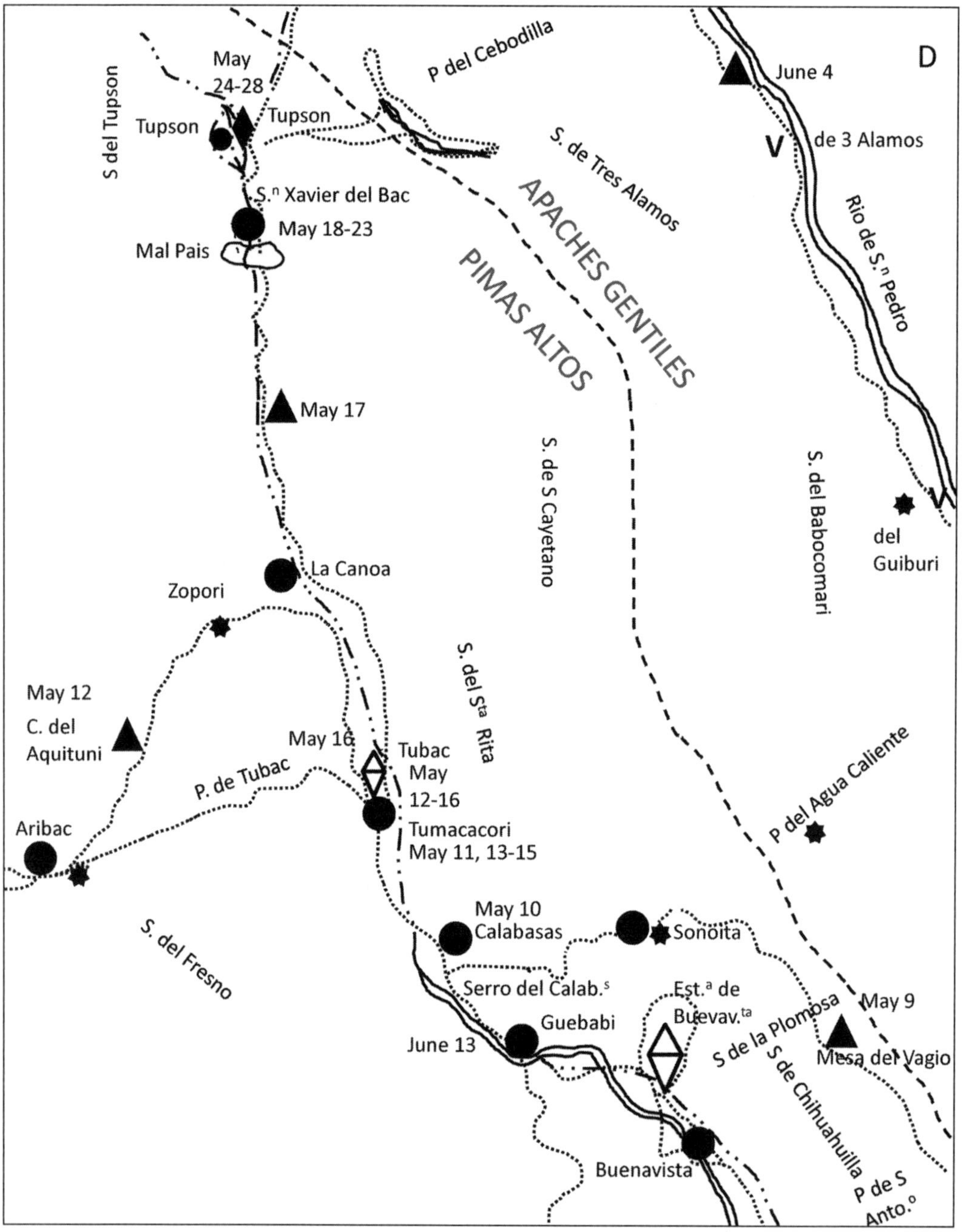

FIGURE 5.6. Map D.

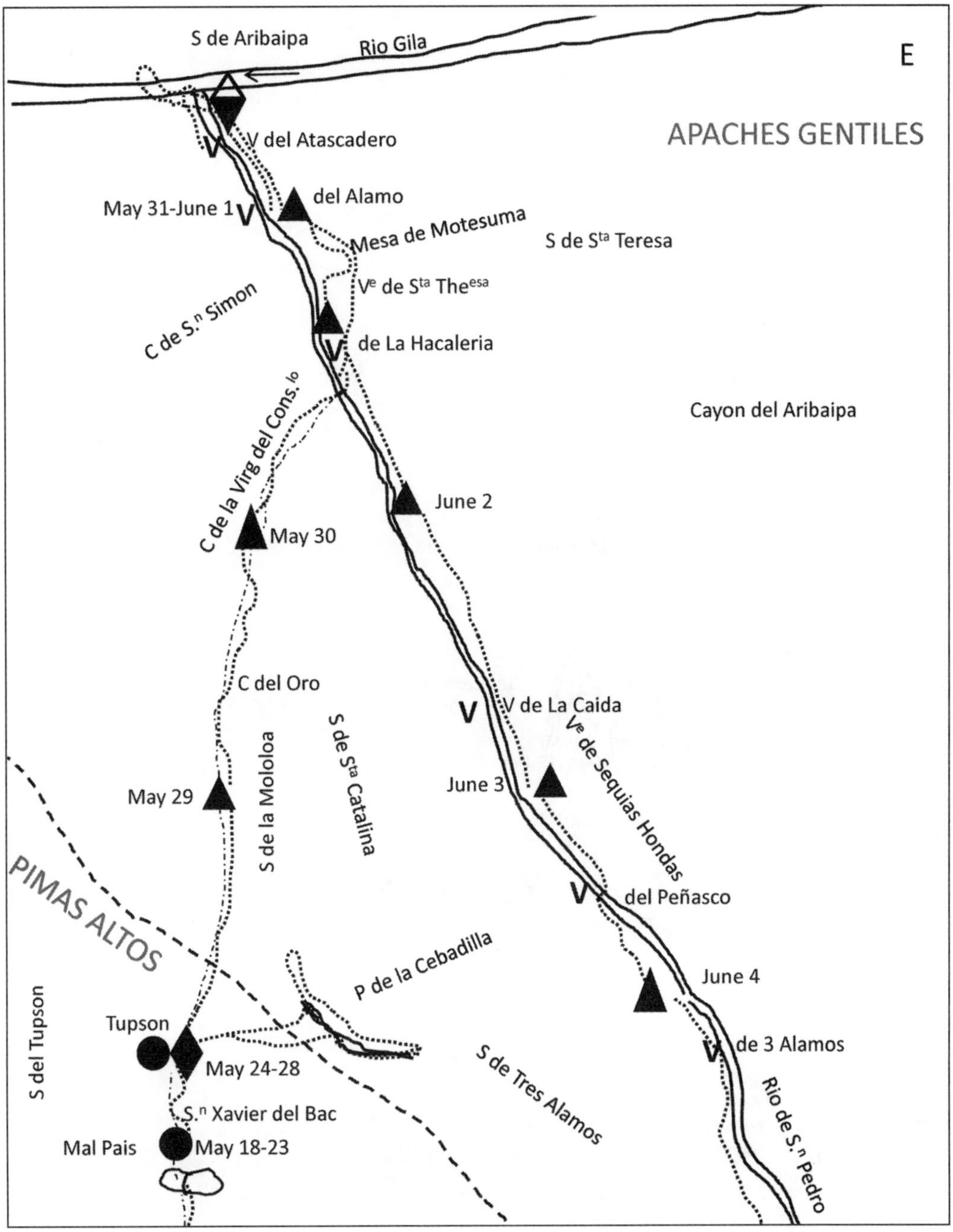

FIGURE 5.7. Map E.

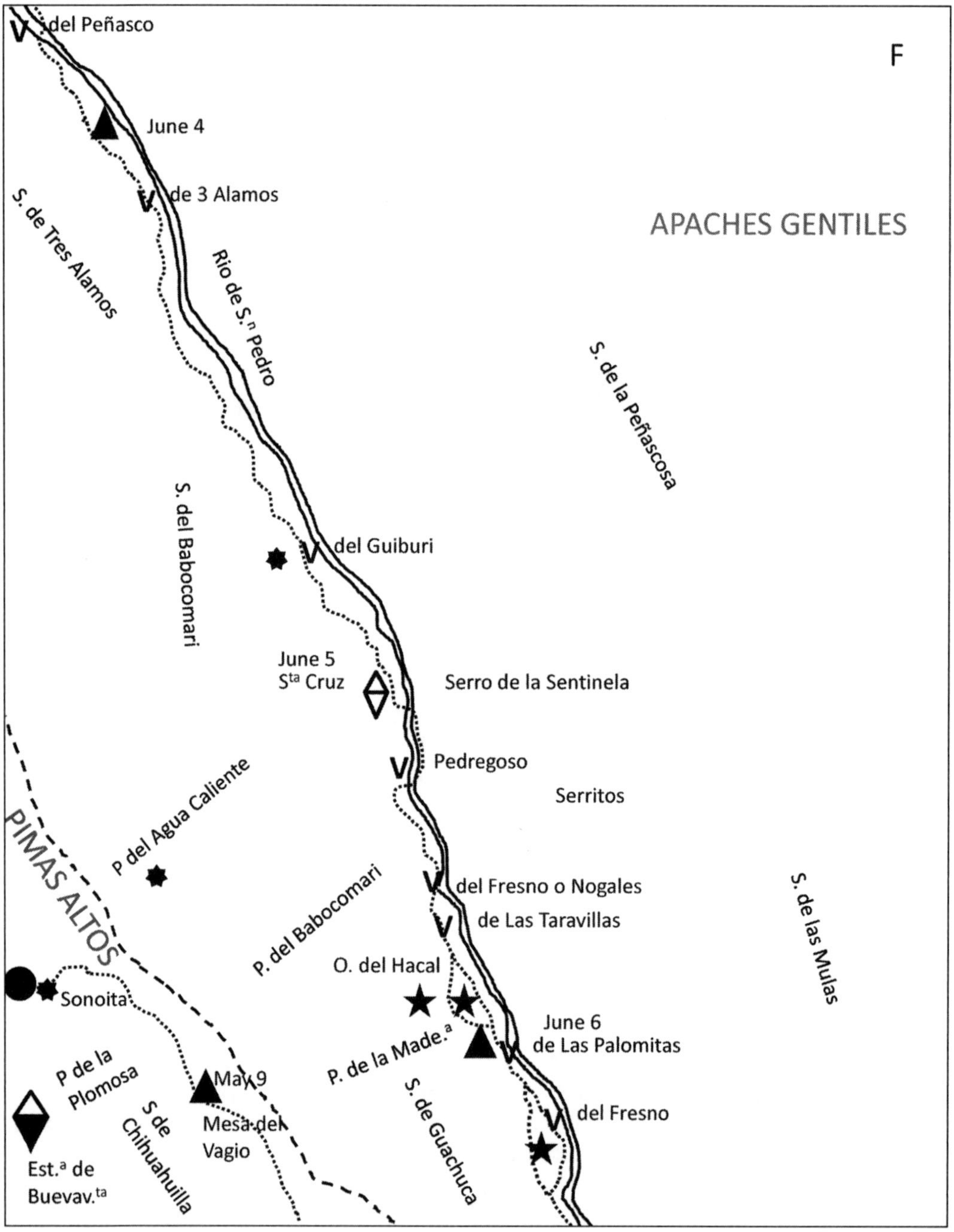

FIGURE 5.8. Map F.

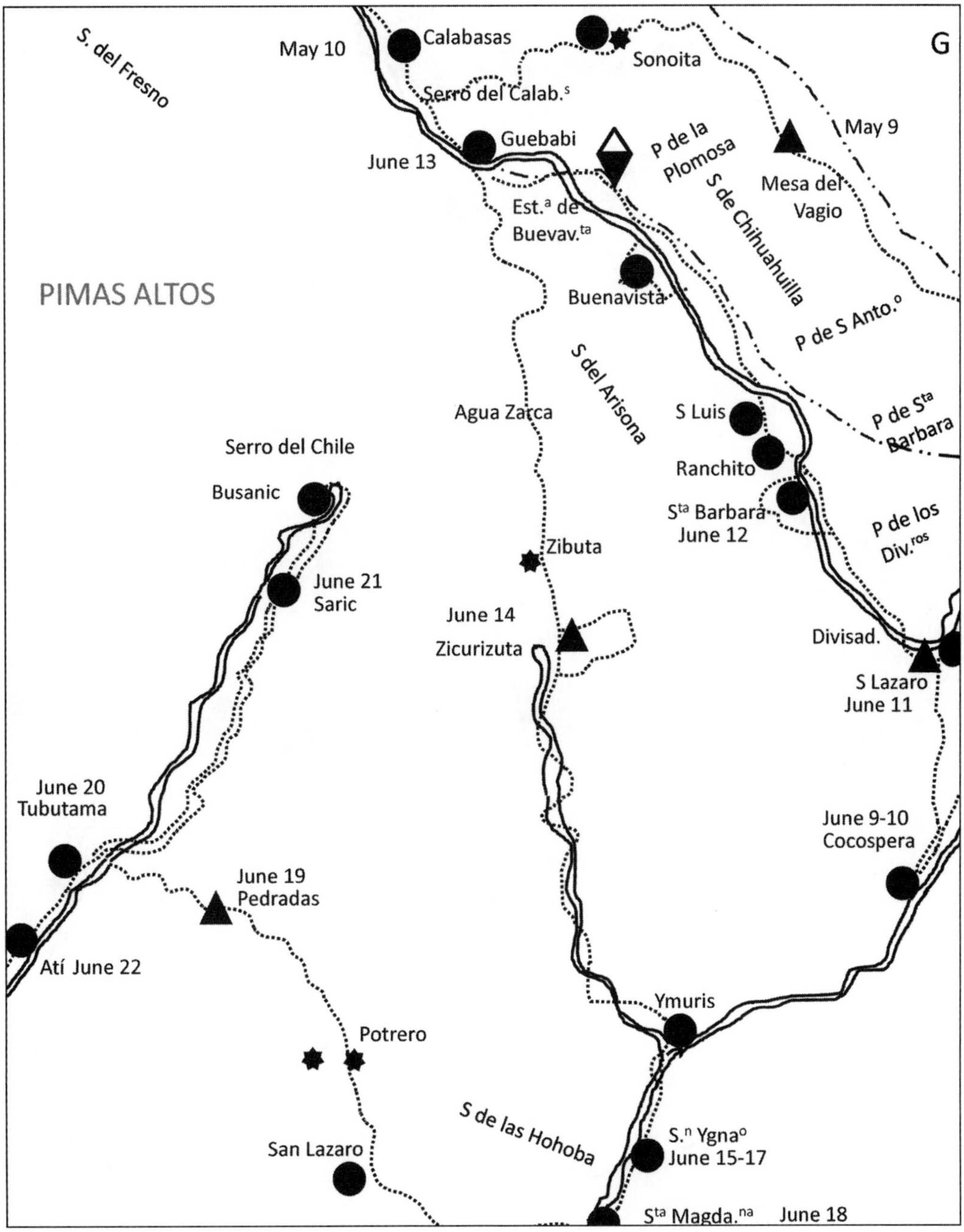

FIGURE 5.9. Map G.

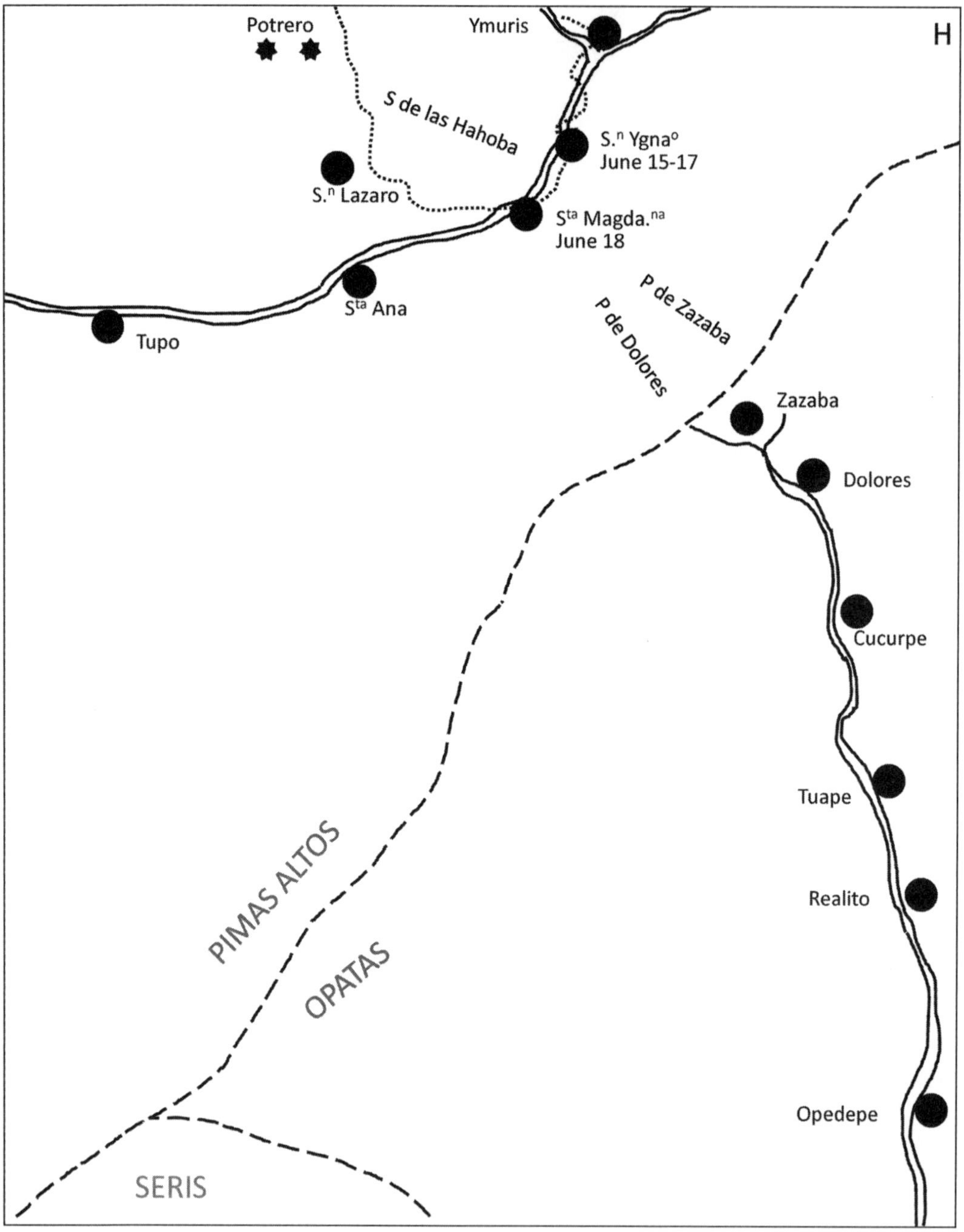

FIGURE 5.10. Map H.

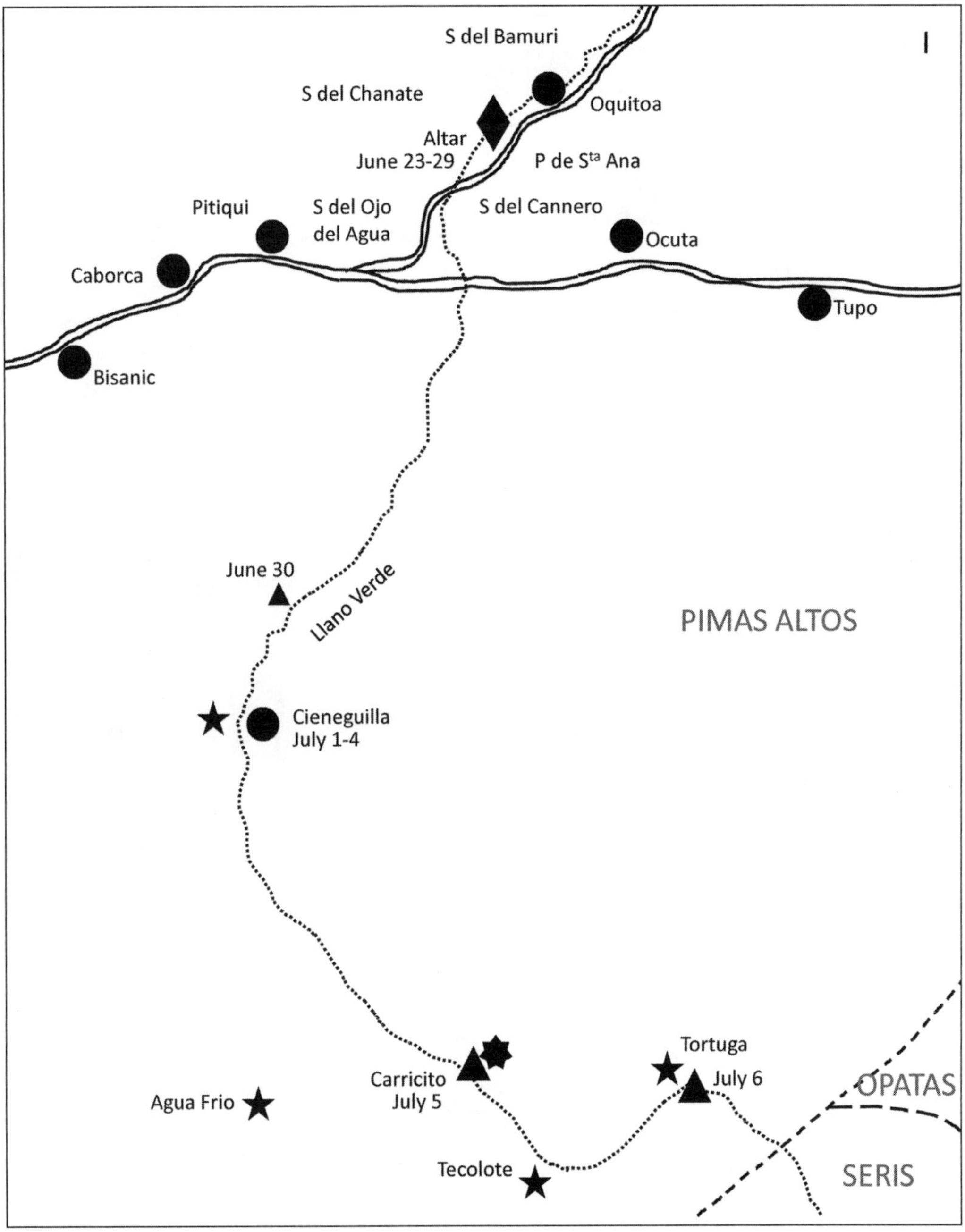

FIGURE 5.11. Map I.

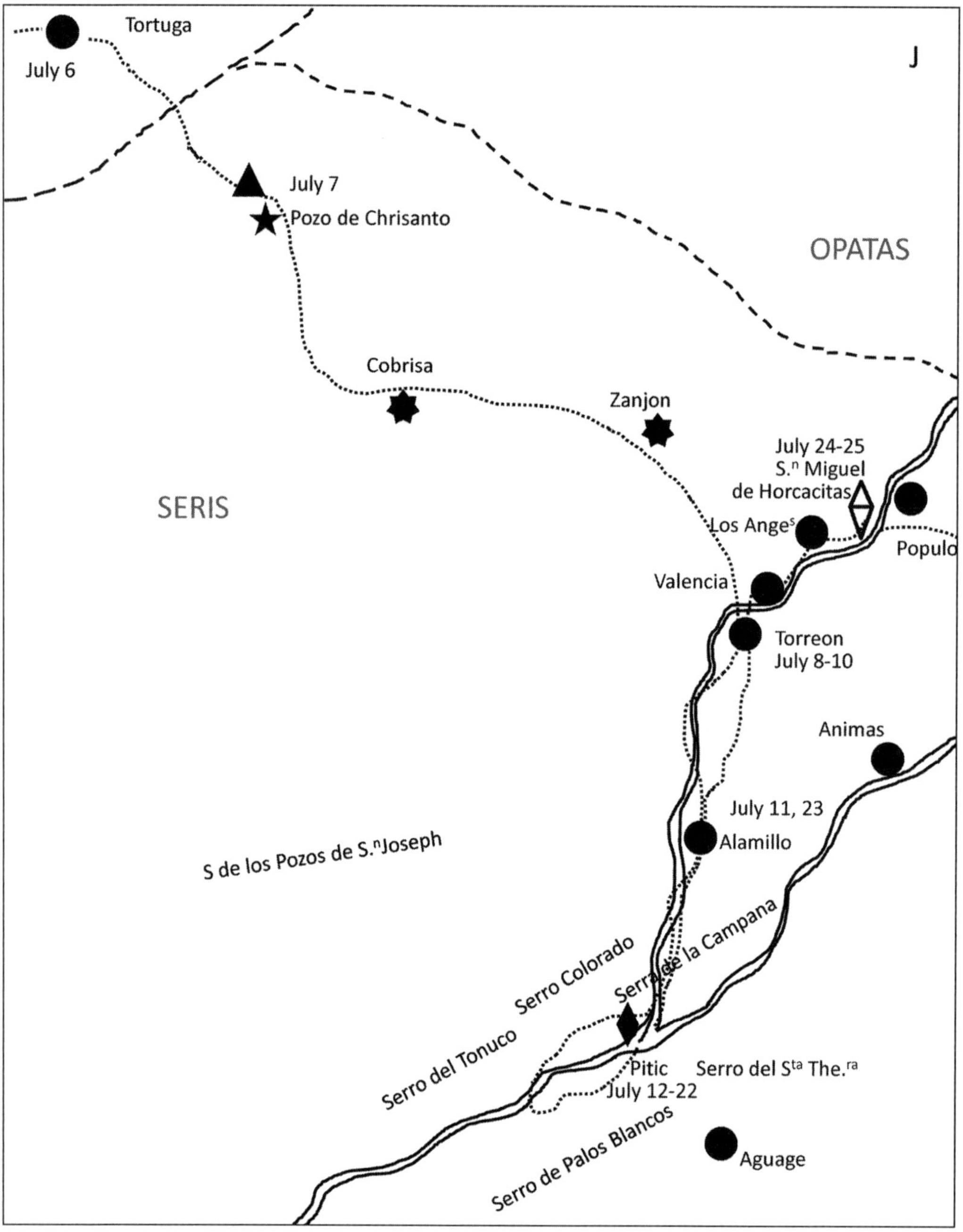

FIGURE 5.12. Map J.

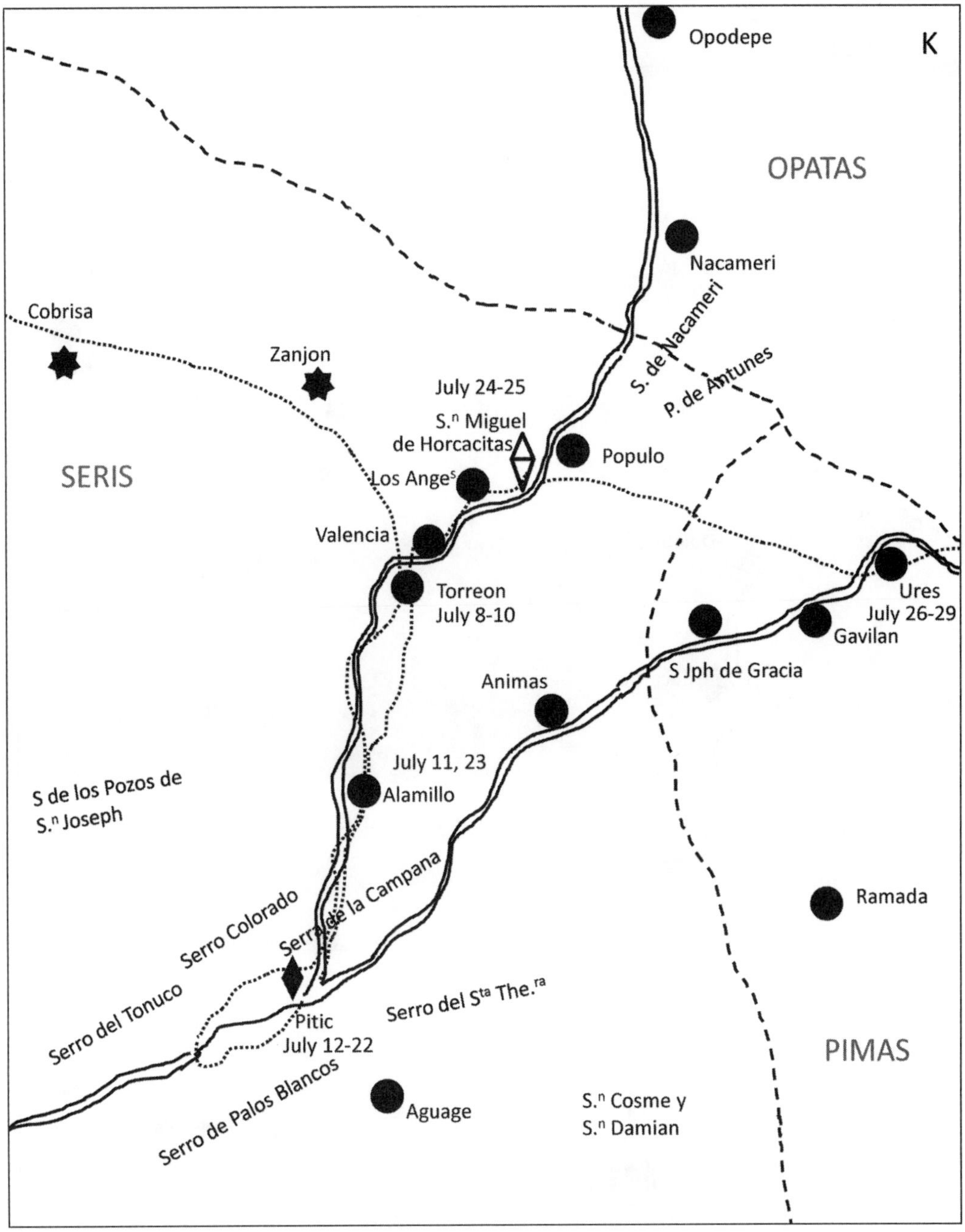

FIGURE 5.13. Map K.

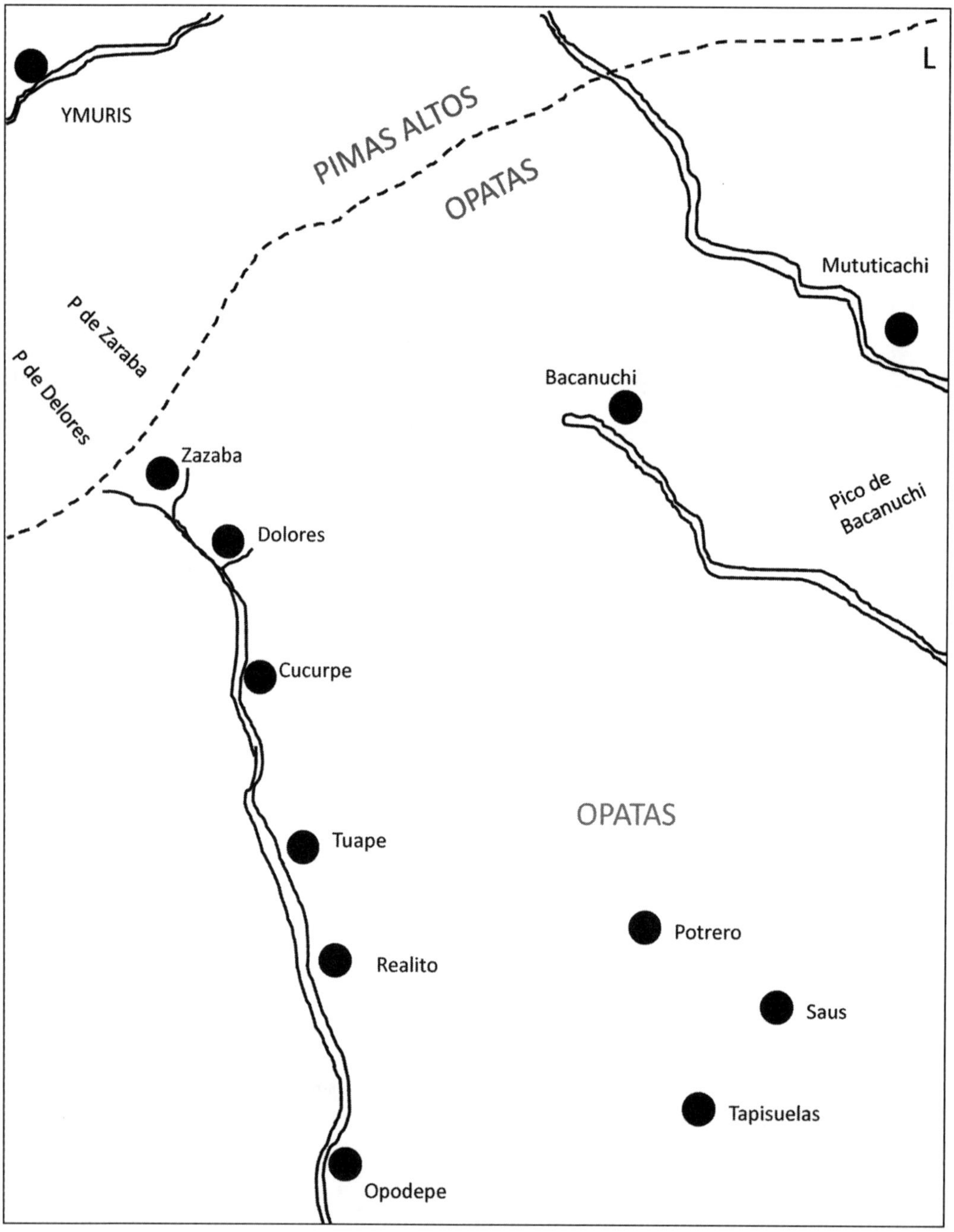

FIGURE 5.14. Map L.

before is the place named La Vieja Cananea ["The Old Canaanite Woman"] where the Sonora River originates.[6]

Four leagues east quarter-northeast are the gold placers where they are presently working but slowly because of the risk and the shortage of water. The known placers are on the slope of the Sierra de Purica ["Flea Mountains"], which are: La Cañada del Tulito, La [Cañada] de Los Alisos ["Alders"],[7] La [Cañada] de San Joseph, San Pedro, Guadalupe, El Puerto ["The Pass"], Las Bolas ["Balls"],[8] and El Cajón del Apache ["Apache Box Canyon"]. The one which has produced most of all (in terms of both the abundance and the size of the nuggets) has been that of Guadalupe.

Day 17 [of April]
We traveled[9] four leagues to the north quarter-northeast to the Puerto de Mababi ["Mababi Pass"][10] and another three leagues to Mababi, where we rested, and we continued another five [leagues] to the east-northeast to the pueblo of Cuquiarachi:[11] 12 [leagues]

One league before the Puerto de Mababi there is a permanent spring they call Los Nogales ["Walnut Trees"]. In the pass, to the right of the trail, there is another very small spring that keeps the water very fresh. Before getting to the place called Mababi, the Arroyo del Chapulin ["Grasshopper Arroyo"], which passes through Cochuta when it is full and joins with the Fronteras River, begins.

Day 18 [of April]
We left to the east-northeast and traveled three leagues to Fronteras:[12] 3 [leagues]

Day 19 [of April]
We did not leave this presidio.[13]

Day 20 [of April]
We started the reconnaissance of this valley along the mesas that are found to the south-southwest and although they [the mesas] are quite extensive, they completely lack water and produce only a thick forest of mesquite. The end of the valley is so extremely broken that a population cannot be located there that might supply itself through two permanent springs in the valley. We went down to the Cuquiarachi River,[14] crossing it by the Vado del Chino ["Chinese Ford"],[15] following along its margins up to where it joins the Fronteras [River]. Wading through it, we headed around the valley to the north, by the foothills of the sierra ["mountain"], examining all its gullies. We returned to wade across the river again, continuing to the west, to the origin of the permanent springs (that are located a quarter of a league south of the presidio). We followed its flow up to the dam that was built for a mill (which today is not useable but at very little cost can be repaired). We got to the presidio, having travelled four leagues: 4 [leagues]

Day 21 [of April]
We continued the reconnaissance by way of the hills that are found to the north quarter-northeast that are extremely broken and sterile. We continued down the valley to the mouth. We examined the cultivated fields from one and the other part of the river,

Figure 5.15. Gardens in San Ignacio, Sonora, with fields on floodplain in background and house gardens and fruit trees fed by a small acequia running adjacent to the house.

and the dam [*presa*, "dam," or "weir"] or old takeout [*saca de agua*, "diversion dam"] for their [the fields'] cultivation, returning to the presidio from which we would carry out the reconnaissance: 6 [leagues]

Days 22 and 23 [of April]
We remained without leaving the presidio.

Day 24 [of April]
We went to reconnoiter the Cochuta and Turicache Valleys which continue to the south of Fronteras Valley without interruption and, passing through the first one, we traveled seven leagues to the pueblo of Turicache. We went back three [leagues] along the same road to Cochuta, where we rested and continued the remaining four leagues to the presidio of Fronteras, having traveled this day: 14 [leagues]

When Fronteras Presidio moved to San Bernardino (see Figure 1.8),[16] the Indians abandoned these two pueblos, gathering in that of Cuquiarachi, which would also have been abandoned had the presidio not been withdrawn to its old place (as I have been informed). The pueblo of Cochuta still has its little houses in good condition and they have only knocked down the roof on the church. Its location is beautiful, and the valley is very appropriate for breeding livestock[17] and maintaining horse herds. It has two *ciénegas* ["marshes"] that they say come from two springs, and other permanent seeps whose waters are conveyed (according to what I have been able to infer by a short irrigation ditch that goes immediately to the houses)[18] (Figure 5.15; also see Figures 3.5 through 3.8); I have no doubt that there could be nurtured orchards[19] and even some cultivated fields that could support a small population or rancho. The river entirely lacks water in dry times. As happens today, from Turicache three leagues on to the south, up to the place they call Corral Viejo ["Old Corral"] two leagues to the north, the waters emerge [burst forth] again and continue by Badeguachi to the valley of Fronteras.[20]

Four leagues to the north of aforementioned Cochuta lies Fronteras Presidio, three leagues to the south [of Cochuta] is the ruined pueblo of Turicache; three leagues to the southwest quarter-south [of Cochuta] is the Turicache Pass (where the Sierra Purica ends). Five leagues to the west quarter-southwest is the Mababi Pass; five to the northwest is the Pueblo of Cuquiarachi, four leagues east is the Pueblo of Teras ["Reeds" (Treutlein 1949:238)].

Turicachi Pueblo has been burned for the most part. It is located at the end of the valley in quite broken and arid land. It is at the entrance of the Real de Nacozari ["Honeycomb" (Treutlein 1949:237)]. It has a good spring where the Fronteras River originates but in a very short stretch it goes dry (as I have said) and it does not come to the surface [burst] in the dry season until Corral Viejo.

Day 25 [of April]
We did not depart the presidio.

Day 26 [of April]
We went to reconnoiter the place called Badeguachi; we were not able to do so when returning from Cochuta because it was night [when we returned to the presidio]. It is a portion of the highest land in the valley, and so it was not flooded by the large flood

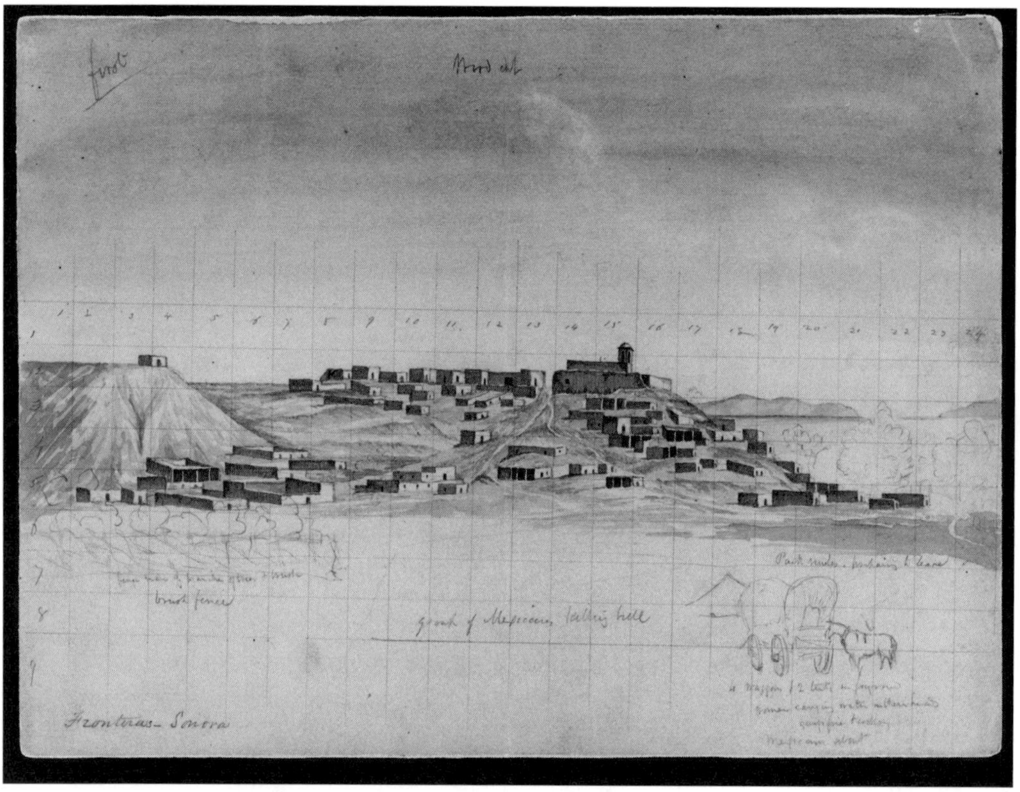

FIGURE 5.16. Fronteras Presidio in May 1851, John Russell Bartlett Collection.

of [17]70 (as I have been assured). It is located at the confluence of the valleys of Fronteras, Cuquiarachi, and Cochuta.[21] It has a good permanent spring capable of supplying a population. The Fronteras River passes eight hundred *varas* [from Badeguachi] without fronting on a ford for more than a distance of a half league. It is on the road to the Puerto del Potrero ["Pasture Pass"] that is used for communication with the [Presidial] Line with [Nueva] Vizcaya (by way of Bavispe ["Snake Cave" (Treutlein 1949:236)])[22] and it is not more than one league south of the current presidio of Fronteras, to which we returned, having traveled 2 [leagues].

The above-mentioned Fronteras is on a narrow ridge (Figure 5.16). The houses are scattered at its foot for not having sufficient expanse of land at the apex. It suffers from the defect of having a rough mountain range to the east, in my opinion, upwards of one thousand and five hundred *varas* from which the Apaches suddenly come out and, crossing the river by the fords that are known to them, they get in the fields and even up to these very houses, as they did yesterday at high noon just a short distance from them.

The valley has enough water and all the attributes that could be desired for the cultivation of their lands being that already much of them are open [being worked].[23]

Days 27 to 30 [of April]

We did not leave the presidio.

First Day of May

We continued our march and travelled ten miles west-northwest to Ojo del Gato ["Cat Spring"]: 10 [leagues]

This place does not allow a settlement because of the broken terrain and the little water that it has.

The first four leagues of the journey we encountered two little permanent springs: Alamito ["Small Cottonwood"] and Turbili, but they can only serve as drinking water for the people [e.g., not sufficient for irrigation or livestock]. The following two [leagues] the Arroyo Hondo ["Deep Arroyo"] was dry, and a league from there the same conditions [prevailed].

Day 2 [of May]

We went five leagues to the west quarter-northwest until the Ojo del León ["Lion Spring"], four leagues northwest quarter-west is the Ojo del Sauz ["Willow Spring"], another four leagues to the northwest to the headwaters of the San Pedro [River],[24] and three more by west-northwest to Campo de Las Nutrias [*nutrias*, "Otters"][25] where the company of the presidio of Santa Cruz[26] is temporarily located: 16 [leagues]

The Ojo de Leon is permanent and there could be a small-sized rancho there. The terrain is somewhat broken, but at a very short distance, plains stretch that continue up to the San Pedro.

The Ojo de Sauz is equally permanent and much more plentiful. The land is expansive and well proportioned for a good pasture.

Days 3 and 4 [of May]

We stayed in this camp.

Day 5 [of May]

We went out to the west-southwest over a distance of two leagues; we went up into the Cerro de Terrenate ["Thorn Bush Hill" (Treutlein 1949:238)]. From there, we went to the reformed [suppressed, repositioned] presidio of Terrenate (Figure 5.17),[27] a league to the northwest quarter-north. Through the valley of this name, we returned to Campo de Las Nutrias two leagues distant, having travelled 5 [leagues].

The situation of Terrenate is quite arid, few abundant waters,[28] and the mountains are very close: The German [Mountains] are at a distance of two leagues to the west quarter-northwest; Las Bolas ["The Balls" Mountains] are another two leagues to the south, the Sierra de la Mariquilla ["Fairy" Mountains] are five leagues to the southeast, and one [league] to the southeast quarter-south is the Cerro de Terrenate. Since this presidio [Terrenate] was transferred to that of Santa Cruz it remained entirely deserted[29] because its few *vecinos*[30] went away at the same time.[31]

Campo de Las Nutrias is pleasant and spacious, abundant in good pasture, and [has] waters in its vicinity.[32] It has a big spring, capable of supplying a population, located at the foot of the mesa, where presently is the company of Santa Cruz. It has, at a very short distance to the west, the Terrenate Valley with two springs with a large flow called La Cruz ["Cross"] and Cabestro ["Halter"] (that in my opinion are of the same water, which cuts off in the first and then springs up again in the second). At a distance of two short leagues are the waters of the Arroyo de Guachuca [or *Huachuca*, *Waw Cuk'a*, "Blacken Cliff"][33] in their own valley, with an abundant spring that is

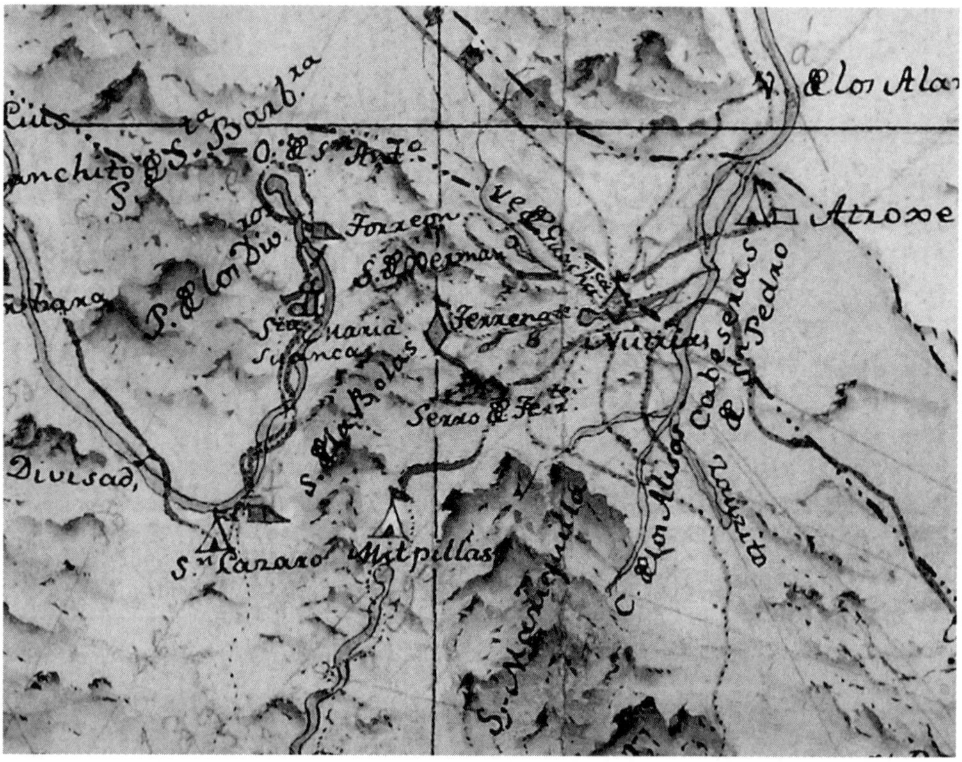

FIGURE 5.17. Enlargement of the old suppressed presidio of Terrenate. Courtesy of the British Library; Shelfmark: Cartographic Items Additional MS. 17,661.a.

part of it (which I reconnoitered during my previous commission).[34] Two and a half leagues to the east are the fields of San Pedro on the margins of its river.[35]

It has the Sierra de la Marquilla five leagues south quarter-southwest, that of Huachuca four to the north, and another four to the northeast quarter-east is that of San Joseph. The three [mountain ranges] have abundant timber and the first two are known for their rich minerals.

Days 6 and 7 [of May]

We remained in this camp.

Day 8 [of May]

The brigadier determined that we would continue our trip through the ruined town of Sonoita, but before daylight the Apaches attacked the garrison's horse herd. And although they failed to take it they hindered our departure this day.

Day 9 [of May]

We followed our course to the northwest twelve leagues to La Mesa del Bagío ["Highland Mesa"] del Alamillo ["Small Cottonwood Tree"]: 12 [leagues]

Within the first six leagues of the journey is found the permanent spring called Los Magueyes ["Agaves"]. And before getting to it, to the right of the trail, there are two ciénegas that in the dry season lack water. The first one is called Ciénega Grande ["Large Marsh"], and the second, Del Medio ["Of the Middle"]. In another three

FIGURE 5.18. San José de Tumacácori Mission situated near the O'odham pueblo of the same name, ca. 1868. Courtesy of the Library of Congress, 3g05667u.

leagues we encountered the Ojo de los Alamos Largos ["Tall Cottonwood Trees Spring"],[36] quite plentiful flow in open terrain, and with many pastures but not much timber or firewood though some quite distant cottonwoods. La Mesa del Bagío, where we stayed for the night, completely lacks water.

Six leagues to the south-southeast of this mesa is San Antonio Spring where the Santa María Suanca River begins;[37] the pass of Los Divisaderos ["Lookouts"] is nine leagues south quarter-southeast; Santa Bárbara Pass is eight [leagues] south; the one of San Antonio is four to the south quarter-southwest;[38] the one of Plomosa ["Lead Colored"] is one and a half to the west; that of Agua Caliente ["Hot Water"] six [leagues] north-northwest;[39] the one of Babocomari ["Bedrock Flat" or "Flat Bedrock" (Bright 2013:12)], three leagues north-northeast, and the one of La Madera ["Timber"] is eight [leagues] northeast quarter-east.[40]

Day 10 [of May]

We traveled six leagues to the northwest quarter-west to Sonoita Pueblo[41] and after resting continued four more [leagues] to the west until that of the Calavazas[42] ["Gourd" or "Squash"]: 10 [leagues]

Sonoita was destroyed by the barbarous Indians and it remains uninhabited. It has a permanent and plentiful spring that flows toward the west.[43] And to the east is a large valley without waters.[44] Their situation is quite bad, being in very broken and hilly terrain, tucked away in a deep ravine.

Calabazas has a very spacious valley but little abundant water in the present season.

Day 11 [of May]

We traveled four leagues to the northwest quarter-north to the pueblo of Tumacácori (Figure 5.18):[45] 4 [leagues]

Day 12 [of May]

We went to reconnoiter the old Real del Aribac ["Little Water" (Bright 2013:9; Lumholtz 1990:388)],[46] passing through the repositioned presidio of Tubac that is located one league north. We continued another four leagues to the northwest quarter-north to the Ojo del Zopori,[47] and four [leagues] to the southwest quarter-west to the Cañada del Aquituni, which lacked water. 9 [leagues}

The Ojo del Zopori is quite plentiful but it has no flow.

Day 13 [of May]

We continue three leagues to the southwest and at dawn we arrived at the origin of the arroyo of Aribac (where I asked permission of the brigadier, and, with him, I went to reconnoiter the old Real del Aribac) and we returned through the pass of Tubac to the pueblo of Tumacácori, distant nine leagues east quarter-southeast: 12 [leagues]

When I went to investigate Aribac the lieutenant of the flying company[48] Don Pablo Romero and two *vecinos* from Tubac went with me. I found the ruins of houses and the terrain so entirely lacking in water that the abovementioned *vecinos* assured me that they had never known it this way before. It is a spacious countryside with abundant grasses. And they assured me that there were in this *real* many and good well-known silver mines and some gold fields.

The Puerto del Fresno ["Ash Tree Pass"] is distant four leagues southeast and eleven [leagues] northwest quarter-west of the flat lands of the Sierra del Babuquiburi [perhaps "Bedrock Constricted in the Middle," (Bright 2013:12) or "Owl Nests" (Treutlein 1949:236)][49] until we joined up again with the men at the source of the creek. I completed: 3 [leagues]

This pueblo of Tumacácori[50] is almost surrounded by a wall in a quadrilateral shape to which are being added several small houses so that they may live in greater security [within]. It [the pueblo] has very good crops but they complained at the time that water had gone scarce because the dryness [drought period].[51] So they [settlers upstream] divert the water that there is, and the flow does not reach Tubac.

Days 14 and 15 [of May]

We remained in this pueblo.

Day 16 [of May]

We continued our march one league north to the old presidio of Tubac (see Figure 3.9):[52] 1 [league]

The referenced Tubac is reduced to nine *vecinos* who have addressed the brigadier, declaring that they could not survive this way because of the total lack of water for their fields as much as because of the hostilities of the enemy. There are quite a number of houses but they are used as entrenchments[53] against the Apaches to defend themselves (Figure 5.19).

Day 17 [of May]

We traveled five leagues to the north quarter-northwest to La Canoa ["Trough" or "Irrigation Flume"][54] and another four to the north-northwest where we spent the night: 9 [leagues]

La Canoa had a small spring but it could not supply enough water for the people, and in the place we slept there was no water.

FIGURE 5.19. Tubac settlement and presidio in 1854, showing protective wing walls attached to housing. The Spanish-period Tubac presidio consisted of a centralized captain's quarters (*casa fuerte*) with somewhat fortified houses scattered in the community around it. There was no perimeter wall. This 1854 lithograph by Carl "Charles" Schuchard is entitled "Tubac in the 1850s" and shows Tubac's houses with wing walls made of adobe that extend outward from the houses. These would have been defensive features that also defined property boundaries. The figure says it is from the SE side but it must be from the SW side looking NE, with the tree-lined river and Santa Rita Mountains in the background. Courtesy of New Mexico State University Library, Archives and Special Collections, #0038.

Day 18 [of May]

We continued six leagues north to the pueblo of San Xavier del Bac:[55] 6 [leagues]

This afternoon a notice arrived with the news that, after our departure [from Tubac], they had been attacked by the Apaches and they killed two *vecinos*.

Days 19 to 21 [of May]

We did not leave this pueblo.

Day 22 [of May]

We went to the south-southeast to investigate the source of this water,[56] a league distant. We also examined many of the cultivated fields and returned having covered: 3 [leagues].

The said San Xavier forms a square shape with its own houses,[57] and it only lacks a few small gates[58] to be entirely enclosed. In the four corners are a kind of towers with rounded gun holes. Despite being in a spacious valley, they came to place it precisely among some hillocks or small hills called El Mal País ["Badlands"] de San Xavier, under which cover the Apaches tended to surprise them.[59] This mission is making great efforts in the cultivation of its good lands. It has an able number of Pima Indian residents, some of them assimilated,[60] and of course I judge it to be among the most thriving. It has a large ciénega immediately to the south, and as this prevailing wind is a bad one I suggest that the waters held therein must be harmful to the health. In this

FIGURE 5.20. Historic and modern photographs of the Santa Cruz River looking south from Martinez Hill at San Xavier. Photograph courtesy of USGS SW Repeat Photography Collection, Stake number 1057, 1913; Photograph courtesy of USGS SW Repeat Photography Collection, Photograph by R.M. Turner, Stake number 1057, 1981; The same general direction taken by the author in 2009.

ciénega are regularly kept the horse herd from the Tucson Presidio and the livestock from the mission [of San Xavier del Bac], and they assure me that there would be no lack of pasture on it even if the horse herd stays all year (Figures 5.20).

Day 23 [of May]
We stayed in this pueblo.

Day 24 [of May]
We continued our march three leagues north to the San Agustín del Tucson[61] Presidio: 3 [leagues]

Day 25 [of May]
We did not go out of the presidio.

Day 26 [of May]
We went to the pueblo of Tucson, distant a quarter of a league southwest quarter-south[62] and as we returned, I left with Captain Pedro Allende[63] to examine the dam and the place where the water divides into three abundant *acequias* ["irrigation ditches"], which serve for consumption and cultivation of the land of the pueblo, and of the presidio, to which I returned having traveled one league: 1 [league]

The construction of this pueblo (although not so advanced) continues in the same terms as San Xavier del Bac.[64]

Day 27 [of May]
I requested permission of the brigadier to go and reconnoiter the woods, under his authority, with an escort of twelve men that he assigned me, and Ensign Don Cayetano Limón, and Captain Don Pedro Allende who offered to accompany me too. I went to the Arroyo de Santa Cathalina at the foothills of the sierra of its [same] name [Santa Catalina Mountains], distant four leagues to the east of the presidio. I found an abundance of *nogal* ["walnut tree"], *alamo* ["cottonwood tree"], and *fresno* ["ash tree"] wood. This arroyo [Santa Catalina] bore very little water, and it tends to lack it [altogether]. Concluding this reconnaissance I returned, having traveled: 9 [leagues].

Day 28 [of May]
We stayed in the said presidio.

The captain of [the presidio] has had the foresight to fence it provisionally with a stockade, forming a square with a ditch on the outside, four feet wide and four deep. At the ends he has raised up a type of *baterías a barbeta* ["battery barbette"],[65] supported with a double palisade, its embankments form small bastions that look like small turrets where he has placed the four small battalion cannons; he has made a powder magazine, a granary, the guardhouse, and a type of chapel that stands in for the lack of a church, without cost to the royal treasury. He also asked me to design a tower to keep a sentry that will watch the camp for a greater distance, and they were left opening [digging] the foundations.

The location is beautiful, in a very unobstructed land with abundant waters and farmlands. It has the proportion of a large corral formed by two irrigation ditches between the pueblo and the presidio where they protect their horse herd, in case they find themselves with limited troop forces; within its immediate vicinity grass is scarce

FIGURE 5.21. Petroglyph of a historic encounter between a rifleman and an Indian on a horse with a bow and arrow.

in the dry season, but they have an abundance at the Ciénega de San Xavier, three leagues to the south, and at other less distant places.

From this presidio that of Santa Cruz is located twenty five leagues to the east-southeast, Tres Alamos seventeen to the east, the Puerto de la Cebadilla ["Wall Barley" or "Sneezewort Pass"][66] nine to the east-northeast, the Moloba four to the north quarter-northeast, El Aquitune sixteen to the northwest, the Sierra del Tucson three to the west, the arroyo and Sierra de Santa Catharina four to the east, the big spring or origin of these waters, one league to the south, and the Pueblo of Tucson a quarter of a league to the southwest quarter-south.

Day 29 [of May]

We continued our course and traveled seven leagues to the north quarter-northeast without finding any water:[67] 7 [leagues]

Day 30 [of May]

We made four leagues to the north quarter-northeast up to the Cañada del Oro ["Gold Canyon"], and five more to the north-northeast where we stayed at night:[68] 9 [leagues]

At the Cañada del Oro (where we rested) there is a small permanent watering hole. In the place where we stopped that night there is no water (Figure 5.21).[69]

Day 31 [of May]

We traveled four leagues to the north-northeast by the Cañada de la Virgen del Consuelo ["Canyon of Our Lady of Consolation"] (Figure 5.22)[70] until we came to the San Pedro River (that we passed when it was dry) (Figure 5.23) and another five leagues by the bank of said river up to the Vado del Alamo ["Cottonwood Tree Ford"][71] (that has already had water) where we stayed the night (Figure 5.24): 9 [leagues]

FIGURE 5.22. Tucson Wash, which is likely the canyon referenced by Rocha as Cañada de la Virgen del Consuelo.

FIGURE 5.23. The lower San Pedro from a terrace overlooking the dry river bed.

FIGURE 5.24. Alamo Ford was probably near Aravaipa Creek, where this image is taken, facing west.

FIGURE 5.25. Enlargement of Rocha's map showing the confluence of the San Pedro and Gila Rivers and the trail's divergence from the river margin. From *Mapa de la Frontera de Sonora para el establecimiento de la linea de presidios.* Courtesy of the British Library; Shelfmark: Cartographic Items Additional MS. 17,661.a.

First Day of June

We continued three leagues to the northwest quarter-north to the Atascadero ["Bog" or "Mire"][72] Ford and one more league up to the confluence of the San Pedro and Gila Rivers (Figure 5.25). We then departed by way of the other side of the river to the Atascadero Ford (Figure 5.26)[73] where we rested, and we continued another three leagues to the southeast quarter-south until the Alamo Ford:[74] 8 [leagues]

Considering it indispensable for the orders I had and to investigate prodigiously [extensively] some leagues to the east and west of the confluence of the said rivers, at which we might have stayed one or two days,[75] [which] I did on repeated occasions in the presence of the brigadier, who not having judged it appropriate ordered that the camp would remain with Ensign Limón at the Atascadero Ford, [while we passed] through with thirty men to the exact confluence of the rivers. Scarcely had I made the observation (although with difficulty because the wind was impeding me), when we returned to the camp.[76]

The place of the confluence is a ravine that, as can be seen, will be flooded at any rise in waters of the Gila, and without any proportion ["size," or perhaps "resources"]. All its surroundings, as far as the eye can see, manifest themselves to be very broken terrain.[77]

Day 2 [of June]

We made four leagues to the south-southeast until the Xacaleria ["Place of the Jacals/Huts"][78] Ford. We rested and continued five more leagues along the margins of the San Pedro where we spent the night: 9 [leagues]

During this entire journey along the *caja* ["channel"][79] of the San Pedro River we did not find water. In the place we slept we made small wells, and the men could drink.

Day 3 [of June]

We traveled six leagues to the south-southwest up to the Cahida [*Caída*, or "The Fall"] Ford. We rested and continued three more by the same course where we camped: 9 [leagues]

Day 4 [of June]

We continued five leagues to the south-southeast up to the Peñasco ["Crag" or "Large Rock"] Ford (Figure 5.27),[80] and three more in the same direction: 8 [leagues]

Day 5 [of June]

We continued to the south-southeast one league to the Tres Alamos ["Three Cottonwoods"] Ford (see Figure 4.16),[81] eight to El Guiburi ["Many Houses"],[82] and after resting, three to the south quarter-southeast until the Santa Cruz Presidio (see Figure 1.7):[83] 12 [leagues]

El Guiburi[84] permits a small population for it is unobstructed [being clear], and with enough water, it has some springs independent of the river (Figure 5.28).

The setting of this presidio seems to me to be quite bad (from the reconnaissance I made for its transfer to Campo de Las Nutrias in my previous commission).[85] It lacks firewood within four leagues of distance.[86] The few pastures, which are called by the intelligent *pajonales* ["sparse grasslands"] and *tovosos* ["tobosa"],[87] which do not suit the horses, are at a long distance [and] cannot survive without a larger garrison because of the broken terrain.[88]

FIGURE 5.26. A crossing that is in the general location referenced as Atascadero Ford.

FIGURE 5.27. Peñasco ["crag" or "large rock"] Ford is recognizable today as an extended and treacherous narrows in the San Pedro River not far from Redington.

Day 6 [of June]

We made three leagues south to the Pedregoso ["Rocky"] Ford,[89] three more to the Nogales;[90] rested and continued one league to the Tarabillas [*Taravillas* on map, "Chatterbox" or "Stonechat," a type of bird] Ford,[91] and four to the south quarter-southeast to the Palominas[92] [or *Palomitas*, "Little Doves" or "Pigeon Droppings," "Black Grapes"] (Figure 5.29): 11 [leagues]

Day 7 [of June]

We traveled two leagues to the south quarter-southeast to the Fresno Ford, three to the south quarter-southwest to La Tienda ["tent or Tipi"],[93] three south-southeast to Los Alamos ["Cottonwood Trees"], and another to the south to the San Pedro agricultural fields[94] (Figures 5.30a and b).

The San Pedro River runs through a spacious valley (without being cut off, except for the part between Los Alamos and La Tienda Fords until passing that of Santa Cruz)[95] from Las Tarabillas Ford the terrain becomes very broken. From Santa Cruz until the Gila River the San Pedro continues forming dry archipelagos in many places,[96] and with few opportunities for settlement from its source to La Tarabillas Ford (although as I have recounted, it is in a spacious valley). It has the defect of being a very deep channel [box][97] and completely lacking firewood.

Day 8 [of June]

We continued to the southwest quarter-west, three leagues to Campo de Las Nutrias, and four more to the southwest up to the permanent spring of Milpillas ["Small Cornfield"].[98]

Day 9 of June

We traveled six leagues to the southwest quarter-south until Cocóspera Pueblo (Figure 5.31): 6 [leagues]

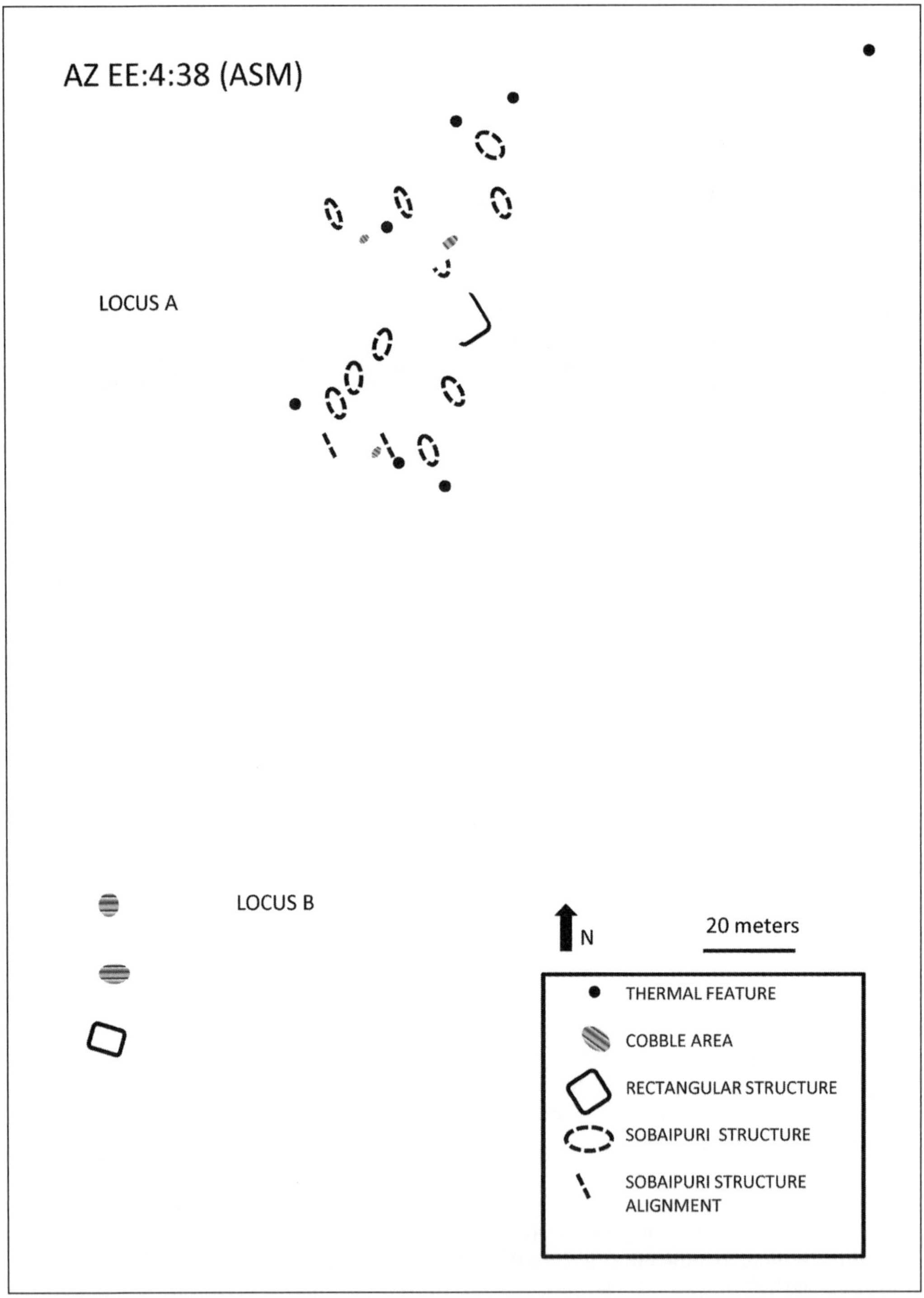

FIGURE 5.28 This is a plan of the Sobaipuri O'odham village of Quiburi occupied when Ugarte and Rocha passed through.

FIGURE 5.29. Enlargement of Rocha map Tienda double-back. From *Mapa de la Frontera de Sonora para el establecimiento de la linea de presidios*. Courtesy of the British Library; Shelfmark: Cartographic Items Additional MS. 17,661.a.

Day 10 of June

We stayed in this pueblo, which has very good crops, and the enemy destroyed all their livestock.

Day 11 of June

The brigadier having ordered me to survey the valleys of the Santa María Suanca River,[99] and assigning me an escort with forty men and flying company Lieutenant[100] Don Pablo Romero,[101] of which ten men were to be reinstated to the Tucson Presidio with the attached Captain Don Juan de Oliva,[102] I left this afternoon to the north-northeast and traveled six leagues up to the old ranch of San Lázaro: 6 [leagues]

Day 12 [of June]

I left the camp in this place, imploring Captain Don Juan de Oliva to arrange what he believed suitable in whatever change in situation might occur, and with Lieutenant Don Pablo Romero and fifteen men went to survey the ruined pueblo of Santa María Suanca three and a half leagues to the north quarter-northeast, I continued another one and a half leagues to the north-northwest until San Antonio Spring, origin of the Santa María River (which is quite plentiful), and after concluding the reconnaissance I returned along the same trail to San Lázaro Valley where I reunited with my men, and after resting I continued five more leagues to the south-southeast until the Santa Bárbara Hacienda.[103] 15 [leagues]

a

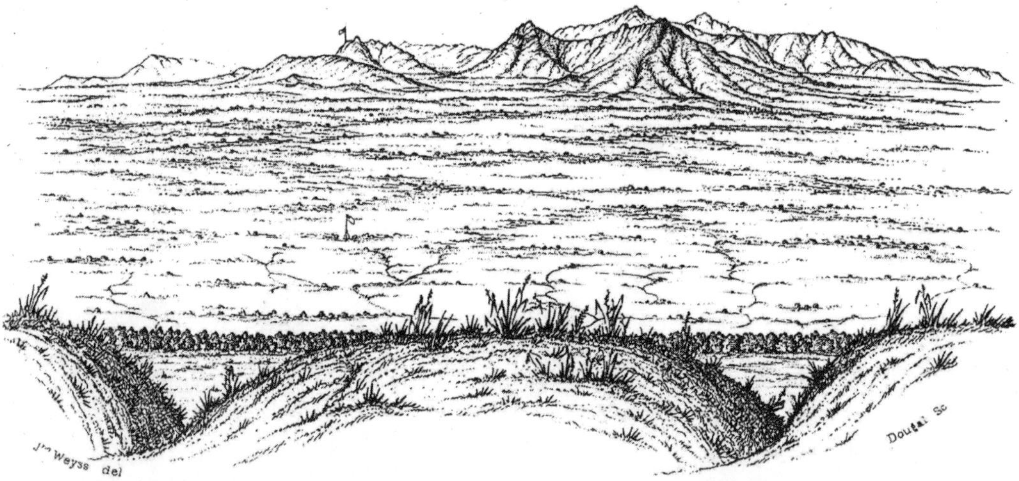

b

Figure 5.30 (*a*) [1857] Sketch from Emory's United States and Mexican Boundary Survey looking west at international border, (*b*) Photo today with border fence facing west in the same general direction as the historic sketch.

a

b

FIGURE 5.31. Cocóspera, Sonora, including (*a*) a portion of the church and (*b*) the Campo Santo with the river valley in the background.

One league to the southeast of San Antonio Spring is the grand pasture or Rancho del Torreón ["Tower Ranch"], three leagues to the south-southeast is the pass or road of Terrenate in the Sierra de German.

Santa María Suanca was the *cabecera de misión* ["head mission"]. It was located in a beautiful valley with the best chance for sowing and livestock breeding. It has Santa Bárbara Pass two and a half leagues to the west-northwest, San Antonio [Pass][104] four [leagues] to the northwest, and the Las Bolas Mountains one [league] to the southeast.

San Lázaro Ranch was in a very spacious valley that formerly they say one could not go through [the valley] because of the numerous livestock.[105] That was equally the case in the valley belonging to Santa Bárbara Ranch, where its fertile lands reveal what may have been.

Day 13 [of June]

I continued one league northwest quarter-north through the pretty valleys to El Ranchito ["Little Ranch"], half [of a league] to San Luis Ranch, three and a half to Buenavista ["Good View"] Hacienda,[106] one to the north-northwest to its estancia,[107] and another three [leagues] to the west quarter-northwest to the ruined pueblo of Guevavi:[108] 9 [leagues]

All of these places mentioned are of the same quality as those on previous parts of the journey; the others, Buenavista Hacienda (which is the most famous of them) has a permanent little spring as well as the river. Their estancia is a large mesa by whose foot the river passes. It has some high hills [*lomas altas*] from which these valleys are visible. The distance from Altar Presidio is thirty-five leagues, from that of Tucson twenty-six, and the place designated Campo de Las Nutrias for that [garrison] of Santa Cruz, twenty-one. You have the Sierra de la Chihuahuilla[109] abundant in woods and rich minerals four leagues to the northeast.

Guevavi has the greater distances between Las Nutrias and the Tucson [presidio], but prolongs that of Altar,[110] and there are not such abundant pastures.

The Santa María River [Santa Cruz River] runs south to San Lázaro that, changing its flow to the north, continues through the referenced places until the pueblos of Calabazas, and Tumacácori.[111] Although it is not very abundant, it always flows and only a short length of about a thousand *varas* (for being sandy ground) cuts off shortly before arriving at Guevavi where water springs again to burgeon out with more strength.[112]

After I arrived at this place I dispatched the ten men from the Tucson Presidio in whose company marched the attached Captain Don Juan de Oliva.[113]

Day 14 [of June]

I started the march at daybreak to the south-southeast. I made six leagues to Agua Zarca ["'Clear' or 'Pure' Water"]. After resting, I continued another three [leagues] to the Ojo del Zibuta, and two more to that of Cicurizuta where I spent the night.

At Agua Zarca a track was cut of quite a large group of Indians coming through with booty all along the Camino Real,[114] and, according to the evidence on the ground, they [Indians] had passed there ten days earlier. In this place we did not have any water. Zibuta Spring is permanent, and with economy can provide something to drink for a horse herd. That of Circurizuta is also permanent, and more plentiful, [and] from it originates the arroyo that goes through Imuris ["Ravens" (Treutlein 1949:237)] and San Ignacio.

FIGURE 5.32. Church at the pueblo of San Ignacio today.

Day 15 [of June]
Before dawn I went out through the canyon of the arroyo, [which is] extremely blocked off by bosque (in which there is a lot of wild livestock). I traveled eight leagues to the south-southeast to Imuris Pueblo, where I stopped to rest, and at the fall of the evening I continued another three [leagues] to San Ignacio Pueblo (Figure 5.32):[115] 11 [leagues]

In Imuris I was told by the Indians that the brigadier had left there a short while earlier,[116] leaving them with the order that they tell me when I arrive I should go without delay to San Ignacio where I was expected; but I was forced to stop until nightfall because of the heavy sun the men had been exposed to, at which time I carried through with [the order] and, appearing before the said brigadier, I informed him of my mission with the corresponding diary, giving him my leave with no major incident.

In Imuris Pueblo the Arroyo of Cocóspera joins with the one of Cicurizuta, and united they go through it [this pueblo] to Magdalena.[117]

The distance from this pueblo to Zazava Pass is five leagues to the south-southeast, to the [pass of] Dolores, five to the southeast, and to that of Jojoba, two [leagues] to the west.

Days 16 and 17 [of June]
We remained in this mission, which is in the most abundant time for fruits and livestock.

Day 18 [of June]
We went out this afternoon to the south-southwest and traveled two leagues to Magdalena Pueblo[118] (Figure 5.33): 2 [leagues]

FIGURE 5.33. Mural depicting an artist's rendition of Father Eusebio Kino at the pueblo of Magdalena de Kino today.

Day 19 [of June]
We traveled six leagues to the northwest quarter-west to El Portero ["The Pasture"] and five northwest to Las Pedradas ["Falling Stones"]: 11 [leagues]

At the pass there are two very good, permanent springs, and at Las Pedradas there are none.

Day 20 [of June]
[Traveled] four [leagues] northwest quarter-west to the Pueblo of Tubutáma [*Tjúvutam*, "High Up" (Lumholtz 1990:394)]: 4 [leagues]

This mission has some good cultivated fields, but the farming of them at this time is the cause of water shortage to those in Santa Teresa [del Ádid], and the Atí ["Brook" (Treutlein 1949, 236), also *Átil* or *Atshi*, meaning "Narrow Mountain" (Lumholtz 1990:388)].

Day 21 [of June]
We made eight leagues northeast to the Pueblo of Saric [*Sháarik*, "Pass" (Lumholtz 1990:393) or "Very Windy Place" (Treutlein 1949:238)],[119] and two more northeast quarter-north to the ruined pueblo of Busanic ["Bat" (Treutlein 1949:236)].[120] We returned by the same route to Saric: 12 [leagues]

At El Busanic there is no shortage of land and water so that a population can survive according to what I was able to see from the place where the pueblo was, next to which originates the stream that passes through Saric.[121] Tubutáma is where you shorten the intervals from one pueblo to the next. El Arivac is distant fourteen leagues north quarter-northeast, the Arizona[122] Mountains [are] eight to the east-northeast,

Guevavi [is] fifteen northeast quarter-north, and the Cerro del Chile ["Chile Hill"] [is] one northwest quarter-north.

Day 22 [of June]

We made eight leagues southwest to Tubutáma ["Defile" (Treutlein 1949:238); see Figures 5.34a and b],[123] one and a half-southwest quarter-west to the Pueblo of Santa Teresa,[124] and one and a half to Atí[125] (Figure 5.35): 11 [leagues]

This Pueblo of Atí completely lacked water that day, so for the necessary consumption of the people they go looking for it near Santa Teresa.

Day 23 [of June]

Five leagues [traveled] southwest to the Pueblo of Oquitoa, and two to the west-southwest to the Presidio of Santa Gertrudis del Altar.[126] 7 [leagues]

The Mission of Oquitoa is maintained in good condition, and water is not scarce (Figure 5.36).[127]

Days 24 to 29 [of June]

We stayed in this presidio without leaving its enclosure.

It has the defect of lacking in water for the cultivation of their land in the dry season (as happens now), that it only has that which is needed for personal consumption, which has caused most of its gardens to dry up, and those which remain show in the abundance of fruits the fertility of the land.

Twelve leagues to the northeast are the Sierra de Santa Teresa, one and a half [leagues] to northwest quarter-north is the Cerro del Bamuri, one and a half northwest quarter-west El Chanate ["The grackle"], six to the west-southwest the Pueblo of Pitic, three to the south-southwest the Sierra del Ojo del Agua, and one to the east-southeast, Santa Ana Pass.

Day 30 [of June]

We made fourteen leagues to the south-southwest to the green plain without finding water: 14 [leagues]

First day of July

We traveled two leagues to the south-southwest to the Real de la Cieneguilla ["Small Marsh"]: 2 [leagues]

Day 3 and 4 [of July]

We did not leave the pueblo.

In this *real* there is no lack of water because the little ciénega is always there, and [because of] the ease with which they have found it [water] in different wells that have been made. Therefore, I argue that using industry they might make use of it to greater benefit.

In the gold placers (that have produced so much) they tend to have great water shortages, according to what I have been assured. Those they work now are one league to the southwest.

Day 5 [of July]

We continued our march to the southeast quarter-south, we made ten leagues until the permanent spring of El Carricito ["Little Reed"]: 10 [leagues]

a

b

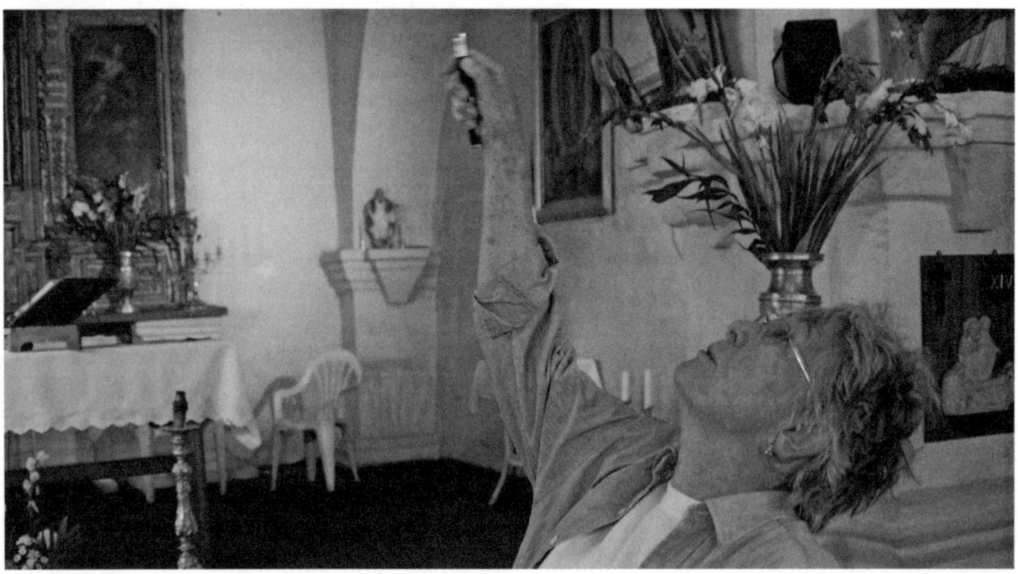

FIGURE 5.34 (*a*) Tubutáma ceiling (*b*) Gloria Giffords at Tubutáma pointing out characteristics on the ceiling.

FIGURE 5.35. Ruins of the church at Atí.

Day 6 [of July]
Three leagues to the southeast to the aguaje ["running spring"] de El Tecolote ["Owl"], and four to the northeast to the [aguaje de la] Tortuga ["Tortoise" or "Turtle"]: 7 [leagues]

They say these two *aguajes* do not remain during dry spells.

Day 7 of July
Eight leagues to the southeast quarter-south to the Pozo de Chrisanto ["Holy Christ Well"]: 8 [leagues]

This well is permanent, but it is necessary to remove the water with buckets.

Day 8 [of July]
We made four leagues to the southeast to La Cobrisa ["Copper Color"], five to the east quarter-southeast to Zanjon ["Deep Ditch" or "Cliff"], and six southeast quarter-south to the Hacienda del Torreón ["Tower"]: 15 [leagues]

In La Cobrisa and Zanjon there is water in the rainy season.

Day 9 and 10 [of July]
We stayed at the Hacienda del Torreón which has abundant crops, vineyards, cane, and other fruits. The Rancho de Las Animas ["Spirits Ranch"] is five leagues to the southeast where they maintain their herds.

Day 11 [of July]
We continued our route to the south, five leagues to the Rancho de Alamillo: 5 [leagues]

Day 12 [of July]
We traveled six leagues to the southwest to the Pitic Presidio:[128] 6 [leagues]

FIGURE 5.36. Church at the pueblo of Oquitoa.

Day 13 [of July]
We started out to the west to reconnoiter the terrain and traveled two leagues: 2 [leagues]

Day 14 [of July]
We did not leave the presidio.

Day 15 [of July]
We left for the east to reconnoiter the entrance of the river [inlet], and the *toma* ["intake" or "source of water" or "headworks" and "dams"] or *saca de agua* ("takeout" or "diversion dam") that are for the cultivation of the land; we traveled: 1 [league].

Day 16 to 22 [of July]
I stayed at this presidio which has much farmland, abundance of waters, and the ability to draw the water they should desire, but the terrain is exposed to flooding, as took place in the greater part of the year of [17]70 at the time of the expedition,[129] [such] that the people had to take refuge in the Cerro de la Campana ["Bell Hill"] (as I have been informed). It has no wood other than mesquite, which is brittle and short in length, and whenever another species of wood is needed it is necessary to bring it from the Sierra de Sonibiate, about thirty leagues distant to the northeast, and I do not consider its conveyance to be very easy.

The Cerro del Tonuco is four leagues to the west, the Cerro Colorado ["Red Hill"] [is] two to the northwest quarter-north, the Pozos de San Joseph [is] ten to the northwest, Santa Teresa [is] three to the east quarter-southeast, Palos Blancos ["White Sticks"] two to the south-southwest, and La Campana very near to the presidio on the other bank of the river to the north.

Day 23 [of July]
With regard to having completed my commissions, and not having in this presidio opportunity to work on the maps and other relevant papers, [it just so happened] that on this day a party would leave to bring the subsidy [pay] of this presidio from the capital of Arispe, the brigadier determined that incorporated with it [the group] I would return to the said capital,[130] by virtue of which we left in the afternoon to the north-northeast and traveled six leagues to Alamillo Ranch: 6 [leagues]

Day 24 [of July]
We traveled five leagues to the north to Torreón Hacienda, and four to the northeast up to the pueblo and suppressed presidio of San Miguel de Orcasitas:[131] 9 [leagues]

Although the presidio that was in this pueblo was transferred to that of the Pitic,[132] it has not wanted for anything major because its local community has grown and has regular commerce.[133] Its condition is good. It has enough cultivated fields, sufficient water, and in its immediate vicinity some known mines of both kinds. Cerro Colorado is located two leagues to the east, Puerto de Antunes [is] two and a half to the east-northeast of that of Nacameri Pasture, Treutlein 1949:237], four northeast quarter-north [is] the Real de San Joseph de Gracia, seven to the southeast [is] the Populo Pueblo (uninhabited),[134] one [league] to the northeast [is] a permanent spring to the northwest next to the pueblo.

Day 25 [of July]
We remained in San Miguel because of the bad weather.

Day 26 [of July]
We left at 1:00 in the evening, and shortly thereafter a strong storm began and a continuous downpour lasted almost our entire journey. We traveled eleven leagues to the east[135] up to the Pueblo of Ures ["Wildcats" (Treutlein 1949:238)]: 11 [leagues]

This mission is located on a large plain with abundant water and land for sewing.[136]

Day 27 [of July]
We were detained because we could not ford the river in this pueblo. From this pueblo the pass and ranch of Soniviate is five leagues to the north, the Sierra de Soniviate [is] two to the northeast, the Pueblo of Los Alamos [is] ten to the southeast, and its pass [is] three along the same course, the Pueblo of Santa Rosalia [is] twelve to the south-southeast,[137] the Real de Nacameri [is] ten leagues to the northwest.

Days 28 and 29 [of July]
Because of the strong storm that occurred the night of [July] 27, the horse herd stampeded, and having been left without any [horses] it was essential to stop these two days until we gathered it.

Day 30 [of July]
We took the rough road they call Los Altos ["The Heights"], fleeing from the infinite impassible fords because of the unceasing sudden rise of waters [flashflood] present along this river and we traveled fourteen leagues northeast quarter-east until the Real de la Concepción: 14 [leagues]

Day 31 [of July]
Continuing the same way of Los Altos, we traveled two leagues north to the Pueblo of Baviacora, three northeast quarter-north to that of Aconchi, four north quarter-northeast to that of Huepaca, three to Banimichi, and three north quarter-northwest to the Real de Motepore ["Deer Leap" (Treutlein 1949:237)]. 15 [leagues]

Although we planned to reach Sinoquipe this evening, it was necessary to stop for having rolled a mule of mine down a slope or cliff to the river, and made entirely useless my papers, books, tools, clothes, and the rest that I was bringing.

First Day of August
We left late to the north and traveled two leagues to the Pueblo of Sinoquipe: 2 [leagues]

Day 2 [of August]
We were detained. Because of the continuation of the rains the river could not be forded, and we were told that the heights were impassable.

Day 3 [of August]
We continued to the north-northwest through the entire river canyon (with considerable discomfort because the water reached up to the cantles[138] of the of the saddle), four leagues up to Tetuachi where we took the heights, because they were presently much easier, and continued another three leagues to the capital of Arispe: 7 [leagues]

Total leagues traveled on this trip: 504

Notes

1st As to the distances of the mountains, passes, springs, as everything that pertains to reports that I have received in this trip, I have little satisfaction for the great inconsistency of the facts of the land, for it has happened to me repeatedly to ask one about a thing, repeat the question to him after awhile, and he contradicts himself regularly in everything; and in wanting them to explain, he satisfies himself with saying, "who knows?" It is true that in terms of distances they are not to be blamed because they have never communicated by the number of leagues [they do not think in terms of the number of leagues].

2nd Do not also take as official leagues those which I mention in my journeys, since it has not been anything other than a reasonable calculation according to the time spent, and the pace [steps] we have taken, but in this there have been so many deviations that I have not been able to assure myself of the estimate of these leagues, which I have considered in accordance with those established in this kingdom.

3rd Anyone that makes the trip from the Pueblo of Ures to this capital by the regular route by way of the river, will in fact find some variation in the distances that I have provided because the flooding [from the recent rains] forced me go through the highlands, in which the infinite amount of detours caused by its breaks in the terrain make the distance vary.

4th As for the latitudes and longitudes noted on my map, I will only say that I tried to make my observations in the places that I have been with the accuracy possible, but I don't have total confidence in them for having lacked the proper instruments that such sensitive observations require.

5th With regard to having made these trips at the time when the drought had been worse than has been experienced in these provinces, which has caused several watering holes that have never lacked water to be found dry, it guaranteed that all the ones I have seen flowing will be permanent, and they are the ones with this expression that will be found in my diary.

6th That which is stated in the preceding note should not be understood for [does not apply to] the portion of road we travelled from the Real of Cieneguilla to the Hacienda of Torreón because the rains started in that *real*, and since then rare has been the day that it has stopped raining, and even though on every route we found water (according to the reports that I have) only El Carricito and El Pozo de Crisanto[139] are permanent, and the latter with the inconvenience of needing to draw water with buckets and make use of small troughs to water the livestock, it so happens that this road in the dry season is grueling owing to the lack of *aguajes*, and in the rainy season to the many mud holes it has.

7th I have no doubt that if today I should make another such reconnaissance, with regard to how much it has rained, perhaps I might find some places very appropriate for settlements that I have not identified as such because of having found them dry or with limited water = Arispe, August 5, 1780= Gerónimo de la Rocha y Figueroa__

This is a copy of the original that I have certified. Arispe, December 31, 1781. Antonio Bonilla.

Notes

1. *Caballero* (gentleman or horseman) was an earned title.
2. The term *Don* identifies him as a person of substance and influence.
3. In 1780 Arizpe was made the capital of the *comandancia general* of the Interior Provinces (Croix 1780a). Situated amid the Ópata, the town takes its name from the Ópata words of *arit* ("fire ant") and *pa* ("place"), meaning "Place of the Fire Ants." It was established in 1646 as the mission community of Nuestra Señora de la Asunción de Arizpe by Jesuit missionary Jerónimo de la Canal. Because Jesuits usually established missions in indigenous communities, it was likely an Ópata settlement long before this. Two years before this reconnaissance (1778) Arizpe had 118 adobe homes and a single stone residence (Corbalan 1778).

   Many of the O'odham place names that Father Ignaz Pfefferkorn has translated (Treutlein 1949:236–238) differ from the translations that linguists and many O'odham suggest today, and so these names should be used with caution. For example, Tubaca ["Soap Tree," "place where soap tree grows in abundance"], Tumacácori ["pepper bush"], Terrenate/Ternate ["thorn bush"], Tucson ["heath"], San Xavier del Vac [from *Cuema Vac*, a Spanish place in New Spain where the picture of St. Francis Xavier is greatly venerated], and Guevavi [Large River] are all names that have been brought into question. In many instances, however, there are no alternative translations so Pfefferkorn's are offered. It is likely that language use has changed through time and also that inferences regarding the original O'odham words are in error, thus rendering inaccurate translations.
4. Chinapa is also referenced as San José de Chinapa. Situated along the Sonora River between Bacoachi and Arizpe, San José de Chinapa was an early Jesuit Ópata mission and served as a *cabecera* or "head" mission briefly in 1685 (Roca 1967:152).
5. *Real* ("royal mining camp"); a *real de minas* is a mining district consisting of a principal community including smaller settlements, and the surrounding area. Unlike land grants for farming and ranching, silver and gold mines were not granted. They were always owned by the Crown and the miners simply had a concession to mine them and share what was extracted.
6. Throughout this diary Rocha used the terms *nacimiento del ojo* to indicate the source or origin of the spring or river. He also discussed the phenomenon where the water goes underground and later emerges. For this emergence he often used the term *brotar*. As is discussed in the next chapter, this is characteristic of the rivers in southern Arizona today, suggesting that while the rivers are and were perennial, the flow was not always on the surface.
7. While some sources say that *aliso* is a "sycamore," the most common use of this word locally is as "alder."
8. "The balls" likely refers to *bolas de plata* or "balls of silver." Stories abounded about "bolas de plata" in the mid-to-late 1700s, a rumor that was again propagated by Captain Juan Bautista de Anza in 1772. This mine was in northern Sonora, perhaps as indicated by this name.
9. *Caminamos* or *caminar* means "to walk," however these soldiers would not have walked, but rather rode horseback. So instead the alternate meaning of "to travel, move along" is implied. The same interpretation is used for *marchar*.
10. Also Mababa or Mavava. Many of these terms are O'odham or Spanish renderings of O'odham words or words resembling the language of other local inhabitants and also indigenous guides and scouts.
11. Cuquiarachi was in Ópata territory, and according to the *Rudo Ensayo*, the Franciscan mission of Cuquiárachi was established in 1660 (Pradeau and Rasmussen 1980:125), although Roca (1967:9) states that Fray Juan de San José established it in the 1642 or 1643.
12. Fronteras was Sonora's easternmost presidio at the time, and was situated in northeastern Sonora on the western slopes of the Sierra Madre range, 150 miles from Janos Presidio (Moorhead 1975:22). The short-lived San Bernardino (1775–1780) and Bavispe (garrisoned by Ópatas in 1781; Moorhead 1975:89 and n30) were situated further east. Fronteras was established in 1692, known at the time as Coro de Guachi, it was not yet formally established and was considered a *compañía volante* with its fifty soldiers (Moorhead 1975:22, 23n27). In 1775 Fronteras Presidio was temporarily transferred to San Bernardino but was then withdrawn back to Fronteras in 1780 (Gerald 1968:21; Thomas 1941:146–147).
13. As noted in the introduction, presidios in this

area and discussed in this journal were garrisoned fortifications.

This, of course, was where Croix ordered that the reconnaissance was to begin.

14. Perhaps the Coroguachi River.
15. It is unclear whether this is named for a Chinese ford or Kino's ford.

    With regard to the importance of fords and the difficulty of crossing rivers in areas that did not possess adequate characteristics for a ford, Kino had noted in 1701 regarding the Colorado River: "We intended to take two or three horses over, also, but when they put the first horse in the river at a bad place, where he was mired, he was frightened, and we left him with the rest" (Bolton 1948:316). And again Kino noted in 1702: "we found very difficult the crossing of the horses, because of the enormous bogs on the banks of the very large volumed river" (Bolton 1948:343).
16. The royal regulations of 1772 assigned the garrison of Fronteras to San Bernardino (Brinkerhoff and Faulk 1965:50, 51; Dobyns 1959:193; Williams 1991:78). In 1775 troops from Fronteras were transferred to San Bernardino but returned to Fronteras in 1780. In the interim, Fronteras remained occupied for a time but was soon abandoned owing to incessant Apache attacks, as were surrounding settlements.

    Dobyns (1959) suggested that this presidio is located north of the US-Mexico border, although this inference is in error. Gerald (1968:21), who visited the location, placed this site just south of the international line, noting period-specific artifacts, an enclosing wall, and bastions that conform to the 1772 regulations. His plan drawing of the presidio along with a discussion of pottery types found there (e.g., majolica, green glazes, etc.) confirm his assessment.

    With regard to San Bernardino, Emory's (1857a:17) account of the United States Boundary Commission Survey states: "This basin, forming, as it is said, the head of the Yaqui River, here shows a wide flat plain, extending from north to south, and having a breadth of three to five miles. On its western edge is situated the deserted settlement of San Bernardino. Adjoining this rancho are numerous springs, spreading out into rushy ponds, and giving issue to a small stream of running water. The valley is covered thickly with a growth of coarse grass, showing in places a saline character of soil. The timber growth is confined to a few lone cotton-wood trees scattered here and there." He continued: "The numerous bodies of wild cattle now running at large over this section of country are the remains and offspring of domestic herds, now widely scattered and hunted by Indians."
17. *Ganado* means "livestock," although perhaps in this case specifically it means "cattle" because he is contrasting them with horses. Throughout this document *ganado* is translated as "livestock."
18. A common practice in Sonora involved directing water through canals into the yard adjacent to or between buildings to water fruit trees and gardens, as well as to supply water for domestic purposes. This was based on the Andalucían garden, as García (2016) points out: "Many of the agricultural and gardening traditions introduced by the European colonists originated in Andalusia in southern Spain, North Africa, or the Middle East. And many of these plantings and traditions blended with American food crops and customs to create the fusion that gave rise to our unique Southwestern gardens. We could also call them Mexican gardens or Andalusian gardens." In fact, Father Kino mentioned this type of garden as a desirable goal at San Xavier del Bac when they were constructing a church in 1700, noting: "And that house, with its great court and garden near by [*sic*], will be able to have throughout the year all the water it may need, running to any place or work-room one may please" (Bolton 1948:236).
19. *Las huertas* can mean "orchards" or "vegetable gardens." In this context and others he was probably intentionally not being specific, but generally in this region it means "orchards."
20. He is describing the flow of the river going underground and then emerging again further downstream.
21. Rocha recommended that a presidio be built at Badeguachi. Construction began in 1781, but was never completed.
22. In 1779 Croix ordered that an Ópata company, made up of former Ópata scouts, be permanently stationed at San Miguel de Bavispe (Moorhead 1975:89).
23. *Ya mucha parte de ellas abiertas* means "already much of them open," but it is unclear if this means that the vegetation has been removed and fields prepared, or whether the land

is available for use but not being worked, perhaps as if they were once cultivated but now are open for others to come in and take them over, as in fallow.

24. During the 1690s and early 1700s the San Pedro River was referred to as San Joseph de Terrenate and a variety of other names, including just the Terrenate or Quiburi River and Valley. Many believe that this river was called the Nexpa by Coronado. Lafora referred to this as "the Sobaipuris Valley, also called the San Pedro" (Kinnaird 1958:106; see Seymour and Stewart 2017 for a discussion of the succession of name changes for the San Pedro).
25. While *las nutrias* means "the otters," this is likely a reference to beavers. Beavers were a common species on the San Pedro River before being hunted excessively. In 1826, James O. Pattie noted that the mouth of (what has been inferred to be) the San Pedro "was very remarkable for the number of beavers, we gave it the name Beaver River. At this place we collected 200 skins" (Batman 1988:39). Emory (1857b:100) crossed the river in the general vicinity of the international line and commented that "though affording no very great quantity of water, this river is backed up into a series of large pools by beaver-dams and is full of fishes."
26. This garrison has a complex history. It began as a presidio at Terrenate, San Phelipe de Guevavi or San Bernardo de Gracia Real de Guevavi in 1741, and then in 1774 the garrison moved to Las Nutrias, only to stay a couple of years when they moved north to Santa Cruz in December 1775. This northernmost location for the presidio is often referred to as simply Santa Cruz or Santa Cruz de Terrenate. Santa Cruz was in use between December 1775 and March 1780, when the garrison moved south again to Las Nutrias (Rocha 1780c). They did not move again until 1787, when the presidio was established on the Santa María River, which is now known as the Santa Cruz River, named after this garrison (Kessell 1966; Seymour 2012b).
27. Lafora noted that in 1766 Terrenate presidio (also called San Felipe de Jesús Guebabi) had a population of 300 (Kinnaird 1958:107).
28. This assessment is consistent with that of Lafora, who noted: "Its climate is unhealthy and the water is not at all good, nor are there any farm lands nearby" (Kinnaird 1958:107).
29. A secondary source says that people stayed here when they moved to Santa Cruz (Brinkerhoff and Faulk 1965).

    The Santa Cruz garrison would not move west to Santa María, near the headwaters of the modern Santa Cruz River, until 1787. For a history of this see Kessell (1966) and Seymour (2011b, 2012b).
30. *Vecino* means a "householder" or "citizen" of a city, town, or a *real de minas*, and usually only referred to Europeans in colonial times.
31. This statement clearly asserts that Terrenate was entirely depopulated by this time. A detachment of ten soldiers had been left at Terrenate Viejo when the garrison moved east to Las Nutrias and then north to Santa Cruz. These soldiers remained behind to protect civilian residents who did not move with the troops (Anza 1777; Williams 1986:136). The final abandonment of Terrenate Viejo may have occurred after it was attacked in 1777 by Apaches, leaving the settlement in ruins, although this place was the target of numerous other Apache attacks through time.
32. Lafora commented that there was a lagoon in the area of Las Nutrias a league above, or south, of the crossing (Kinnaird 1958:106).
33. The origin of the name for the Huachuca Mountains has many intertwined elements. The range is called Thunder Mountain in some Apache dialects, and in Mescalero this derives from the term *da'dindi dzil* (Jacob Daukei, personal communication, 2017; Willem de Reuse, personal communication, 2017). The term *Huachuca* is O'odham and in the O'odham dialect most closely related to and deriving from the Sobaipuri O'odham it means "blackened cliff," from *Waw Cuk'a* (Tony Burrell and Felicia Nunez, personal communication, 2017). This is similar to an interpretation of *Huachuca* by Winters (2012:616) as derived from *Chukadag*, which "is an old word for grime" (i.e., possibly a Sobaipuri O'odham word for grime). This term appears in the Lower Pima Nevome dialect as *tucurhaga* (Pennington 1979:82). Other O'odham translations have been suggested but these are not appropriate for the O'odham dialect that would have been spoken in this area (see for example Barnes 1935:215; Bright 2013:43; Winters 2012:340–341, 615–616).
34. He is referencing the commission during February and March of 1780 in which he moved families and settlers at Santa Cruz de Terrenate

south to Las Nutrias (see Chapter 1, Introduction).

35. In 1766 Lafora noted that there were no farmlands near Terrenate Presidio. He stated: "For this reason, and despite the danger, settlers plant on the banks of the San Pedro river in the Sobaipuris Valley, five leagues away. They maintain a storehouse there which had been burned two or three times by the enemy. This valley is very suitable for settlement and it would be well to move the presidio there so that settlers might gather under its protection. Undoubtedly, they would be attracted by the good and abundant land there" (Kinnaird 1958:107).
36. This may be the elongated blob shown on his map, perhaps indicating a spring just southeast of his camp for the night.
37. Santa María was the name Kino gave to the modern-day Santa Cruz River. For a history of the river's name see Seymour (2012b). Although Lamberton (2011:52) says that *Suamca* means "immaculate" in O'odham, Pfefferkorn (Treutlein 1949:237) states that *So'amca* means "the black one" because an image of the Virgin of Loreto is venerated there. On the other hand, Felicia Nunez says that *s-uam ma* means "nasty" in O'odham, perhaps a reference to the drunken nature of one of its priests (Keller).

    Emory (1957a:19) noted: "The situation of the town of Santa Cruz is highly picturesque, lying embosomed amid lofty wooded mountains. Its soil is fertile, abundantly watered, and susceptible of easy irrigation; its elevation gives it a cool temperature, suited to the production of northern fruits and cereal grains."
38. San Antonio Pass was used by Lafora in 1766 and is known by this name today. It passes through the Patagonia and San Antonio Mountains south of the international line.
39. The Agua Caliente shown on Rocha's map is probably the same Agua Caliente noted by Lafora, shown on the latter's map as being upstream or to the northeast of Sonoita or *Zonzita* (see note below). This notation references a pass and a spring. Puerto del Agua Caliente shown on the map is probably the route east from Patagonia toward Sonoita and on to the San Pedro through Rain Valley or the Babocomari River. The spring indicated on the map is likely Cottonwood or Monkey Springs near Sonoita, as discussed below.
40. This could be the modern-day Madera Canyon in the Santa Rita Mountains.
41. This pueblo is discussed further in Chapter 7. The route indicated by the map suggests they may have traveled through the Patagonia Mountains arriving at Sonoita Creek via Harshaw Creek. If this is so, they would have intersected Sonoita Creek at the north edge of modern Patagonia, and then traveled downstream to visit the ruined pueblo of Sonoita. Sonoita Creek bends noticeably to the north at the point where Harshaw Creek flows into it, which is a terrain feature noted by Rocha and is even hinted at by Kino on his maps.

    Lafora did not mention this pueblo in his text but did show a village in this area on his 1769 map (Urrutia 1769). This village is not shown on the later (1771) edition of his map. The village is labeled *Zonzita* (the equivalent of Sonoita and a commonly made copying error; Urrutia also incorrectly referenced San Xavier del *Paz*). A second location is labeled Ojo Caliente, as noted above. The latter is a reference to water that comes out warm in a spring between modern day Sonoita and Patagonia. This may be Cottonwood Spring, used by the later Crittenden and Buchanan Forts of the late 1800s, from which flow *acequias* that can be seen today on the ground and on historic maps. It could also be Monkey Spring, the name apparently a reference to the coatimundi. Historical sources indicate that this is a derogatory reference to Tom Hughes' Mexican laborer/cowboy. More recently it is said to reference Captain Manje, Kino's military companion, which the Americans translated into "monkey" (Barnes 1935:284; 1982:318). One map shows this as Monje Spring, which may be a reference to Manje. Hendrickson and Minckley (1984:153) commented that: "Faults in this intrusion presumably help produce both the thermal Cottonwood and Monkey springs." These springs were important through time and are near many known Sobaipuri sites that occur downstream, including one that was probably Kino's San Gerónimo.

    Fray Bartolomé Ximeno noted in 1772 that Sonoita Pueblo "is located in a mountain range where, because of distance from the other villages, it can neither give help nor be succored during the frequent and repeated attacks of the enemy; neither does this village serve as a stopping place on the road to anywhere else" (Kessell and Ximeno 1964:309).

There was discussion among Croix and others as to whether a presidio should be placed in the Sonoita area, but these discussions were never actualized.

42. This pueblo is discussed further in Chapter 7. It is of interest that on Rocha's map of this area he showed Calabasas north of a side drainage that appears to be Sonoita Creek, being the largest and most important in the area. This places it north of the commonly accepted location for Calabasas, which represents a later ranch. Lafora noted that in 1766 Calabasas was one league (three miles) from Tumacácori Pueblo (Kinnaird 1958:109; see discussion in Chapter 7). In 1773 the O'odham pueblo was located four leagues from Tumacácori (Kessell and Ximeno 1964:307). This is consistent with what we know about the regular movement of O'odham villages over time. In 1780 it was further north than is now recognized.

    It is also noteworthy that his map identifies the Cayetano and Santa Rita Mountains as distinct ranges, with the Santa Rita Mountains to the south of the Cayetanos. This seems to indicate the difference between the high peaks of Mount Wrightson and Mount Hopkins while the Cayetanos are the lower part of the range to the north. The Cerro del Calabasas seems to be what today we refer to as the Cayetano Mountains; these are drawn from the north-looking southward perspective.

    In 1766 Lafora noted that the Pimas Altos (Sobaipuri) inhabitants of Calabasas Pueblo had died in an epidemic, and that the village was repopulated by the Papago (Tohono O'odham) (Kinnaird 1958:108–109).

43. The passage can be read two ways. The first is that there is a spring separate from Sonoita Creek that flows to the west, and that the village was located in this deep tributary drainage. Areas around some of these springs were examined for Sobaipuri O'odham evidence. Alternatively (and more likely), Rocha was discussing the westward flow of Sonoita Creek itself. Rocha's map supports this interpretation as does the stream flow characteristics of Sonoita Creek (see Chapter 7).

44. This references Sonoita Creek between Cottonwood and Monkey Springs, on the one hand, and the spring south or west of Patagonia in the creek channel, on the other. The water goes back underground in this zone and is therefore inaccessible for surface use.

45. By the mid 1770s San José de Tumacácori had replaced Guevavi as the head mission or *cabecera* for the area (Kessell and Ximeno 1964:304n2). According to Fray Ximeno "3 out of 4 of the Indians of the 4 small villages are of the Papago tribe, recently converted and settled in the villages" (Kessell and Ximeno 1964:309).

    In 1773 a letter by Fray Bartolomé Ximeno, we learn that Tumacácori "has 23 families. This is the village, it may be said, that has a certain advantage with regard to its crops; because, although the water is not the most abundant, this is relieved by having it near the village. For that reason, Tumacácori's inhabitants are not so imperiled as those of the other villages by the continual attacks of the enemy Apache" (Kessell and Ximeno 1964:307).

    In 1774 Fray Antonio Ramo visited this mission and others in the area and "the Visitor found that the number corresponds to the census, which is 98 souls of the Pima nation, baptized from childhood, some born in the same pueblo while others were from abandoned pueblos. There are 21 married couples, 5 widowers, 7 widows, 14 boys over twelve years old, 21 of minor age, and 9 girls under twelve" (Baldonado 1959:22).

    Father Thomas Eixarch's 1775 account of visitation to Tumacácori stated that "the number of persons who live in this village of Tumacácori is 91—that is, ninety-one—Indians, and 26—that is, twenty-six—*de razón*, as they say here" (Kessell 1965:79).

46. Aribac is present-day Arivaca.

47. *Zopori* or *Sopori* is sometimes suggested to be derived from the word *Sobaipuri* (Barnes 1935; Bright 2013:96), but there is really no basis for this assertion other than the fact that these names share a few letters. The name may derive from the Spanish word *sopor*, meaning "peaceful" or "calm"; or the O'odham word *sopolk* for "short," referencing a short wash or stream.

48. *Volante*, "lieutenant of the flying or traveling company." Rather than being garrisoned at a presidio, flying companies tended to be headquartered in towns (rather than defending a fortified position) behind the presidio lines and patrolled the roads, intercepting hostiles who penetrated the Presidial Line, although

they sometimes reinforced a presidial garrison and regularly worked with presidial soldiers. These tended to be small detachments of mobile, lightly armed mounted troops (Moorhead 1975:180; Thomas 1941:53n170).

49. This is a distinctive mountain and the sacred mountain of the O'odham, where I'itoi/Elder Brother resides. I'itoi lives in a cave on the northwest side of the mountain. Traditional stories indicate he came from a world on the other side, leading his people, whom he had turned into ants, through an ant hole. He then changed them back into the O'odham. The O'odham still regularly make pilgrimages to the cave, leaving offerings and prayers for I'itoi. Father Kino called it Noah's Ark.

50. Dobyns (1959) suggested that the name Tumacácori originated in the O'odham words *Tchookum Kavolik*, "where the Caliche Curves." Yet modern Wa:k O'odham suggest that Tumacácori comes from *Chemaj Galolig* and means "Small Bending or Small Bent," perhaps a reference to its placement at the bend in the river. Bright (2004:520) suggests that the term comes from *cemagı ˇ gakolig*, which means "caliche bending," or perhaps *cem ko'okolig*, which means "place of little chili." The archaeological site (AZ DD:8:19, ASM) thought to be San Cayetano del Tumacácori is situated at a substantial bend in the river—known by locals as a unique characteristic of this river segment. It therefore seems most reasonable to accept a definition that includes *bending* or *crooked* in its name (Seymour 2011a:53).

51. Rocha's note at the end discusses the drought, and the *vecinos* at Arivaca had just noted (May 13) that they had never seen such a dry year. Stream flow records for this period show this was a drought year, but many years were low flow years, so this was an expected type of event.

52. Tubac (now Tubac, Arizona) was originally a Piman (Sobaipuri O'odham) settlement that in 1731 became a *visita* of Guevavi. Bright (2013:113–114) argues that Tubac derives from the O'odham *cewagĭ*, meaning "cloud," a translation that current Wa:k community members suggested. Dobyns (1959, Chapter 1) suggested that the name Tubac derives from the O'odham word *Tchoowaka*, which translates into English as "rotten." The explanation given is as follows: "Some enemies attacked Tumacácori (*Tchookum Kavolik*, "Where the Caliche Curves") and then *Tchoowaka*, where several of them were killed by the Pimans, as the story goes. Their bodies lay there and rotted, so that place came to be called *Tchoowaka* or literally "rotten" (Ríos 1959:2). By extension, the place name carries the connotation "Place Where Some Enemies Rotted" to a speaker of northern Piman familiar with the explanation. This does not make sense, however, because the O'odham would not have occupied a village where so many were killed. It would have taken such a name only after being abandoned, not when still occupied.

The presidio at this time was known as San Ignacio de Tubac and was established in 1752 after the 1751 Pima Revolt, though Moorhead (1975:52) gives the date of 1753. San Ignacio de Tubac was established in an effort to contain unrest and to guard the border against Apache incursions. After the presidio's first captain (Juan T. Beldarrain) was killed in a battle against the Seri in 1759, Juan Bautista de Anza became its commander, maintaining this position for over seventeen years. Tubac today is around twenty miles north of the US-Mexico border in Arizona.

Its garrison was transferred to Tucson in late 1775 or early 1776, but a small settler population remained behind, maintaining residence there through 1783 (Dobyns 1959). They were required to stay and had to get permission to move, which is the intent of the following paragraph (see following note).

Built prior to the 1772 regulations, Tubac was a dispersed presidio without an enclosing defensive wall. The captain's house was fortified and could be used for defense in case of attack. The numerous houses of soldiers and settlers were scattered around this fortified house (*casa fuerte*), forming the north neighborhood or *barrio*. A second clustering of houses was situated to the south, forming a second barrio. The arroyo that separated the housing areas runs through the modern Tubac community today.

53. *Trincheras* means "trenches" or "entrenchments," and in this region often references rock terraces or walls, and in this case, walls that extend from houses that could have served a defensive function. Here Rocha may be specifically referring to the wing walls recently

encountered during excavation of an area north of the commander's house, adjacent to what later became the Poston house (Seymour et al. 2010). An 1854 image by Charles Schuchard shows Tubac's houses with wing walls that extend outward from houses (see Figure 5.19). The one encountered during recent excavations just north of the *casa fuerte* shows that these were made of adobes (unfired mud bricks) set on a foundation of mud (*zoguete*) and cobbles, typical of the period and earlier (Seymour et al. 2010). These wing walls would have been defensive features that also defined property boundaries. At Tubac, many were later incorporated into house walls, forming enclosed spaces while at the same time masking their original appearance.

54. A fault crosses the riverbed near Canoa, which is why the flow disappears under the sand here.

    The reference to irrigation troughs in the place name may relate to the water being channeled from the small spring or from a well within the channel. Alternatively, the name may reference earlier canals that may have been taken off at this last reliable point, before the water disappeared too deeply into the sands.

55. This pueblo is discussed further in Chapter 7. San Xavier del Bac is named after the O'odham village of Wa:k. Contrary to common opinion, Wa:k means "come in" or "goes in." The O'odham understand Wa:k refers to San Xavier, but the meaning itself does not say where the water goes underground. Maybe "where the water goes back in," according to Tony Burrell, a Wa:k O'odham Elder. Bright (2013:88) suggests it means "standing water" but this is one of many misinterpretations. This O'odham community has been continuously occupied for centuries. The people who live there know the meaning of the term.

    This was the largest O'odham settlement, with eight hundred people when first visited by Father Kino in 1692. The community remained important through time, accepting O'odham migrants from throughout the Pimería Alta as a result of relocation orders, Apache attacks, and the reduction of more mobile O'odham from the west. It eventually was called a Papago, then Tohono O'odham settlement, but it was originally occupied by Sobaipuri O'odham. The residents refer to themselves as Wa:k O'odham and, being by the river, they are *Akimel*, or River O'odham. In the 1690s Wa:k was the residence of some of the most influential leaders. Manje mentioned people coming from all over, showing respect to the elders and leaders at this village.

    During Fray Antonio Ramo's 1774 inspection he said of San Xavier: "160 souls born and baptized in said pueblo, except for one gentile who is being prepared for baptism. There are 38 married couples, 17 widowers, 7 widows, 9 boys over twelve years old, 30 boys of minor age, 7 girls over twelve, and 14 of minor age" (Baldonado 1959:23).

56. Today this place is known as Punta de Agua.
57. Here he means that the square is formed by the residential housing. This layout is consistent with *casa muros* described for the period that consisted of walled plazas that were formed by contiguous buildings. This fortified village is illustrated in early nineteenth-century images (see Seymour 2019a).
58. *Portillos*; in this case he means that if they put gates up, the fortified square of housing would be entirely enclosed.
59. The significance of this is enormous because it tells us that by 1780 the settlement had already moved south of its original location on the floodplain (see Seymour 2019b).

    These hills include Martinez Hill and Black Mountain, both of which have *trincheras*, relating to the prehistoric Trincheras culture, on their summits and slopes which, according to oral history, were used for defense into the Historic period.

60. *Yndios Pimas vecinos, con algunos de razón. Indios de razón* usually refers to indigenous people of central Mexico, or natives who were considered peaceful, reasonable, or sensible by the Spanish. This is an interesting statement by Rocha because, in the absence of commas, it appears as if Rocha is saying that the Pima Indians are *vecinos*, including some of reason. Generally, *vecinos* (meaning citizens in this region) refers to community members with full rights to community resources, such as land, and is a term reserved for non-Indians as distinguished from *Indios*. In this case, Rocha may be stating that these are converted Indians who have bought into the colonial agenda. It is also likely that these represent people in marriages

of mixed race, between people of settler or *vecino* status and those of Piman ancestry.

Gente de razón, meaning "people of reason," was a label reserved for non-Indians and suggests these were influential non-Indian settlers (Jackson 1999:98, 102, 105, 120). On the one hand, it is doubtful that Rocha was referring to the Pima as *vecinos* and *gente de razón* because the caste system specifically differentiated between local indigenous populations and non-indigenous settlers. On the other hand, application of the caste system varied considerably throughout the Spanish world (Jackson 1999:109–110). Rocha may be saying there is a mixed community residing at San Xavier, which would be explained by a change in law just a few years before that allowed non-Indians to live in these communities, reversing an earlier law that isolated the indigenous residents so they would not be influenced negatively or taken advantage of (Jackson 1982:147, 149). Alternatively, he may be referring to mixed bloods or mestizos, as noted. On the other hand, Brinkerhoff and Faulk (1965:31n) discuss the difference between Apaches: "Apaches *de razón*—reasonable Apaches—were those who made treaties and kept them. Apaches *gentiles*—heathen Apaches—were those who refused to enter into covenants of peach with the Spaniards."

In the context of this journal it is difficult to know if Rocha is referring to mestizos or to O'odham who had adopted Spanish ways and therefore were reasonable, had good sense, and were Indians of reason. This suggests a finer set of distinctions than was often used where reference was simply made between Spaniards, Indians, and mixed bloods.

61. Tucson is a modification of the O'odham word *Cuk son*, meaning " black base." This name references an indigenous village that was situated at the base of the black hill referred to today as A Mountain or Sentinel Hill. Hugo O'Conor had recommended shifting the Tubac garrison to Tucson as a result of the royal regulations of 1772, and the move was accomplished in late 1775.

    In 1774 Fray Antonio Ramo inspected the San Agustín del Tucson *visita* and noted: "239 souls, born of the Pima nation, and baptized in that pueblo. There are 60 married couples, 17 widowers, 14 widows, 21 boys over twelve years old, 40 boys of minor age, 7 girls over twelve, and 19 of minor age" (Baldonado 1959:23). Neither this pueblo or San Xavier had any Spaniards or people of any other nationality living within their bounds.

62. This place is the pueblo of Tucson in what is now known as the mission garden area, located at the base of Sentinel Hill or at the base of the black hill.

63. Captain Don Pedro de Allande y Saabedra was assigned the command of the Tucson post in February 1777, at the age of thirty-five or thirty-six (Dobyns 1976:63).

    Allande had been a lieutenant in the dragoon regiment of Mexico and wanted to be reassigned to that outfit. An inspector in 1779 reprimanded him for using cruel and improper punishments to maintain discipline, and for employing soldiers and Indian scouts in his private business affairs, yet he was not then transferred (Dobyns 1976:63).

    "Allande y Saabedra was a nobleman born in Spain. He had entered the royal army as a cadet in the Navarre Infantry at the age of 14, and had spent 220 years in the service by the time he assumed command of the presidial company at Tucson. Allande was a veteran of Spain's war with Portugal in 1762, battles against the Moors, and the drawn-out Sonoran campaign against the Seri Indians on the Gulf of California coast between 1767 and 1777" (Dobyns 1976:63).

64. This suggests that both San Xavier and the Tucson pueblos were being built anew.

65. *Baterias* is a pile, heap, or something built up, while *barbeta* is a section of a parapet, uncovered so as to be able to place artillery. This references a raised or built-up area, a heap, on the uncovered parapet where guns could be placed.

66. La Cebadilla Pass, now called Redington Pass judging from its location, and according to McCarty (1976:11), had its name as early as 1768. Barnes (1982:261) credits Roskruge's 1893 map as the first appearance of the name and interprets *cebadilla* to mean "wild lily," but this word has several other botanical associations as well.

67. This is consistent with Emory's observation of the area and the character of the channel north of Tucson today: "The settlement of Tucson occupies the lowest line of constant running water, and consequently the last fertile basin

lying in the course of this valley. Below this, on the north, succeeds the extensive desert tract lying between Tucson and the Gila River" (Emory 1957a:19).

68. They followed along the foothills of the Santa Catalina Mountains. This approximate route later became a wagon road between Tucson and Camp Grant Military Reservation. In fact, where Rocha and his men likely camped was in the general vicinity of where an ambush occurred on May 11, 1869, between the Aravaipa Apache and the Tully and Ochoa Company wagon train en route to Camp Grant (for a discussion of this later event see Van Orden and Barnes 2014).
69. The placement of the label for C [Cañada] del Oro on the map is consistent with them stopping at Romero Canyon to take advantage of the water pools in the *tinajas* or natural rock tanks, or the spring in Sutherland Wash. Cañada del Oro's headwaters are on the northwestern slopes of the Santa Catalina Mountains, near Oracle and the Biosphere 2. The water flows northwest until it leaves the mountains, but then turns abruptly south and flows along the margin of the foothills until reaching Catalina State Park (between the towns of Catalina and Oro Valley) where it flows southwest to intersect with the Santa Cruz River. Flow along this foothill margin is intermittent and there is permanent water only in the side canyons.
70. Cañada de la Virgen del Consuelo would have been accessed at modern day Oracle, where several washes originate at this high point on the terrain. These initially flow to the north before turning east to intersect with the San Pedro. One of the main washes is Tucson Wash, and most of the other washes flow into this main wash. Tucson Wash flows into the San Pedro at Mammoth. This general area is likely where the Ugarte-Rocha expedition intersected the San Pedro. There is no crossing here as the channel is relatively wide and hosts a rich mesquite bosque with patches of cottonwoods. This explains why they traveled north for another five leagues before crossing.
71. This crossing is probably north of modern day Aravaipa Creek. Just south of Alamo Crossing on Rocha's map is the Mesa de Motesuma and to the east is Valle de Santa Theresa. Valle de Santa Theresa is likely Aravaipa Creek, where there is generally a reliable flow during the winter months and early spring when the trees are dormant, leaving sufficient water to flow on the surface. The reliability of water from both the San Pedro and Aravaipa Creek allows for luxuriant cottonwood and mesquite stands in this area, with a mix of other tree species. The Aravaipa Creek Valley goes through to the Klondyke area and the Santa Teresa Mountains (the name of this range has been retained since Rocha's time to the present, though it was known by other names earlier), and so the name of the valley makes sense from this perspective.

    The mountains to the north of the Gila River, which are now known as the Pinal Mountains and others, were labeled the Sierra del Aribaipa on Rocha's map. On Rocha's 1784 map the modern day Galiuro Mountains, which are immediately east and parallel to this part of the San Pedro, were labeled the Sierra del Aribaypa. These are examples of a name being transferred over time to a new unrelated location either intentionally as the names were adjusted or as corrections for earlier mislabeling. The name Aravaipa is now used exclusively for the valley to the south of the Gila that in Rocha's document is referenced as Valle de Santa Theresa. Today the Aravaipa and Klondyke Valleys are subsumed by the location referenced then as the Valle de Santa Theresa.

    Arivaipa is an O'odham name deriving from *Ali Waika*. *Ali* means "small, short, or child;" *waika* means "ditch, stream, or canal (also see Barnes 1935:26; Bright 2013:8; Lumholtz 1990:388; Winters 2012:722–723).

    The trail, as shown on Rocha's map, bowed out to the east in this area, probably adding a league or two to his distance.
72. In 1697 Manje mentioned passing this location on his way to Casa Grande, veering out away from the river owing to the bog, where, he said, "[we] took our course toward the west because the guides of the Sobaipuris, who were accompanying us, told us that we could not travel the bank of the river as there were many miry places. They guided us through a clear beaten track, and through broken mountainous county, but always kept in sight of the river" (Karns 1954:285).

    Because 1780 was a drought year there was likely a useful crossing in this area, which Rocha identified as Vado de Atascadero.

73. This was in the area of Dudleyville, although it is difficult to discern whether it was north or south of or at this modern town. Today there are several crossings, only some of which would have been appropriately rocky at the time. Fords probably changed in character and location through time, with the most reliable ones found in locations where bedrock outcropped or where there was a rocky flow from a tributary wash that dumped cobbles and gravels into the San Pedro channel.
74. Alamo Ford is almost certainly north of Aravaipa Creek.
75. The route taken by Rocha at the confluence is visible on his map as the darkened line demarking a loop. Much of this portion of this route loop is now under mine tailings piles.
76. This paragraph indicates that this version of Rocha's journal was the one forwarded secretly to Croix, along with the summary, which has similar statements that would not likely have been made in the journal sent through Ugarte.
77. Along this portion of the San Pedro and to the south, from the junction with the Gila to about the modern Benson area, Lafora commented that "there is a great deal of farmland and plenty of water" (Kinnaird 1958:106). This view in 1766 is just the opposite of the impression Rocha was providing. The drought may be partially responsible for Rocha's notion, as might the season during which Rocha and Ugarte passed. It seems equally likely, however, that Rocha and Ugarte were predisposed to determine that the lower and middle San Pedro were inappropriate for placement of a presidio as a result of their discussions with the troops at Las Nutrias (who had just relocated from Santa Cruz de Terrenate not more than two months before) and their desire not to stretch the Presidial Line too far north. Additional comments as they proceeded along this river provide the same dismal impression of this river as do Rocha's and Ugarte's summaries. Most likely the settlers and soldiers then at Las Nutrias would not yet have had time to recover from the malnutrition and lack of food toward the end of Santa Cruz de Terrenate's occupation, and so Rocha and Ugarte would have seen the distended bellies and skin and bones described by the garrison's captain Vildosola (see Thomas 1941:153).

    The king's instructions were prepared as a result of work in the late 1680s and were published in 1772, but remained in force despite the fact that Santa Cruz de Terrenate Presidio had just failed (with the soldiers and settlers ultimately moving south in March 1780). Thus, work undertaken, including this reconnaissance, was driven by old knowledge. Policies often lagged far behind events taking place on the frontier, and so Rocha's and Ugarte's recommendations were required to address the old orders, but were also significantly influenced by current events. They would have known before this trip that a presidio at the confluence of the San Pedro and Gila Rivers was folly but would have been required to fulfill the orders anyway. This reconnaissance is a perfect example, among many, of the commonly cited reasons for the failure of the Spanish empire and the waste of the crown's resources. Authority was too centralized, there was too much lag time, and many decisions that should have been made on the spot required the king's review.
78. This probably means that there were unoccupied huts or housing here. It is unclear whether this means these were huts of an Apache or Jocome ranchería or whether they were the domed elongated structures of the Sobaipuri O'odham. This was within the Sobaipuri O'odham homeland, and this type of landform which Rocha and Ugarte walked along would have been appropriate for Sobaipuri O'odham settlement. There are numerous Sobaipuri O'odham sites along the river margins, which make it surprising that only this one is mentioned. Because they do not state that they encountered indigenous people here, this may indicate that it was recently depopulated, which perhaps made it more visible by the standing frameworks of these structures. A 1732 map, resulting from when Padre Keller and Juan Bautista de Anza came through the area on their way to Santa María del Suanca, shows a village named Naideniba in this general area that presumably could have been an occupied settlement at that time.

    Apache and Jocome sites have been found along this river as well, although they tend to be more ephemeral. It is possible that this was the location where Oliva spotted smoke that resulted in the capture of the only prisoners taken during the campaign, although this is doubtful (Croix June 23, 1780; Dobyns 1976 Tubac, Chapter 6; see note below).

This Xacaleria would have been across the river from the vicinity of modern Mammoth.

79. *Caja* is used throughout these texts to denote a river channel or the box of the channel. This usage is consistent with Spanish geological terms (e.g., Long 1991:C-1). See the discussion in Chapter 6.

80. This ford is likely at the bedrock outcrop between Cascabel and Redington that was known as The Narrows during Kino's time (see Bolton 1936:364) and that was described as having "many *embudos* between two cliffs where the river narrows its course [for] about a half a league" (Karns 1954:79). More recently the Tres Alamos Narrows has also been referred to as The Narrows. The Cascabel-Redington Narrows involves a longer stretch of the river and would have been much more dangerous from the standpoint of ambush. The Tres Alamos Narrows is one of several short narrows along the river where the borders of the river constrict and, as discussed elsewhere in this book, was a key feature of the river that allowed for Sobaipuri O'odham irrigation and therefore settlement (also see Seymour 2011c).

81. This ford is formed by the intersection of rocky Tres Alamos Wash and the San Pedro in the general area of modern-day Willow Lake. This was a common stopping place for expeditions, including for Kino and Manje in the 1690s. The area did not possess the necessary river channel characteristics suitable for irrigation agriculture for the Sobaipuri O'odham so their settlements were not present in the area, although many are known to the north or downstream. Local lore indicates that this upstream area may have been swampy until the 1887 earthquake, although such recollections are vague. Geological evidence of a swamp is present even farther south, upstream from this location.

    Lafora did not mention an occupied settlement here at Tres Alamos in 1766. He indicated that this and other settlements were abandoned "because of constant robberies and murders committed by the Apaches from the shelter of the Chiguicagui sierra [Chiricahua Mountains] where they have never been pursued" (Kinnaird 1958:106).

82. This is Quiburi, the largest Sobaipuri O'odham village on the San Pedro in Kino's time and the only remaining Sobaipuri O'odham village on the San Pedro during Rocha's time. The village was once further south, in the vicinity but not at Santa Cruz de Terrenate Presidio. A Sobaipuri O'odham village called Santa Cruz was located where the presidio was eventually placed, and it was called this after it moved from the south owing to the 1698 battle that occurred at Santa Cruz de Gaybanipitea.

83. This is Santa Cruz de Terrenate Presidio, whose garrison was transferred to this location in December 1775. It was occupied for four short years, as by March 1780 Rocha had moved the people of the presidio south to Las Nutrias. The adobe ruins of this presidio are visible on Bureau of Land Management land north of Fairbank. Excavations have been undertaken at the site by Charles Di Peso (1953) and more recently by Seymour (2011a, 2011c). The presidio is known as Santa Cruz to distinguish it from Terrenate (Terrenate Viejo) nearer the headwaters of the San Pedro and as shown on Rocha's map. Commandant-Inspector Hugo O'Conor had selected this more northern location in 1775 to comply with the revisions in presidio placement required by the royal regulations of 1772. Santa Cruz de Terrenate Presidio was placed on a site known as Santa Cruz (Thomas 1941:181), owing to the former presence of a Sobaipuri O'odham village by this name (see Seymour 2011a). After numerous Apache attacks, including the burning of buildings and fields and attacks on supply trains, the presidio was abandoned and the garrison moved south again to Las Nutrias.

    The distance between places mentioned in the journal is probably somewhat greater than the actual on-the-ground distance, because their trail diverged to the west, probably to avoid arroyos that were already deeply incised. The arroyos in this area today are excessively deep, up to a point on the west where their erosion is stopped by a bedrock shelf (see discussion in Chapter 6).

84. Quiburi was a Sobaipuri O'odham settlement occupied in 1692 when Father Eusebio Francisco Kino first visited the area. *Quiburi* means "Many Houses" in an ancient O'odham dialect and it was aptly named, for it was the largest settlement on the San Pedro. By 1780 it seemingly was the last settlement on the San Pedro and was about half its former size. It is significant during this period because it remained occupied after the Sobaipuri O'odham were said to have abandoned their villages along this river because of Apache attacks. In fact, while

the Spaniards ordered these San Pedro Sobaipuri O'odham to relocate, only about half the population complied (Seymour 2011b). Rocha's journal and map confirm the continued occupation of this area by the Sobaipuri O'odham. Archaeological data provide evidence that the Sobaipuri O'odham occupied the San Pedro throughout this and the following century. It is possible that the area was "abandoned" for a time in the 1760s, as it was briefly after the 1698 battle (Seymour 2014, 2015a), because with reference to this part of the San Pedro in 1766, Lafora stated: "Here are the ruins of the pueblos of Santa Cruz, Quibori, Tres Alamos, and Acequias Hondas. They were inhabited by the Sobaipuris Indians, who were compelled to abandon them because of constant robberies and murders committed by the Apaches from the shelter of the Chiguicagui sierra where they have never been pursued" (Kinnaird 1958:106).

85. Again, Rocha is referencing the March 1780 move of the soldiers and settlers of Santa Cruz de Terrenate south to Las Nutrias.

86. One of the criteria for initially selecting this location for the relocated presidio of Santa Cruz (or any presidio) was that it had sufficient firewood. O'Conor noted in a summary report of 1775 just prior to the relocation of Terrenate, then at Las Nutrias, to Santa Cruz, that "the spot of Santa Cruz, destined for the location of the presidio of Terrenate, besides having abundant pastures, waters and woods, it is at an average distance of thirty-three leagues west of San Bernardino" (Thomas 1941:181). Throughout his diary Rocha repeatedly comments on the disposition of water, pasture, firewood, and timber for building, as well as lands for planting, consistent with Croix's orders. O'Conor (1775) had certified that this defensive location of Santa Cruz had sufficient firewood as of August 1775 when he conducted his inspection. Consequently, this means that either the occupants of the presidio stripped the area clean of firewood during their four-year stay, or that Rocha's criteria of adequacy were more attuned to the firewood densities further south. Vegetation densities and thickness of riparian areas increase as one travels south out of the more arid frontier areas. The distance Rocha mentions means that he is referencing the surrounding mountains, the Dragoons to the East, and the Whetstones and Mustang mountains to the west, as sources of firewood.

On his approach to the San Pedro Valley from San Bernardino on the east, Emory (1857a:17–18) described the eastern branch of the San Pedro near its source (Las Nutrias is the western branch), stating: "The country here begins to assume most attractive features. To the north and west rise high mountain ridges clothed with pine and oak groves; the intervening country is everywhere carpeted with fine grama grass, the nutritious quality of which is exhibited in the well-conditioned character of the numerous wild horses and cattle that luxuriate over this favored region. Water is frequent in the valleys, and everything indicates a capacity for cultivation, the grazing capabilities being unequalled by any tract heretofore passed over." His description was from a little south of the international line, but clearly contrasts with Rocha's statements, suggesting the terrain had recovered in the intervening years as Apache depredations left the area less densely settled, or that the two men evaluated from different baselines.

Emory's (1857a:18, 30) account of the United States Boundary Survey noted of the San Pedro River Valley and high elevation valleys near the boundary line: "These upland valleys are only sparsely wooded by occasional cottonwood or walnut trees. As we approach the mountains, however, the timber growth becomes more abundant, and the lower ridges are occupied by extensive groves of oak, which, on the higher points, are associated with pine and cedar."

87. Tobosa is a coarse range grass (*Hilaria mutica*) whose name means "rocky with limestone."

88. The Serritos shown on Rocha's map to the east of this location is probably the modern-day Tombstone Hills.

89. This seems to be in the vicinity of present-day Charleston.

90. This is about where Highway 90 crosses the San Pedro. This may be in the vicinity of the crossing that is currently labeled San Pedro Crossing near Lewis Springs.

91. The captain of Santa Cruz de Terrenate Presidio (Captain Don Francisco Ignacio de Trespalacios) apparently failed to move against the Apaches when they were encountered in this ford in 1778 (Croix's General Report of 1781 in Thomas 1941:139).

92. This is probably near present-day Herford, perhaps a little south toward modern-day

Palominas. This is the crossing along the route suggested for fifteen-day patrols between Santa Cruz and San Bernardino presidios by O'Conor (O'Conor 1994:75). Rocha's map referenced this as *Palomitas* ("Little Pigeon," "Popcorn"), but the journal used *Palominos*, as did O'Conor (see O'Conor 1994:75, Appendix:71). This is where O'Conor suggested they cross the river and head out either across the desert or toward La Soledad ("solitude," or perhaps in this instance "desert"), across flat land to the Chiricagui (Chiricahua) Mountains and on to San Bernardino. La Soledad is not shown on any maps, including those by Urrutia and Rocha. This suggests that this is a reference to the broad expanse of desert, perhaps reinforced by the fact that *la* is not capitalized in the original (see O'Conor 1994:71). It is also possible that *la Soledad* is an extension of the name of the *vado* (i.e., Las Palominas de la Soledad). Finally, another possibility is that La Soledad represents a prominent landform referenced in the 1850s by Emory (1857c:17): "A remarkable tower-shaped peak rises in the centre of this ridge, a short distance south of the road, forming a conspicuous landmark. This ridge is seen to be composed of one or more of the variable forms of volcanic products so often noticed heretofore; the prevailing character is here a reddish brown granitic mass." In any event, this route would have taken them south of the Burro Mountains, toward modern-day Douglas, and on to San Bernardino Presidio.

Just beyond this crossing may be where Santa Cruz de Terrenate's Captain Don Francisco Ignacio de Trespalacios and nineteen soldiers and settlers were killed. On September 24, 1778, they likely passed across this ford, proceeding toward San Bernardino on their routine patrol when they were killed on an open, level plain (Thomas 1941:144).

It is likely that Captain Don Francisco Tovar similarly died along this route in an ambush in 1776, as Croix noted: "the road from this presidio [Santa Cruz] to San Bernardino has become impassable to regular parties of troops, as one party of ten men detailed to take mail bags had perished at the hands of the Apaches. Likewise did thirty others [sic, actually 24] and their captain, Don Francisco Tovar, suffer the same fate in the year '76" (Thomas 1941:151). If this can be read as a discussion about atrocities that occurred along the road between Santa Cruz and San Bernardino, then it is reasonable to argue that it was at the Palominas Crossing that the ambush occurred.

Rocha's map shows what looks like a second trail that bows out in this area, just north of the crossing. There is also a spring named Hacal a little further west, suggesting that they found a *jacal* ("hut") or a ranchería here. This may be the place mentioned by Croix (June 23, 1780, Dobyns 1959) where, during this reconnaissance, Oliva spotted smoke that resulted in the capture of the only prisoners taken during the campaign. Rocha did not mention this encounter.

In another report Emory (1957a:18) commented that: "At the point where the main valley of the San Pedro is reached we find an alluvial belt, variable in width, and occasionally marshy. These bottoms are flanked by terraced tableland of unequal heights, composed of a hard, gravelly soil, and supporting a close sward of grama grass, giving a peculiarly smooth shorn look to the general face of the country.

"Occasional exposures of igneous rock, or the projecting spur of some mountain ridge, serve to diversify the scene; and quite constantly in the higher branch valleys is exposed a form of igneous conglomerate. This latter formation is exposed in irregular bluffs along the edges of these valleys, presenting washed faces and precipitous walls crowned with terraces. These higher points are frequently set off with the remains of deserted dwellings, plainly located with a view to defense. Other eminences, commanding extensive views, are occupied by rocky breastworks, serving the double purpose of watchtowers and strongholds of retreat. Associated with these are also extensive rocky enclosures, in which the cattle were secured. All these points are suggestive of the condition of constant warfare to which this commencing civilization was subject, and under which it was at last obliged to succumb."

93. The league distances from here south to the San Pedro fields do not add up. The difference cannot be accounted for by changes in river course. Instead, it seems they traveled some extra distance in this area that they did not specifically mention in the journal. Just south of Las Palomitas Crossing the trail shown on Rocha's map splits and does not come together again until the *vado* at La Tienda. This split

may indicate a doubling back, perhaps to find a way around the possible obstruction or explore the four darkened areas on the map (which are also shown on his 1784 map and are likely springs). Also, north of Las Palomitas Crossing the trail diverged to a spring labeled "Ojo del Hacal." This could relate to the smoke seen by Oliva mentioned above, and perhaps the discovery of a ranchería near a low-flow spring as explained in the map key and the word *Hacal* (see note above).

This explanation of these divergent trails likely accounts for the extra distance indicated in the journal. The distance traveled (as stated in the journal) between Santa Cruz Presidio and the San Pedro fields, both known places, is too great as compared to the actual distance, even when accounting for curves in the river channel. When subtracting the doubled distance (approximately 10.50 miles) along this segment between these three crossings, the league distances match quite well, eliminating approximately 10.50 miles of the distance between Las Palominas and the San Pedro fields. This indicates that the map illustrates travel not noted in the journal.

94. This is shown as *Atroxe* [*A troje*] on Rocha's map along with a rectangular box, perhaps referencing a granary or barn at the San Pedro fields. This general area of the San Pedro fields was likely where the river obtained its name. Originally called the Nexpa, then the Quiburi, San Joseph de Terrenate, and Terrenate River, it then became the river of the Sobaipuris or Sobaipuri River before becoming the San Pedro. This name change was gradual, but likely corresponds to the official removal of the Sobaipuri from the river in 1762. While about half stayed, the official position is that they left, and the Sobaipuri O'odham certainly did not dominate the river as they had for centuries before. Beginning in about the 1730s the indigenous village of San Pedro began to show up in documentary sources and was located in this general area. This suggests that as the Sobaipuri O'odham were removed, the San Pedro village name was transferred to Spanish fields, a ranch, a fort, a land grant, and then to an ejido.
95. This passage indicates that the ford just south of Santa Cruz de Terrenate Presidio was in fact referenced as Santa Cruz.
96. This contrasts with later observations during much wetter years (and during the month of February) wherein it was noted that "beyond this the San Pedro valley spreads out in diverging branches to the east and west, thus drawing tributary a very extended mountain drainage. It is this latter character which sufficiently accounts for the fact that the San Pedro is the only branch of the Gila River, coming from the south, which furnishes an uninterrupted stream of running water along its whole course" (Emory 1957a:18). Rocha's account is a more accurate description of the intermittent nature of the modern flow of the San Pedro.
97. This description may suggest that the San Pedro channel was already deeply incised at this time (see Chapter 6). The channel today is steep sided, because of arroyo incision and because of cliffs along the borders of the wash that narrow the channel.
98. At this point they had left the San Pedro, transiting to the headwaters of the Río Cocóspera (each valley segment was sometimes also referenced by other names) within a tributary channel which (after accepting the flow of other tributaries, going underground, and re-emerging) eventually forms the Río Magdalena and rivers or valleys of other names. The name (Milpillas) indicates that there were fields in this location as well as at the June 7 location shown as *Atroxe*.

    Rocha's map references the heads of the San Pedro, illustrating the three sources or channels at the head of the river that flow north to form a single channel. These three tributary channels are clearly visible today in satellite images.
99. This is the modern-day Santa Cruz River, which originates in the San Rafael Valley in southern Arizona.
100. Lieutenant of the "flying company" or *compañía volante*.
101. Don Pablo Romero would become captain of the presidio of San Agustín del Tucson after Captain Pedro de Allande y Saavedra. He had been lieutenant at the presidio of Santa Cruz in 1778, staving off abandonment of that post. Also lieutenant in the flying company of Sonora in 1780, Romero commanded the Ópata Company at Bacoachi at that rank. He became captain in command of the Buenavista Presidio. When Lieutenant Colonel Pedro de Allande left Tucson, Romero moved there as acting captain (Dobyns 1976:93).
102. Lieutenant Juan María de Oliva commanded the Tubac garrison at the time of its relocation

to Tucson (Dobyns 1976:59–60). He served under Juan Bautista de Anza, who at the time was away on his second California expedition. Oliva was illiterate and so pertinent records are not available, but he probably continued to serve as post commander of the Tucson Presidio until his replacement arrived in 1777 (Dobyns 1976:59–60).

Captain Oliva was retired and sixty-five years old when on this reconnaissance. This was quite old for the period when women had a life expectancy of forty years and warfare made life expectancy uncertain for men (Cruz 1988:130). He had been elevated to the rank of captain upon his retirement in 1776. According to Dobyns (1959), during a reconnaissance, possibly this one, Oliva spotted smoke that resulted in the capture of the only prisoners taken during the campaign (Croix June 23, 1780b). Rocha did not mention this encounter.

103. A *hacienda* is a large agricultural establishment using day laborers. These were large landed estates typically based on a mixture of grain farming and livestock production, usually including smaller properties and employing many families in raising crops or livestock. Not every hacienda is a ranch, nor is every ranch a hacienda.
104. This is the pass between the San Antonio and Patagonia Mountains.
105. This statement suggests that the valley may have been overgrazed at an earlier time, which may have begun the degradation of the watershed and entrenchment of the river channel.
106. This is the namesake of the Mexican land grant of Buenavista, issued October 24, 1831 (Barnes 1982:315).
107. An *estancia* used to be a certain type of livestock ranch. It was different from the generic rancho or hacienda in that it was defined geographically. The typical estancia was a narrow valley bounded by steep mountains, unfordable rivers, or canyons. The *hacendado* ["landowner, rancher"] relied on these features to contain his livestock by fencing the few exits and letting the stock graze within the estancia with minimal effort to keep them in place. While some estancias were indeed ranchos and haciendas, not all ranchos and haciendas were estancias. Some ranchos and haciendas also operated estancias, but as a side feature of the entire operation. Another characteristic of an estancia was that it was attended by staff who camped on site temporarily or came and went after checking on the penned herd. A permanent ranch community that came with the typical hacienda and rancho was not a central characteristic of an estancia. This was possible because estancias were usually located within a day's travel from a nearby permanent community or presidio.
108. When Lafora reported on Guevavi in 1766 it was inhabited by fifty Pimas Altos (Kinnaird 1958:108). While it was said to have been abandoned for the last time in 1775, archaeological evidence indicates that it was occupied by O'odham and others after this, consistent with the Sobaipuri O'odham practice of living in one location, moving, and then re-establishing residence at the old location, perhaps ten to forty years later. Thus the abandonment did not really relinquish the village location but reflected a temporary and regular decadal movement along the margins of the irrigation and field system (see Seymour 2011a).
109. This is the modern-day Patagonia Mountains.
110. He was saying that Guevavi was on the trail between Las Nutrias and Tucson and so divided the trip, but Guevavi was out of the way to Altar when going from either Las Nutrias or Tucson.
111. He was discussing the flow of the Santa Cruz, which originates in the San Rafael Valley in southern Arizona, curves south into Sonora, and then heads north, flowing through Tubac and Tucson and then emptying into the Gila River in central Arizona.
112. The water gains more force because of bedrock outcrops at Guevavi that push water to the surface. This phenomenon is an important factor in Sobaipuri O'odham settlement placement (see Chapter 6; Seymour 2011a). The bedrock that forces the water to the surface gave Guevavi its name. Jane Hill, linguist of the O'odham language, noted that Guevavi likely derives from *ge: waw*, meaning "big cliff/bedrock" (as in the *Babo* part of Baboquivari, from *Waw Giwul(i)k*). In discussions with her it became clear that the reason this name has not been suggested is that there was no reason to think that a "big cliff" would be present in the valley, so consequently other suggestions for the meaning of the name have prevailed (such as gi-vavhia, meaning "big well," "big water," or "big spring"; see Kessell 1970; National Park Service 2007, or "large river" Treutlein

1949:237). When the senior author showed Dr. Hill an image of the bedrock outcrops in this area she said that these clearly qualify: "The outcropping is a pretty decent size, good enough for "gue…" (ge:)!"

113. Oliva and ten men continued on to the Tucson presidio north via the Santa Cruz River while Rocha and the rest of his thirty men went south to Santa María Suanca.
114. "Royal Road" or a "royal highway" was a principal road or trail for mounted travelers or pack trains.
115. San Ignacio was the head mission for the area. Lafora noted that in 1697 it had three hundred Upper Pimans and sixty native soldiers (Kinnaird 1958:113).
116. Ugarte had taken a different route to Imuris. Rocha had gone with the men from Tucson Presidio to explore to the west, including to Guevavi, and then his intention was to meet up with Ugarte at Imuris, after many of the soldiers and officers returned to Tucson. This more direct route by Ugarte may be an indication that he was aging and less inclined to the rigors of field exploration (see Moorhead 1968:48).
117. It is unclear here whether he is referencing the Magdalena River or Magdalena Pueblo.
118. Magdalena is where Father Eusebio Kino became sick and died in 1711. His burial is said to be on display in the plaza. Magdalena was a *visita* of San Ignacio. Lafora noted that Santa Magdalena was inhabited by thirty-six Upper Pima families in 1767 (Kinnaird 1958:113).
119. Lafora referred to this settlement as Sariqui. In 1767 the mission was inhabited by 300 Upper Pima plus another 300 Tohono O'odham who camped in its vicinity. He noted they came in the winter "to escape the barenness and drought of their country and they return to their homes in summertime during the rainy season. He noted that "among the people of the Sariqui settlement there are sixty armed men" (Kinnaird 1958:110–111).
120. Lafora referred to this settlement as El Busani, which at the time (1767) was a *visita* of the mission of Sariqui. He noted that the village had recently been depopulated because of an epidemic, leaving only four families (Kinnaird 1958:110).
121. Lafora stated that this spring was to the left (east) of the road and about a quarter of a league from Busani (Kinnaird 1958:110).
122. *Arizona* likely derives from an O'odham word for a small base which they called *Ali*-shon. These mountains are the modern-day Sierra La Esmeralda, and seemingly also the Atascosa and Tumacácori Mountains.
123. Tubutama mission had 300 people when Lafora passed through in 1767 (Kinnaird 1958:111).
124. Santa Teresa had been a *visita* of Tubutama with the same number of Upper Pimans as the mission. Here too Lafora mentioned that there was a Tohono O'odham village "with grass huts like those in the pueblos" (Kinnaird 1958:112).
125. The distance between settlements differed between Lafora and Rocha's time. In 1767 Atí was three leagues from Santa Teresa (Kinnaird 1958:112). Several distances between settlements differ between the Spaniards, probably indicating that the settlements had shifted, as O'odham settlements tended to do.
126. This presidio was established not to contain the Apache, but rather, as Lafora noted, "to restrain the Seris, rebellious Pimas, and Pápagos should they at any time attempt to unite, as happened in the uprising of 1752" [sic 1751] (Kinnaird 1958:112). He noted that besides the soldiers there were twenty-five families and ten armed men (Kinnaird 1958:112). Santa Gertyudis de Altar was established in 1752 (Moorhead 1975:52).
127. Atí and Oquitoa (Oquilva in Lafora's text) had the same population as the preceding settlements during Lafora's time (Kinnaird 1958:112).
128. Pitic is situated in the modern municipality of Hermosillo, which was inhabited by the Seri, Tepoca, and Pima. The first missionaries arrived in the state of Sonora around 1614. San Pedro de la Conquista was established at El Pitic in 1741 but its garrison was moved to San Miguel de Horcasitas in 1748 (Moorhead 1975:51). Croix had moved the presidial company of San Miguel de Horcasitas to the pueblo of El Pitic because the Seris were concentrated there (Moorhead 1968:51).
129. This references the expedition by Inspector-General Don José Gálvez.
130. This route, of course, would take them northeast to Arizpe.
131. In 1767 Lafora made the following statement about the Horcasitas area: The Seris and Pimas are "gradually destroying it [Sonora] like thieves in the house. Together with the Gileño Apaches, who attack from the north, they are penetrating farther and farther every day, and

have now reached the neighborhood of San Miguel de Horcasitas" (Kinnaird 1958:125). He further stated that "this area is more dangerous than any part of Sonora" (Kinnaird 1958:116).

132. This transfer occurred earlier in 1780, following a January order by Croix (Thomas 1941: 146–147).
133. In 1767 Lafora noted that at San Miguel de Horcasitas "a cavalry company was garrisoned with the same number of soldiers and the same allowance as the other presidios. . . . There are also sixty civilians and various Indian families who are the servants. All are very poor" (Kinnaird 1958:116). At this time, it was the capital of Sonora, but by 1780 the capital had shifted to Arizpe.
134. This had been a Seri mission, initially established in 1679 by Jesuit missionary Juan Fernández on the San Miguel River and referred to at the time as Santa María de Pópulo. In 1688 Father Adamo Gilg served this mission (Spicer 1981:105–106).
135. Here they were going cross-country to the Sonora River Valley.
136. In 1767 Lafora described the Mission of Los Ures as being inhabited by as many as 200 families of Ópatas and Pimas and thirty civilized people (Kinnaird 1958:117).
137. In 1767 this pueblo had been abandoned because of Seri attacks. Lafora also stated that "these places are seldom visited by the Apaches who are not usually in the vicinity of Ures" (Kinnaird 1958:117). Thirty Upper Piman families resided at Santa Rosalía in 1767 along with a detachment of twenty men and an officer (Kinnaird 1958:117–118).
138. *Borrén* means "saddlecloth," "saddle," or "straw cushion," as in *borrenes de la silla*. It is found at the meeting of the saddle tree and the bridle in military saddles, is filled with stuffing, and would be uncomfortable when wet, so the water probably came up to the cantles.
139. A place of this name is present in Sonora today, at or near the one visited by Rocha, west of Highway 15, the road between Santa Anna and Hermosillo. It is situated east of an intermittent arroyo.

CHAPTER 6

Environmental History

The contents of the journal, summary reports, and map allow us to combine historical and indigenous information to develop a fresh understanding and deeper view of the environmental history of the region or at least establish a new baseline from which to assess historical changes. These texts are especially relevant with respect to the far northern portion of the frontier, that which currently lies mostly north of the international line, and which encompasses the San Pedro and Santa Cruz River Valleys. This was the zone where the Presidial Line in Sonora was located from 1775 to 1780 and also where the proposed changes were designed to take place. We are fortunate to have these early sources because, as Herford and Betancourt (2009:234) note, information relevant to environmental history and channel cutting along the San Pedro has been restricted to the administration of Terrenate presidio, which was established in 1742 near the headwaters in Sonora and later moved (as Santa Cruz) to the middle San Pedro near Fairbank in late 1775. Thereafter documents are from the 1820s and 1830s and relate to the establishment of the San Juan de las Boquillas y Nogales and the San Rafael del Valle Mexican land grants. The Ugarte and Rocha documents provide insights into this intervening timeframe, highlighting the character of the landscape after an intensive four-year occupation on the middle San Pedro and an even longer exploitation of the upper reaches of the river. This time period is important for a number of reasons. For one, other documents show us how quickly conditions could change on the frontier, given the ebb and flow of population levels, impacts of Apache attacks, changes in colonial and military policies, and natural drought cycles, to name a few. Notions are that environmental changes, such as arroyo cutting, channel entrenchment, and devegetation, occurred rapidly once initiated (see Turner et al. 2002:xiii), which is borne out by the Rocha journal data. Yet, as these 1780 texts indicate, most understandings situate the commencement of this—or at least one historical cycle of dramatic changes in the natural landscape—much too late in time. Examination of these documents allows us to see that many processes attributed only to the late-1800s actually occurred as well in the mid-to-late-1700s, and were seemingly initiated as a result of both occupation of Terrenate and Las Nutrias south of the modern international line, and Santa Cruz Presidio to the north. Specifically, while documents relating to the establishment of Santa Cruz de Terrenate Presidio paint a bountiful picture of the terrain on the Middle San Pedro, with plenty of wood, water, and pasture, Rocha's journal provides evidence of the impacts of the presidio's population on the local ecosystem. The journal text suggests that presidial and settler activity were the potential triggers for initiation of this phase of rapid change on these segments of the watershed. Rocha's observations

FIGURE 6.1. Deep arroyo north of Santa Cruz de Terrenate presidio along the west side of the San Pedro, which would have obstructed travel along the river margin.

seemingly relate to an important transitional period wherein it is possible to see the impacts to surrounding mountains and valleys following an intensive period of use and occupation at Terrenate Viejo, Las Nutrias, and Santa Cruz de Terrenate. Because one of the journal's goals was to report on the availability of water, pasture, fuel wood, timber, and other resources for settlement, we have an in-depth perspective on a time previously poorly represented. Apparently, the ecosystem was able to restore itself sufficiently after the residents moved south, and later when the Santa Cruz garrison left Las Nutrias for the modern Santa Cruz River. The reduction in pressure on resources and the surface and near-surface water table were beneficial to the repair of local impacts. This series of intensive occupations may have activated a decades-long degeneration or change of the river system, but this is a question left for future research and examination of other historical accounts that may be found and analyzed.

Arroyo Cutting, Incised Floodplains, and Environmental Degradation

Because Rocha demarcated the course traveled on his map with a dotted line it is possible to follow their general route today along certain segments, assessing the basis for decisions made as to route and the implications with respect to environmental conditions. One especially good example is provided by Ugarte and Rocha as they approached Santa Cruz de Terrenate Presidio from the north. They rested overnight at the presidio before heading south, crossing over to the east side at a ford, and then farther upstream (south) they passed back over. Along most of the way, their route paralleled the river course. The dotted line suggests that, at least four times at various points along the southward segment north of Santa Cruz de Terrenate Presidio, they had moved toward and away from the terrace edge and floodplain (see Figure 4.17). These deviations in path, both outward from the terrace edge and back inward, likely correspond to deep washes, bends in the river, and other terrain features and obstructions that can be mapped today. Rocha's route adjustments suggest that these especially deep arroyos presented obstructions to their travels at the time, even though the arroyo channels would have been presumably less incised than they are today. The causes of arroyo formation are certainly not settled (Turner et al. 2003:32-34, 261), but these data suggest that it is inappropriate to date the inauguration of arroyo cutting to the period from 1875 to 1895, as Turner and others (2003:261) do. Rather, Rocha's repeated remarks on the broken nature of the terrain, how it made travel difficult, and how the channel was deep—potentially meaning entrenched—all suggest that these arroyos were present in the 1780s and that the main channel was incised at this time. This would also suggest that some of the side arroyos, washes, and channels were already present and of fairly consequential depth along this portion of the Middle San Pedro. Specifically, terrace travel in this area is especially difficult today owing to a series of side drainages and, in particular, one deeply incised arroyo. Rocha's dotted-line trail substantially diverges from the river at about 2.25 miles north of Santa Cruz de Terrenate Presidio, where there is an arroyo many meters deep, which would have obstructed travel in this area even if it were much shallower (Figure 6.1).[1]

Archaeological data may also reinforce this evidence of arroyo cutting in the recent historical past. A large circular historic cairn is present upstream on this most deeply embedded tributary wash segment. This cairn marks the location where a bedrock shelf has limited the depth and occurrence of erosion upstream, providing resistance for down-cutting further west. The flat area to the west can be easily crossed by foot, horse, or wagon, suggesting that this was an important point along the trail where travel diverged from the riverside to avoid obstruction. The presence of this historic cairn, of unknown age but clearly weathered, in this location suggests that this feature marked the route around these impediments as the trail diverged from the river (Figures 6.2a and b). Smaller cairns, perhaps trail markers, are situated further north as well at the approximate location where the trail would have rejoined the river margin, near one of the ciénegas, at the Quiburi

a

b

FIGURE 6.2. A historic cairn, (*a*) present at the point at which the bedrock impedes further upstream erosion and therefore would allow passage to the west. (*b*) A deeply cut arroyo stops abruptly at this cairn owing to a much harder buried sandstone shelf which has stopped further erosion to the west.

vado, and near the late (1780s) Sobaipuri village site of Quiburi.

This specific reroute and other information in the journal provide substantial insights into the character of the landscape these men encountered, the stage of the river's cyclical changes, and also important aspect of environmental conditions and change. The conventional wisdom is that channel entrenchment did not begin for another hundred or more years, not until the 1870s (Bryan 1925, 1940; Turner et al. 2003:34, 261). While Waters and Haynes (2001) are careful to state that the San Pedro and other major rivers have down-cut and backfilled at least five times, recent notions are that the current cycle began in the mid-1800s: "Dramatic changes in channel geometry during the last 150 years" have been documented for the San Pedro, such that "prior to the mid-1800s, the San Pedro River flowed over an unincised surface and had a larger area prone to flooding" (Huckleberry et al. 2009:259–260; also see Turner et al. 2003). Hereford and Betancourt (2009:233) suggest that in the 1850s the channel became entrenched at Saint David, Tres Alamos, and below the Redington Narrows, with perpendicular banks three to six meters deep. Webb and others (2014:68; also see Turner et al. 2003:xiii) similarly attribute arroyo cutting and other drastic changes in the natural landscape to the 1880s. Yet, Rocha's journal suggests that at a minimum we should carefully re-evaluate the timing and episodic recurrence of arroyo cutting and channel entrenchment and the role which humans played in initiating an earlier historic cycle. Rochas's observations indicate that the San Pedro River as a whole did not flow over an unincised surface in the 1780s, but that owing to localized conditions, some areas were in fact marshy and unincised. Rocha seemingly commented on down-cutting and channel entrenchment with reference to the San Pedro River Valley. This seems especially apparent when compared to conditions for the Gila, which he described as having a shallow floodplain where flood waters spread widely—that is, over an unincised surface. Thus, with Rocha's diary we now have what can be interpreted as evidence of entrenchment and arroyo cutting as early as 1780, probably initiated in early 1775 with the settlement of the garrison at Santa Cruz, or even earlier (beginning in 1742) by activity related to Terrenate Viejo and Las Nutrias which may have begun the current cycle much further upstream at the headwaters. Unresolved is how far along the river these impacts spread; it is not known if they were localized with short-term consequences or whether they initiated, or were the consequence of, river-wide or watershed-wide changes.

Plainly, these historical data lack systematic depth and width measurements. They suffer from lack of clarity as to whether arroyos were active channels or were formed by much earlier erosional episodes.[2] Like all historical data derived from narrative texts, Ugarte and Rocha's comments suffer from the shortcomings inherent in such limited observations. Nonetheless, this anecdotal evidence is on par with other later historical records that are frequently used to assess the timing and character of stream entrenchment and arroyo formation. These sources from 1780 provide an opportunity for another look deeper in time at the role of human agents in relation to natural erosion cycles characteristic of streams with intermittent surface flow like the San Pedro. If, as is argued later, the process of "overgrazing, trampling of springs and marshes by cattle, eradication of beavers, draining of marshes through ditch diversions, and fuel harvesting in the 1870s and 1880s . . . preconditioned the watershed to arroyo cutting in the 1890s" (Herford and Betancourt 2009:241), then many of these same processes operational in the 1770s likely contributed to erosion, entrenchment, and arroyo cutting visible in the 1780s. We suggest that assessments of historical sources have focused too late in time and so, because of a lack of earlier historical sources, have assumed a lack of similar human impacts and resulting environmental processes earlier in time. We will return to this issue below.

Rocha also commented on how the areas surrounding Santa Cruz Presidio were devoid of grass and trees for many leagues [Diary, June 5, June 7]. Presumably the barrenness of pasture

a

b

FIGURE 6.3. Monkey Spring as shown from the same approximate location in (*a*) 1889; Photograph courtesy of USGS SW Repeat Photography Collection, George J. Roskruge collection, Stake number 157, 1889; and (*b*) 1962; Photograph courtesy of USGS SW Repeat Photography Collection, J.R. Hastings, Stake number 157, 1962.

relates in part to the grazing livestock associated with the Santa Cruz Presidio occupation, as well as the burning of fields and pasture by the Apache as acts of war. Since the presidio had just been abandoned in March, the landscape would not have had time to regenerate and devastation would have been at its worst, having been exacerbated by the excessive drought.

Rocha's journal also seemingly provides insights into the character of climax vegetation, as well as vegetation and groundcover reduction earlier than we have had evidence for previously. Many modern environmental scientists are under the impression that the regional landscape was once grasslands (e.g., Cox and Thacker 1996: 306; Stromberg and Tellman 2009:423; Turner et al. 2003), which only in late historic times was invaded by mesquite and other brush and trees. While these landscapes are currently managed with this notion in mind, especially to enhance grazing values, there is considerable textual evidence to suggest that when Ugarte and Rocha passed through the area much of the terrain was covered with brush and trees rather than grasslands, and the floodplains were not dominated by sedges and grasses except in specific areas. For example, Rocha mentioned that the mesas around Fronteras Presidio were covered with thick forest of mesquite (Diary, April 20). His journal also indicated that substantial environmental degradation had already occurred by 1780. Rocha stated that around Santa Cruz there was no wood and no grass (Diary, June 5) in areas where they were previously abundant. His words seem to be evidence for reduction of perhaps already sparse pasture near the presidio as a consequence of overgrazing and subsequent erosion. He also reports what amounts to clear-cutting of timber and firewood. This substantial overuse of the landscape resulted from both cultural conceptions of the role of the natural environment as consumable and endlessly abundant resources, as well as the considerable stress and restriction of movement caused by Apache pressure on the inhabitants of Santa Cruz de Terrenate Presidio. People were afraid to tend to their fields, grazing horse herds were stolen, and pack trains that supplied the presidio were attacked (Thomas 1941:204–205). Moreover, crops and houses were burned (Thomas 1941:153), suggesting that some areas immediately around the presidio were a charred and denuded landscape, which would have encouraged erosional processes under the right rainfall regime. This kind of intense pressure would, no doubt, tend to focus activity as close to the presidio as possible, resulting in excessive overuse and, in turn, substantial point-focused environmental degradation.

Rocha's journal provides evidence for overuse and destruction of the environment around Santa Cruz de Terrenate in the late 1770s as a result of this special type of siege, where resources became unavailable in the vicinity of the presidio. Yet the documentary record suggests that this terrain, the terraces in particular, was cloaked with spiny and brushy vegetation even earlier. The vast, waist- or chest-high grasslands illustrated in Hastings and Turner (1965) seem in many instances to be a consequence of a stressed and overused landscape along this river or one stage in a cycle of change, not the native climax community for this area. Severe overuse of these terraces and valley bottoms, through timber and firewood harvesting, overgrazing, and trail impacts quickly leads to barren and trodden landscapes, where grass may be the first species to become re-established. The absence of vegetation and the moonscape-like settings seemingly resulted, in part, not from original or normal desert conditions, but from abuse and overexploitation. This likely accounts for the condition of the terrain surrounding Monkey Spring along Sonoita Creek, shown in a historical photograph from 1889 (Figure 6.3; also see Hastings and Turner 1965:68–75; Turner et al. 2003:54–59).

In all likelihood, Marcos de Niza and Francisco Vázquez de Coronado traveled up the San Pedro River Valley (Seymour 2009a, 2011a). When Pedro de Casteñada de Nájera of the 1540 Coronado expedition commented on the boundary formed just after Chichilticali "where the spiny forest disappears" (Flint and Flint 2005:417), he was probably referencing the thick cat claw, whitethorn acacia, and thorn-ridden mesquite that drapes the rocky terraces of this river valley and adjacent bajadas. Nowhere has the senior author surveyed in the American Southwest where the vegetation is so brutal and thorny as along the San Pedro and some of the rocky bajadas sloping up to the foothills. Documentary sources, including these cited, provide evidence that this has likely been the norm for this valley for quite some time (also see Segesser in Truetlein 1945:183). The rocky nature and shallow soils of the river terraces (as on the bajadas and in the foothills) are suitable habitats for this type of thick spiny vegetation, as can be seen in other river valleys.

Rocha is clear that 1780 was a drought year across the region. He states that several settlements were experiencing water shortages. The few residents of Tubac were suffering because all the water had already been diverted by irrigation and settlements upstream (Diary, May 13, May 16). The pueblo of Atí lacked water, and its residents had to go upstream to Santa Teresa to obtain it (Diary, June 22). Farming at Tubutáma was causing water shortages at Santa Teresa as well (Diary, June 20). The presidio of Santa Gertrudis del Altar had no water for crops, only to drink, and so the gardens had dried up (Diary, June 24–29). At another place Rocha notes that with economy the spring could provide something to drink for a drove of horses (Diary, June 14).

From a reconstruction of the Southwestern Drought Index (Cook 2000) it is possible to see that this region fell within a below-average rainfall regime around the time of this reconnaissance and during the occupation of Santa Cruz Presidio. In particular, the period between 1773 and early 1782 was a period of pronounced and prolonged dryness, which likely contributed to the hardship experience by the residents visited at Tubac, Atí, Santa Cruz Presidio, and elsewhere. Droughts are cyclical in this region, but no less stressful on area residents when the rivers did not flow and the springs dried up. During the 1761 drought Padre Manuel de Aguirre at San Xavier del Bac wrote to the civil authorities stating that there was "plenty of land for everyone, but not enough water to sustain the existing Spanish and Indian population" (Meyer 1984:55–56). While this is said to be the first recorded incidence of insufficient surface flow to satisfy the needs of settlers (Logan 2002: 50), it is likely one of many reoccurring sets of low-flow periods throughout the centuries. Indigenous peoples adapted to this fluctuation through a variety of means, and this is probably one of the primary reasons for the shifting of Sobaipuri O'odham settlements along river segments and for the intermittent depopulation of places, including mission sites, that were soon reinhabited as conditions improved.[3] In fact, this is probably why Guevavi was found abandoned when Rocha passed through, but archaeological evidence and chronometric dates indicate that it was soon repopulated.

Rocha's descriptions, and the inferences we draw from them, are in direct contrast to statements about the specific terrain prior to the construction of Santa Cruz de Terrenate Presidio. In 1775, when O'Conor inspected the area for the proposed presidio, he certified that it had abundant pastures, waters, and woods (Thomas 1941: 181). This assessment provides a comparative basis with which to evaluate Rocha's descriptions. The overgrazing and overuse described by Rocha (within less than three months of the garrison moving south from this location in 1780 and less than five years of O'Conor's statement) is of the type and scale usually attributed to the later Territorial period, and is often cited as the cause of channelization and arroyo cutting. Intensive use of these rivers can result in such degradation and probably has done so off-and-on for centuries, but the river has stabilized each time, establishing a new equilibrium until the next series of events, being able to repair itself because the water table remained sufficiently close to the surface that vegetation could take hold once again. As it healed itself it took on new forms, cutting arroyos in one area, while depositing sediment in another. A reason for one of these cyclical periods of recovery on the San Pedro may be the forced depopulation of the area owing to enemy (Apache) hostilities, which may have provided time for the river to stabilize. The San Pedro habitat experienced a gradual lessening of impacts following the movement of the Santa Cruz garrison south to Las Nutrias in 1780 and then again to Santa María on the modern Santa Cruz River in 1787. These moves may have allowed the watershed to heal itself to a new balance. No doubt considerable environmental devastation took place in the nineteenth century, some of which continues to degrade the terrain today; the river valley has not fully recovered, or more accurately, the river has not returned to its pre-European or even it prehistoric state. Degradation during the nineteenth century is thought to have occurred on a much more widespread basis than in the Colonial period and had watershed-wide, rather than just local, and long-term effects. Some of the descriptions provided by Ugarte and Rocha, however, bring this inference into question and suggest that similar processes occurred much earlier, but perhaps not at such an industrial level.

The San Pedro River is one area where the impacts of historical populations and resource extraction have been extensively examined. The environmental history of this river has been written about numerous times. In addition to a variety of other topics, a number of authors discuss the substantial woodcutting for fuel related to mining and charcoal production that occurred in the San Pedro River Valley in the late nineteenth century (Bahre 1991; Bahre and Hutchinson 1991; Noonan 2011; Studnicki-Gizbert and Schecter 2010; Tellman and Hadley 2006). During the 1880s, as nearby Tombstone was at its height, woodcutting depleted forest stands within a 60 km (thirty-seven mile) radius of the mines (Nabhan 1985:65). Nearby settlements of Contention City and Charleston also contributed to this deforestation. Wood was taken from the mesquite bosques and mixed species stands along the San Pedro and the Babocomari Rivers, from the evergreen forests found in the Huachuca and Whetstone Mountains to the west, and the Dragoon, Burro, and Chiricahua Mountains to the east and south. As Noonan (2011:3) notes:

> There are no authoritative studies about the impact on the San Pedro River of wood removal from the San Pedro River Valley and nearby hills and mountains. However, it is logical to conclude that the extensive timber cutting increased runoff into it during floods. The extensive harvesting of mesquite, including the digging up of its roots, may have made the ground more susceptible to erosion. The removal of woody plants from the San Pedro River Valley and adjacent hills and mountains is one of a complex set of natural and anthropogenic factors that influenced arroyo formation along the river.

Noonan (2011:3) stated that while woodcutting occurred locally on the floodplains, the extent of this cutting and its impact on the riparian zone is unknown. He cited Turner and others (2003), who concluded that riparian species, especially cottonwood, were largely avoided for fuelwood because they did not burn as hot as did other available woods. Yet Rocha references the depletion of wood near Santa Cruz de Terrenate, in a zone assessed earlier as having plenty of it. Moreover, since some places are called "Cottonwood" (*Alamo* and *Los Alamos*) and "Three Cottonwoods" (*Tres Alamos*), it may be that these trees and others were mostly depleted in all but a few locations, seemingly at persistent marshes, which made these exceptions standout and therefore worthy of these names. This seems apparent when on May 9 Rocha notes: "we encountered the Ojo de los Alamos Largos ["Spring of the Tall Cottonwood Trees"], quite plentiful flow in open terrain, and with many pastures but not much timber or firewood, though some quite distant cottonwoods."

Even though the eighteenth-century devastation around Santa Cruz de Terrenate in the Colonial period was relatively local, it did have more widespread effects. Wood cutting may have been restricted to a smaller radius around Santa Cruz de Terrenate than it was in the later historic period (although Rocha reports of little firewood and timber all along the river, including in areas without marshes that had surface flow), but the locations of Terrenate Viejo and Las Nutrias were probably even more intensively used because they were occupied for longer periods. They were also at the headwaters, affecting stream flow and channel cutting in areas downstream. Livestock grazing would have also impacted riparian areas and the ability of trees to regenerate, especially cottonwoods and willows, whose seedlings would have been especially susceptible. Rocha states with reference to Santa Cruz de Terrenate Presidio: "It lacks firewood within four leagues [sixteen miles] of distance" (Diary, June 5).[4] As Rocha indicates, this was one reason a presidio was not again placed along this or the northern portion of the San Pedro in 1780 when this relocation was considered. He states with reference to the lower San Pedro and portions of the middle San Pedro (between the Gila River and Santa Cruz Presidio) that the valley was "completely lacking firewood." The captain of Fronteras Presidio, Don Francisco Tagle y Bustamante, reiterated this opinion when, according to Croix, he stated: "the valley of the Pimas Sobaipuris [e.g., San Pedro Valley] is fertile in lands, waters, and pastures, but scarce in wood" (Thomas 1941:203).

Debate continues as to whether historically the San Pedro floodplains were essentially devoid of trees, either entirely or just along certain segments (Hastings and Turner 1965 and Turner et al. 2003). Turner and colleagues (2003:xiii, 25,261) suggest that the marshy and largely unchanneled valley habitat would have suppressed tree growth. Such conditions, however, would not have been useful for agriculture either, and it is known that key stretches of the San Pedro were cultivated for centuries, including by the Sobaipuri, who were full-time irrigation farmers. Irrigation canals and fields downstream from the Santa Cruz Narrows (Seymour 2003, 2011a) and the absence of signs of saturated sediments are evidence that these areas were farmed and were not marshy. Moreover, when Santa Cruz de Terrenate Presidio's location was sited, Croix's basic selection criteria were adequate crop land, water, wood, and pasture (Moorhead 1975:226), and the presidio was said to have been placed where there were "abundant pastures, waters, and woods" (Thomas 1941:181). O'Conor's (1775) inspection certified that Santa Cruz was not only defensable but had sufficient firewood as of August 1775. Yet, in 1780 there were no trees, no pasture for miles, no firewood except in the adjacent mountains many miles away, and seemingly considerable arroyo cutting and channel entrenchment. Rocha comments that while the valley was very spacious, "it has the defect of being a very deep channel [*caja*]," which has relevance to the issue of the San Pedro's channel entrenchment. Of the Gila River he said that the channel [*caja*] of its current was so shallow that the waters would spread during a downpour (Rocha's Summary Report, Chapter 3). This wording and comparison between the San Pedro and Gila suggest that the box Rocha is referencing is the channel, rather than a box canyon, as we perceive the term's use today, because on the whole the San Pedro River is not a box canyon, but rather has a fairly wide old floodplain situated between the terrace margins. Rocha's description of the Gila indicates that the river channel was not entrenched (as it seemed to have been on the San Pedro), allowing the waters to spread across the floodplain, despite the course of the river in a canyon.

In this context it is useful to examine Rocha's use of the term *caja*, since it is so central to this interpretation. His summary report and journal mention the terms *barranca*, *cajón*, *caja*, *arroyo*, and *río*, among others, from which it is reasonable to assume he is deliberately referencing different geographic characteristics, some of which may vary from our understanding and word usage today. *Caja* is one of these terms that had different meanings, but as a geological term can be translated as "river channel," consistent with its use in New Mexico and Colorado (Cobos 2003:37; Long 1991:C-1). It is also likely that only certain types of river channels, those with a box-like character, were meant by such usage. This interpretation is also reinforced by the definition of the term *caja* in a geographical dictionary as channel or canal box (Madoz 1847: 26–27). This usage seems consistent with Rocha's use of the term for *caja* as "channel," especially when the sides were vertical, steep, or rocky. On the Gila River Rocha uses the term *cajón*. This is consistent with modern-day observations of steep-sided canyons upstream to the east of the confluence, and also with Rocha's comment that the mountains came right down to the river. Here he aptly mentions that "the channel [*caja*] of its [the Gila's] current" is in a *cajón* (compare Diary, June 1 to Summary Report).

Rocha uses *barranca* to describe Sonoita Creek, where there are rocky steep slopes in some areas, many of which are vertical. While *barranca*, or "ravine," is not appropriate as a description based on current use of these terms, the area Rocha refers to (where the Sobaipuri O'odham village of Sonoita was located) fits to a considerable degree with his observations, and so this equation can be made, providing a baseline for his perceptions of landscape features.

In the area of the San Pedro where Rocha used the term *caja*, there are no extensive box canyons, which is the modern translation of the term. With reference to the upper San Pedro (a stretch from just south of Sierra Vista to the mouth) Rocha states, as just cited above: "(although as I have recounted, it is in a spacious valley). It has the defect of being a very deep channel [*caja*]" (Diary, June 7). This area is not characterized today (nor was it then) as a box canyon, but this area's attributes are consistent with *caja* translated as "channel," or a box-shaped or entrenched channel. And when Rocha is referencing the San Pedro as a whole he uses *caja* to reference the channel, saying: "During this entire journey along the channel [*caja*] of the San Pedro River we did not find water. In the place we slept we made small wells and the men could drink" (Diary, June 2). For these reasons it seems apparent that Rocha was describing the channel characterized as a box, as in a canal or channel box, or perhaps what we refer to today as an arroyo.

With all this in mind, there are three options for Rocha's use of *caja* in his reference to the channel of the San Pedro River: (1) he is simply using a generic term for river channel, (2) he is referencing the terraces that run along and parallel the river margin, that contain the river flow in many areas of the valley, boxing in the river and its floodplain, or (3) the channel of the river forms a box because it is entrenched, which we have argued herein when discussing arroyo cutting. The second suggestion is not likely, given that the terraces that border the river were viewed for centuries as a positive defensive attribute for settlement, not a defect, including by O'Conor when siting Santa Cruz de Terrenate Presidio. That the river may have formed a box-shaped channel this early may attest to the rapidity with which channel entrenchment can occur under intense land-use pressure, or perhaps this description simply relates a stage of the river's natural cyclical development. These interpretations are important for our considerations of the historical character of the San Pedro and the timing of changes in its entrenchment and characteristic of overflowing its banks. Geological studies should be able to address these issues directly, providing independent data with which to evaluate these inferences. At a minimum, tributary washes seem to have incised the terrain by this point, which is viewed as a step in the process in watershed change by some, degradation by others.[5]

It is likely that one of the reasons Sobaipuri settlements moved up and down specific segments of the river was periodic depletion of fuel wood and building materials; other reasons, such as adapting to low-flow periods and allowing fields to fallow, should not be discounted. Although we are not arguing that indigenous land use practices were always perfectly in tune with the environment (e.g., Denevan 1992; Whitmore and Turner 2001), it does seem that they had mechanisms to counteract extreme overuse of resources in these river valleys so that resources and channels would recover within a reasonable period. One cultural response was settlement shifting up and down the river margin, as noted. Importantly, this is not the type of movement discussed by Hastings and Turner (1980:26), who present these Sobaipuri O'odham residents as transitory. Rather, their settlements were permanent and movements were on the order of a decade or two or even a generation, and they shifted along specific river segments where their improvements—canals, dams, and fields—could be maintained (Seymour 2011a). It is important to convey an accurate characterization of populations who inhabited these rivers if we want to understand specific and long-term impacts.

It is important too that indigenous population levels were so low by the time Santa Cruz de Terrenate Presidio was established in December 1775 that the Spanish probably did not notice an appreciable degradation. In point of fact, during his inspection of the frontier in 1766, Nicolás de Lafora noted with regard to the upper portion of the valley: "there is a great deal of farmland and plenty of water... This valley is very suitable for settlement" (Kinnaird 1967:106, 107; Thomas 1941:204). Lafora's and O'Conor's statements cited above are both in direct contrast to Rocha's comments a few years later, demonstrating the rapid rate of degradation and excessive resource use. Mostly likely, as well, Rocha was making specific efforts to counter Lafora's and O'Conor's assessment of the viability of settlement in the area since Santa Cruz de Terrenate Presidio had already failed. There is little doubt that he heard of the horrors and scarcities of life at Santa Cruz, terminated just months before, and that he saw with his own eyes the poverty and vulnerability of the post when he moved the garrison from there back to Las Nutrias (Rocha 1870c). Still, different observers have dissimilar impressions and so it is possible that conditions were not as dire as conveyed, though both Ugarte and Rocha express similar impressions.[6] It is probably relevant to their perspectives and interpretation as well that, as compared to modern Sonora, southern Arizona is arid and lacks the rich riparian stands characteristic further south.

The coincidence of intensive land use (overgrazing and excessive wood use) in stationary population centers (such as Santa Cruz de Terrenate, Terrenate Viejo, and Las Nutrias) with a period of extreme drought may have initiated a cycle of erosion, including the topsoil loss and stream and tributary entrenchment that is recorded in these documents.[7] During these prolonged periods of lower-than-average precipitation, stream flow levels diminish while water tables may drop. At the same time vegetation is reduced as a result of this drier landscape, which means the soil is more susceptible to erosion. High river flows may have a much greater impact on channels under such conditions, causing changes in channel morphology, such as down-cutting and lateral erosion (Graybill et al. 2004:9, 210). It is possible that the concurrence of intensive land use by the soldiers and their livestock at a time of severe drought was an important historical event that initiated the sequence of river channel changes that we see today and that were reported for the late 1800s.

If nothing else, these documents from 1780 convey that if we want to understand historical changes in environment along these rivers, we must look deeper in time. We'll need to consider the earliest intensive European use to determine when potentially unsustainable practices were initiated, if not even earlier to investigate indigenous forms of land use and misuse. The eras preceding the Territorial period were not ones of benign use and the San Pedro was not a pristine environment before Territorial period events. An adjusted perspective is likely when analyses are solidly grounded in accurate environmental and land use history, to which this diary is a contribution. Current notions about the timing of the initiation of arroyo cutting and channel entrenchment on the San Pedro (in the 1890s) suggest rapid channeling which then declined substantially after 1955, when the channel largely stabilized (Herford and Betancourt 2009:248–250). Yet, if arroyo cutting and channel incision were actually initiated much earlier on the San Pedro (and scholars admit that the timing of arroyo initiation is uncertain, see Herford and Betancourt 2009:249), then rates of entrenchment may be much slower over a longer period of time, which in turn could influence interpretations of modern data and management strategies.

Interrupted Flow

A characteristic of the north-flowing Santa Cruz and San Pedro Rivers is that seasonally the flow along various portions of these rivers goes underground to emerge again further north where it is pushed to the surface by bedrock, faults, or at

FIGURE 6.4. Historic image of Guevavi Mission, by Geo. Roskruge, July 15, 1889; Photograph Courtesy of Arizona History Museum, #15823.

springs. These perennial reaches occur at several points along the San Pedro and other rivers and represent places where there is an intersection of groundwater with the ground surface (Webb et al. 2014). These perennial reaches occur at several points along the San Pedro and other rivers, such as Sonoita Creek and the Babocomari River. In many places Rocha's journal mentions water going underground and re-emerging. Rocha uses the words *brotar* and *vuelven a reventar,* indicating that the water would bud, burst, and spring forth. Rocha was describing and illustrating which reaches of these episodic streams had perennial surface flow as compared to those that did not. Importantly, these descriptions indicate that surface flow was interrupted along certain segments or reaches of the San Pedro as early as 1780, and that this has been a longstanding characteristic of the river.

Rocha comments that this interrupted flow also occurred on the Santa Cruz River, for example at Guevavi, where a short length "cuts off shortly before arriving at Guevavi, where water springs again to burgeon out with more strength" (Diary, June 13). Guevavi was initially a Sobaipuri O'odham settlement that Father Kino, often with his military escort, visited many times in the 1690s and early 1700s. Several of the Sobaipuri O'odham villages and the later mission church are visible today along the east margin of the Santa Cruz River just northeast of Nogales, Arizona (Figure 6.4). Here irrigation canals are visible, along with field plots, many of which are still in use today. A portion of these systems represents one of four known and recorded canal systems used by the indigenous Sobaipuri O'odham (Seymour 1990, 1993, 2011a). One reason the canal headgates are situated where they are at Guevavi and why Rocha noticed that the water "burst out" here is that the channel to the south (upstream) is sandy, but at Guevavi a bedrock outcrop pinches the river channel (Figure 6.5). Rock, rather than deep sand, underlies the river channel in this location, accounting for the O'odham name for this location, which means Big Cliff or Big Bedrock (see the endnote in Chapter 5). When the underground flow encounters this bedrock it is forced to the surface,

Figure 6.5. Bedrock where canals originated at the Sobaipuri O'odham settlement and mission of Guevavi.

re-emerging for use even during the dry season, although 1780 was an especially dry year and settlers upstream had siphoned off too much of the flow so there was no water apparent and no villagers. Of course, during the wet season the entire river would have flowed, often in violent flash floods that scoured the river channel and sometimes breached the low banks, spreading wide across the floodplain.

Rocha noted this phenomenon of submersion and reappearance on his map, demarcating the intermittent characteristic of river flow (including of the San Pedro specifically). Inspection of many of the river courses on his original map shows a narrow strip to indicate a stylized outline for each river. This strip is variably shaded dark (green) in areas where the flow was visible. The dark (green) shading is clearly demarcated and cuts off with a definite line, changing to lighter (tan) shading where river flow disappeared (shown here in black and white; Figure 6.6).[8] Comparison of this map to his journal content, and also to modern-day river channel and stream flow characteristics, indicate that these represent accurate markers of where even today the water emerges, where it goes underground, and where it re-emerges. The journal and map indicate continuity through time in these river flow characteristics. Other rivers without good flow, such as the lower Santa Cruz, are demarcated only with a line and dots, to indicate the course of the dry wash.

In fact, careful examination of Urrutia's 1769 map illustrates this phenomenon as well (see Figures 1.12 and 1.13). He drew the trajectory of both the Santa Cruz and San Pedro Rivers for a distance north, downstream, using dotted lines, only to terminate them before reaching the Gila River. This is a representation of the termination of surface flow for a sufficient distance that he felt confident in his representation for the reminder of their courses.

The inference drawn from Rocha's diary and his map (as well as Urrutia's map), that there were alternating stretches with and without flow, is in direct contrast to modern notions, such as: "Historical records suggest that water flow in the Upper San Pedro River was formerly perennial" (Noonan 2012:10). This seems a reiteration of an earlier statement:

> The historical record suggests that in the mid-nineteenth century the San Pedro was a continuously perennial stream from its source near Cananea to just beyond the Narrows [Tres Alamos Narrows].[9] Flow was interrupted (spatially intermittent) in the lower reaches, with dry discontinuities outdistancing limited surface flow from groundwater outcroppings (Hereford and Betancourt 2009:249).

Other sources also suggest that at one time the flow of the San Pedro was permanent (e.g., Barnes 1982:150; but see Dobyns 1981:60). The intermittent nature of surface flow now seen is attributed to the most recent cycle of arroyo cutting and channel entrenchment. This assumption also forms the basis for assuming that the length of the San Pedro was mostly treeless due to saturated soils. Yet Rocha's map and journal indicate that wet and dry stretches and an inconsistent flow were intrinsic characteristics of this river (and others in this region), and that these characteristics have considerable time depth.

Rocha's notes and map indicate that surface flow was intermittent quite far south, or upstream. His map shows an interruption of flow along a segment of the upper San Pedro between La Tienda and Los Alamos (parallel to the southern end of the Huachucas between Sierra Vista and Palominas) and then again beginning just north of Quiburi Vado (then in the general Saint David area) and north. Rocha's diary from June 7 states: "The San Pedro River runs through a spacious valley (without being cut off, except for the part between Los Alamos and La Tienda Fords until passing that of Santa Cruz) and from Las Tarabillas Ford the terrain becomes very broken." This statement reiterates the information provided by the map.

As will be discussed in greater detail in the next chapter, this river flow characteristic also explains the distribution of Sobaipuri O'odham settlements, indicating that this attribute of flowing and then going underground exemplified

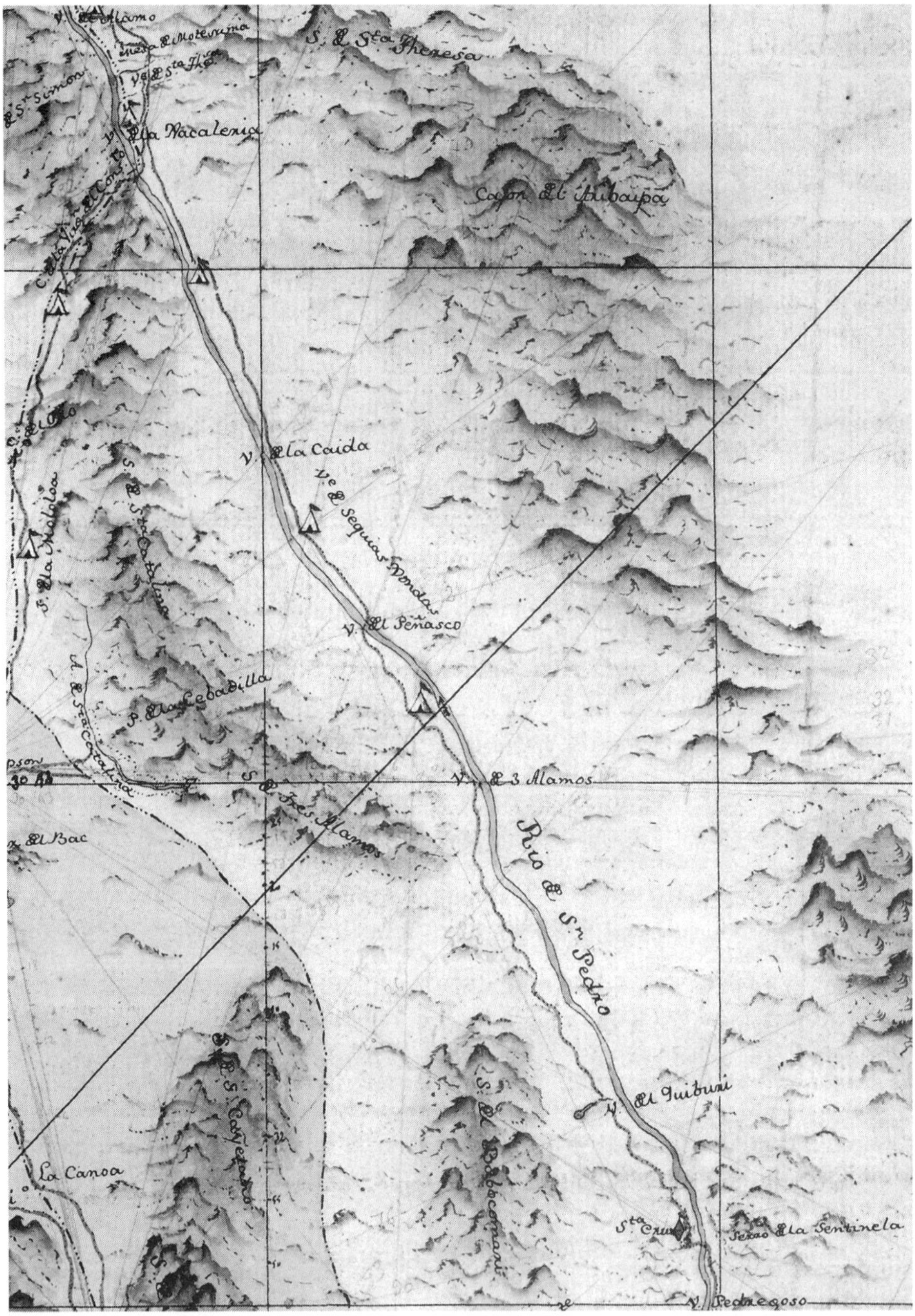

FIGURE 6.6. Close-up of Rocha's map showing banding on river to show surface flow and areas where the river submerges. (Dark areas are green on original map, while light bands are tan.) From *Mapa de la Frontera de Sonora para el establecimiento de la linea de presidios.* Courtesy of the British Library; Shelfmark: Cartographic Items Additional MS. 17,661.a.

this river at least as early as the early 1300s CE (Seymour 2011a, 2011d). Croix's pre-trip instructions also clarified, with specific reference to the San Pedro, that Ugarte and Rocha were to continue their march to the place where the San Pedro River starts to flow without interruption, or where it flows continuously. This statement itself acknowledges awareness that the surface flow of the San Pedro was intermittent at least along certain of its segments.

It is of interest that the modern-day Santa Cruz River is mostly shown by Rocha as a dotted line, indicating that this was considered intermittent, without a reliable flow. A ribbon representing the stream course is shown all the way to Tubac, and thereafter (to the north) the course is shown as a dotted line. The change in representation likely relates to his journal entries (Diary, May 13 and May 16), which indicate that people residing at Tubac were having difficulty getting enough water during this dry period owing to the water being diverted by farmers upstream. Typically, the point at which the Santa Cruz River flow sank underground was a bit farther north, somewhere between Agua Linda and Canoa. The Santa Cruz River comes alive on the surface again just south of San Xavier del Bac, or Wa:k, as it is known by its O'odham residents. As was noted in the preceding chapter, *Wa:k* references the place where the water re-enters the ground after having flowed on the surface for a few miles. This name confirms the intermittent surface flow of this river since prehistoric times. This name is one of the most misinterpreted in the area, with dozens of incorrect translations. Interestingly, in our Western way of thinking and from a downstream perspective, we would say this is where the water emerges, but the O'odham look upstream and note that just north (downstream) of their settlement is where the water disappears. It is two to three miles to the south, upstream, where the water emerges (see below).

The *Hikdan* or "channel that cuts the earth" is how these indigenous residents refer to the Santa Cruz River that once flowed abundantly (Austin Nunez personal communication, 2012). Yet the river flowed abundantly only intermittently and only along certain segments of the channel. These reliable segments are where the Sobaipuri O'odham, and the prehistoric populations before them, placed their settlements and fields fed by extensive irrigation canals. On May 22 Rocha rode a league or 2.6 miles south-southeast to investigate the source of the water that formed the ciénega at San Xavier. This zone around San Xavier was one of the most reliable sources of water along the Santa Cruz. This is the first known historical mention of the marsh and its thick mesquite bosque upstream from the narrows at Martinez Hill, a full twenty-four years before the previously cited example thought to be the earliest reference (e.g., Webb et al. 2014:38, 42). The character of the channel indicates that this was a long-present feature of the river channel because of the bedrock constriction provided by volcanic hills in the area. As noted, and as will be discussed in greater detail in the next chapter, Sobaipuri O'odham settlement placement along the Santa Cruz and San Pedro Rivers were always keyed to these river attributes. The reliability of the surface flow here and the lushness of the riparian setting also explain the size of the San Xavier, or Wa:k, settlement, the largest and most important in the region during the mission period, although, contrary to common understandings (e.g., Webb et al. 2014:36), Wa:k was not the only Sobaipuri O'odham settlement along this river, nor was it the first as one travels north or downstream (Seymour 2012f).

The water came back to the surface reliably at Wa:k but only after flowing underground for twenty-three miles (beginning its descent south of Canoa). Thus, the water goes back into the ground between Canoa and Wa:k. Being dry along this more than twenty mile segment was not a measure of the river's health, but simply an attribute of its character. This explains why there were no Sobaipuri-O'odham settlements noted historically in this expanse (see Chapter 7).

The bedrock constrictions that force water to the surface for human use also create ciénegas in many other places, including in the Benson-Tres Alamos and Río Rico areas. One reason for the placement of the Wa:k village where it was

a

b

FIGURE 6.7. The area that used to be a marsh south/upstream from San Xavier del Bac (*a*) as seen from Martinez Hill in 1942. Image notes state: "This mesquite forest near Tucson, Arizona, is one of the oldest stands for nesting and roosting of the white wing in the U.S." Photograph courtesy of USGS SW Repeat Photography Collection, Arizona Game and Fish Department, Stake number 937, 1942; (*b*) as seen from Martinez Hill in 1978. Photograph courtesy of USGS SW Repeat Photography Collection, R.M. Turner, Stake number 937, 1978.

(north of the present location) is that south or upstream from there was an extensive marsh referred to as Agua de Misión. At Wa:k, the water emerged to create an expansive and life-giving ciénega east of the community, just south of Martinez Hill (Figures 6.7a and b). This marsh is mentioned by Rocha (Diary, May 22) as being a place with reliable water and verdant pasture for livestock grazing, including presidio horses. Yet the standing water also made the air and water unhealthy and so Sobaipuri settlements were placed a bit downstream, where the water began to flow more freely, that is, downstream from the constrictions or narrows. Because of this wet spot on the river and the band of riparian vegetation formerly between there and north of Tucson, this was a valued residential area where crops could be reliably grown in abundance. Even in dry years, such as 1780, this ciénega was reliable. And because of its maturity, the ciénega and its vegetation, including the trees surrounding it, would absorb much of the high flow of the river, shielding the community from devastating floods and protecting the floodplain from erosive incision (Dobyns 1981:61). The waters would flow more broadly, taking in expanses on either side of the now deeply entrenched channel, and infiltrating into and replenishing the water table. Today the Wa:k community uses Central Arizona Project (CAP) allocations to recharge the aquifer and the water crops and to invest in the repair of the riparian zone that was once the ciénega. Consequently, just as past residents of Tucson pumped water from the aquifer to supply the city and their farms, now the Wa:k O'odham pump water back into the ground to have a reliable water source for the farm at Wa:k during CAP maintenance outages. They also hope to revive the riparian habitat, perhaps eventually recreating the ciénega and decreasing the severe erosion. As the mesquite bosque begins to thicken and the cottonwood and willow gallery takes hold, the Wa:k O'odham have begun to rejuvenate the river that is so interconnected with their unique heritage.

Notes

1. As of the 1870s this arroyo was clearly not as deep and wide as it is today. Such depth and width are cumulative and increase exponentially through time as large chunks of the arroyo walls are undercut and collapse in. A corral and associated features and fire pits are present adjacent to this arroyo and are currently collapsing into the arroyo. The presence of this archaeological site indicates that this arroyo was less substantial at that time.
2. Interestingly, historic width and depth measurements obtained from cadastral surveys between 1873 and 1933 lack information on this critical segment between Fairbank and the area around Curtis Flats (see Herford and Betancourt 2009:Figure 12.1).
3. Consequently, historical accounts of abandonment of places, such as Guevavi, probably have little actual relevance because we know from archaeological work and documentary sources that such places were soon reoccupied.
4. At this distance he is referring to it being present in the Huachuca Mountains and perhaps the Dragoon Mountains, but probably not the Whetstones and Mustangs, which are closer and probably were already depleted. On May 5 in his journal Rocha notes that the Huachucas had abundant timber, so perhaps the Dragoons or Peñascosa [Rocky] Mountains were depleted by then as well.
5. Luminescence dating of the sediment under the rocks of the cairn noted at the deep arroyo head and examination of channel cutting and in-filling episodes should provide definitive evidence in support or correction of these suggestions.
6. As Seymour (2009a:405) has discussed before, their accounts are not really independent accounts because they were in agreement on most points and likely discussed them in advance, while the reconnaissance was underway.
7. Shifts in the location of the Santa Cruz garrison resulted in these settlements being less permanent than they might have otherwise been. Still, the way the landscape was used, the intensity of this use, and the aggregate effects of this overuse from all three locations seems to have been more impactful than previous

occupations that shifted more routinely and instituted other land management policies.

8. Some of this detail is lost in the reproduction of the larger map.
9. Presumably they mean the narrows on the lower San Pedro, but this is not clear from their document because there are several narrows, one just below Fairbank, one just below modern Tres Alamos (and above the historic Tres Alamos), and another north of Cascabel. Often earlier historical accounts refer to the northernmost narrows as the Redington Narrows or simply as The Narrows. Hereford and Betancourt's Figure 12.1 indicates "The Narrows" in a location that would be the Tres Alamos Narrows, which is considered by many to be the beginning of the lower San Pedro. This Tres Alamos Narrows is not as extensive and therefore as dangerous as the Cascabel-Redington Narrows and it was not unique in that there were several narrows along this river, a characteristic which allowed Sobaipuri irrigation and consequently settlement.

CHAPTER 7

Insights into Indigenous Practices and Local Customs

Perhaps the most valuable information contained in the diary and reports is that which pertains to indigenous practices and local customs. This might not be immediately apparent given the brief nature of many of the observations, but placed in the context of the times, and combined with what is known historically and archaeologically about these groups, these texts and the map are a treasury of information. The deeper one probes into the details, the more insights are gained. In some instances the content of these documents fundamentally changes our understanding of the period.

Of course, emphasis is often placed on the enemy by these military men (as discussed in the next chapter), but there is also considerable attention paid to tribes who cooperated with the Europeans and what they viewed as improvements and advances made in frontier settlements. These documents by Ugarte and Rocha are especially informative when it comes to understanding one branch of the Sobaipuri O'odham, the historic indigenous inhabitants of the river valleys in the northern portion of the frontier, residents whose villages were bisected by the northern extent of the Presidial Line. These officers spent most of their time in what is now southern Arizona, and the king in particular was interested in the San Pedro-Gila confluence area for the placement of a new presidio, so special attention was paid to this area and the current population and defensive centers.

Most environmental histories written about the San Pedro and Santa Cruz Rivers and their tributary drainages incorporate a cursory prehistory and history of occupation along the rivers, acknowledging the role of human population in changes to and interactions with the environment. Regrettably, many are uninformed and often quite wrong about the O'odham because they have relied on out-of-date information. So much new information has been obtained over the past three decades from archaeological research and re-evaluation of ethnohistoric and ethnographic data that our understanding of this group has changed significantly. For example, Logan (2002:43) refers to San Xavier del Bac as a Papago (Tohono O'odham) settlement, as is often done, whereas in Kino's time it was a large Sobaipuri O'odham (Akimel or River O'odham) village and even acknowledged Sobaipuri O'odham headmen up until at least the late 1800s.[1] Other researchers emphasize different groups at the expense of discussion of the O'odham, even when focusing on the core of the O'odham occupation area, the San Pedro and Santa Cruz River Valleys (e.g., Tellman and Huckleberry 2009), or skip from discussing Hohokam to Spanish irrigation systems (Logan 2002:47) without mention of the extensive Sobaipuri O'odham systems that were central to their way of life and their settlement system (Seymour 1993, 1997, 2011a). This is a common mistake, even made by ethnohistorians who rely on late historic labels and conditions when referencing earlier historic peoples (see discussion

a

b

c

FIGURE 7.1. Historical maps showing the location of Sonoita: (*a*) The placement of the Pueblo of Sonoita in Kino's time (1695-1696) relative to Sonoita Creek, (*b*) A slightly later placement of the Pueblo of Sonoita in Kino's time (1696–1697) relative to Sonoita Creek, (*c*) Rocha's placement of the pueblos of Sonoita and Calabasas in 1780 relative to Sonoita Creek.

in Seymour 2011a). The Sobaipuri O'odham were a sedentary farming group who lived along the Santa Cruz, San Pedro, and middle Gila Rivers, and along Sonoita Creek, Aravaipa Creek, and the Babocomari River. They were a subgroup of the Upper Pima (see Seymour 2011a). In contrast, the Tohono O'odham were mobile and semisedentary people who hunted and gathered full time and planted seasonally. It is important to the people themselves and for accurate historical understanding to distinguish modern political representations from distinct historical ethnic groups who practiced different lifeways, lived in discrete areas, and therefore left distinct archaeological and historical records.

Regrettably, many environmental sources continue to state that evidence of these O'odham is generally missing from the archaeological record and that their "scattered rancherías... left no trace for further archaeologists once the inhabitants had died or moved on" (Logan 2002:45). In some cases, as noted, Sobaipuri O'odham history is glossed or entirely skipped over (Tellman and Huckleberry 2009). Even many archaeological references insularly focus on much outdated notions, failing to cite more current data and interpretations. In fact, considerable work had been completed along both the Santa Cruz and San Pedro Rivers and along the Sonoita Creek and the Babocomari River, exposing the recognizable evidence of the Upper Piman/Sobaipuri O'odham populations (Seymour 2011a). Their places of residence are far from invisible. We now have recorded more than ninety residential sites related to the Sobaipuri O'odham alone, and Seymour's work has focused on this group for over thirty years.

The 1780s documents contained in this book provide evidence of incalculable value in understanding changes for indigenous populations as they were occurring on the far northern frontier. These sources chronicle a slice in time, providing an important perspective into culture change, including the effects of violence and colonialism on the Sobaipuri O'odham. They provide a supplement to the archaeological and geographic evidence that together allow more effective interpretations. The diary and accompanying texts and map provide important insights into the location of particular villages, the types of landforms they settled on at this time, changes in village organization, and varying forms of farming practices throughout the region.

O'odham Settlement Placement and Landscape Use

One of the most important contributions is the information Rocha's map and journal provide on the character and location of indigenous settlements. Many of these Sobaipuri O'odham settlements were now missions (or had been prior to their recent abandonment), and so these sources document a period of time during which the character of the settlements themselves and their locations were undergoing substantial change.

Sonoita

A good example is the placement of the Sobaipuri O'odham settlement of Sonoita, which had already been depopulated when the reconnaissance party passed through the area. Father Kino and Captain Manje mentioned Sobaipuri O'odham villages in this area in the 1690s, and two named villages (Los Reyes [del Sonóidag] and San Gerónimo) were plotted on Kino's "Saeta martyrdom" map dated 1696–1697 (Bolton 1948; Karns 1954) and on an earlier (1695–1696 Teatro) map (Figures 7.1 a and b). Kino plotted both settlements south or east of Sonoita Creek. On-the-ground investigations and archaeological surveys indicate that each of these two Kino-period villages is located near the only reliable water sources in the valley. In Kino's time the Sobaipuri O'odham residents occupied zones similar to those they used along the Santa Cruz and San Pedro, along raised landforms overlooking their fields and irrigation canals, avoiding areas where surface water was not available. Historic maps from both the early and late 1800s roughly plot what were referred to as "Sonoita Ruins" and "old mission ruins" (Gonzales 1821; Roskruge 1893; San Jose de Sonoita Land Grant papers). As such they provide corroborative evidence of Sonoita's Kino-period location relative to that which is made available

FIGURE 7.2. Rocha describes Sonoita Creek and the general placement of the abandoned village of Sonoita as a *barranca* or ravine, a description that is applicable to portions of the river valley.

by the archaeological record and earlier historic documents.

Increased population and possibly two new villages were added to the existing two when Headman Coro and the Sobaipuri O'odham residents of Quiburi and Santa Cruz de Gaybanipitea retreated to this general area after a 1698 battle (Seymour 2011b, 2014, 2015b). The Kino-period settlement in this area occupied by the Quiburi and Santa Cruz de Gaybanipitea residents would have had to be sizable because nearly six hundred people migrated. It is likely that these newly arriving San Pedro residents joined residents already in the area, probably establishing new villages. These are likely two of the numerous Sobaipuri O'odham sites identified along Sonoita Creek. Here, as found along the San Pedro and Santa Cruz Rivers, repeated and intensive use through the years is indicated, by either dense populations or shifting settlements, an inference that is being supported by luminescence dates on these Sonoita Creek sites. These San Pedro Sobaipuri moved back to the middle San Pedro sometime after the turn of that century, presumably bringing all or most residents with them.

Comparisons between Rocha's and Kino's maps suggest that settlements called Sonoita (actually a variation of the name Sonóidag) were in two different locations in the 1690s and 1770s. Maps indicate that they were on opposite sides of Sonoita Creek. Kino's 1696–1697 map (Saeta's martyrdom map, see Figure 7.2b; Burrus 1965: Plate IX) shows the settlement on the south or east side of the river, whereas on Rocha's 1780 map it is clearly placed to the north or west (see Figure 7.1c). Both Kino and Rocha visited the settlement, so it is unlikely that they would have plotted it incorrectly relative to Sonoita Creek. They probably even used the creek margin to guide their travels and would have watered their mounts in the creek. These map data indicate that two distinct places were occupied in the 1690s and the mid-1700s, respectively.

It is not documented when the Sonoita settlement moved, but archaeology has determined that each of these Sonoita settlements were situated within the same valley segment set back from the floodplain. Reuse of the same river segment was the norm for the Sobaipuri O'odham throughout the centuries. This practice ensured that they could take advantage of the infrastructure, such as canals and fields, at old locations while allowing fields to lie fallow and firewood and other plants and animals to rejuvenate for a decade or more while they were away. Seymour has previously discussed movement of Sobaipuri O'odham settlements along certain river segments (Seymour 1989, 1990, 1993, 1997, 2011a), involving the processes of village drift, intervallic sedentism, and serial settlement reuse. Since settlements were placed near reliable water sources (where the water was on the surface), good agricultural land, and along river channel segments that possessed certain characteristics, there were only so many places considered ideal for settlement.

The village visited by Ugarte and Rocha was depopulated, presumably for the last time, sometime before Rocha's 1780 visit because of an attack, as he records, by "barbarous Indians" (Diary, May 10), meaning they were enemies that were unsettled and unconverted. Documentary sources tell us that as of 1775 Sonoita's residents had already moved, for as Fray Thomas Eixarch noted: "Calabasas in which live the Indians of Guevavi and Sonoita, [is] depopulated because of the furious hostility of the Apaches" (Kessell 1965:79). Other documentary sources indicate that the battle occurred in 1770 or 1771, because on March 5, 1773, Fray Bartolomé Ximeno, at Tumacácori, wrote that

> Sonoita (Sonoytac), which is 11 leagues from the cabecera Tumacácori, has 26 families; but in all of these families only 11 women are counted, for during an attack that the Apaches made 2 years ago they killed most of the women in the house that they call the Father's, where they had taken refuge (Kessell and Ximeno 1964:307–308).

Elsewhere, Fray Juan Crisóstomo Gil de Bernabé recorded this, or perhaps an earlier attack, by the Apache on Sonoita, in the Tumacácori mission register for 1770, recording the deaths of nineteen people (Gil de Bernabé 1770; Kessell 1976:56–58).

The Sonoita settlement mentioned by Rocha in 1780 is of interest because of its placement in "very broken and hilly terrain, tucked away in a deep *barranco*" (Diary, May 10). In 1773 the village was located far from their fields: "These people of Sonoita do almost all of their planting more than two leagues from the village" (Ximeno 1773:308). This placement seems to be a defensive aspect of the Sobaipuri O'odham settlement pattern adopted by midcentury or at least by the third quarter of the eighteenth century. This type of village placement at a distance from fields and on higher landforms was also noted in Font's journal from his travels along the Gila River during the 1775–1776 Anza expedition (Bolton 1930:46). Font mentions why the settlement was placed so far from the river:

> The Indians were asked why they lived so far from the river, since formerly they had their pueblo on the banks, whereas now they had moved it to a place apart. They replied that they changed the site because near the river, with its trees and brush, they fared badly from the Apaches, but now being far away they had open country through which to follow and kill the Apaches when they came to their pueblo (Bolton 1930:46).

Major river courses were travel routes not only for the Spaniards but also for indigenous groups, as they had been for centuries. Residence in relatively low-lying areas along these routes had proven indefensible as animosities increased and population densities decreased. Thus, the age-old pattern of landscape use on raised terraces and hills adjacent to the rivers, near their fields and water, was abandoned in favor of more defensible locations that were more remote from the key travel routes.

Rocha's passage ("their situation is quite bad, being in very broken and hilly terrain, tucked away in a deep *barranco*," May 10) can be read two ways. The first is that there is a spring separate from Sonoita Creek that flows to the west and that the village was located in this deep tributary drainage, away from the creek. Rocha's map can be interpreted this way; he provides a distinctive marking to the right of the symbol for the pueblo of Sonoita. This particular interpretation was initially thought attractive because the site had not been previously found along Sonoita Creek and Rocha does not discuss the village placement near irrigable land, as he often does elsewhere. While this provides one possible interpretation of Rocha's statements, areas around a number of springs and tributary drainages were examined for Sobaipuri O'odham evidence, and none of the springs, seeps, or drainages to the west or north of Sonoita Creek produced evidence of Sobaipuri O'odham occupation. Furthermore, these are inconsistent with league distances from other known locations.

Sites found during archaeological investigations indicate that Rocha was referencing the westward flow of Sonoita Creek itself rather than the westward flow of a spring located away from the river in a side canyon. Rocha's map supports this interpretation as do the stream flow characteristics for Sonoita Creek and the incredibly rough and craggy nature of portions of Sonoita Creek (Figure 7.2). When Rocha's map is compared to a satellite image of Sonoita Creek it is possible to see that he captured two of the drainage's most important turns. The first or northernmost turn is a southward reorientation near several springs, including two important ones with reliable flow, recorded as a single spring by Rocha (perhaps not surprising given the dry season during which he passed and also that he passed through the area quickly). The second is a turn to the southwest just north of Patagonia. If these two indicated turns are accurately mapped and appropriately interpreted, this places the pueblo of Sonoita visited by Rocha to the southwest of Patagonia, after the westward turn. This also fits most appropriately with Rocha's league distances to Calabasas (which is located north of where it is recognized today and so the location is not precisely known; see below).

Today, there are only three sources of reliable water in this valley, two are springs that flow into the creek bottom and the other is a spring in the river bed itself at a single location. The Patagonia area is where the permanent flow of Sonoita Creek begins at this riverbed spring (Figure 7.3). While the creek flows for thirty miles both above and below ground, it comes to the surface and flows above ground here, below Patagonia. Upstream from Patagonia the flow is only intermittent during the rainy season (Nassereddin 1967:1). The other locations with potentially reliable water flows are near Cottonwood and Monkey Springs (Figures 7.4 and 7.5). Water diverted from Cottonwood Spring was used by the soldiers of Forts Crittenden and Buchanan in the late 1800s and later by hay farmers. The acequias that drew water from this spring may have joined the flow of Monkey Spring, providing ample irrigation water for the fields now evident, and possibly present in the 1600s and before, just below the bend. This is where several archaeological Sobaipuri O'odham sites are situated, indicating that Kino's San Gerónimo was located south or east of the creek, but league distances preclude this from being where Rocha's Sonoita was positioned. The presence of two strong and reliable springs separate from the river and the emergence of the underground flow of Sonoita Creek at the northernmost bedrock projection would have made this stretch attractive for Sobaipuri O'odham settlement. Relatively broad expanses of floodplain adjacent to Sonoita Creek in each of these areas provide suitable lands for irrigation agriculture (Figure 7.6). This is an attribute important for Sobaipuri O'odham settlement, which means that Ximeno's statement about the field being two leagues away must reflect the fact that they were so arranged to protect the fields from attack by placing them further from the enemy.

Just west of Patagonia, the terrain is especially uneven for roughly two miles, with deep canyons created by high hills, ridges, and mountains. This fits well with Rocha's description of the area where the village of Sonoita was located and also contributes to the perennial flow of Sonoita Creek near Patagonia. As Nassereddin (1967:ix, 1) states, this reliable perennial flow is

FIGURE 7.3. Stream flow in Sonoita Creek just downstream from its place of emergence.

due to the impervious andesite volcanic rocks below ground, which outcrop five hundred feet south of town. Here the alluvial deposits of the channel terminate abruptly. For this reason it is reasonable to infer that historically this segment of the creek had the most reliable stream flow as well. This bedrock outcrop provided reliable surface water that was fed by precipitation in the Patagonia Mountains, which provide the majority of water to Sonoita Creek, although chemical analysis suggests the water originates from a variety of sources (Nassereddin (1967:1). The Patagonia Mountains parallel and are closest to the creek along this segment.

The results of archaeological survey indicate that Rocha was not referring to a spring in a side drainage, but rather the spring that flows forth from the creek bed itself. As Nassereddin (1967:34) notes, Sonoita Creek in this area below Patagonia is the only perennial stream in the area. The distinctive marking on Rocha's map between the symbol for the pueblo of Sonoita and the name "Sonoita" represents the shape of the side canyon near where the village was located, or may indicate the beginning of the flow. A good fit is established between his statement about the bad, broken, and hilly terrain and the character of the canyon segment along which this archaeological site is situated. The Sonoita Creek canyon itself is the "deep *barranca*" to which Rocha referred. The village overlooks but is set back from Sonoita Creek, with its population dependent on the underground flow coming to the surface that acts as a spring that feeds Sonoita Creek, rather than a separate spring located up a side canyon. No other locations in this zone exhibit archaeological evidence of a Sobaipuri O'odham village.

Calabasas

Once Rocha reached the O'odham pueblo of Calabasas on the Santa Cruz River from Sonoita, the inaccuracy of the league distances mentioned in Rocha's second note at the end of the diary become apparent. Today the distance between Calabasas and Tumacácori is twice that of the distance between Calabasas and Guevavi, yet Rocha's map shows Calabasas at about halfway between the two. One likely possibility is that Calabasas was located farther north in 1780

Figure 7.4. Historic nineteenth-century *acequia* in the Sonoita Creek channel at Cottonwood Spring.

FIGURE 7.5. Spring head at Monkey Spring in the Sonoita Valley.

FIGURE 7.6. Farmland in the floodplain of Sonoita Creek near Patagonia.

FIGURE 7.7. Adobe structure from the later historic Calabasas ranch, upstream and south of the O'odham village of Calabasas in 1780. Courtesy of the Library of Congress, http://hdl.loc.gov/loc.pnp/hhh.az0127/photos.008600p

than the currently recognized later historic ranch location. As noted above, it was common for settlements to shift up and down the river. In fact, the 1780s Calabasas on Rocha's map is shown north of the confluence of Sonoita Creek and the Santa Cruz River, whereas the location currently referenced as Calabasas (and recognized as such in the later historic period; see Figures 7.1c and 7.7) is located south of this junction. Rocha would have correctly indicated this relationship to the river channels, so this map provides strong evidence that at least one indigenous village called Calabasas was located near the current community of Río Rico north of Sonoita Creek. Given that the Sobaipuri O'odham residents died of epidemics, it is likely that the new Papago or Tohono O'odham settlement was moved to a new location, consistent with their custom, and then even later the ranch referred to as Calabasas was established to the south. The geographically distinct residential sites retained their name because the area was known as Calabasas.

Yet this explanation still does not solve the problem entirely because Rocha's journal indicates Calabasas was four leagues from Tumacácori, which would place Calabasas halfway between the modern Calabasas and Guevavi. This distance is seemingly more consistent with the currently accepted location. Yet, because of the map plot it is useful to consider other explanations, and in this case the movement of Guevavi may provide the answer. Most scholars believe that the indigenous settlement at Guevavi Mission was abandoned by about 1775. Yet chronometric dates and artifacts from Seymour's excavations in one locus and surface evidence in others indicate that indigenous residents occupied at least two locations near the old mission after this date. The area was abandoned frequently as epidemics raged or as attacks or insurgencies occurred and probably also as stream flow subsided, as was apparent in 1780. Importantly, however, there are at least a half-dozen indigenous residential loci in the general vicinity of and surrounding Guevavi Mission, each probably occupied at different times, and then reoccupied repeatedly. There is also another locus to the north that postdates 1775. It may be to this location that Rocha was referring, thereby clarifying what are otherwise discrepancies in distances. If this or another village was occupied by Guevavi's residents and positioned further north than Guevavi Mission itself, then Rocha's map and text make considerably more sense.

It is reasonable to accept the map plot of Calabasas north of Sonoita Creek because as an engineer and seasoned field man, Rocha would have known his position relative to Sonoita

Creek, especially since he had just traveled the distance. Further, while he acknowledges that his leagues are potentially faulty, there are many interpretations of the archaeological and documentary record that explain these village placements and are consistent with Rocha's map plots of the villages. In fact, Rocha's map shows his trail route and documents the position of Calabasas pueblo to the east and away from the river or at a large bend in the river. Two little hill symbols suggest it is to the north of the Cayetano Mountains, or at least north of the first peak of this range, referenced as the Sierra de Calabasas on his map, although the hills depicted could be the Cuates Buttes (see Figure 7.1c). There are two major indents in the river north of Sonoita Creek, one of which is in the area of a ciénega and is likely the location for this village in the drought year of 1780. Modern development in the area has seemingly eradicated all evidence of its placement, as archaeological survey through the years has produced no evidence. Another possibility is that Calabasas in this era was situated further north, at a key bend in the river that had earlier served as the location of San Cayetano del Tumacácori, where dates from different contexts provide evidence of a 1690s and 1770s occupation.

It is likely that the 1780s Calabasas was located to the north of the currently recognized historic site, in a zone that would place it appropriately with reference to both Guevavi and Tumacácori during this period.[2] There is mid-century evidence in support of this suggestion. When Nicolas de Lafora traveled through the area in 1766 he noted that Calabasas was two leagues from Guevavi (Kinnaird 1967:108), which places it north of the currently recognized National Park Service site and historic rancho and in the vicinity or north of the modern Río Rico nucleus. Tumacácori was one league south of Tubac, which is three miles, indicating that for Lafora the league was equivalent to three miles. Unfortunately Lafora's map is no help in this regard as the scale is too large. In 1780 Calabasas contained a small population, but Lafora indicated that as of 1766 the Pimas Altos (Sobaipuri) villagers had succumbed to an epidemic and the village was then (as of his visit) repopulated by Papagos (Tohono O'odham) (Kinnaird 1958:108–109). This difference is critical because the material culture is sufficiently different between these O'odham groups to distinguish this temporal difference or to identify these two villages if they occupied different locations.

San Xavier del Bac

Rocha's journal is also of interest to the location of San Xavier in 1780 relative to its current placement and the position of the Kino-period settlement (Figure 7.8). Other sources tell us that the Jesuit-period settlement noted by Kino and Espinosa was on the floodplain and to the north of the current community. In 1700 Kino describes how the irrigation canals would be able to run through the courtyard of the new church buildings (Bolton 1948:I:236). Even as late as 1772 Antonio de los Reyes mentioned that it is in a flat pastureland: "The mission at Bac…is located on a long, flat lowland.… The village…is situated on open ground with an abundance of water"(Reyes 1772). These and other documentary sources indicate that the Kino-period and later Jesuit-period mission was located north of the current community and church. Archaeological evidence supports this interpretation as well, as Seymour has documented a sizable community situated to the north. Oral historic sources recorded by Father Bonaventure Oblasser around the turn of the twentieth century indicate that local community members would play on the adobe walls and that they observed the mission walls collapse into the Santa Cruz during a sizable flood (Oblasser 1931; Silver Belt 1931; Tucson Citizen 1930, 1931). These same sources tell us that the Franciscans moved the community to the south, where it is now located, but the timing of this move is not provided.

Using Rocha's map along with a passage in this journal provides a strong hint that this shift to the south had already occurred by 1780. Rocha writes: "Despite being in a spacious valley, they came to place it [the community] precisely among some hillocks or small hills called El Mal Pais de San Xavier" (Diary, Day 22). *Malpaís*, a Spanish name meaning "badlands," was a term introduced in the historic period

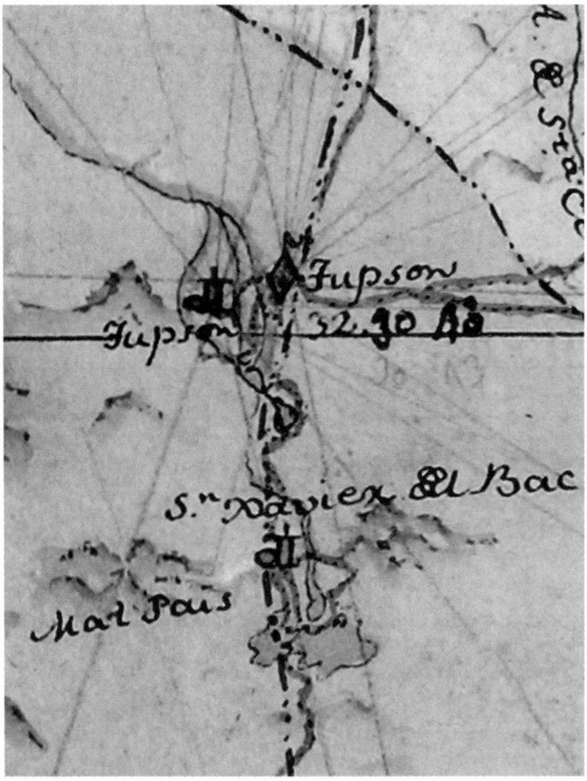

FIGURE 7.8. Close-up showing San Xavier del Bac and Tucson. San Xavier del Bac with Martinez Hill, *malpais* of Black Mountain, and *cienega* (the oval shape to the south), and Tucson showing the canals, O'odham pueblo, and the presidio, from *Mapa de la Frontera de Sonora para el establecimiento de la linea de presidios.* Courtesy of the British Library; Shelfmark: Cartographic Items Additional MS. 17,661.a.

because such lands are unsuitable for cultivation. Even today this term is used to reference "badlands" characterized by eroded rocks of volcanic origin found in arid environments. In this instance *malpaís* references the dark boulder-studded hills prominent within the modern Wa:k community. If this statement can be taken literally, it is evidence that the indigenous community by this time had moved south to its current location, situated between the malpaís hills, because there are no hills for the community to sit between a mile to the north where the earlier community and Jesuit-period churches were positioned. The malpaís hills Rocha is referring to are either Martinez Hill (or Little Black Mountain, Cem S-Cuk Du Ag) and Black Mountain (S-Cuk Du Ag), the largest features on the landscape, or the smaller hillocks within the community itself, which are also composed of malpaís (Figures 7.9 and 7.10). These include Grotto Hill and several that are situated in the heart of the Wa:k community. This relationship is shown even more clearly on Rocha's 1784 map (Figure 7.11).

Kino referred to this distinctive rock as *tezontle*, which at the time was about a quarter-league from the community and the church he was attempting to build (Kino 1698; Bolton 1948:I:235–236). Kino used this tezontle to form the foundation of his capacious church in 1700. Tezontle is a reddish porous or vesicular volcanic (igneous) rock that is used in construction.

This interpretation, that the settlement had moved south by the time of this reconnaissance,

a

b

FIGURE 7.9. San Xavier del Bac: (*a*) from Martinez Hill, facing west toward Black Mountain and the community, showing placement of the current community among the hills. The volcanic rock present on nearby *malpaís* hills is distinctive and so was mentioned by Rocha, who placed San Xavier exactly between hillocks or small hills, as it is today, indicating that the shift south noted in oral histories had already occurred. This *tezontle* was also used in construction of building foundations, as noted by Kino in 1700. (*b*) View from Grotto Hill and San Xavier Mission east toward Martinez Hill.

a

b

FIGURE 7.10. San Xavier del Bac then and now: (a) 1981, Photograph courtesy of USGS SW Repeat Photography Collection, R.M. Turner, Stake number 1058, 1981; and (b) same view of the community from about the same location in 2009. Wa:k O'odham elder Tony Burrell in foreground.

is consistent with other documents that suggest that construction on the current church, the White Dove of the Desert, began around 1783. Father Juan Bautista Belderrain, a Basque Franciscan, initiated construction in that year, but it was thought to have been completed under his replacement, Father Juan Bautista Llorens, in 1797. Thus, it seems that an earlier Franciscan church had been started near this location after community members complained to Captain Anza about the lack of a church, and a food subsidy was provided for its construction by Father Garcés (Dobyns 1976:32; Ezell 1955; translation of archival copy of Anza, May 1, 1770). This would have also been after Reyes' 1772 report, but before Rocha and Ugarte's visit.

These sources narrow the shift of the community and church from north to the current location to an eight-year period between 1772 and 1780. In 1797 the priest Bartolomé Socies (1797) noted that the new church (White Dove of the Desert) had been placed "in the old church," presumably in the foundations of this post-1772 Garcés church. Latitudes derived from Rocha's map suggest this scenario has merit (as was discussed in Chapter 4). Rocha's plot of San Xavier is consistent with its current location, not its position during the Jesuit period, indicating that by 1780 the community had moved south and a new church had been or was being built.

Some misconceptions that pertain to San Xavier del Wa:k, such as the former course of the river "channel," are clarified by this understanding of the placement of the ancestral village. For example, Lamberton (2011:175, 177) states that prior to 1880 the West Branch was the main channel, which, situated west of the current channel, runs from Los Reales Road to the Santa Cruz at Sentinel Peak. Yet this statement is not supported by the geological literature for the Santa Cruz nor the position of the indigenous settlement. The 1690s village on Kino's maps was always plotted west of the river, consistent with archaeological evidence of the ancestral village. The generalized course of the Santa Cruz in this area has, since Kino's time (and, as chronometric dates and archaeological sites indicate, long before) been restricted to its current course by the volcanic outcrops at Martinez Hill. Lamberton (2011:167, 175) states that the main course used to flow closer to the church, and while it did, this was made possible by the position of the Jesuit church on flatter ground, in pasture lands to the north of its current location, as Reyes said, not by a shift of the channel. Historically, the river would have been broader, less entrenched, and closer to the O'odham community to allow the canals to run through the churchyard, as Kino envisioned. South of Martinez Hill, the upstream course did shift as the ciénega and springs were exploited and dried up with the pumping of groundwater, water development projects by José Martinez and by Tucson residents and politicians, and the 1887 Bavispe earthquake (Castetter and Bell 1942:163-167; Dobyns 1981:62-63; Webb et al. 2014).

FIGURE 7.11. Close up of a section of Rocha's 1784 map showing San Xavier del Bac and Tucson.

Quiburi

Quiburi was the only Sobaipuri settlement occupied on the San Pedro at the time Ugarte and Rocha passed through the area, at least according to their diary, which presents a new source of Spanish documentary evidence regarding this issue of Sobaipuri O'odham occupation of this river at this time. It has been thought for centuries that no Sobaipuri O'odham remained on the San Pedro River after 1762 because the

Rudo Ensayo, attributed to Father Juan Nentvig, stated that the area was abandoned after that time (Pradeau and Rasmussen 1980). It is true that the San Pedro Valley's Sobaipuri O'odham residents of the villages of Santa Cruz and Quiburi were ordered to move west to occupy San Xavier, Santa María, and Guevavi along the Santa Cruz River. Rocha's 1780 diary and map and his 1784 map (see Chapter 1) indicate, however, that many of them remained. Other sources confirm this and indicate that only half of the Sobaipuri residents relocated in 1762, perhaps thirty families remaining (Seymour 2011b). The lingering San Pedro Sobaipuri population congregated at Quiburi.

Rocha's map plot of El Quiburi Crossing and his notes about distance from Santa Cruz de Terrenate Presidio to the village provide evidence that the Quiburi settlement was positioned much further north than it was in the Kino period. This placement is seemingly confirmed by San Juan de las Boquillas y Nogales land grant maps and descriptions that plot and discuss the *Ciénega del Quiburi* in the same general area as a site recorded by Seymour (see Howard and Hearst 1881). The 1780s village of Quiburi was about half the size of its Kino-period predecessor.

The absence of wood and grass around the Santa Cruz Presidio discussed in the preceding chapter may explain why Quiburi's residents relocated so far north of the presidio. The new location also provided privacy from the Europeans settled at the presidio and was more defensively situated on high, steep terrain and surrounded by a swamp. This village was also close to a water source separate from the river, as Rocha's journal notes and archaeological survey confirms, so the residents were not dependent solely on the flow of the San Pedro. As was noted, these considerations of resource availability (firewood, wood for building, and grass) probably contributed to the degree to which Sobaipuri settlements moved in the historic period. Flooding and the need to let fields lie fallow were also probably important environmental factors that, along with political and social issues, caused regular shifts in settlements up and down this segment of the river margin. The moves of the Sobaipuri O'odham residents, however, were usually limited in extent. They stayed along a specific segment of the river because they had made costly improvements to the channel in the construction and maintenance of canals and fields, and because this is where surface water was available and reliable (Seymour 2011a). Rocha's diary records an important chapter in Sobaipuri O'odham use of the San Pedro because it documents a persistence and continuity of their occupation and claim to this valley.

Tres Alamos

Perhaps one of the most used names in the journal is Alamos ("Cottonwoods"). This term makes reference to the cottonwood trees that today line the rivers and apparently were distinctive characteristics of the riparian strip in Ugarte and Rocha's day. Fremont cottonwood (*Populus fremontii*) is native to the area and is one of the dominant species, along with willow and mesquite (Figure 7.12). When Rocha visited, as now, there was a discontinuous distribution of cottonwoods, although his journal hints that their distributions might have been even more restricted than today. This restricted distribution is indicated both by the fact that some locations were named Alamos (indicting that these trees were lacking or occurred in much lower densities elsewhere, making them distinctive) and that at one point Rocha commented that in the distance they could see some cottonwoods at the Alamos Largos Spring with "quite plentiful flow in open terrain, and with many pastures but not much timber or firewood, though some quite distant cottonwoods" (Diary, May 9). Most references are to Los Alamos, but one location on the Lower San Pedro was called Tres Alamos, as it is today. This locale was important through time and has an interesting history.

The primary importance of Los Alamos or Tres Alamos stems from the fact that it was a shady and watered camping location with a good rocky ford. In the rainy season it is best even today to cross at known rocky locations because elsewhere there is a risk of encountering quick-

FIGURE 7.12. Cottonwoods at the Tres Alamos Narrows on the middle San Pedro River.

sand. The ford at Tres Alamos seems to have been reliable because of the heavy rocky load carried down from the adjacent mountains (see Figure 4.16).

The name Tres Alamos implies that there would have been cottonwoods to provide some respite from the sun. In Rocha's time this was called Tres Alamos, but in Kino's time about a century earlier it was Los Alamos, perhaps indicating a reduction in stand size through time. During the Kino era he and his military escorts, such as Manje, mentioned a *paraje* or "camp." They stayed over in this location, which was a known and frequently visited stopping place. It was not until the 1730s that Spaniards began to reference an indigenous settlement here, although archaeological evidence documents Sobaipuri O'odham villages here much earlier as well. A new settlement of Tres Alamos had been established in Padre Ignaz Xavier Keller's time. Keller and Juan Bautista de Anza went through this settlement in 1732 on their way from San Xavier del Bac to Santa María as Keller was being installed as the area missionary. On their way Keller was introduced to various villagers in the Pimería Alta (Di Peso 1953:38; Hammond 1929:224, 229, 231). Tres Alamos is also shown on a map of this region by Francisco Javier Saviñon, which dates to 1733 (González Rodríguez 1977:26) and seems to have been made from knowledge obtained from this Anza and Keller trip. Moreover, in 1746, Governor Don Agustín de Vilsósola listed Tres Alamos as an active village when he wrote about the San Pedro Valley (Thomas 1941:203; Di Peso 1953:39). These sources indicate that the *visita* of Tres Alamos was first mentioned as a settlement in 1732, the year in which three German Jesuits were assigned to the Pimería Alta: Johann Baptist Grazhoffer, Phelipe Segesser, and Ignaz Xavier Keller. The presence of these strong-minded German Jesuits may have encouraged continued resettlement of this area, far from centers of European interference. The location was also mentioned as a refuge during the 1751 Pima Revolt, suggesting its remoteness from Spanish institutions was a perceived advantage.

Rocha's map and local lore indicate that this was one area that tended to have reliable surface water. One reason for this is because just to the south or upstream from the villages there are bedrock outcrops that pinch the river, forcing water to the surface so canals can be easily taken off downstream (north) and also causing some pooling to the south or upstream before the constriction (see Figure 7.12). This constriction, or narrow (Tres Alamos Narrows), explains the string of Sobaipuri O'odham sites in this general downstream area, eleven documented by archaeological survey. It also explains why this was such an important crossing. The pooling upstream from the constriction, which according to local lore was impacted by the late nineteenth-century earthquake, would have provided suitable water and shelter for travelers and so probably served as the *paraje* of Kino's time.

O'odham Village Layout

Important changes in O'odham village layout are indicated in descriptions from Rocha's journal regarding Tumacácori and San Xavier. Both are described as defensibly arranged: (a) "This pueblo of Tumacácori is almost surrounded by a wall in a quadrilateral shape to which are being added several small houses so that they may live in greater security [within]" (Diary, May 13) and (b) "San Xavier forms a square shape with its own houses, and it only lacks a few small gates to be entirely enclosed. In the four corners are a kind of tower with rounded gun holes." (Diary, May 22).

Similar types of arrangements were described by Father Joseph Och a bit earlier in the 1750s and 1760s: "we influenced them to build their villages in complete squares, one house next to the other…such a quadrangle…protected them against enemies" (Treutlein 1965: 151). This arrangement is a substantial departure from the traditional village layout, where houses were paired and arranged in rows but spaced relatively widely, a couple to perhaps ten meters apart.

The archaeological manifestation of the pattern described in these historical sources was examined at the native settlement around Guevavi Mission (AZ EE:9:132, ASM). Seymour's excavations revealed that O'odham houses were paired, situated in rows, as they always had been, but here they were positioned especially close to one another (Seymour 2009b, 2011a, 2014; see Figure 7.13). The wall of one is fifty centimeters from the adjacent house wall, effectively restricting access to the common area and providing some degree of protection from outside incursion. The low ridge on which the village was situated creates a somewhat defensible setting. Still these slopes are not anywhere near as steep as those at Santa Cruz de Gaybanipitea, a village on the San Pedro that was easily overrun by a horde of enemy mobile groups in 1698. So while being on a low rise probably provided some measure of advantage, it was not a highly effective defensive posture. Like Santa Cruz de Gaybanipitea, Guevavi too shows evidence of widespread burning, either from an enemy attack or as a result of an O'odham uprising, or both. The original Kino-period chapel burned and some of the latest houses at the site also show evidence of having been destroyed by fire, suggesting that this mission site was the focus of considerable ire from those opposing Spanish presence and missionization (Seymour 2009c). All of the later structures show signs of having been burned as well, as do both of the latest occupied housing areas located elsewhere around the mission.

Indigenous Agriculture and Irrigation

When taken, together Rocha's written accounts and map provide more than the sum of the parts in many other ways, including providing insights into agricultural and irrigation practices on the colonial frontier. Despite many shortcomings, as Rocha himself acknowledged, the level of detail is sometimes notable. One impressive example is provided on the 1780 map, where the three canals Rocha mentions in Tucson in his journal are depicted in detail:

> We went to the pueblo of Tucson, distant a quarter of a league southwest, quarter-south and as we returned, I left with Captain Pedro Allende to examine the dam and the place where the water divides into three abundant *acequias* ["irrigation ditches"], which serve for consumption and cultivation of the land of the pueblo (Diary, May 26).

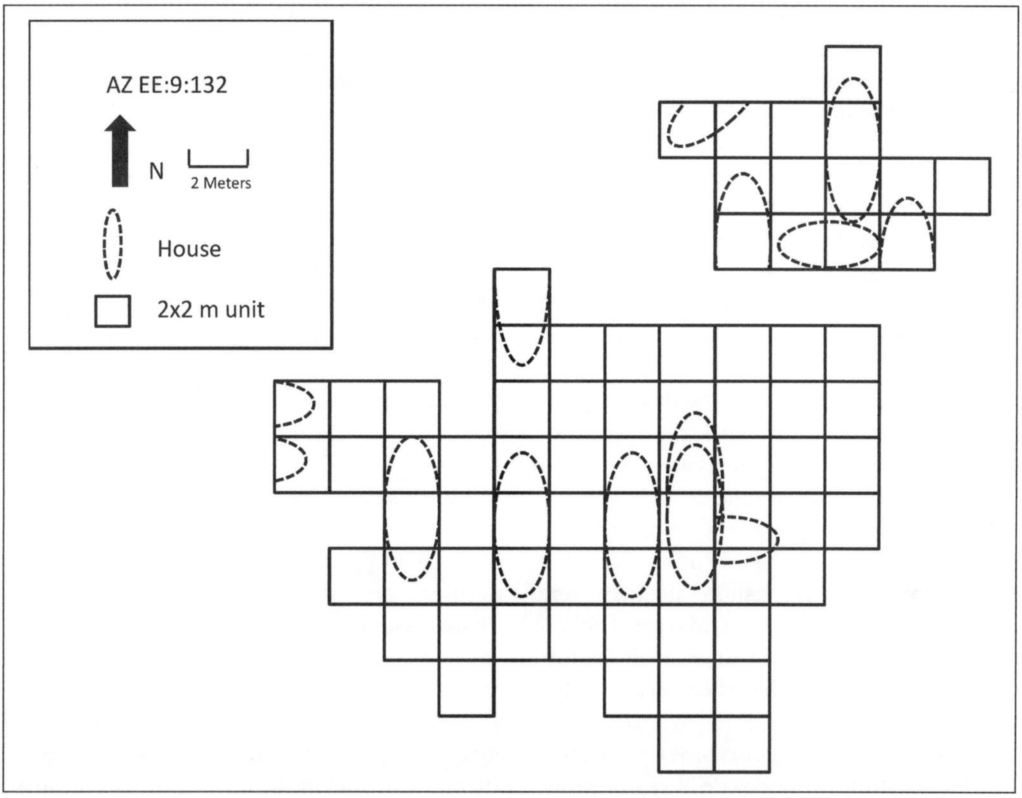

FIGURE 7.13. Housing layout at Guevavi Mission through time, showing the close spacing of structures in the late 1700s. This arrangement is a substantial departure from the traditional village layout, where houses were paired and arranged in rows but spaced relatively widely, at two to perhaps ten meters apart.

Were it not for the journal, the significance of these lines might not be recognized. This division into three channels independent from the river is shown clearly on Rocha's 1780 map, all three radiating to the west of the river from a place upstream or south of the presidio and native pueblo (see Figure 7.8). Because of the scale on Rocha's 1784 map we see only the main acequia splitting off from the river channel, and curving to the west of the mission (see Figure 7.11). On the more detailed 1780 map it is possible to see two of the canals that extend between the pueblo and presidio, as Rocha notes in his journal:

> The location is beautiful, in a very unobstructed land with abundant waters and farmlands. *It has the proportion of a large corral formed by two irrigation ditches between the pueblo and the presidio* where they protect their horse herd, in case they find themselves with limited troop forces (Diary, May 28; emphasis added).

Each of these three larger lines probably represents an *acequia madre* (literally "mother ditch," meaning the main irrigation canal from which lateral ditches fed). Lateral channels are also probably depicted on his map by the shorter lines radiating from the main three. Williams (1986:115) had created a hand-drafted sketch of a small portion of the original Rocha map for use in his article on San Agustín del Tucson. Yet, in doing so, he illustrated only one channel bowing to the west of the mission and the Santa Cruz River instead of the three actually discussed in the journal and shown on the map (along with some lateral canals).[3] As Williams (1986:115) points out in the same figure, the point of divergence for these canals upstream from Tucson was likely where the dam was placed to form the diverted channel that made the Sobaipuri O'odham pueblo an island.[4]

Other important aspects of local agricultural practices are mentioned by Rocha. In his diary text Rocha references water control features in several areas and by several different names. He mentions *acequias*, or canals, at Cochuta (Diary, April 24) and the Tucson pueblo and presidio (Diary, May 28), but fails to mention them at several places known to have such features. For example, San Xavier del Bac would have still been using the same fields and canals as were established many decades and centuries beforehand. In 1699 these canals were described by Kino as extensive: "The fields and lands for sowing were so extensive and supplied with so many irrigation ditches running along the ground that the father visitor said they were sufficient for another city like Mexico" (Bolton 1948:I:205). Many of these that probably continued in use through time have been documented on the ground at San Xavier (Deaver 2007) and elsewhere, such as at Guevavi (Seymour 1993, 1997, 2011a).[5] In 1539 Marcos de Niza was probably referencing similarly extensive fields and canals for the village of Quiburi's predecessor on the San Pedro when he said: "It is all irrigated and is like an evergreen garden" (Flint and Flint 2005:72). Quiburi's residents would also have almost certainly still used canals when their village shifted to the north, yet these are not mentioned in Rocha's journal. We know of their earlier existence because a system thought to have been used by the Sobaipuri O'odham during Kino's time has been documented north of the Santa Cruz Narrows on the San Pedro, where there are also later (1880s) irrigation features, including canals, that relate to Contention City, a settlement contemporary with Tombstone (Seymour 1990, 2003, 2011a; also see Croix's comment below about the canals here). This is a prime example of the fact that just because Rocha did not mention canals does not provide evidence of the absence of their use. It seems that in some of these well-known locations he was more focused on other aspects of the villages or water sources and neglected to mention their often extensive systems, that were probably so well known or so ordinary they did not merit attention.

Although not mentioned in this diary, information about the presence of Sobaipuri O'odham (and Hohokam) canals and the possibility of their reuse was likely discussed among the Spaniards. In a letter to Gálvez in February 1780, Croix discusses an earlier report (1778) by Adjunct Inspector Don Roque de Medina in which he proposed various means for encouraging settlement at Santa Cruz de Terrenate Presidio "and for the cultivation of many lands which the Sobaipuri Indians sow, as he [Medina] recognized by means of the mother ditches which remain open and which at a little cost could be put into use" (Thomas 1941:204).

Of considerable interest is that at two recently established presidios Rocha does not mention acequias, per se. Rather, at Fronteras Presidio he discusses the diversion dams and headgates, *la presa o saca de agua*, that is, "the dam or old takeouts [diversion dam]" (Diary, April 21). At Pitic Presidio he uses the terms *la toma o saca de agua* (Diary, July 15) to denote intake or takeout dams on an inlet of the main river. This change from noting the acequias to noting the headgates likely conveys information about the age of the community and their agricultural infrastructure:

> As part of the initial inspection [for planning and establishing a town], when needed, an *alcalde* would help locate suitable places where one or more diversions could feasibly be built to take water from the river source (Carlson; Wozniak) in order to irrigate alluvial flood plains by means of gravity flow. Once determined, this *toma* or *saca de agua* (the diversion dam and headgate) was the first public works construction project undertaken in the formation of most communities, begun even before the building of the local church, presidio, or other government buildings. To complete the infrastructure for irrigation, the settlers excavated an *acequia madre* (main canal) off one or both banks of the river, thereby extending the irrigable lands adjacent to the watercourse for several miles downstream (Rivera 2006:4).

Additional detail provides further clarification:

> Each commons ditch, described in the Spanish of the times as the *acequia de común*, was the main force that established a distinct place, defined the community boundaries, and bonded the irrigators, obligating them to the collective management of the local water system and their corporate village as a whole. The idea of a common property ditch for all irrigators in any new settlement was replicated time and again in the province and, in fact, was the key to both the development and economic survival of local communities (Rivera 1999:22, 2006:4).

As conveyed in these quotations, as part of the initial inspection, an *alcalde* (mayor), or in these cases, the military governor (Don Jacobo de Ugarte y Loyola), would help locate suitable places where diversions could be built to take water from the source, which at Pitic Presidio was an inlet of the river. The fact that these are presidios, and recently established ones at that, most likely accounts for Ugarte's and Rocha's headgate inspection and the reference of different aspects of the irrigation system. The recent relocation of the presidial company of Horcasitas to El Pitic earlier in 1780 (Moorhead 1975:86) and the withdrawal of San Bernardino to Fronteras (Moorhead 1975:88; Thomas 1941:146–147) probably account for why canals were still being established or had been recently established but not inspected. It is also possible that the canals were already in place, the soldiers using existing canals dug by previous occupants, so that the headgates and dams were the only parts of the system that needed to be constructed anew, the originals having been washed out or otherwise made inoperative. As Rocha notes for Pitic Presidio, at modern-day Hermosillo, the area was subject to flooding and therefore they may have had to routinely reconstruct headgates, which are one of the first components of the irrigation system to wash out in high waters.

Not all places had an adequate amount of reliable and accessible water for irrigation canals. In other locations this type of agriculture was not possible because of terrain or was not practiced because of local customs. At Pozo de Crisanto residents had to use buckets (Diary, July 7). In Note 6 at the end of the diary Rocha mentions the use of buckets and that they use a few small conduits or troughs to transport or distribute the water after drawing it from the wells. It is not clear from the diary whether this mode of water extraction related to current drought conditions, a growing population and the need to place villages in less than ideal locations, the customary adaptation of the local people, or new technologies being adopted owing to intervillage disputes where water was being diverted upstream (as at Tubac). Hamilton (1882:22) notes that "On the road from Hermosillo to the port of Guaymas, in the dry season, no water is to be had for thirty-six leagues, except at La Posa and La Cieneguilla, and it is occasionally so scarce at these places that foot passengers perish from thirst." This fact suggests that at least in the region around Pozo de Crisanto (and Cieneguilla), where surface water was not available, wells were the only way agriculture could be conducted and drinking water made available.

Ethnographic information on the lower Pima or Pima Bajo provides useful insights into this practice of hand irrigation. *Canoas* are mentioned as being used as part of a bucket-lift form of irrigation among the Onavas Pima (Pennington 1980:154). As Pennington (1980:145, 355) points out, many areas, including along reaches of the Yaqui River, are unsuitable for large-scale gravity-fed irrigation. The gradient along many rivers would have made it difficult for these groups to benefit from gravity-fed irrigation.

In the Rio Grande Valley of New Mexico, where many terms from an older Spanish are still used, the Spanish term *canoa* references the irrigation flume (Wozniak 1998:52). From photographs it is possible to see that these are often used to transport water across divides (canyons, arroyos, and gullies) or to change elevations (Figure 7.14). This *canoa* at Pozo de Crisanto would have allowed the water to be poured from buckets at the well into the wooden trough for distribution into ditches at the fields.

FIGURE 7.14. Historic canoa, shown as an irrigation trough or flume. Courtesy of the Library of Congress, 364416pu.

It is unclear whether La Canoa *paraje* along the Santa Cruz River (Diary, May 17) was the same type of trough, although evidence suggests it was. The reference to an irrigation trough, by use of this place name, may relate to the water being channeled from a small spring, well, or pool, as variably referenced through time by Rocha, Manje, and Bernal (Burrus 1971:246, 431; Smith et al. 1966:45, 77–78). Alternatively, canoas may have fed canals in a system being taken off at this last reliable point for miles in the north-flowing Santa Cruz River, before the water disappeared into the sands, or from deep wells known to have been excavated elsewhere by the O'odham (e.g., Kino and Manje) and here later in time. At San Xavier del Bac some of the canals seem to have been taken off the river near where the water disappeared back below the surface, providing a parallel historical example. As the modern Canoa community's Master Plan (2006) notes, "Beginning at Elephant Butte [*sic*; Elephant Head] Road, a major fault crosses the riverbed. Water begins its descent downward underground into the Tucson water basin and does not resurface until it reaches Martinez Hill close to San Xavier Mission" (also see the discussion in Chapter 5 about this and in Chapter 6 regarding the interrupted character of the Santa

Cruz and San Pedro Rivers). In 1852 John Bartlett (1965:302) with the U.S. Boundary Commission noted this characteristic about this section of river as well, stating that the Santa Cruz River "was quite dry...notwithstanding all the rain that had fallen." A fault line near Canoa is visible today both on the ground and from the air or on Google Earth upriver or south of the modern Canoa community and just north of Amado, where the riverbed is green with irrigated land to the south (upriver) of Elephant Head Road and dry brown to the north (downstream) until reaching the community of Green Valley, which is abundantly fed by pumped groundwater.

Interestingly, because of the presence of water here but not upstream for some distance, the Canoa area may be where the 1690s O'odham village of San Martín was located.[6] Kino's earliest map shows a settlement called San Martín on the east side of the river a third of the way between San Cayetano [del Tumacácori] and San Xavier del Bac that may have been in this general vicinity (see Burrus 1965:Plate VIII), a fitting location for the last irrigable location south or upstream of San Xavier. If an O'odham village of this name was present, it would have been located on the upper portion of the floodplain, as searches along the terraces in this zone have produced no evidence of a Sobaipuri presence. Many terraces have been bulldozed, but still some evidence might be apparent if such a village was present.

This place visited by Ugarte and Rocha was already being called La Canoa when Anza passed through on his way to California in 1775. Both Anza and Font mentioned the *paraje*, and Anza stated that "we halted at the place which they call La Canoa" (Bolton 1930:6, also see page 211; Coues 1900:63). The wording of this suggests that the locale had this name for some time, that La Canoa was already a designated location along a well-known route, as indicated also by the much earlier references to water here by Kino and Manje. Both Bolton (1930:6n1) and Coues (1900:74) suggest that in this context the term means "canoe," although Bolton clarifies that, "Local tradition says that in this case *canoa* meant trough" (Bolton 1930:6n1). The revised version of Will C. Barnes' *Arizona Place Names* says: "In Spanish the word designates 'canoe,' and it has been suggested that at one time there may have been an irrigation or watering trough hewn from a large tree, hence the name, since such a trough resembles a canoe" (Barnes 1982:261).[7] Although all the names derive from a common root and concept, it is clear that at that time in this area the term *canoa*, in fact, was also the name of a watering trough or flume commonly used for irrigation. While this cannot be definitively determined, it seems quite likely that a flume was used here given that this was the northernmost place of reliable surface water for some distance to the north, and residents would have likely taken advantage of this by utilizing spring or pooling water, much as they did in the Sonoita Valley near the Kino-period settlement of San Gerónimo, whose fields were fed by spring water, perhaps also with the assistance of irrigation troughs. As the spring at the Sonoita Pueblo shows us, water pooling in the channel may look like a pool, well, or spring, depending on personal definitions and conditions that month or year. Yet Rocha was likely suggesting that he did not notice modifications, as would characterize a well.

This information does not address whether this well-and-bucket system of irrigation was an ancient practice or one introduced by the Spaniards. This journal reference is rather late and numerous influences had already transformed many other aspects of Lower Pima culture. By the time Álvar Núñez Cabeza de Vaca passed through the Corazones area (near present-day Ures on the Río Sonora) in the 1630s the area had already been devastated as a result of slaving raids. He repeatedly mentioned that the indigenous people could not farm for fear of Christians and that they wandered throughout the area or coalesced in pluralistic communities in rugged terrain to avoid capture (Hodge 1990: 109–110). There are also examples of missionaries teaching some groups to irrigate (Reff et al. 1999:590, 687) who presumably had not previously irrigated or perhaps used different techniques. Consequently, this question will remain unresolved by Rocha's journal.

Rocha's journal and map and his and Ugarte's summary reports provide insights into the late colonial period after many changes had already occurred among indigenous peoples. Consequently, from these documents it is often not possible to assess which practices being described were of indigenous origin, which were introduced or encouraged by the Spaniards, or those which local populations might have borrowed from other indigenous groups. Other sources will be required to address these types of questions relating to change, and fortunately this region provides a rich record of the local history that clarifies many of these issues, especially when combined with archaeological evidence. The latter has provided insights into changes in village layout, irrigation features, technology changes, and a range of other aspects of Sobaipuri O'odham life that are simply not conveyed in the documentary record or, in other instances, that are clarified when examined in the context of textual data. From studies of various O'odham lifeways as they lived earlier in time it is possible to understand that the conditions Ugarte and Rocha observed were in many ways substantially different than a mere century before. This was a critical decade for the Sobaipuri O'odham, owing to the increasingly firm Spanish hold on this frontier region and the escalating resistance of the Apache.

Notes

1. Owing to past historical references to the descendant populations of Sobaipuri and their villages as Papago and current political absorption of Sobaipuri descendant populations and places into the Tohono O'odham Nation, there is a commonly held misconception that the Sobaipuri and their descendants are not River O'odham. In fact, they were the archetypical River O'odham and most other O'odham were either Desert O'odham or practiced a part-desert, part-river adaption.
2. In considering these distances it is important to remember that Rocha went to Guevavi then back to Las Nutrias, and then up to Sonoita (via the San Rafael Valley) and down to Calabasas. Consequently, the distance between Guevavi and Calabasas was estimated, as he did not travel it during this reconnaissance.
3. In copying the Williams' map, Jonathan Mabry of Archaeology Southwest (2001:14) duplicates this error and shows only the river and the westernmost channel that bows around San Agustín Mission. The original shows three channels, as can be seen in the figure provided.
4. The word *acequia* is derived from Arabic *as-sāqiya*, meaning "water conduit" (Fernald et al. 2012:2999). And while some authors suggest that *acequia* is the Spanish word for the physical and social water management system brought to the New World by the Spanish colonists who migrated from the central valley of Mexico to north-central New Mexico" (Fernald et al. 2012:2999), in fact, canal irrigation systems and irrigation management communities were used widely throughout this region by indigenous people long before Europeans arrived. In fact, the prehistoric Hohokam had massive and complex irrigation systems as did their successors the Sobaipuri O'odham, although these later systems were at a much smaller scales than the Hohokam ones. Thus, it is important to differentiate between the unique Spanish-introduced management systems and the physical and organizational systems already present for millennia.
5. These are the canals discussed by Mabry (1999: 11) as originally recorded by and reported in Seymour (1997). Until recently these at Guevavi and the system Seymour recorded along the middle San Pedro were the only canals known for the Sobaipuri O'odham. Systems have since been reported at Santa Cruz de Gaybanipitea, Tumacácori, San Xavier del Wa:k, and Tucson.
6. Barnes says that Garcés referred to an O'odham settlement here, but it seems to be a footnote added by Coues.
7. Sheridan (2006:190; also Hadley 2000; Sheridan 2000; Willey 1979) suggests that Canoa along the Santa Cruz derives its name much later in time from "the hollowed-out log that some enterprising pilgrim had placed there to water horses." In this he is (and the others are) referencing one of the other meanings of this term as a watering or feeding trough, but La Canoa had the name long before the time they are referencing, and it was even called *La Canoa* by the Anza party.

CHAPTER 8

Understandings of the Enemy Apache

Rocha's diary is as much of interest with respect to the types of groups he, Ugarte, and his men did not encounter as it is for those they did. Mention is made of Apache and O'odham (Pima and Papago, now known as Akimel and Tohono O'odham, respectively) in the journal. He does not mention the Jano, Jocome, Manso, Suma, or any of a number of other groups who once dominated the area and the journal pages of local Spaniards. This absence is consistent with the long-held notion that by this time these other non-Apache groups had been absorbed into surrounding groups. For the most part, all had merged their identities with the Apache, O'odham, Piro, Jumano, or Tigua, at least as far as the Europeans were concerned.

Both Ugarte and Rocha mention the Seri in their *informes*, which as a group was a particularly recalcitrant and powerful foe to the Spaniards. Ugarte specifically mentions the Tiburones and Tepocas, which were subgroups of the Seri, all hunter-gatherer-fisher bands who roamed the coast and were within and on the border of the area discussed during Ugarte and Rocha's journey. As Ugarte notes in his summary report, the presidios of Pitic, Altar, and Buenavista were indispensible for the containment of these rebels. Rocha mentions how some of these indigenous occupants had been reduced to mission life but "remain in the pueblo...only... in appearance; maintaining communication and dealings with those who harass us, and it will not be strange if they serve them as faithful spies. To let them do so without risk, and in order to avoid these known evils that each day will be greater, because of the rising number of those that desert and return to the sierra" (Summary Report, Chapter 3), Rocha suggests that rebels should be removed from the area, exiled to the south, "to places where they will not even have the hope of returning to their homeland or soil."

In this period the enemy was attacking from two fronts, the Seri along the southwest and the Apache from the north and east. Meanwhile there were uprisings internally, among the Pima/O'odham and others. One of the greatest concerns was that the Gileño Apache would ally themselves with the Pima and Seri, coalescing these now independent areas of resistance into a more cohesive and powerful crisis.

Previous notions have the Apache arriving fairly late from the north, not pushing south into this area until the mid- to late 1700s (e.g., Logan 2002:49 and many others). With reference to 1748, Moorhead (1975:49, emphasis added) discussed this issue, stating: "From the Bolsón de Mapimí, in the east, and from the Gila River Valley, in the northwest, the *new invaders* [Apache] began to ransack the very heart of Nueva Vizcaya." Of course the routes and depth of Apache penetration differed between areas, but in northern Sonora (what is now southeastern Arizona) the Apache were not new invaders. It is possible that Plains Apache groups did

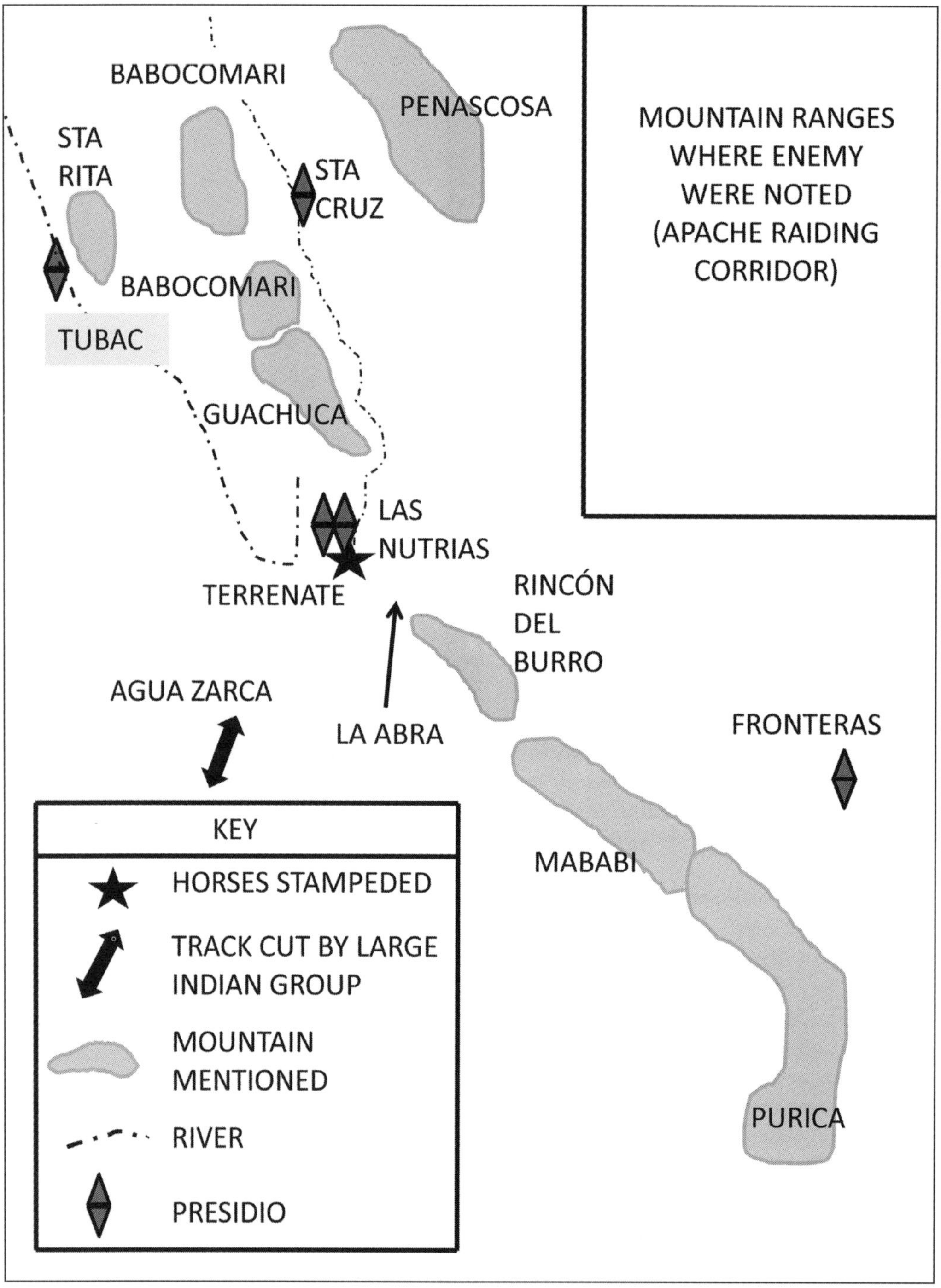

FIGURE 8.1. Apache raiding corridors as conveyed by Rocha and others of his time.

not reach as far south as the Río Grande until after Apachean groups who were further west did. In the documents included in this book, Apache groups that resided in vastly different geographic areas are referenced, but their histories differed markedly, as did their lifeways in many instances. In some areas, other indigenous groups effectively blocked Spanish contact with the Apache, or at least lessened its intensity, whereas here the Apache were the largest threat on the northern border. We now know from archaeological evidence that these impressions about the recent arrival of the Apache into southern Arizona, New Mexico, Chihuahua, and Sonora are incorrect (Seymour 2011b, 2012c, 2012d, 2013a, 2017a, 2017b). Thus, when a presidio captain or the viceroy discussed a recent uptick in Apache depredations, we must consider this as a possible reassertion after a quiet period, a new spurt of invigorated activity; alternatively, some other factor changed that might have pushed the Apache into a new area, encouraged shifts in their raiding patterns, or removed an obstacle or deterrent that had previously existed. In the specific 1748 case referenced by Moorhead (1975:49), he even noted that these Apache were being "aided and abetted by restless bands and the now unsupervised Tarahumara," which provides a hint as to the complicated interaction of groups that likely confused the Spaniards. In the late 1760s, Apache had taken advantage of a Seri rebellion to invade in large numbers (Moorhead 1975:61). Both examples demonstrate the importance of not assuming that recent invasions mean a recent arrival (e.g., migration), but rather represent new alliances or a taking advantage of the unrest or movement of another group (also see Seymour 2011b).

The identity of the enemy is often not specifically stated. In his summary, Rocha very clearly indicates several mountain ranges by name that were frequented by "the enemy." He does not identify who these enemies were, but these locations were clearly north of the range for the Seri, including the Tiburones and Tepocas. They were in the heart of the area used and occupied by various Apachean groups, and it seems fairly clear that it was one or more bands of the Apache whom they were referencing (Figure 8.1). Recent research indicates that ancestral Apachean groups (Chiricahua and Mescalero) were in the southern Southwest (Peloncillo, Dragoon, Chiricahua, Whitlock, Florida, Hueco, Organ, Franklin, Sacramento Mountains, and others) by the 1300s CE, if not earlier (Seymour 2008, 2012d, 2013a, 2017a, 2017b), and by this time in the late eighteenth century they were raiding into Mexico (Seymour 2011b).

If Spanish perceptions were accurate, the main route of Apache movement at this time was toward the Sierra Madres. This seems apparent from the sightings and problem areas mentioned by Rocha, for example, the Sierra Purica, up to the slopes of the Mababi. These and other areas mentioned as enemy terrain were to the south and southeast of Fronteras Presidio. Rocha also references the Rincón del Burro, where the enemy interfered with the Spaniard's agenda and where the enemy began most of their operations.

Ugarte suggests that a presidio be placed at Bavispe because the Sierra Madres to the east provided an important and protected route for invasion between Sonora and Nueva Vizcaya and a place of retreat for the enemy (also see Moorhead 1968:53). Lafora provided a detailed statement about the placement and movements of the Apache, which seems relevant in 1780 (Kinnaird 1958:127–128). He described the "customary hideouts and entries" of the Gileño Apache as follows:

> The Sierra Madre lies between the presidio of Janos in Nueva Vizcaya and the presidio of Fronteras in Sonora. The Gileños have a free passage through these mountains by the Carretas ridge [shown in Figure 1.3], which they frequent, and over the Caguiona mountains [Kinnaird talks about El Tinaja being beyond Caguiona, the former shown on maps], by El Potrero in the Fronteras chain and by other passages named in the diary. From the shelter of these immense and rugged mountains they sally forth to attack all the neighboring valleys and settlements belonging to the two districts.

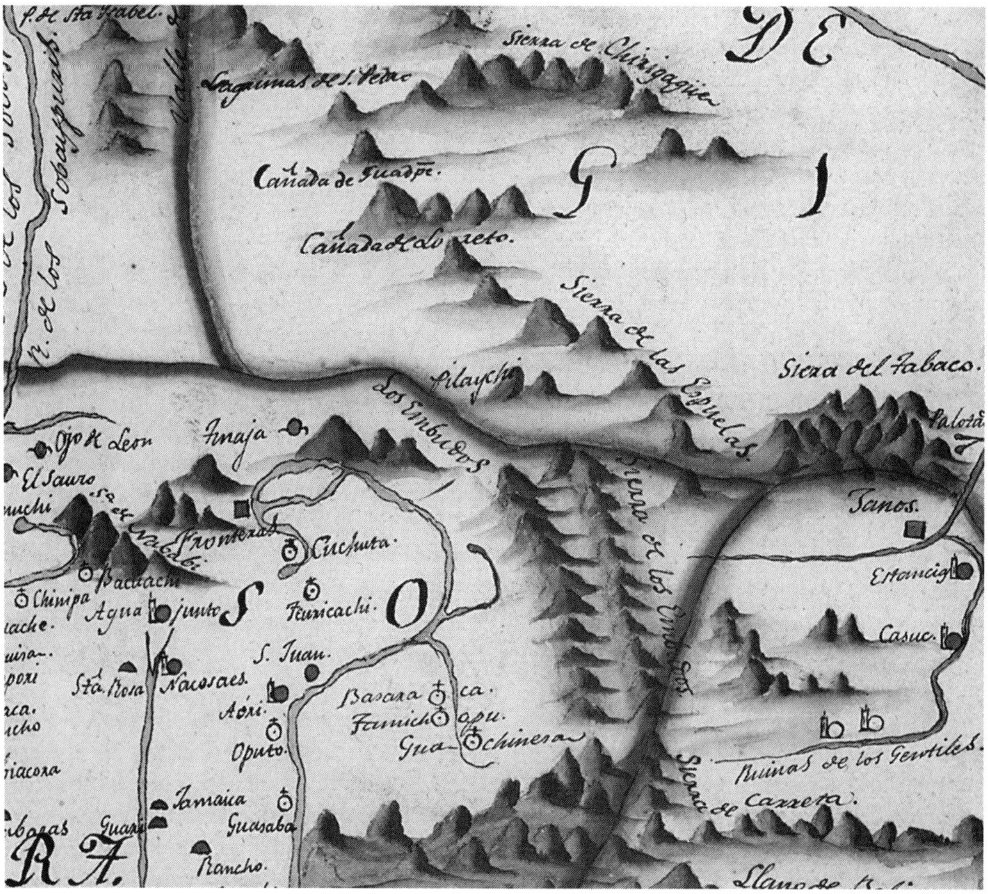

FIGURE 8.2. Close up of Urrutia's 1771 map showing Mountains used by the Apache as understood by the Spaniards at this time. [*Mapa de toda la frontera de los dominios del rey en la America septentrional*, 1771.] Courtesy of the Library of Congress; https://www.loc.gov/item/2001622423/.

Between Fronteras and the presidio of Terrenate, the most prominent mountains where the enemies usually seek refuge are Mababe or Tesocomáchic [west of Fronteras; shown in Figure 8.1], Magallanes [west of Fronteras], Chiguicagui [Chiricahua and related ranges; a bit misplaced on the Urrutia map relative to the Animas range and others], where there are always many Apache villages, and Ague Verde (Figure 8.2).

From Terrenate to Tubac presidio their sallies are over Las Bolas Ridge, the San Antonio Pass, and San Luis Valley. In the neighborhood of the [Tubac] presidio are the San Cayetano and Santa Rita Mountains. In the last named is the Consumidero Pass, ten leagues northeast of the presidio and much used by the enemies.[1] These mountains continue as a chain four or five leagues beyond Tucson pueblo, located twenty-one leagues north of Tubac and five from San Xavier del Bac, which precedes it. Both are inhabited by Pimas Altos Indians and administered by a Jesuit missionary....

From Tubac presidio looking toward Altar one sees the ruins of the Real de Aribaca, the Longoreña mine, and the Real de la Arizona. The first two were abandoned during the uprising of the Upper Pimas...Longoreña mine was abounded because of the constant attacks of the Apaches who frequent the cordillera where it was situated....

> Altar presidio is free from Apache attacks, but not from those of the Series and rebellious Pimas (Kinnaird 1958:127–128).

In his comprehensive 1781 report Croix states that as of 1777 the "Gila Apache were attacking [all the way] from the presidio of Santa Gertrudis del Altar in Pimería Alta as far as the neighborhood of the Real del la Trinidad [now Yécora, Sonora; not shown, but southeast of Pitic on Figure 1.1] in Lower Pimeria" (Thomas 1941:134). These descriptions were intended to convey a representation of the far northwest and southeastern reaches of Sonora, emphasizing the impact of the Apache and the degree to which they penetrated behind the Presidial Line. His point was that the enemy were everywhere and their penetration could not be halted, despite the objective of the Presidial Line, which was to keep the Apache to the north. This is apparent both before and after the reconnaissance, for in 1781 Gileño Apache attacks had reached Arizpe (Moorhead 1968:52).

A bit earlier, in 1775 O'Conor clarified that Apaches, or at least enemies, were in the rugged mountains that cut like a lance head through the Presidial Line. They were securely hidden in the mountains overlooking the missions and presidios, when he noted

> the ease with which the enemy can enter by way of the sierras of Guachuca, San Cayetano, and Santa Rita, along the cordillera which overshadows the entire trail. They will, with advantage, repeatedly attack our troops from the many hiding places and passes which the sierras provide (Thomas 1941:180).

These mountain ranges provided relatively unfettered access to the settlements in Sonora. These Apache distributions are reinforced by the content of Rocha's journal and his summary, wherein he notes that the Apache routinely moved from the Santa Rita Mountains to attack Tubac and that,

> being very near the foothills of the Santa Rita Mountains where its slopes extend, they form many breaks and ravines that allow the enemy to enter clandestinely right up to the houses, from which they have pierced with arrows, and killed a few *vecinos*, reducing them to such a small number that no more than nine remained by the time of my transit through that pueblo. And even of these [nine remaining residents], I learned the news that the day following my departure the enemy had killed two (Summary Report Chapter 3).

Rocha also provided information about their movements around the flanks of Tucson Presidio, suggesting the presidio could

> even provide aid to prevent the entry of the enemy by its flanks and especially via the south... [which is the point of entry that] needs the most guarding because there are located the populations of San Xavier del Bac, Tumacácori, and Calabazas. And because it is in the same direction as the uninhabited [places] of Sonoita, the passes of Agua Caliente, Babocomari, and other places where the enemy penetrates, launching from the mountains of Guachuca, Santa Rita, Babocomari [Mustang and Whetstone], Peñascosa [Dragoon], and other places [mountain ranges] that lie at their backs, which is why I consider it very useful to keep it [Tucson Presidio] in the place where it is located, and I have not seen another [place] where it would be better (Summary Report Chapter 3).

These adjacent mountain ranges were especially problematic for the Spanish because they allowed enemy entry into areas behind the Presidial Line. They served as conduits for travel, as Rocha makes clear when describing that the mountains between the Santa Cruz and San Pedro provided cover for their free passage. As settlements and presidios moved, so did enemy residences, routes of travel, and targets of raiding. The Spaniards did not necessarily grasp the full importance of this Apachean behavior, as seems clear when they described these mountain ranges as routes of travel rather than places of residence and refuge, as archaeological research suggests. The Spaniards continued to operate with the conceptual model that if they just had the presidios in the right place with the correct spacing, manned with sufficient troops, with manpower distributed appropriately, and were able to maintain settled populations in areas behind and in front of the line, they could stave off the attacks, the incursions, the southward travel from haunts to the north.

They were doomed to fail for so many reasons, including because their conceptions of Apachean distributions were faulty. European settlements attracted more raids (and the residential sites that followed the raiders south) and the thrust of the Spaniards northward meant a more diversified, intensified, and dispersed resistance. There were too many fronts that required Spanish attention because the raids were not organized along predictable fronts, but hit here and there, using small, mobile groups. Spanish fortresses were stationary, while the enemy was not and could move with ease to accommodate new raiding targets. The enemy was much more flexible and adjusted their movements accordingly, a problem that could not be solved but by more concentrated, widespread, and persistent opposition. Thus, tactics effective in 1768 were ineffective in 1775 or 1780, and as the overall strategy changed, as it often did, the enemy must have at times read into it their own triumph. Disadvantages in presidio placement were soon remedied by shifting presidios but then the abandoned location or points beyond became problematic once again. The shifts designed to obtain better positions undoubtedly sent messages of success to the enemy, encouraging future resistance as they advanced their raiding reach. Despite all the investment in establishing presidios, the line was stretched too far and had to be pulled back.

Rocha (Diary, June 14) also mentions seeing signs that a large group of Indians had intersected the royal road (*Camino Real*) ten days before south of Nogales in the Agua Zarca area. One implication of this is that this trail, inferred to be Apachean, followed a different course than the *Camino Real*, suggesting, as expected, that enemies of the Spaniards followed a different set of trails that sometimes intersected those of the Spanish. Apachean trials would have been in the highlands, in areas out of the way, and would have crossed the valleys quickly or at night unless they were in remote areas not used by indigenous or Spanish enemies.

In 1774 Governor Crespo conveyed his impressions of the source of the problem of Apache incursions. In doing so he provided insight into a critical misunderstanding of Apache practice, largely because he was overlaying European assumptions on Apache behavior:

> I consider the junction of the rivers of San Pedro and Gila (looking only at the Apache enemies) as the final point of the frontier. Although on the other side of the Gila there are some Apache, they cannot enter the province because they are opposed to the Gila, Pima, and Papago (Thomas 1941:175).

Crespo was contrasting the Apache groups north of the Gila (that we now call the Western Apache e.g., Cibecue, White Mountain, San Carlos) with the Gila Apache or Gileños whom he perceived as residing exclusively at or south of the Gila. At first glance it sounds like he was saying that this was the southern edge of the Apache distribution, and from there the Apache raided south, but in fact, he was saying that the Gila River was the geographical division between Apachean groups, the Gileños to the south and the Western Apaches to the north. If this place (San Pedro/Gila confluence) is occupied by the Spaniards, he thought, it would be near the north edge of Gila Apache territory, and also perhaps at the west edge of residential distribution for other Apaches. He understood that Apaches were present throughout the area, but incorrectly believed the Gileños and O'odham groups to the south of the Gila would prevent the more northern Apaches from moving south.

Crespo was also acknowledging the important role played by Sobaipuri O'odham groups, specifically those along the San Pedro, which likely still provided some resistance to Apache movements. This role for the Pima/O'odham has been argued for some time, although until recently it has been suggested the Pima/O'odham left the area entirely in 1762, though we now they remained (see Chapter 7; Seymour 2011b). In fact, it is this Rocha journal and map (as well as chronometric dates on Sobaipuri sites) that clarify without question that these residents were still present, and Crespo's words suggest these Sobaipuri O'odham were still allied with the Spanish. Crespo was also asserting that this corridor along the San Pedro was in itself limiting to Apache movement:

> Besides, even if there was not this block [by the Gila, Pima, and Papago], it is not possible for them [the Apache north of the Gila] to enter because the extensive land they would have to cross is so scarce in water that at certain times it is impassable, even for the natives themselves (Thomas 1941:175).

This underestimation of the landscape knowledge and differences in cultural practice of Apachean and other indigenous groups was likely one of the fundamental reasons the Spaniards were ineffective in subduing them. This specific valley was later a travel corridor for the Apachean groups north of the Gila as they moved south into Sonora and Sinaloa, Mexico (Ball 1970; Seymour 2012c, 2012e). It is unlikely that this favored route south was any less attractive fifty or one hundred years earlier. Moreover, had the Spaniards understood Apache behavior more thoroughly they would have understood that the Apache had a much more intricate landscape knowledge that allowed them to maneuver safely through lands the Spanish would find barren. They were able to find water in places that seemed waterless and they could survive on significantly less water than their European counterparts.

Crespo was correct that the mountains bordering these proposed presidios were in the heart of heavily used Apache territory:

> The three indicated spots [for presidios: Gila-San Pedro confluence, Santa Cruz, and San Bernardino] have the advantage of being points which, if not absolutely necessary, are the ones most utilized by the enemies for entering and departing, especially if they have [raided] herds and if they find themselves very close to their principal points of reunion. These advantages can facilitate the retrieval of stolen property which they have and their frequent punishment (Thomas 1941:175).

It should be no wonder, then, that attacks were so frequent at the presidios and on routes of travel between them and that so many men were lost in ambushes. The Spaniards followed predictable routes and practiced the routines characteristic of stationary settlers. Rather than bolstering the number of men and perhaps even adding a presidio or two along this north and eastern margin, they advanced only two presidios (Santa Cruz and San Bernardino) and then within a few years ended up pulling both back to or near their original southern locations.

As Fray Díaz pointed out in early 1775, many settlements at this time were either beyond the Presidial Line or were insufficiently protected. This latter point meant that enemies could insert themselves from beyond the Presidial Line, come down from the mountains, or, equally importantly, rise up with impunity:

> With the presidios established in the spots proposed all the missions and Spanish settlers are within their cordon or line...in this case the settlers of Tubac, the pueblos of Tumacácori, Calavazas, San Xavier, Tupson and those which can be established all along the Rio Gila and Colorado are exposed... the missions having been founded under the protection of these presidios, all the Papago country on the Rio Gila will be surrounded by Christianized pueblos. For this reason they are closest to the Catechism. Thus there is less danger that they may attempt some revolt because they will not have the refuge of the roving Indians which up until now has served them as an alternative and asylum for their evil activities (Thomas 1941:178).

Rocha's journal and also the summary reports provide insights into Spanish perceptions at the time of Apache behavior and movements. The Sierra Madres provided a highly attractive cover because the Apache could easily raid from these protected mountains into the heart of Sonora. This brought them to the far southeast, into what Croix had referred to as the "neighborhood of the Real de la Trinidad" in the Lower Pimería. Further north, the Santa Ritas provided direct access to Tubac and Tucson. The Huachucas and other ranges along the San Pedro were favored for their proximity to Terrenate, Las Nutrias, and Santa Cruz. With these strings of rugged mountains to hide them, the Apache had free access to valley settlements. The buildup of occupation in one area made it even more attractive as a target. The shift of a presidio to one of these locations left another area or settlement unprotected, changing the formula each raiding group used to assess risk and return. A presidio cordon was not likely to succeed in the face of exceptionally flexible Apache resistance and raiding tactics. Furthermore, the Apache were drawn to the herds, the unprotected fields, and the supply trains of these presidio outposts in ways that substantially supplemented their coffers.

Notes

1. This might be a reference to the pass through Madera Canyon, or perhaps north of the Santa Ritas and south of the Rincon Mountains, though this latter pass (where Interstate 10 lies) is probably too far north.

CHAPTER 9

Both Conceded and Contested

Each time an expedition entered these lesser known lands on the northern margin of the Spanish colonial empire, it was asserting claim to its resources and governance over its people. This 1780 reconnaissance was no exception, but by now a reality had set in. Part of this reality was starkly evident to Rocha when he arrived in February 1780 to help transfer civilians and troops back south to Las Nutrias from Santa Cruz de Terrenate Presidio on the San Pedro River. The residents were starving and terrorized, the landscape was barren and used up; the enemy had successfully undermined this part of the Spaniards' plan. Rocha was reminded of this again during the 1780 reconnaissance when stopping off at Las Nutrias, where the resident soldiers and settlers of Santa Cruz Presidio had withdrawn and no doubt remonstrated against the idea of establishing a presidio at the confluence of the San Pedro and Gila Rivers. It must have been clear to Rocha that if the Santa Cruz post had been too far north and too distant from adjacent presidios, then one established even further into enemy territory at a greater distance from supply lines and aid would be even more disastrous.

Each administration was faced with new circumstances involving a shift in presidio locations or intensity of enemy resistance, because, as noted in the preceding chapter, the enemy readily adapted (also see Worchester 1951:18). The frequency of enemy attacks was not constant, nor was the location of their raids consistent. These realities may have given the Spanish a false sense that their troop patrols and presidio shifts were having some consequential effect, and these might have had some result, but only for a short time after a transfer owing to the new circumstances presented to the enemy. Soon after news of an accomplishment or success was committed to paper and forwarded to higher authorities, the Apaches adapted their strategy and Spanish field and tactical responses were immediately less effective, if not obsolete. The Spanish authorities' need to consult the king and adhere to royal regulations in all matters made their responses to fluid situations exceedingly slow, in direct contrast to the expedited and ever-flexible action of the Apache. The quick-changing circumstances, even the location of the front of encounter, made it look like earlier Spanish claims were overstated or that previous officers had misread the situation. Moorhead (1968:34, 36, 46) and Thomas (1941:22–23, 28–35) describe the rancor and differences of opinion between Croix and Ugarte, on the one hand, and Bucareli and O'Conor, on the other, with respect to frontier conditions. No doubt some of this was purely politics and personalities, but the adaptability of the Apache should not be underestimated, as it often is in discussions of nineteenth-century Apache tactics. By then, in particular, the Apache had centuries of responding to and inciting responses from invaders, which laid the foundation for a highly developed system of Apachean field tactics in diverse theaters of conflict. This was understood by many of the Europeans as well, for a few years later Bernardo de Galvez would concede Apache superiority in weapons and tactics, and would acknowledge the shortcomings of past efforts to subdue them (Worchester 1951).

The Spanish were adaptable as well, however, despite the burdensome nature of their administrative structure. Both local officials and high-ranking authorities in central Mexico continually modified frontier policies to respond to ever-changing threats, changing royal orders, and new personnel. This is certainly true of Croix, who studied and learned from predecessors' reports, explored areas under his jurisdiction, and made more efficient use of available resources to modify the frontier army and its tactical response (also see Weber 1992:226, 443n100). One example implemented by Croix in 1778 was that *tropa ligera* (specialized light troops) were used to augment the leather-jacket soldiers, allowing for a much faster response to an agile enemy, whose fleetness they attempted to approximate. The particular expedition discussed in this book was an example of exploration that provided intimate knowledge of the area under Croix's jurisdiction. From this and other efforts Croix obtained firsthand information about frontier conditions, both with respect to resources and the enemy. In this case, the primary objective was to assess the movement of a presidio far to the north so that it could be most effective in the king's larger strategy to connect the California settlements to Sonora.

But this flexibility was also detrimental, particularly when expressed as vacillations in policy and action. As José de Gálvez changed policies in rapid succession, from defensive war to offensive war, then to peace, and then back again to offensive war (Weber 2005:156), the Apache had opportunities to regroup and were emboldened. This 1780 reconnaissance was carried out during a time when Carlos III and Gálvez had ordered "kindness, good treatment, and benevolence" toward the enemy. Rather than conveying power and resolve, these changes in policy must have looked fickle, for, if nothing else, periods of peace and defensive war were a welcome reprieve for the enemy.

The Conceded Colonial Landscape

To the Apache, the Spanish had conceded terrain when they moved the Santa Cruz and San Bernardino garrisons back south. It probably looked this way as well when Tubac was moved northwest to Tucson, away from the mountains and further from their trails, leaving a tiny cadre of settlers to fend for themselves. For centuries indigenous peoples had forfeited their homelands in the face of conflict or after a defeat in battle. Even after prevailing in the 1698 battle at Santa Cruz de Gaybanipitea, the Sobaipuri O'odham left the San Pedro Valley to the enemy for several years as they retreated to the Sonoita Valley. Ugarte and Rocha may have quietly sensed that Spanish tactics were being misread, although they provide no hint. Nonetheless, deserted presidios, settlements, and missions were part of the reality of the colonial landscape encountered by this expedition. These were clear reminders of resources expended, lives lost, and the momentary (they hoped) setback in progress. This reconnaissance would help determine where resources would be directed, which settlements would be re-established, and where presidios would be placed, but still within the confines of the clearly laid-out strategy decided upon more than a decade earlier. Options for these administrators and field men were limited as they moved pieces within the confines of the king's chess board, while begrudgingly recognizing the elusive enemy had the upper hand.

The character of the discarded colonial landscape was one of melting adobe ruins, burned-out churches, harassed villagers, and valleys surrendered to violence. Yet it was also one of hope, of founding new settlements to the northwest at Yuma, of extending a line of support along the route to the Californias, and establishing a stronger, more unified front with more closely spaced presidios, supported by *compañias volantes*, *tropa ligera*, and towns garrisoned with militias. Many of the relinquished places would soon be revived, reclaimed again, as part of the newest frontier strategy.

Ugarte, Rocha, and their party visited many forsaken places, some in ruins, others with small populations remaining, struggling. Many old ranchos, pueblos, haciendas, estancias, and presidios were described by these men as abandoned, ruined, old, or ancient places. These descriptors acknowledge that these places no longer served as they had originally or as intended. Many of these lacked populations because the people had fled to safer locations, including larger settlements, presidios, or further from the entry points of the enemy. Nonetheless, many of these locations were still of use and formed a part of the expedition backdrop, providing temporary shelter that tethered the soldiers to a named and familiar place. These familiar places helped orient the direction of travel and these places were registered by being committed to Rocha's map. Ugarte and Rocha evaluated the terms of the failure of each and in doing so were assessing the future of hundreds of natives, *vecinos*, and solders who would be asked to repopulate some of these places.

Many of these familiar and defensible places were used as camps along the way, especially those that provided comfort or safety. Ugarte and Rocha stopped over at the suppressed Santa Cruz de Terrenate Presidio, which provided both relief and protection, despite its perilous history. The still-standing walls provided greater security than the open terraces bordering the river. As noted, it had only been a few months since Santa Cruz's population had left, moving back south to Las Nutrias. Consequently, features of this defensive site were still fresh in military consciousness and in Rocha's especially recent recollection. Even the middens that bordered the gate would have still been ripe with offensive smells and the items left upon removal of the population were there for the use or intrigue of the soldiers. Some of the suppressed presidio's attributes were noted on Rocha's map, including Sentinel Hill (*Serro de la Sentinela*) across the way from the presidio, and his men probably used this as a lookout post during this reconnaissance. A few years later, during the 1795 Zuniga expedition, Santa Cruz was used as a jumping off point again, where troops gathered from many different areas before proceeding on an expedition (Hammond 1931; Holterman 1956:2). In fact, a sizable lump of flux and a majolica game piece found in the lower fill of rooms during Seymour's recent excavations there may attest to the quotidian details of preparing for an extended campaign by military personnel who regrouped in the presidio ruins. Even though the presidio had been suppressed, it was still perceived as a feature of the military expedition landscape, though its role within the colonial setting had changed. This reuse of abandoned places shows how even the landscapes of Europeans remain imbued with meaning and value despite a movement of residence (Seymour 2011b:n61).

Frontier Defense

The documents included in this book provide evidence of the treacherous conditions in the late 1700s and are especially informative about the northern margin of the frontier. Spanish strategies required adjustment, and the indigenous populations that lived beside the Spanish were also forced to adjust to accommodate the increasingly intense conflict. For centuries the Sobaipuri O'odham had lived in settlements consisting of loosely arranged but formally distributed house pairs on flats overlooking their river bottom fields (Seymour 2011a). By the 1780s they were building and occupying fewer and larger settlements with housing defensively arranged. A description by Padre Joseph Och (Treutlein 1965:151) suggests that this type of arrangement may have begun by midcentury or shortly thereafter, at least further south. This defensive arrangement consisted of closely spaced houses, as seen in the archaeological record as a result of excavations over the last decade at Guevavi Mission (Seymour 2009b, 2011a, 2013b), adobe row houses at Wa:k, and in the passages of Rocha's journal (also see Seymour 2019a). Whereas for centuries the Sobaipuri O'odham had occupied elevated landforms near the river, by the last quarter of the eighteenth century they occupied even higher landforms with steeper slopes, landforms that had until then been avoided. Their settlements were also situated a little farther from rivers, as is apparent at villages on the Gila that were positioned far away from their former locations (see Chapter 7). Rather than being situated along major thoroughfares to engage in commerce and serve as gatekeepers into and across their homeland, the Sobaipuri O'odham moved their settlements to places where they would be less vulnerable, could not be as easily accessed by Apaches, and where vegetation would not as easily obscure an enemy approach.

Some mission settlements, like San Xavier and Tumacácori, even incorporated guard towers (but see Seymour 2019a). The guard towers in particular may reflect European influence, although defensive structures had been used throughout the region for some time (Seymour 2014). Traditional accounts indicate that Casa Grande along the Gila River was built by the prehistoric Hohokam to protect against enemies from the east, and early accounts captured by both Kino (Bolton 1948:I:128) and Manje (Karns 1954:287) reference Apache attacks as a basis for disruption at the end of the prehistoric period. This is, of course, consistent with early dates that show an ancestral Apachean presence in this area during this late prehistoric period, at least as early as the 1300s CE. Padre Andrés Pérez de Ribas and other early missionaries and expedition members also discussed defensive features throughout Sonora and Sinaloa, suggesting they represent a traditional defensive strategy and an established form of architecture that may precede Europeans, although the effects of European presence occur much earlier in those areas (see Seymour 2014 for a discussion). Several Sobaipuri O'odham villages, including Santa Cruz de Gaybanipitea, Santa Cruz del Pitaitutgam, and Quiburi on the San Pedro River, all had defensive structures in the 1690s. It is difficult to know at this point if these defensive adobe-walled structures were newly adopted, owing to increased violence in this period, because earlier communal structures are apparent in these and other Sobaipuri O'odham sites. More research is needed to determine whether these later forms were encouraged or even introduced by the Europeans, or whether such structures simply changed in character as new building techniques, materials, and details were incorporated. Seymour's recent research at these specific sites suggests that the latter is true, because use of adobe structures for defense follows a long indigenous tradition in Sonora and Sinaloa; structures dated much earlier seem to have served a similar role to these later adobe-walled structures. So while indigenous settlements in this frontier area became increasingly fortified through the years, fortification was not a new concept for regional indigenous residents. Violence did not begin with European entrance into the region, but the nature of this violence changed and long-standing balances and alliances were disrupted. In any event, the descriptions provided in Rocha's journal are indispensible for understanding the dynamic circumstances facing mission-based indigenous groups at the time, which in southern Arizona/northern Sonora pertained largely to the Sobaipuri O'odham.

Naming and Claiming the Frontier

Ugarte and Rocha traveled to places already known to themselves at the time, if only vaguely, and to others. Many of the routes taken had been trails first worn by indigenous peoples, although this fact is not mentioned by either Ugarte or Rocha. The soldiers at the former presidio of Terrenate (San Felipe de Gracia Real de Guevavi, or Terrenate, established in 1742), then Las Nutrias (est. 1774), and Santa Cruz (1775–1780) moved through and across these valleys along regular patrol routes between presidios and on campaigns (see O'Conor 1994:75, also endnote in Chapter 5). Even in this region distant from European society *caminos* had been established and served as travel routes between known waterholes or as supply routes up from the south or between population centers. Ugarte and Rocha traveled specific routes rather than engaging in random walks, thereby saving effort and assisting in the preparation of the requisite map. In this way they further inscribed the landscape with order, committing the world around them to parchment and through their words, bringing decisiveness to their observations. In 1780 the resulting documents attested to their passage and their commitment to their commission. The retracing of existing routes, previously charted and named, reinforced the king's claim to a land that otherwise lay neglected by his subjects. Their footsteps and pen strokes incised the indigenous landscape, leaving indelible marks as invasive as knife jabs at a deer-skin shield. Exploration of lesser known areas and the knowledge gained strengthened the crown's claim as well, at the same time circumscribing and crosscutting the indigenous realm.

Nonetheless, this area beyond the Presidial Line was less known than zones to the south. These two officers were sent north to analyze this terrain and to descriptively and cartographically capture its essence in a manner that had relevance to military strategy. This effort as an initial step in taming this frontier is reflected as Ugarte and Rocha named specific places along their route. As the reconnaissance team moved throughout the region they recalled existing, long-used names for places and committed them to map and journal. Many pueblos, mountain ranges, and waterholes had indigenous names which they retained and whose origins can be discerned in their spellings. Those to the north are Sobaipuri O'odham names, while those to the southeast are often Ópata, some Tarahumara. Names to the south are also O'odham and then others further to the southwest are Yaqui and Seri. While the Hispanicized spellings often distort the original names, many times the original meaning can be discerned, as has been conveyed throughout this book. In some cases, modern O'odham speakers provide some of the best links to the original meanings, either through a continued use of the terms (such as Wa:k, e.g., San Xavier del Wa:k) or because those who still speak various dialects of the language convey the many possible variations in meaning. Still, interpretation of the meaning varies across the O'odham world because pronunciation and dialects differ throughout.

In a number of other instances, the meaning has been lost, though many suggestions have been proffered for the original intent (e.g., see endnotes regarding Guevavi, Tubac, Tumacácori, Babocomari, Huachuca, etc.). One example is the name Arizona or Arizonac, which as a place south of the international line in Mexico became a focus of Basque settlement before the name was transferred to the American state. Several suggestions have been made as to its original meaning, the first made by Padre Pfefferkorn, who in the mid-1700s suggested this meant "sand dune" in O'odham (Treutlein 1949:236). Yet many of the names Pfefferkorn suggested have since been legitimately questioned. Following Granger (1982:xv), Bright (2013:9) suggests that Arizona derives from "al sonag" which means "having a little spring" or "place of the little spring," although he suggests that this could be a Basque word meaning "good oaks," as suggested by Garate (1999) from miners who settled the area. Given that most names for known places of the period were referenced by their existing indigenous names by the Spaniards, it is most likely that Arizona derives from an O'odham word. This interpretation was suggested by historian James McClintock (1915:3), who recorded that an Arizona pioneer named Isaac D. Smith stated that it was an O'odham word for a small stream which they called Aleh-zon (young spring), but some modern O'odham suggest ali shon (small base). Rocha's journal and map make this practice quite apparent, in that the indigenous names for existing places were commonly maintained and incorporated into the European system of reference. In fact, many of these names have been maintained to this day.

In some instances familiar names were used in 1780 but the landforms to which they refer have changed. One example of this is the modern-day Santa Rita Mountains: in Rocha's time the north end was called the San Cayetano Mountains while the south end and highest part were known as the Santa Ritas. Today it is just the opposite.

In still other cases modern names are recorded on the map, such as the Santa Teresa Mountains, replacing the older name Sierra de

Santa Rosa de la Florida. Yet some of the more ancient names are retained or ranges were named anew, including the mountains north of the Gila River, which the map labels Sierra del Aribaipa, an area that today is known as the Pinal Mountains.

Ugarte and Rocha also provided new names for places that lacked labels or whose names they had not heard. *Vados* or river crossings were mostly referred to by Spanish words, perhaps even as they were "discovered" by this expedition as a way of claiming the landscape. In fact, Rocha noted regular river crossings on his map and in his journal, as per his instructions. Some of the names seem to have been long-standing references, and so while they were Spanish names they were not "discovered" by Ugarte and Rocha. For example, as already noted, Tres Alamos was referenced as a camping place, sometimes called Los Alamos in Kino's time (1690s). Only one of the crossings in Arizona was given an indigenous name, suggesting that many additional places were crossable on foot and so specific crossings were not memorialized with names, or at least these were not conveyed to the Spaniards. This may simply reveal which portions of landscape knowledge had been conveyed by indigenous residents, rather than an absence of intersecting interest in these types of geographic places. On the other hand, crossings had special relevance for military men whose considerations required unencumbered crossings for their mounts, and routes of escape so as to preserve their lives, their horses, and their possessions. Natural crossings allowed them to avoid having to make bridges to cross rivers and swamps in order to take the horses and baggage across (e.g., Machuca 1892).

Most *vados* held Spanish names that characterized some special attribute of the crossing, for example, *Atascadero* ["Bog" or "Mire"] and *Caída* ["Fall"], or Tres Alamos, Los Alamos, or Alamo, are the most commonly used names on San Pedro, along with *Fresno* ["Ash Tree"]. Names that convey the physical characteristics of the crossing are most common, such as *Peñasco* ["Crag or Large Rock"] and *Pedregoso* ["Rocky"], each of which is a different way of conveying the rockiness of the area. Given the characteristics of the San Pedro with quicksand, it is not too surprising that they would select the rockiest places that would provide stable substrate to cross. The bed of the San Pedro is only intermittently rocky; the rockiness is usually caused by tributary washes dumping rocks into the main channel. Occasionally a crossing will be a place where the bedrock outcrops or where the channel has been scoured exposing deep deposits of cobbles.

Some place names have survived to this day, including those for the Sonora River, Fronteras, San Pedro, Cañada del Oro, Tres Alamos, Canenea, Sonoita, and Babocomari, though the latter reference for an adjacent mountain range has been changed to the Whetstone and Mustang Mountains. The San Pedro was once known by other names, the Nexpa during Coronado's time, and as the Quiburi, Terrenate, and San Joseph de Terrenate River during Kino's time (Seymour and Stewart 2017). The Santa Cruz River was once known as the Santa María, labeled by Kino in 1691 (Seymour 2012b). Some places visited by Ugarte and Rocha and earlier Europeans have long been forgotten, but have since been found again. For example, the archaeological location of Quiburi from this period has been identified, which was the only Sobaipuri O'odham settlement on the San Pedro at the time of Ugarte and Rocha's visit. Despite these changing names, these places and rivers remain lively in the imaginations of local residents and indigenous peoples who once called these places their home.

Borders and Boundaries

At the time of this Ugarte-Rocha reconnaissance the international border that is so prominent in today's conceptions of this region did not exist. Fronteras Presidio was guarding the border (as its name suggests) in the northeastern sector of Sonora, facing the Sierra Madres. Tucson, as Ugarte said, was at the northwest corner of the province. All of these presidios and new settlements were in the frontier region, pushing the boundaries of the barely known, attempting to tame the fringes of the Spanish empire, to extend the area of protection without breaking the increasingly brittle defenses. Even so, these campaigners probably knew this land better than most present-day residents of Tucson. Slow and deliberate travel, perhaps at least one man counting each pace, brought them to direct awareness and sometimes into agonizing connection with each laborious league within this prickly, desiccated, and dangerous land.

At that time portions of this region were probably more desolate than they had been, with few residents along the San Pedro River. However, this valley was not entirely devoid of population, for, as noted, the Sobaipuri O'odham remained to hold their traditional lands and enemy families found refuge and resources throughout this zone. Sobaipuri O'odham clung to their homeland, perched on an elevated landform, while attempting to manage the ever-changing realities that had taken hold, as they had done for centuries. In fact, these residents of Quiburi stayed long after the Spaniards fled south, and their descendants were still present when others came to use this river valley throughout the next century, as archaeology attests (Seymour 2011a, 2014).

The Spaniards did not mention seeing the Apaches who were now lords of these hinterlands and the reason for their labors. The exception is a single reference to an encounter, probably on the San Pedro (Diary, June 23, 1780; Dobyns 1976, Chapter 6), although they did see tracks (Diary, June 14). Settlements in the Santa Cruz Valley were gaining traction as Europeans huddled near Sobaipuri O'odham population centers, sharing scarce water resources, tapping into their canals, appropriating agricultural lands, and pasturing their horses in the extensive ciénega near San Xavier. They also shared the burden of defense, mustering forces from the Sobaipuri O'odham settlements of San Xavier and the pueblo at Tucson.

As these officers looked out on the blue mist settling on the mountains and the fiery sunset gracing the western sky, they may have thought of the enemy's smokescreen descending on the land and the flames of their retribution on friends and family. This was still a land filled with many peoples that, they believed, remained to be tamed by the wits and swords of gentlemen. Their Presidial Line was intended as a lariat cast around the wilderness in a transcontinental effort to break the enemy, convert those who were friendly, establish bastions of security as far out on the frontier as possible, and repel or expel those who might make parallel and competing claims. It is no wonder that, after hearing the stories of terror and privation from the unnerved men of the Santa Cruz garrison and their families, Rocha was so clearly opposed to establishing a presidio at the confluence of the San Pedro and Gila. All of the atrocities and hardships experienced at Santa Cruz de Terrenate would be compounded, they reasoned, by the even more remote placement recommended by predecessors and desired by the king. Tucson Presidio and its environs were, by contrast, a shiny *concho* along a much more reasonable expanse of land. And so the fate of Tucson was decided by this reconnaissance. It would stand as a bastion positioned "at the corner of the province," as Ugarte commented, until the places between Tucson and Monterey could be established.

APPENDIX

Transcriptions of Primary Documents

Artículos 1.º y 2.º titulo 10 del Real Reglamento de Presidios
Titulo Decimo.

Trato con los Yndios enemigos, o Yndiferentes.

1,, Deviendo la Guerra tener por objecto la Paz, y siendo el de mi mayor atención el bien, y la converción de los Yndios Gentiles, y la tranquilidad de los payzes de Frontera, el inspector Comandante, y los Capitanes, y Tropa de presidios tendrán siempre presente, que los medios mas eficaces de conseguir tan útil y piadosos fines, Son el Vigor, y actibidad en la Guerra, y la buena fee, y dulzura de trato con los Rendidos dados de paz, o prisioneros: por tanto, la primera atención de to--dos hade ser con los Yndios declaradamente Enemi-gos mantener una viva, é incesante guerra y en quanto sea posible atacarlos en sus mismas Rancherías, y terrenos; pero con los prisión--eros que de estos se hagan en las funciones de Guerra, prohíbo todo mal trato, é impongo pe--na de muerte al que los matase a sangre fría; y mientras no se remitan á las cercanías de México, para que mi Virrey los destine como–convenga: Mando se les asista con la Ración de Víve--beres diaria que se da á los Yndios Auxiliares; y las Mujeres, ó parbulos que se aprehendan, se--ran igualmente tratados, y asistidos, procurando su converción, y enseñanza.

2,,. Pero habiendo acreditado la experiencia, que la suabidad, y buen trato con los prisioneros particulares es tan util, como perniciosa la contemplación con la nación enteras; y la facilidad de conseder pases ó Treguas, que no sean cimentadas, y seguras, maior--mente á los Apaches, que con distintos nombres hos-tilizan las Fronteras, demostrando el deseo de la paz, ó Reducción quando se hayan inferiores en fuerzas ó atemorizados por los sucesos, y abusando después á la primera ocasión, interpretando como debilidad la clemencia con que se les ha tratado, y admitido, prohíbo al inspector Comandante y á los Capitanes de Presidios, que puedan consederles Paz; y en el caso de que la pidan con seguridades ó señales que la persuadan estable, ó berdadera, ó que quieran sugetarse a mi Dominación, solo se les concederá por los Capitanes una Tregua, ó suspención de Armas (dando rehenes), por los días suficientes para tener la confirmación del Inspector Comandante, y por este no se les alargará tampoco sino por el tiempo necesario, para con la aprobación de mi Virrey, forma--lizar las circunstancias, y condiciones, exigiendo siem--pre, durante las referidas treguas, la total sesa--ción de hostilidades; y si se pudiere, la restitución de Prisioneros, Españoles, Españoles, ó Yndios Amigos.

[Text continues but is not relevant.]

[Only a portion of the following text is included.]

CORDON DE PRESIDIOS.

Altar.

2. Es el primero de los fronterizos el Pre--sidio de Altar, que hallandose actualmen.[te] situa

-do á treinta leguas de Vizani, y Pitiqui, Pue -blos pertenecientes á la antigua mision de Caborca. destruida por los Apaches, se deve remover, y colocar en otro paraje mas inmediato á la Costa del Golfo de Californias, procuran -do establecerlo en terreno llano donde hay a agua, y pastos suficientes para la Caballadas y en que no sea dificiles á sus Destaca- -mentos recorrer y batir los distritos que han- -de quedar por Derecha é izquierda desde este Presidio a las Orillas del mar, y al inmediato de la Linea, para impedir que los Enemigos del rumbo del Norueste internen á hostilizar Ia Provincias.

Tubac.
3,, A menos distancia de quarenta le- -guas del anterior Presidio se halla el de Tubac, con un competente, vecindario, que sea congrega -do á las sombras de su Guarnasion, y los Vecinos pueden subsistir en aquel parages trasladandose La Compaña á otro de sus cer canías donde ofrece el terreno las propor -ciones
indispensables, y la de situarse precisamente a la misma distancia de quarenta leguas de Altar, acercandose á este fin quanto sea posible asi a el oeste con el objecto de ase -gurar su reciproca comunicación, cortar promis -cuamente rastros en el terreno intermedio, y em -barazar las entradas de los Enemigos del País interior.

Terrenate.
4,, Se halla establecido este Presidio en me -nos distancia de Tubac, de las quarenta le- -guas, que acortas diferencia han de tener entre sí todos los de la Línea, y por lo mis= -mo deve removerse, y situarse, precediendo indibidualo reconocimiento de los terrenos, en al guno de los muchos Valles que bañan los Ríos de San Pedro, las nutrias, Guachuca Terrena -te, y otros, procurando dexar casi a su espalda las Sierras de Magallanes, y Mababe, y en mas cercanía al Presidio de Frontera, para que asi puedan impedir las invasiones de los Apaches, y auxiliarse mutuamente sus Destacamentos de los dos Colaterales.

Fronteras.
5,, Respecto de hallarse tan mal situ- -ado este Presidio, en que haí un mediano vecindario, que dista sesenta leguas del de Janos, dejando por consiguiente descubierta – una gran parte de la Fronteras mas expu- -esta á las incursiones de los Apaches Jileños se hade trasladar con la posible brevedad al Valle de San Bernardino, a otro paraje in- mediato, si lo huviese mas ventajoso, con el pre- -ciso destino, de que crusándose, y uniéndose sus destacamentos con los de Janos y Terrenate con- tengan las entradas de aquellos Barbaros, cayendoles con frecuencia sobre sus cercanos Aduares õ Rancherías.

6,, Los sitios en que actualm.[te] se hallan los referidos quatro Presidios de la Frontera de Sonora han de quedar á la traslación de ellos, ocupados con el Vecindario que tuvíeren y además se deverán agregar otros Pobladores Españoles, ẽ Yndios opatas, dandose atodos re- partimiento de tierras, y Casas, õ solares para fabricarlas, con las precisas condiciones de man -tenerse equipados, y dispuestos ã defender sus respectibos distritos, y auxiliár los destacam.[tos] de la tropas que hande Resguardar la Fron- -teras; ácuio fin se proveera á los españoles de las Armas que necesiten por el mero costo que tuvieren ami R.[l] Haz.[da] [Real Hacienda]; y a dhos
Yndios opatas se les dará de cuenta de ella Escopetas, õ Carabinas, por su notorio valor y la constante fidelidad que tienen acreditada desde que voluntariam.[te] entraron en mi Do- minio.

Californias.
29,, Arreglados ya los Presidios del continente, y sus situados annuales: (pues los dos interiores de Sonora, que solo deven subsistir interín se radican en Pueblos los Yndios rendidos, quedan sugetos en todo ã este Reglamento) Declaro, q.[e] los de Californias hande continuar por a ora sobre el pié que se hallan, conforme ã las pro- -videncias dadas por mi Virey, despues de haverse extendido la conquista, y Reducción hasta el Puerto de Monterrey; y supuesto de tener provisionalmente señalada la cantidad annual de treinta y tres mil p.[s] para la atencion y resguardo de aquella Península Ordeno, y Mando, que este situado se continúe pagando al fin de cada año en la R.[l] Caxa de Guadalajara, como se ha practicado ultimamente y que mi Virrey Sostenga, y auxilie por todos los medios posi- -bles los antiguos, y nuevos establecimientos

de dha Provincia, y me informe de todo lo q.[e] Regulare conducente, y util para su fomento posible, y extencion de las nuevas reducción.[es] de Yndios Gentiles.

[Text continues but is not relevant to this.]

[Begin orders, summary reports, and diary.]

Copias de las ordenes comunicadas al Gov.[or] Militar Dn Jacobo Ugarte y Loyola, y al Ingeniero Dn Gerónimo de la Rocha para los Reconocimientos de la Frontera de Sonora y traslacion de sus Presidios, y de los Informes de aquel Gefe y este Oficial.

Orn Ynstructiva al Govern.[or] Militar. [Croix=Ugarte]

En los Articulos 2.º 3.º 4.º y 5.º de la R.[l] ynstruccion inserta al Reglamento de Presidios se digno resolver S.M. la traslacion de los de Santa Gertrudirs del Altar, Tubac, Terrenate, y Fronteras äla nueva Linea propuesta por el exmo s.[or] Marques de Rubi, y en el Articulo 29. de la misma Ynstruccion la reforma de los de s.[n] miguel de Orcasitas, y san Carlos de Buenavista.

Correspondiendo del cumplimiento de estas Soberanas resoluciones al difunto Comandante Ynspector d. Hugo Õconor practicó este Gefe las diligencias requisitas resultando de ellas que variada en parte la prevenida direccion de la Linea de Frontera se trasladara el Presidio de este nombre al valle de s.[n] Bernardino, el de Terrenate al arruinado Pueblo de Santa Cruz, y el de Tubac, al Tucsón; que conservara

su Puesto el del Altar, y que se suspendiese la reforma de los de Orcasitas, y Buenavista.

Sobre todas estas providencias, y las succesivas que se discurrieron para mejorarlas y asegurar la defensa de esta Provincia expusieron sus dictamenes el referido comandante Ynspector, y el Governador D. Fran.[co] Antonio Crespo, pero nada pudo adelantarse por que no lo permitieron las inquietudes de los Seris, y las hostilidades del Apache.

Unas y otras obligaron al Teniente Coronel d.[n] Juan Bap.[ta] de Ansa siendo comandante de las Armas de la Provincia a representarme la necesidad de que volviesen los Presidios (que havian transmigrado) ã sus antiguos terrenos, y Yo accediendo ã su solicitud, determine que procediera como que tenia las cosas presentes, y con la justa responsabilidad

ã que desde luego le contrageron sus proposiciones.

Di cuenta de ellas ã S.M. y aunque en R.[l] orden de 30,, de Diz.[re] de 77. se digno aprovar mi determinacion, no ha podido verificarse hasta ahora en que conferida ã V.S. la comision de reconocimientos de la Frontera, espero que sus resultas sean el feliz cumplimiento de las Soberanas resoluciones del Rey.

Para proporcionarlo es indispensable que V.S. egecute el examen mas escrupuloso y prolijo, no solo de los terrenos que actualmente ocupan los Presidios de la Provincia, sino también de los que cubrían antiguam,[te] de los que previo la R.[l] Ynstruccion para la nueva Linea, y de los que puedan ser ventajosos para continuarla hasta darse la mano con los nuevos establecimientos del Rio Colorado, y abrirse la comunicacion

con la California septentrional, pues la importancia y gravedad de los fines ã que se contrahen las R.[s] resoluciones exigen los insinuados indispensables reconocim.[tos]

Lleva V.S. ã sus ordenes para que le ayude al Yngeniero d.[n] Gerónimo de la Rocha, y deviendo V.S. empezar su comision por el Presidio de Fronteras, luego que se haga cargo de la situacion, proporciones, y ventajas del citado Presidio, continuará V.S. su marcha por el camino derecho, Õ de costado al parage en que empieza ã correr sin intermision el Rio de s.[n] Pedro y desde alli examinando los arroyos de Guachuca, Las Nutrias, y Terrenate al nacimiento del Rio, despues se dirijira V.S. por sus margenes hasta el parage donde se une con el Gila, y retirandose al Presidio de san Agustin del Tucson, reconocerá V.S. antiguo de

Tubac, volviendo al de Terrenate.

Concluido este examen podrá V.S. trasladarse al Pitic por el Presidio de s.[ta]

Gertridir del Altar, reconociendo en este retroceso el valle del Arivac, Busanic, Saric, Tubutama, y demas misiones de esta ruta, y me remitirá con el Plano õ Croquis correspondiente que formara el Ingeniero d.ⁿ Gerónimo de la Rocha un Ynforme claro y bien circunstanciado de las distancias, Sierras, Puertos, Cajones, Rios, Ojos de Agua, Arroyos que las conserven todo el año, y los que carezcan de ella en la estacion de seca, circunstancias del Rio de s.ⁿ Pedro, numero y nombres de su pasos vadeables, calidades de las tierras de sus margenes, posibilidad, õ imposivilidad de fecundarlas.

Consiguiente ã esta prolija disertacion del Pais, me expondrá V.S. lo que

se le ofreciere y pareciere sobre los Parages que deben ocuparse en la Linea que verdaderamente lo sea de Frontera para la defensa de la Provincia, teniendo presente la circunstancia precisa de que al abrigo de los Presidios puedan establecerse Poblaciones respetables que con el tiempo no necesiten los auxilios de la Tropa.

En el mismo Ynforme õ con separacion me expondrá V.S. su dictamen ã cerca de la ereccion del Presidio que han solicitado los Opatas, y ultimamente como quiera que V.S. va a conocer practicam.[te] los Territorios de la Frontera, espero hallar en sus Ynformes todo quanto pueda desear y sea conducente al beneficio de esta Provincia, cumplimiento de las R.[s] Resoluciones de S.M. y arreglo de mis succesivas providencias.

Cerca del Arroyo de las Nutrias

hallara V.S. trasladado el Presidio de s.[ta] Cruz, y al capitan d.ⁿ Jph Vildosola con la orden de levantar algunas Barracas para alojamiento interino de la Tropa, h.[ta] que V.S. me informe si será conveniente situar allí el Presidio.

Assi el mencionado capitan, como el de san Agustin del Tucson d.ⁿ Pedro De Allande acompañaran ã V.S. si lo considerare necesario, y podrá V.S. confiarles los reconocimientos que tenga por convenientes pues aunque he detallado todos los que deben egecutarse con presencia del Yngeniero Don Gerónimo del la Rocha, dejo ã V.S. el arbitrio de hacerlos por si, õ por los Oficiales que merezcan su concepto para la mas pronta conclusion de los importantes encargos que hago al acreditado zelo de V.S.

Dios guarde ã V.S. muchos años. Arispe 15. de Abril de 1780= el cav.[ro]

de Croix=s.[or] d.ⁿ Jacobo Ugarte y Loyola__

Otra acompañandole Docum.[tos] y avisandole la comisión del Yngeniero D. Geronimo de la Rocha [Croix=Ugarte]

Mui señor mio: Tengo por conveniente remitir á V.S. las adjuntas Copies de Ynformes que hicieron del difunto comand.[te] Ynspector D. Hugo Õconor, el Coronel d.ⁿ Fran.[co] Crespo, el Ayunante Ynspector d.ⁿ Antonio Bonilla, y el R.P.F. Juan Diaz sobre el establecimiento de la Linea de Presidios de esta Provincia, para que V.S. los tenga á la vista en la comision que le he conferido, y me los devuelva luego que la haya finalizado, previnien do a V.S. franquee los referidos Documentos al Yngeniero D. Gerónimo de la Rocha.

Dios que a V.S. mu.[s] an.[s] Arispe 16. de Abril de 1780= BLm. de V.S. su mas at.[o] seg.[o] serv[or]= el cav.[ro] de Croix= s.[or] d[n] Jacobo Ugarte y Loyola___

Orñ al Yngeniero. [Croix=Rocha]

Por orden Verbal he prevenido a Vm

que bajo las del s.[or] Brigadier D.ⁿ Jacobo Ugarte y Loyola, egecute los mas prolijos reconocimientos de la frontera de esta Prov.[a]

Deven empezarse por el Presidio de Fronteras, repitiendo los que acaba Vm. de hacer para la traslacion del de s.[ta] Cruz hasta el nacimiento del Rio de s.ⁿ Pedro y desde alli continuarse por las margenes de dicho Rio hasta el parage donde se junta con el Gila, siguiendo ã este escrupuloso examen, el del terreno en que actualmente se halla el Presidio de san Agustin del Tucson, el que ocupava antiguamente en Tuvac, y el de Terrenate.

Concluidos estos esenciales reconocimientos, y trasladandose Vm al Pueblo del Pitic por los llanos del Arivac, Busanic, Saric, Tubutama, y demas misiones, Presidio del Altar, y R.[l] de la Cieneguilla formara un Croquis de todos

Los Terrenos examinados, entregandolo al citado señor Brigadier para que me lo dirija con los correspond.[tes] Ynformes, deviendo Vm remitirme reservadamente los suyos.

Para que Vm los instruya con la perfeccion que deseo, recivira del Secret.[o] de la Comandancia gen.[l] un exemplar del Reglamento de Presidios, un Plano gen.[l] de estas Provincias, y otros Documentos necesarios para ilustrar las noticias q.[e] deseo, y han de contraherse a una clara disertacion de todo el Pais que ha de examinar; ã exponer su estado, y los medios de contener las hostilidades que sufre de los Apaches, y Seris, en inteligencia de que no haviendose verificado en esta Provincia el establecim.[to] de la Linea prevenida en la R.[l] Ynstruccion inserta al Reglam.[to] de Presidios

es necesario que Vm me diga los parages que considere ã proposito para situarla, teniendo presente que el Rey ha resuelto la ereccion de un Presidio en las Juntas del Rio de san Pedro, y Gila para que dandose la mano con los nuevos Pueblos del colorado se abra el camino, y comunicaz.[n] de esta Prov.[a] con la de Californias.

Y pues repetidas veces he dicho a Vm verbalmente que las ideas que medito para el cumplimiento: de las soberanas resoluciones de S.M. se dirigen ã que los Presidios se establezcan en terrenos capaces de mantener Poblaciones respetables que con el tiempo no necesiten del auxilio de la Tropa para su propria defensa, espero que los ynformes de VM, completen el logro de los deseos, y los justos fines ã que aspiro del mejor servicio del Rey.

Dios guarde ã VM mu.[s] años.

Arispe 15. de Abril de 1780= El Cav.[ro] de Croix= s.[r] d.[n] Gerónimo del la Rocha___ Señor comand.[te] Grãl=

<u>Ynforme del Gover-</u>
<u>nador Miliar.</u> [Ugarte=Croix]

Mui señor mio:

Haviendo pasado ã poner en practica los reconocimientos de esta Frontera acompañado del Teniente de Yngenieros D. Geronimo de la Rocha conforme ã lo que V.S. se sirvió prevenirme en su superior de 15. de Abril último, di principio ã esta comision por el Presidio de Fronteras, segun lo denota el Diario prolixo, claro, y circunstanciado que con el croquis correspondiente habrá ya pasado ã manos de V.S. el insinuado Yngeniero, expresandose en el con la mayor puntualidad las Sierras, Puertos, Caxones, Rios, Ojos de Agua, Arroyos que la conservan todo el año, y los que carecen de ella en la estacion de seca, parages proporcionados para Poblacion, Siembras, Estancas de Ganados, y demas circunstancias que

en la citada me ordena V.S. le comunique.

Desde el expresado Fronteras hice pres.[te] ã V.S. con fecha de 29. del mencionado Abril que haviendo pasado ã reconocer el hermoso Valle de Cochuta lo Juzgava el mas proporcionado para la ubicacion del Presidio de Fronteras por su grande extension en la q.[e] se encuentra mucha abundancia de Pastos, suficientes Tierras de labor, y mucha facilidad de conducir ã el desde Fronteras los bastimentos necesarios aun quando las Aguas del valle no fuesen bastantes ã dar el fruto necesario; añadiendo en mi oficio de 6. del corriente haver adquirido nuevas noticias de Sugetos al parecer veraces, y de conocimiento que aseguran que con solo el Temporal (ahun sin hacer uso de las aguas del valle para el riego) eran abundantisimas las Cosechas que recogian los Yndios Pobladores que lo desampararon, concluyendo los mismos ser aqui el Agua mas

abundante que en Badeguachi.

A estas razones deben agregarse las siguientes ventajas que expuse en el citado y repito en compendio.

1.[a] Viviran las Familias sin el continuo sobresalto de ser sorprehendidos por los Enemigos como lo han hecho varias veces por las proximidad del cerro.

2.ª Queda cubierto en lo posible el territorio ē impedido el transito continuo de los Enemigos que por el Puerto de Teras y los que forman la Sierra Purica se introducen ã lo interior de la Provincia.

3.ª Que reconocidos desde aquí por un capitan de conducta y resolucion los Aguages de dicha Sierra, la de los embudos (donde por esta parte se halla el Puerto de Batepito) y los caxones que forma su aspereza, donde por largo tpo, y con seguridad suelen arrancharse se les quitará esta rochela y alexandose

de estas inmediaciones serán por consecuen cia menos frecuentes sus irrupciones.

4.ª Podran ser sostenidos los que se dediquen al util trabajo de los muchos Placeres que segun el Ynforme de los vecinos de Bacuachi se hallan inmediatos á dhá sierra Purica desde el Puerto de Turisachi hasta cerca del de Mabavi.

Y ultimamente colocado en el Valle de Babispe el idéado Presidio de Opatas, (lo que tengo por ventajoso segun hago presente á V.S. en oficio separado) podrán mutuam.[te] auxiliarse assi para dichos reconocimientos, como para otros que podrán practicarse en las Sierras de las espuelas, en la de s.[n] Luis, y otras cercanas.

Colocado en este sitio, õ (si á V.S. no pareciere conveniente) en Fronteras, õ Badeguachi el primer Presidio de esta Linea expondré me dictamen con sencillez, ē

ingenuidad sobre los demás que deben completarla, valiendome de las noticias que experimentalmente he adquirido en el prolixo reconocimiento que acabo de practicar, y proponiendome el solo fin de obedecer á V.S. é informarle según lo que alcanzo lo mas conducente al Real Servicio, felicidad de la Provincia y castigo de los Enemigos.

Baxo de este supuesto de segundo Presidio deberá colocarse en el parage de las Nutrias donde actualmente se halla acampada la compañía del abandonado Presidio de santa cruz. Las razones q.[e] apoyan la preferencia de este sitio expuse ã V.S. en mi oficio de 7. del pasado Mayo, añadiendo ahora solamente que este Parage dista del de Cochuta por el camino De Magallanes de 25,, ã 26. leguas, y por el del ojo del Gato (que es mexor terreno) de veinte y ocho ã veinte y nueve.

En la espaciosa y proporcionada Mesa de Buevavista juzgo conveniente se coloque el tercero: está situada ã las margenes del Rio de san Antonio con todas las Proporciones para una buena Poblacion, y dista legua y media de la despoblada Haz.[da] de Buenavista; treinta y cinco del Presidio de Altar, veinte y seis del de el Tucsón, y veinte y una del sitio de las Nutrias. La ubicacion de un Presidio en este sitio animaría a las Gentes y con el tiempo podrán poblarse los ventajosos parages de s.[ta] maria Suanca, san Antonio, Rancho del torreon, valle de san Lázaro, Hacienda de Santa Bárbara, Rancho de san Luis, Buenavista, Pueblo de Guevavi todos situados ã una regular distancia del propuesto Presidio, lo que verificado servirá ã la Provincia como dice en su Diario el indicado Yngeniero de las mayor utilidad

por las siembras y crias de Ganado.

A mas que asi quedan cubiertas las Misiones y Pueblos de calabazas, Tumacacori, y Tubac que forman Linea desde Bue navista al Tucson, cuyos Avitadores podrán cooperar con la Tropa de los Presidios á una mutua defensa.

Los tres Presidios de que he hablado hasta ahora los considero ventajosos para formar una nueva Linea que verdaderam.[te] lo sea de Frontera para la defensa de la Provincia, sin perder de vista la precisa circunstancia de que al abrigo de ellos puedan establecerse Poblaciones respetables que con el tiempo no necesiten los auxilios de la tropa; pero sirviendose V.S. prevenirme en el citado, exponga mi dictamen sobre los que pueden ser ventajosos para continuarla hasta darse la mano con los nuevos establecimientos

del Rio colorado, y abrirse la comunicacion con la california septentrional, debo decir en obedecimiento de esta superior orden que para estos fines tengo por mui preciso y ventajoso el actual Presidio del Tucson.

Aunque este Presidio que se halla

en un rincon de la Provincia, puede servir muy poco á su defensa á excepcion de las misiones de s.[n] Xavier del Bac, y del Tucson que están ã el inmediatas, es sin embargo el mas proporcionado para seguir la sobre dicha Linea dirigiendola en este caso p.[r] las casas grandes de motezuma, por donde hasta aquí han caminado, y ban ã caminar los Religiosos, y demas que transitan al Rio Colorado, en cuyo sitio, õ en sus inmediaciones podrá establecerse un buen Presidio, no siendome posible hablar de este sitio, ni de los subsecuentes con la certeza que de los anteriores, respecto

ã no haverlos reconocido.

Lo cierto es que no soy de dictamen se dirija la Linea por las orillas del Rio de san Pedro, õ Terrenate, ni se ubique Presidio alguno en las juntas de este Rio con el de Gila. El Presidio que aquí se colocase quedára muy abanzado y distante del interior Pais; de ninguna defensa podria servir ã la Provincia; necesitaria para sostenerse de una numerosa dotacion; y seria preciso que condugese desde el Tucson todo lo necesario por no ofrecer aquel Parage proporcion alguna para Siembras, y mucho menos para que á su abrigo se establezcan en lo succesivo nuevas Poblaciones.

Y aunque en el valle de s.[ta] Teresa distante como legua y media de este sitio podrán verificarse algunas siembras siempre serán tan cortas que no

evitarían la escacez de Bastimentos del Presidio, ni atraerán las Gentes ã ubicarse en un Parage que les ofrece tan poco proporcion y comodidad.

La unica ventaja que aquí puede encontrarse, es la de dirigir la sobre dicha Linea que se dé la mano con los nuevos Establecimientos del Rio Colorado; pero dejo ya dicho ã V.S. que por el Tucson podrá continuarse con mayor comodidad, y mas en derechura.

Lo mismo ã proporcion juzgo debe decirse del Rio de s.[n] Pedro, õ Terrenate, nada menos á proposito para seguir la Linea de Frontera, porque aunque en sus orillas se encuentran varios sitios donde parece pudieran colocarse los Presidios como so el Guiburi, tres Alamos, Cequias jondas, y otros, siempre sería nada ventajosa, y mui perjudicial aquesta Linea. Lo primero por

que estos parages no ofrecen proprocion sino para pequeñas Poblaciones que nunca podrán sostenerse sin los auxilios de la Tropa.

Lo segundo por que sería inevitable colocarlos con notable distancia los unos de los otros ã menos que se aumenten, lo que ocasionaria considerables gastos al Real erario.

Lo tercero porque quedaria desamparada la Provincia, y sin defensa los Pueblos interiores, abanzados los Presidios á una larga distancia desde la que ni pueden auxiliarse mutuamente, ni ocurrir en caso de imbasion ã sostener los Pueblos Fronterizos.

Y ultimamente se haria indispensable que en estos (como he dicho del de las juntas de los Rios) se colocase Dotacion numerosa, õ quedaven inutiles para

hacer la guerra al enemigo defendiendo solo las cascos de los Presidios.

Ninguno de los expresados inconven.[tes] antes por el contrario las mayores ventajas y proporciones presenta la linea que dejo detallada; con la que quedan mas á cubierto en lo posible los Pueblos interiores; con mas facilidad podrán mutuamente auxiliarse los vecinos, Yndios amigos, y soldados; quedan colocados á regular distancia los Presidios; son menos arriesgados del uno al otro los transitos; pueden establecerse á su abrigo respetables Poblaciones que además de no necesitar con el tiempo de los auxilios de la tropa, sirvan de utilidad á la Provincia, cultivando los fertiles terrenos que aora estan despoblados; y finalmente dará la mano por camino mas corto y a proposito á los sobre dichos nuevos establecimientos segun los Ynformes con que me hallo.

Y aunque segun concibo nunca se evitara enteramente la hostilidad del Apache, coloquese la Linea donde se colocase; sin embargo dirigiendola por donde dejo expuesto, debemos persuadirnos será menos frecuente, especialmente si se reduce á practica la providencia que V.S. se sirve comunicarme en el superior suyo de 16. de Mayo, de señalar dos puestos de Asamblea sobre la Frontera que hagan la guerra al Enemigo conforme á las cortas fuerzas con que nos hallamos, interin S.M. proporciona los auxilios que son necesarios para hacerla en los terminos que su R.^{l} piedad se sirve prevenir en los articulos 1.º y 2.º tit.^{o} 10 del R.^{l} Reglamento de Presidios.

En quanto á esta Frontera de los seris nada tengo que añadir á lo que varias veces he hecho presente á V.S. á quien consta que las fuerzas del Pitic, Altar, y Buenavista son aqui indispensables para la posible contension de estos Rebeldes, y de los Tiburones, y Tepocas, y en mi concepto aun haciendoles con ellas las mas posible viva guerra no llegara á lograrse sus verdadera sugecion õ exterminio, interin no se verifique su transmigracion ultramarina q.^{e} en mi Dictamen reservado de 15. del pasado Enero propuse á V.S. en contestaz.^{n} al superior suyo de 31. de Diciembre de 1779.

Este mi dictamen contrahido a los terrenos que he reconocido el que sugeto en todo al superior y mas prudente de V.S.

Nuestro Señor guarde la vida de V.S. muchos años como le pido. Presidio del Pitic Agosto 14. de 1780.=s.^{or} com.^{te} gen.^{l} = Blm. de V.S. su mas atento y reconocido servidor= Jacobo Ugarte y Loyola= Sor Comand.^{te} gen^{l}= Caballero de Croix___,,_________,,_______,,_____
Sor Comand.^{te} general= Mui s.^{or} mio: obedeciendo La superior de V.S. de 28. del pasado Ag.^{to} acompaño los Documentos que V.S. me pide en la citada, y son los dictamenes del difunto Comandante Ynspector d.^{n} Hugo Õconór; del Governador que fue de esta Provincia d.^{n} Fran.^{co} Crespo; del Ayudante Ynspector Dn Antonio Bonillo; y del R.P.F Juan Diaz.

Nro s.^{or} que la vida de V.S. mu.^{s} años como le pido. Pitic sep.^{re} 1.º de 1780=8^{l} com.^{te} Gral=Blm. De V.S. su mas atento y recon^{do} sen^{or}= Jacobo Ugarte y Loyola= s.^{or} Comand.^{te} gen.^{l} Caballero de Croix______,,_____,,______,,____

Informe de Yngenie
ro Dn Gerónimo de la
Rocha. [Rocha=Croix]

Mui s.^{or} mio: En orden de 15. de Abril pasado de este año se sirvió V.S. mandarme que bajo las del s.^{or} Brigadier D. Jacobo Ugarte Y Loyola, hiciese los mas prolixos reconosimientos de la Frontera de esta Provincia empezandolos por el Presidio de Fronteras, siguiendo por los que acababa de egecutar para la translacion del de s.^{ta} Cruz hasta el nacimiento del Rio de San Pedro, y por las margenes de este hasta su junta con el Gila, y de allí el del terreno que actual mente ocupa el de san Agustin del Tucson, el de Tubac, donde estubo antiguamente, y el de Terrenate; que haviendolos evacuado me trasladase al Pueblo del Pitic por los llanos del Aribac, Busanic, Saric, Tubutama, y demás misiones, Presidio del Altar, y Real de la Cieneguilla, y formase un croquis de todo, entregandolo al s.^{or} Brigadier Loyola para que lo dirigiese á V.S. con sus Ynformes, debiendole Yo pasar reservadamente los mios; que las noticias que devia de dar en ellos, y deseava V.S. havian de con de contraherse á una clara diser tacion de todo el Pais que examinase, y á manifestar su estado, y los medios de contener las hostilidades que sufre de los Apaches, y seris, en la inteligencia de que no haviendose establecido en esta Provincia la linea preve nida en la R.^{l} Ynstruccion inserta al Reglamento que se me entregaria en Secretaria, era necesario digese los parages que considerase oportunos para situarla, teniendo presente haver resuelto S.M. la ereccion de un Presidio en la Junta de los Rios San Pedro, y Gila, para que dandose la mano con los nuevos Pueblos del colorado, se abra el camino y comunicacion de esta Provincia con la de Californias; y finalmente que dirigiendose las idéas de V.S. en cumplimento de las soberanas resoluciones de S.M. á que se establezcan los Presidios en terrenos capaces de mantener Poblaciones respetables que con el tiempo no necesiten del auxilio de la tropa para su propria defensa, esperava que mis informes completasen el logro de estos justos fines á que aspiravan

sus deseos.
En el mismo dia que recivi esta orn.
emprendi mi marcha al Pueblo de Sn Joseph
de Chinapa, donde encontré y me presenté
al s.^{r} Brigadier D^{on} Jacobo Ugarte, y Loyola
y debiendo egecutar bajo las suyas los referi-
dos reconocimientos, se ha invertido por obede-
cerlas el orden con que se mandaron egecu-
tar, como lo advertirá V.S. por el Diario q.^{e}
acompaño, y tambien no haverme sido posi-
ble evitarlo, por no haver tenido arbitrio p.^{a}
dejar de cumplir la de V.S. que me preve-
nia estubiese á las de aquel Gefe á quien
no entregué el mapa de los Terrenos reco-
nocidos que igualmente paso á manos de
V.S. por que no haviendo podido formarlo
durante nuestra dilatada marcha, no tu-
be tampoco proporcion ni tiempo para
egecutarlo en el poco que permaneci en el
Presidio del Pitic, desde donde regresé

inmediatamente á esta capital.
De los Terrenos que he reconocido
son á proposito para Poblaciones los Va-
lles de Fronteras, Badeguachi, Cavece-
ras de Sn Pedro, Nutrias, Guachuca,
y Terrenate, Sta María Suanca, Sn Laza-
ro, Santa Bárbara, Sn Luis, Buenavista
y su estancia, Guevavi, Calavazas, Tuc-
son, Zicurizuta, y Busanic, por tener
todos abundantes aguas permanentes,
muchas tierras fertiles, que beneficiadas
con el riego y cultivo producirian copio-
sas cosechas; Pastos, Piedra, Leña, y Ma-
dera áa excepcion de las Caveceras de s.^{n}
Pedro donde escasean los dos ultimos ren-
glones, y seria forzoso buscarlos en las Sier-
ras de Guachuca, Las Mulas, y s.^{n} Joseph,
distantes de dos á tres leguas: Entre es-
tos podrían establecerse Ranchos utilisi-
mos para la cria de toda especie de Ganado

en los parages llamados Nogales, Capulin,
Valles de Cochuta y Turicachi, ojos del Leon
del saus, y de los Alamos largos, Sonoyta,
ojo de San Antonio, Torreón, y el Guiburi, q.^{e}
todos producen abundantisimos pastos, agre-
gandose á algunos el fruto de la Bellota, que
con el ramon de sus Encinales fomentarian la
cria de los de Cerda, y Cabrío, sumamente pre-
cisos para el abasto de manteca, sebo, y cueros
de que se hace tan conocido consumo, como lo es
la escaces que se experimenta en la Provincia:
Todos tienen agua permanente que aunque no
es suficiente para Poblacion basta para abre-
baderos de multitud de Ganados, para el con-
sumo de sus Pastores, Baqueros y demas gente
que regularmente abita en semejantes Estancias
y aun podria alcanzar en alguno para regar
sus Huertas, y hacer pequeñas labores, que
las proveyesen de frutas, Verduras, y semillas
para sus consumos: Y como en el Diario

expongo menudamente la situación y rum-
bo de todos, y la distancia que media de unos
á otros escuso repetirla en este Informe.
Las margenes del Rio de Sn Pedro
no tienen sitio alguno oportuno, ni con las
proporciones necesarias para fundar Po-
blaciones hasta su junta con el Gila, y lo
mismo sucede en esta, cuyo terreno es suma-
mente quebrado y aspero en el corto espacio
que alcanzó la vista á examinarlo, sin
que pueda decir si las habrá en las Rive-
ras del Gila siguiendo su corriente, õ subien-
do contra ella, por no haverme permitido
el s.^{or} Loyola detenerme á reconocerlas con
la escrupulosa proligidad que lo deseava
para lo qual le pedi con varias instancias
que me diese escolta y Licencia, y no tubo
por conveniente concedermela, y aunque-
las inmediaciones de ambos Rios tienen
varios Sitios muy oportunos p.^{a} Estancias

de Ganados, no puede pensarse en establecerlas
sin destruir õ rendir al Apache Gileño que
avita en ellas, y las aniquilaria como lo ha
egecutado con otras ubicadas en lo interior de
la Provincia que por lo mismo gozavan de
mayor resguardo y defensa.
Esta nacion con sus continuos robos,
y muertes ha logrado destruir las pequeñas
antiguas Poblaciones de Cochuta, Turicachi,
Sonoitá, Santa María Suanca, Guevavi, el
Busanic, Cananéa, y Aribác, de que solo
han quedado los vestigios de sus ruinas; ha
minorado considerablemente las de chinapa
Bacuachi, Cuquiarachi, Fronteras, y demás
contiguas a la Linea, y ha despoblado entera-
mente las Haciendas, y Ranchos de s.^{n} Pedro,
Terrenate, Torreón, San Lázaro, s.^{ta} Bárbara,
Ranchito, San Luis, Buenavista, Sn Lázaro
de la magdalena, y otros varios que se hall.^{n}
desiertos, y desamparados y podian reponerse

õ repoblarse sino lo impidiesen los insultos que repite con frequencia, los quales han embarazado igualmente los progresos de las misiones y demás Pueblos que he examinado y se hallan en estado bien decadente y con especialidad en quanto á las cria de Ganados que hay suma falta, por ser el obgeto en que siempre se ha cebado mas la ambicion del Enemigo.

La situacion del Presidio de Tubac trasladado al Tucson carece de proporciones para Poblacion, por que aunque tiene algunas tierras utiles para labor y sementera les falta el beneficio del riego, sin el qual son escasas õ se pierden las cosechas, y hallandose mui inmediato a la falda de la sierra de s.^{ta} Rita donde desembocan sus vertientes, forman estas muchas quiebras y Barrancas que sirven al Enemigo para introducirse ocultamente hasta las mismas

Casas, desde las que han flechado, y muerto á algunos vecinos, reduciendolos á tan corto numero que no excedian de nueve los q.^{e} quedavan á mi transito por aquel Pueblo, y aun de estos tube noticia que el dia siguiente al de mi salida mataron dos los Enemigos, por cuyos irremediables inconvenientes no considero á proposito aquel sitio, ni para Presidio, ni para Poblacion, y segun tengo hecho pres.^{te} á V.S. anteriormente, seria de conocida utilidad y beneficio á los Ynfelices que han quedado hacerles trasladarse al Tucson, õ s.^{n} Xavier del Bac, donde hay suficientes Tierras y aguas para darles suertes, y proporcionarles mejor y mas seguro establecimiento.

El Terreno del Tucson á que se trasladó, y donde se halla el Presidio de Tubac, es de los mas utiles, y á proposito para la subsistencia de la compañía y parage asu abrigo se fomente una buena Poblacion que con el

tiempo pueda defenderse por si misma, y aún facilitar auxilios para impedir la entrada al Enemigo por sus constados y especialmente por el del sur que es el mas frecuentado, y que necesita de mayor resguardo por hallarse en el las Poblaciones de san Xavier del Bac, Tumacacori, y Calabazas y por tener al mismo rumbo el despoblado de Sonoita, los Puertos del agua caliente, y Babocomari, y otros parages por donde se interna el Enemigo, desprendiendose de las sierras de Guachuca, s.^{ta} Rita, Babocomari, Peñascosa, y otras que quedan á la espalda por cuyo motivo considero mui util su subsistencia en el parage donde está ubicado, y no he visto orto alguno en que pudiera mejorarse.

Persuadiendome que con lo expuesto he dado á V.S. quantas noticias he podido adquirir relativas al estado de los

Terrenos que he reconocido y de las proporciones que cada uno goza para fomentar Poblaciones õ nuevos establecimientos, considero preciso sentar que no podrá afianzarse su subsistencia, ni harán los progresos que deben esperarse sino se castiga y aleja al Enemigo cuya hostilidad ha sido y será, mientras dure, la causa principal de la ruina de tantas Poblaciones, Haciendas, y Ranchos, y del atraso y decadencia en que se miran otras: Desde que se internaron los Presidios al País del enemigo se retiraron de las Poblaciones que debian abrigar y cubrir, y abrazando por consecuencia la mayor porcion de terreno aban zado resultó por necesidad ser mayor la circunferencia de la linea que debian formar y ocupar, y mas dilatada la distancia en que quedaron colocados unos de otros, y a la dificultad de que sus cortas guarniciones pudiesen impedir la entrada al Enemigo por

el mayor claro õ descubierto que quedaba á sus costados, se añadió la de no poder emplearse toda la fuerza en este preciso y primitivo objeto por que no haviendo bastim.^{tos} en las nuevas ubicaciones para proveher á la Tropa y sus Familias, ha sido y todavia es necesario salir á buscarlos á la distancia en que se hallan las Poblaciones que los cosechan, y ocupar gruesas Partidas en conducirlos y escoltarlos, sin que puedan hacer otro servicio, ni emplearse en la defensa, ũ ofensa; y de este principio ha provenido en mi concepto la facilidad y frecuencia con que han repetido sus insultos por que hallando la entrada libre por el terreno descubierto entre los Presidios colindantes se introducen sin embarzo en lo interior del Pais, y egecutan los daños sin encontrar resistencia, por no ser bastantes á hacerla las Poblaciones por si solas y sin el abrigo de la Tropa de que se les privó por abanzarla.

Quando para ocurrir á este daño sea suficiente el numero de Tropas que guarnecen la Frontera, parece indispensable que no tengan otra ocupacion ni destino que la de defenderla, impedir la entrada al Enemigo, perseguirle, y castigarle haciendoles viva, ē incesante guerra, y atacandolos en quanto sea posible en sus mismas Rancherias y terrenos como lo previene el articulo l.º tit.º 10. del Reglamento, por que si mucha parte de la fuerza se emplea como ha sucedido hasta ahora en buscar y escoltar Remontas y bastimentos hará forzosamente falta á aquel primer objeto de su instituto, y nunca llegará el caso de que pueda llenarle como lo exige el estado de la Provincia, y no siendo asequible esta idéa sin colocar los Presidios en terrenos capaces de producir cosechas

para su abasto y consumo, y sin fomentar en ellos, y á su abrigo la agricultura, y cria de Ganados, paso bajo de este principio á señalar los que he encontrado con estas calidades y me parecen mas á proposito para formar la nueva Linea.

En mis anteriores Ynformes de 29. de Abril y 25. del presente, he hecho presente á V.S. la mala situacion del Presidio de Fronteras, que es el primero de ella, y las ventajas que lograría trasladándolo al sitio de Badeguachi distante solo una legua al Sur de su actual ubicacion, y refiriendome á ellos nada tengo que añadir sobre este establecimiento, y lo mismo sucede con el de Santa Cruz de Terrenate que es el segundo puesto, y trasladado al campo de las Nutrias como igualmente tengo informado á V.S. reducirá á veinte y cinco leguas la distancia de cerca-----

cincuenta leguas á que actualmente se halla de su colindante Fronteras; facilitará la comunicacion de ambos, y la reunion de sus fuerzas para la defensa y ofensa, cubrirán mejor los Puertos y cañadas mas frecuentadas por los enemigos; al abrigo de ambos, y con el beneficio de las fertiles dilatadas tierras, y abundantes aguas de sus inmediaciones podrán fomentarse dos buenas Poblaciones que los provean de lo necesario, y auxilien sus Armas en caso de necesidad, y ahún debe tambien esperarse que bajo la proteccion del primero, renazcan las destruidas de Cochuta, Turicachi, y R.[l] de Nacosari, se mejoren las de Cuguiarachi, Baquachi, Sn Joseph de Chinapa, la Haz.[da] de Bacanuchi, Cumpas, y otras mas internadas, y finalmente que con la defensa, y amparo de los dos se travagen con libertad y teson los Placeros de Oro de Bacuachi, la cananea,

y otros varios que en el dia solo dan constantes pruevas de su prodigiosa riqueza y por no dejar buscarla y adquirirla el riesgo y temor que han infundido los insultos del Enemigo.

Tambien tengo informado á V.S. ser mui bentajosa la actual ubicacion del Presidio del Tucsón que goza quantas proporciones pueden apetecerse para una buena Poblacion, y para fomentar á su abrigo y defensa las que se hallan en sus inmediaciones, por cuyos motivos concivo no puede, ni deve removerse; pero quedando descubierto el largo espacio de quarenta y cinco leguas que median hasta su colindante colocado en el campo de Las Nutrias, y no siendo posible que la fuerza de ambos impidan las entradas y salidas del Enemigo que tiene muchas y muy frecuentadas en los Terrenos

intermedios, considero precisa para lograrlo la situacion de otro Presidio en el centro, õ mitad de aquella distancia, y no haviendo encontrado ni reconcido otro Paraje mas oportuno para ubicarlo que la estancia de Buena-vista, en esta me parece seria muy conveniente la nueva ereccion por que sobre tener bellas proporciones para una mediana Poblacion, y para muchos Ranchos y Haz.[das] parte con igualdad á corta diferencia la expresada distancia de las Nutrias al Tucson quedando á veinte y seis leguas de este y á veinte y una de aquel, con la bentaja de cubrir los Puertos de la Plomosa, chihuahuilla, Divisaderos, y san Antonio, defender los Pueblos de Calabazas y Tumacacori, facilitar que buelvan á su antiquo sér los destruidos de Guevavi, Sonoitá, y s.[ta] María Suanca, que se cubran de Ganados los hermosos valles y arruinadas Haciendas y

Ranchos de Buenavista, s.^{n} Luis, Ranchito, Santa Bárbara, y San Lázaro; y por ultimo proporciona tambien la mejor comunicacion de la Linea, y la reunion de sus fuerzas con las de sus dos colindantes, y aún si fuere necesario con las del Presidio del Altar, que situado fuera de la Linea biene á quedar á la distancia de treinta y cinco leguas al Sudueste.

Ya dejo hecho presente á V.S. que en las margenes del Rio de san Pedro no he encontrado Sitio alguno á proposito para establecer Presidio, ni menos para fundar Poblacion, y que lo mismo sucede en su junta con el Gila, por cuyo motivo no puedo señalar el que será oportuno para la nueva ereccion resuelta por la piedad de S.M. y para poderlo hacer con conocimiento y acierto, tengo

por indispensable proceda un nuevo y mas prolijo reconocimiento de las margenes del Gila hasta su junta con el Colorado, pues además de que el examen de aquellos terrenos dará luces para elegir el que sea mas ventajoso, conducirá tambien para preferir el que á los demás proporciones fuente la de facilitar mejor la comunicacion, y reunion de sus fuerzas con las destinadas á cubrir igualmente los nuevos Pueblos de Colorado.

Formada la linea en los Parages que ban propuestos quedará el actual Presidio de Fronteras colcado en Badeguachi á los treinta grados 57 min.^{s} y 52. Seg.^{dos} de latitud, libre de las inundaciones que han padecido aquellos valles en sitio muy desejado, y con extension suficiente para una buena Poblacion en el punto donde concurren y se juntan los valles de Fronteras, Cuguiarachi, y Cochuta sobre el camino del Puerto

del Potrero que sirve para comunicarse por el Pueblo de Babispe con la linea de la Vizcaya, y tendrá á distancia de una legua al Norte el Pueblo de Fronteras, dos al Oeste el de Cuguiarachi, tres al Sur el despoblado de Cochuta, y como ochocientas varas al Eeste el Rio de Fronteras, que careciendo de vado alguno en el espacio de mas de media legua es muy apreciable por cubrir, y resguardar del enemigo todo aquel frente, y además se halla sobre él una cuchilla alta donde colocada una pequeña torre õ vigia se domina y descubre la extension de los tres valles, cuyas labores pueden sostenerse; y fomentarse tambien los Placeres de Bacuachi, haciendo frecuentes contadas desde la sierra purica, hasta las vertientes de la de mavavi, para impedir la entrada

al Enemigo, á cuyo fin seria mui conducente colocar un Destacamento den el despoblado de Cochuta que tiene tres leguas al Sur el de Turicachi, tres al Sudueste quarta al sur el Puerto de turicachi, cinco al Oes sudueste el de Mababi, y quatro al Eeste el de Teras que son los parages por donde se introduce.

El de Santa Cruz trasladado al campo de las Nutrias quedara á los treynta y un grado 24. minut.^{s} y 10. segund.^{s} de latitud distante del anterior veinte y cinco leguas al Oes norueste por el camino que llaman de Magallanes, situado en terreno fertil, abundante, y descubierto; tendrá los valles de Guachuca dos leguas al Norueste, las caveceras de san Pedro y sus Labores dos y media al Eeste, el Pueblo õ antiguo Presidio de Terrenate dos al Oes-Noroeste, ocho al sur la Abra que se forma entre la vieja Cananea, y el rincon del Burro

por donde se introducen y sacan los Enemigos la mayor parte de sus robos y será fácil cortarlos saliendoles al encuentro con qualquiera aviso que se tenga de las Poblaciones que podrán mui bien darlo por hallarse á la distancia de veinte y cinco leguas; y por ultimo en caso de hacerse Campañas para buscarlos y atacarlos en sus proprias Rancherias, será el punto mas importante para la reunion de las Tropas, asi por la facilidad de poder acuartelarlas, y proveherlas, como por hallarse mas inmediato á las sierras donde se arrochelan y ser mas pronto su encuentro.

El nuevo y tercer Presidio colocado en la estancia de Buenavista, se hallara á los 31. gr.^{s} 40. minut.^{s} y 25,, segundos de latitud en una grande mesa, cuya falda riega el Rio de santa María Suanca que tiene su origen en el ojo de san Antonio, y aunque no es muy caudaloso nunca pierde su corriente aun entiempo de seca; tendrá un hermoso, y ameno valle en que una legua al Sur, estubo la Hacienda despoblada de Buenavista que fue abundantisima en frutos y Ganados, tres al Oeste cuarta al Noroeste al arruinado Pueblo de Guevavi, quatro al Nordeste la sierra de la Chihuahuilla fecunda en ricos y conocidos minerales, quedará á distancia de veinte y una leguas al Noroeste quarta al Oeste de las Nutrias y en la mejor disposición para cubrir los Puertos de la Plomosa, Chihuahuilla, Divisaderos y san Antonio; defender los Pueblos de Calabazas, y Tumacacori, y fomentar la repoblacion del arruinado de Sonoita, y la de los amenos valles de Buenavista, s.^{n} Luis Ranchito, s^{ta} Bárbara, s.^{n} Lázaro, s.^{ta} María Suanca, Torreón, s.^{n} Antonio, y otros mas internados en la Provincia, debiendo advertir que aunque el sitio de Guevavi divide mejor la distancia entre Las Nutrias y el Tucson elijo con preferencia el de la Estancia por ser mas abundante en Pastos y tener mas cerca el Presidio del Altar.

El quarto y ultimo que es el de s.^{n} Agustin del Tucson se halla á los treinta y dos grados 31. min.^{s} y 50,, seguno.^{s} de latitud en terreno mui despejado, abundante de aguas y Tierras de labor con un Potrero islado por dos Cequias donde con corta Guarnicion está bien resguardada la Caballada, defiende y sostiene las misiones õ Pueblos de Tucson y san Xavier del Bac que á su abrigo han hecho conocidos progresos, y decaerian enteramente si les faltase; y por ultimo es el preciso punto q.^{e} por el Rio Gila abre, y facilita la comunicaz.^{on} de esta Provincia con el colorado y la de Californias; tiene el parage de tres Alamos á distancia de diez y siete leguas por el Eeste, el Puerto de la Cebadilla nueve al Ees Nordeste, el de la Mololoa quatro norte quarta al Nordeste, el Aquitune diez y seis al Noroeste, la sierra del Tucson tres al Oeste, el ojo grande oõ nacimiento de sus aguas un quarto de legua al sur Sueste, y veinte y seis leguas al sur sueste el Presidio de las Nutrias, teniendo otras veinte y nueve al Norte la junta de los Rios de San Pedro y Gila.

Esta se halla á los treynta y dos grados y veinte y un minutos de latitud en un cajon cerrado que forman las asperas sierras que llaman del Aribaipa, y por ser copioso el caudal del Gila y poco profunda la caxa de su corriente se inundan en qualesquiera abenida los terrenos inmediatos, que en lo que alcanzó la vista y pude reconocer demuestran ser mui quebrados, y siempre q.^{e} en el nuevo reconocimiento que debe hacerse de las margenes del Gila, se encuentre muy al Oeste parage oportuno para ubicar el Presidio mandado erigir por S.M. quedara á demasiada distancia de su colindante el Tucson, y tal vez no pudiendo establecerse la comunicacion de ambos por el camino que llaman del Aquitune (que ahora se transita para el Rio colorado) á causa de no tener Aguages permanentes, será forzoso abrirla por las Cañadas del Oro, y de la Virgen del Consuelo, õ bien por las de s.^{n} Simon á salir al Rio de s.^{n} Pedro, y valle de s.^{ta} Teresa, y despues seguir por las margenes del Gila al nuevo establecimiento, en cuyo caso concibo indispensable para sostener este transito demasiadamente dilatado formar un nuevo Puesto, con un fuerte Destacamento en el valle de s.^{ta} Teresa que aunque no tiene las mejores proporciones es el mas oportuno de los que he reconocido en aquellos Terrenos.

La situacion del Presidio de s.^{ta} Getrudis del Altar se halla á los treinta grados, 53,, minutos y 25,, segundos de latitud en terreno bastantemente despejado pero escaso de Pastos y de Aguas, y especialmente en tiempo de seca en que se corta el Rio, pero nunca le han faltado las precisas para el consumo de la Tropa y vecindario, que en algunas ocasiones las buscan y conducen de bastante distancia, como sucedió quando estuve á reconocerle; tiene barias Huertas que abundan en Frutos por la mucha fertilidad de aquel suelo, y al Oes sudueste esta mision de Caborca con sus Pueblos de Visita, el Pitiqui, y Bisanic, la sierra de s.^{ta} Teresa, doce leguas al Nordeste; el Cerro del Bamuri una y media Noroeste quarta al Norte; el Puerto del Chanate una y media Noroeste cuarta al Oeste; La Sierra del ojo de Agua tres al Sur Sudueste; el Cerro del Carnero una al Sueste quarta al Sur; y otra al Ees Sueste el Puerto de s.[ta] Ana; y aunque este Presidio se halla internado en la Provincia y fuera de la Linea de frontera, lo considero indispensable así para contener y castigar las irrupciones de los Seris y Tiburones, y conservar libre el camino del R.[l] de la Cieneguilla, como para mantener en el debido respeto y obediencia los Pimas altos y demás Naciones de los Pueblos de su circunferencia

cuya fidelidad es muy sospechosa, y no seria extraño de alzasen si les faltase el freno de la fuerza que los obliga á permanecer con una quietud que tiene mas de fingida, y aparente que de real y verdadera.

El Presidio del Pitic se halla á los veinte y nueve grados y once minutos de latitud en situacion mui espaciosa, abundante de tierras y aguas, bien que expuestas á inundaciones, como la que se experimentó en el año pasado de mil setecientos setenta, en que fué preciso acogerse al Cerro de la campana, cuyo riesgo se evitaria ubicandole en el parage donde los seris tienen actualmente sus Jacales: Dista el Presidio de s.[ta] Gertrudis del Altar mas de sesenta leguas al Nor Noroeste, el Cerro del Tonuco quatro al Oeste, el colorado dos al Noroeste quarta al Norte, el de los Pozos de s.[n] Joseph diez al Noroeste, y el de Santa Teresa tres al Eeste quarta al Sueste; el de

Palos blancos dos al sur sudueste, y muy poco el de la campana que está al Norte; y convinadas õ unidas sus fuerzas con las de el del Altar podrán emplearse en castigar á los Seris alzados, y á los Tiburones sus Amigos y aliados; cuyos daños concivo no cesarán interin subsistan en al Pueblo los que se llaman reducidos porque segun lo que he podido observan, lo son solo en la apariencia; mantienen comunicacion y trato con los que nos hostilizan, y no será extraño les sirvan de fieles espias para que lo hagan sin riesgo; y para evitar estos conocidos males que cada dia serán mayores p.[r] aumentarse el numero con los que desertan y buelven á la Sierra; no encuentro medio mas oportuno que el de trasplantarlos á todos á bien largas distancias, y a parages donde no les quedare ni aun la

esperanza de bolver á su Patria õ Suelo.

Con lo expuesto he dado á V.S. quantas noticias he podido adquirir de los terrenos que he reconocido; de los que he hallado mas á proposito para el establecimiento de la nueva Linea, y de los medios que segun mi corto conocimiento, y practica pueden ser conducentes á la mejor defensa de lo interior de la Provincia; y para que V.S. pueda instruirse con mayor facilidad de los parages en que se hallan y deben permanecer los Presidios, y los señalados para la ubicacion de los que deben removerse, y aumentarse, acompaño un Croquis de cada uno, y otro de la junta de los Rios s.[n] Pedro y Gila, en cuyo trabajo no he tenido otro obgeto que el mejor servicio del Rey, y los vivos deseos que me asisten de acertar á desempeñar las superiores ordenes de V.S. que si lo he conseguido como lo espero

será la mayor satisfaccion que apetezco.

Dios guarde á V.S. los muchos años de mi deseo. Arispe 31,, de Octubre de 1780. Blm. de V.S. su más subordin.[do] servidor= Gerónimo de la Rocha y Figueroa=Señor Governad.[r] y Com.[te] gen.[l] en Gefe__________

Diario de los Reconocimientos hechos en la Frontera de la Provincia de Sonora en consecuencia de la superior orn del 15,, de Abril del presente año, del s.[or] Comandante general de las Provincias Ynternas de Nueva España el Mariscal de Campo Cavallero de Croix, egecutados a las ordenes del Sor Brigadier y Governador Militar de dha Provincia Dn Jacobo de Ugarte y Loyola por el Teniente de Infant.[a] ē Ingeniero extraordinario de los R.[s] Exercitos d.[n] Geronimo de la Rocha y Figueroa.

<u>Dia 15. de Abril de 1780,,</u> <u>Leguas.</u>

En virtud de la citada superior orn
pasé desde la capital de Arispe al Pue-
<#>
blo de Sn Joseph de Chinapa, donde me
presenté al señor Brigadier Dn Jacobo
de Ugarte y Loyola para continuar a sus
ordenes mi viage hice cinco leguas por
el N.D.4.[a] N.......................... 5„

Dia 16.

Continuando por el mismo caxon
del Río dè Sonora caminamos ocho leguas N.
4.[a] N.D. hasta el pueblo de Bacuachi.............. 8„

Como unas dies y ocho leguas al
N.O. está el R.[l] de Minas de la cananea des
poblado y dos leguas antes el parage llamado
la vieja Cananea de donde nace el Río de
Sonora.

Cuatro leguas S.4.[a] N.D. están los
placeres de oro donde actualmente se travaja
pero con lentitud así por el riesgo como por la
poca agua. Los Placeres conocidos están en
las vertientes de la sierra Purica que son
la cañada del Tulito, la de los Alisos_______ „13.

la de san Joseph, San Pedro, Guadalupe, el 13„....
Puerto, las Bolas, y el Cajon del Apache: la
que mas ha producido de todas (asi en la
abundancia como en el tamaño de los gra-
nos) ha sido la de Guadalupe.

Dia 17.

Caminamos cuatro leguas por
el N.4.[a] N.D. hasta el Puerto de Mababi,
otras tres hasta Mababi donde sesteamos
y continuamos otras cinco por el E. N.D.
hasta el pueblo de Cuquiarachi ....12.

Una legua antes del Puerto de
Mababi, hay un ojo de Agua permanen-
te, donde llaman los Nogales; en el Puerto
hay otro mui pequeño ā la derecha del ca-
mino que conserva el agua mui fresca,
poco antes de llegar al parage llamado Ma
babi nace el Arroyo del Capulín que
pasa por Cochuta quando esta crecido, y se
une con el Río de Fronteras. 25„

Dia 18„ ________________________________25.

Salimos por el E. N D. y cami-
namos tres leguas h.[ta] Fronteras..................... 3.

Dia 19.

No salimos de este Presidio.

Dia 20.

Empezamos el Reconocimiento
de este valle por las mesas que se ha-
llan al S. SD. que aunque tienen bas-
tante extensión carecen totalm.[te] de
Agua, y solo producen un monte espe-
so de mesquites, su extremo sobre el
valle estan sumamente quebrado q.[e]
no puede colocarse una Población, q.[e]
podría surtirse de dos ojos de agua
permanentes que hay en el valle; ba-
jamos al Río de Cuquiarachi, cru-
zandolo por el vado del Chino, se-
guimos por su margen hasta donde
se junta con el Fronteras badean-
do este nos dirigimos por todo el 28.

valle hacia el N. por la falda de la 28.
Sierra reconociendo todas sus quiebras,
bolvimos á badear el Río continuan-
do por el O. al nacim.[to] de los dos ojos
de agua permanentes (que se hallan
como un quarto de legua al S. del Pre-
sidio) seguimos sus corrient.[s] hasta
la presa que se hizo de ellas para un
molino (que en el día está sin poder-
se usar, pero ā mui poco costo puede
recomponerse) suvimos al Presidio ha-
viendo caminado quatro leguas..................... 4„

Dia 21„

Continuamos el reconocimiento p.[r]
las Lomas que se hallan al N.4.[a] ND.
que son sumamente quebradas y es-
teriles, y bajando al valle seguimos
hasta la boca, reconocimos las Tierras
de labor de una y otra parte del río
y la presa ō saca de agua antigua
para el cultivo de ellas, regresandonos 32„

al Presidio en cuyo reconocimiento ca- 32„
minariamos .... 6„

Dia 22„ y 23„

Nos mantubimos sin salir de es-
te Presidio.

Dia 24.

Fuimos á reconocer los valles de
Cochuta y Turicache que siguen al
S. del de Fronteras sin intermision, y
pasando por el primero caminamos
siete leguas hasta el Pueblo de Turica-

che, retrocedimos tres por el mismo camino hasta el de cochuta, donde sesteamos, y continuamos las quatro restantes hasta el Presidio de Fronteras haviendo caminado este día.................. 14.

Quando se trasladó el Presidio de Fronteras á Sn Bernardino, abandonaron los Yndios estos dos Pueblos reuniendose en el de Cuquiarachi, el qual tambien se huviera despoblado ã no haver retirado el Presidio 52„

52„ ã su antiguo Parage (según me han informado) el Pueblo de Cochuta tiene todavía sus casitas en estado de servir, y solo á la Iglesia le han derrivado el Techo: Su situacion es hermosa, y el valle mui ã propósito p.^{a} cria de Ganados, y mantener Cablladas; tiene dos cienegas que dicen proceden de dos manantiales y otros veneritos permanentes, cuyas Aguas vienen conducidas (segun lo que he podido inferir de una corta Azequia que pasa inmediata ã las Casas) no dudo que pudieran cultivarse las Huertas, y aun algunas labores, con las que podría subsistir alguna corta Poblacion õ Rancho. El Rio carece enteramente de Agua en tiempo de seca, como en el día sucede desde Turicache tres leguas al S. hasta 52.

52„ donde llaman corral viejo dos leg.^{s} al N. que buelven ã rebentar las Aguas y siguen por Badeguachi al valle de Fronteras.

Tiene el citado Cochuta quatro leguas al N. el Presidio de Fronteras tres al S. el arruinado Pueblo de Turicachi, tres al S.D.4.ª S. el Puerto de Turicachi (donde finaliza la Sierra Purica) cinco al O.4.^{a}SD. el Puerto de Mababi, cinco al NO. el Pueblo de Cuquiarachi, y otras quatro al E. el Pueblo de Teras.

El Pueblo de Turicachi lo han quemado la mayor parte; está situado al extremo del valle en un terreno bastante quebrado y arido. Se halla ã la entrada del R.^{l} de Nacosari, tiene un buen ojo de Agua de donde nace el Rio de Fronteras pero ã mui corto trecho se seca (como .52.

llevo dicho) y no buelve ã reventar en el tiempo de seca hasta Corral viejo. .52.

Dia 25.

No salimos del Presidio.

Dia 26.

Fuimos ã reconocer el parage llamado Badeguachi, que no pudimos hacerlo quando nos retiravamos de Cochuta por que hera de noche. Es una porcion de terreno de lo mas elevado del valle, ã la qual no bañó la grande inundacion del año de 70. (segun me han asegurado) está en el concurso de los valles de Fronteras Cuquiarachi, y Cochuta, tiene un buen ojo de Agua permanente capaz de abastecer una Poblacion; como ã distancia de ochocientas var.s pasa el Rio de Fronteras sin tener ã su frente vado ninguno en mas de media legua; se halla sobre el cami- .52„

no del Puerto del Potrero para la comunicacion con la línea de la vizcaya (siendo por Babispe) no dista mas q^{e} una legua al S. del actual Presidio de Fronteras al que nos regresamos haviendo caminado.......................... 2. 52„

El referido Fronteras se halla situado sobre una Cuchilla en que están esparramadas las casas hasta su pie por no tener en el Bertice sufíciente extension, padece el defecto de tener por el E. una asperísima cordillera de Sierras que no dista en mi concepto arriva de mil y quinientas varas de donde repentinamente salen los Apaches, y atravesando el Río por los vados que tienen conocidos, se introducen en las labores, y ahun hasta las mismas Casas, como lo egecutaron ayer ã mui corta distancia de ellas al punto del medio 54.

día. El valle tiene suficiente Agua y quantas proporciones pueden apetecerse para el cultivo de sus Tierras estando ya mucha parte de ellas abiertas. 54.

Dia 27. hasta el 30.

No salimos del Presidio.

Dia 1.o de Mayo.

Continuamos nuestra marcha y caminamos diez leguas al O. NO. hasta el ojo del Gato..................... 10,,

Este parage no admite Poblacion assi por lo quebrado del terreno, como por la poquísima agua que tiene.

A las quatro leguas primeras de esta Jornada se encuentran dos ojitos de agua permanentes, el del Alamito y el de Turbili, pero solo pueden servir para vever la Gente, ā las dos siguientes el Arroyo hondo que estava seco, y ā otra legua 64.

el de la parida en los mismos termnos. 64.

Dia 2,,

Hicimos cinco leguas por el O. 4.ª NO. hasta el ojo del Leon, quatro NO. 4.ª O hasta el ojo del Sauz, otras quatro al NO. hasta las caveceras de San Pedro, y tres mas por el O. NO. al campo de las Nutrias donde interinamente se halla la compañia del Presidio de s.^{ta} Cruz........... 16.

El ojo del Leon es permanente, y puede haver en el un corto Rancho pues aunque el terreno es algo quebrado á mui corta distancia se estiende en llanos que siguen hasta san Pedro.

El ojo del Sauz es igualm.^{te} permanente y mucho mas caudaloso, está en terreno muy desplegado y proporcionado para una buena Pastoría. 80.

Dias 3,, y 4,, 80.

Permanecimos en este Campo.

Dia 5,,

Salimos por el O. S.D. ā distancia de dos leguas, subimos al Cerro de Terrenate, desde el pasamos al Presidio reformado de Terrenate una legua al NO. 4.ª N. y por el valle de su nombre nos regresamos al campo de las Nutrias dos leguas distante haviendo caminado.................... 5.

La situacion de Terrenate es bastante arida, poco abundante de aguas y las sierras mui inmediatas, la de German ā distancia de dos leguas p.^{r} el O.4.ª NO. la de las Bolas ā otras dos por el S. la de la Mariquilla a cinco por el S. E. y una por el S.E. 4.ª S. el cerro de Terrenate. Desde que se trasladó este Presidio al de Santa Cruz quedó enteram.^{te} despoblado por haverse hido al mismo 85.

tiempo los pocos vecinos q.^{e} tenía. 85.

Este Campo de las Nutrias es sumamente ameno y espacioso, abundante en buenos pastos y aguas en sus inmediaciones; tiene un grande ojo, capaz de abastecer una poblaz.^{n} al pie de la mesa donde actual.^{te} se halla la comp.^{a} de Sta Cruz; tiene por el O. ā mui corta distancia el valle de Terrenate con dos ojos de Agua caudalosos llamados de la Cruz y Cabestro (que en mi concepto son de una misma agua que se corta en el primero, y buelve ā brotar en el segundo) ā distancia de dos leguas cortas, se hallan las Aguas del Arroyo de Guachuca en su proprio valle, con un abundante ojo que se le agrega (el qual reconocíen mi anterior comision) dos leguas y media al E. están las labores de San Pedro á las margenes de su Río. 85.

Tiene la sierra de la Mariquilla cinco leguas al S. 4.ª SD. la de Guachuca quarto al N. y otras quatro al ND. 4.ª S. la de s.^{n} Jph, las tres abundantes de maderas, y ricos minerales conocidos en las dos primeras. 85.

Dias 6. y 7.

Nos mantubimos en este Campo.

Dia 8,,

Tenía determinado el Sor Brigadier que continuasemos nro viage por el Pueblo arruinado de Sonoita, pero antes de amanecer atacaron los Apaches la Guarnicion de caballada, y aunque no lograron quitarmela, nos estorvaron el marchar este día.

Dia 9„

Seguimos nra derrota por el NO. doce leguas hasta la mesa 85.

85.

del bagio del Alamillo..................... 12.

A las seis leguas primeras de esta Jornada se encuentra el ogito de agua permanente de los Magueyes, y antes de llegar á él á la derecha del camino hay dos cienegas que en tiempo de seca carecen de agua, ã la primera llaman Cienega grande, y ã la segunda del medio; ã otras tres leguas se encuentra el ojo de los Alamos largos bastante caudaloso en terreno abierto y con muchos pastos pero sin mas madera, ni leña, que algunos Alamos bien distantes. La mesa del bagio donde hicimos noche carece totalmente de agua.

Seis leguas al S. SE. de dha mesa se halla el caudaloso ojo de agua de San Antonio donde nace 97.

el Río de Santa María Sianca; 97.

el Puerto de los Divisaderos nueve leguas al S. 4.ª SE. el de Sta Bárbara ocho al S. el de San Antonio cuatro al S. 4.ª SD. el de la Plomosa una y media al O. el de el Agua caliente seis al N. NO., el del Babocomari tres al N. ND. y el de la madera ocho al ND. 4.ª S.

Dia 10.

Caminamos seis leguas por el NO. 4.ª O. hasta el Pueblo de Sonoitá y continuamos despues de haver sesteado otras quatro al O. hasta el de Calavazas..................... 10„

Sonoitá lo destruyeron los Yndios Barbaros, y se mantiene despoblado, tiene un ojo de agua permanente mui caudaloso que corre hacia el O., y por el E. tiene un grande valle sin aguas; su situa 107.

cion es bastante mala por hallarse en terreno mui quebrado y montuoso, metido en un profundo barranco. 107„

Calabazas tiene un valle muy espacioso pero poco abundante de agua en la estación presente.

Dia 11.

Caminamos cuatro leguas por el NO. 4.ª N. hasta el Pueblo de Tumacacori .... 4.

Dia 12.

Fuimos ã reconocer el antiguo R^{l} del Aribac pasando por el Presidio reformado de Tubac una legua al N. seguimos otras quatro por el NO. 4.ª N. hasta el ojo del Zopori, y quatro por el SD. 4.ª O ã la cañada del Aquituni sin agua................. 9„

El ojo del Zopori es bastante caudaloso pero sin corriente.

Dia 13„

Continuamos tres leguas por 120„

el SD. y amanecimos en el $nacim.^{to}$ del arroyo del Aribac (donde solicité permiso del $s.^{or}$ Brigadier, y con él pasé ã reconocer el antiguo $R.^{l}$ del Aribac) y nos regresamos por el Puerto de Tubac al Pueblo de Tumacacori distante nueve leguas al S. 4.ª SE................................. 12. 120.

Quando pasé ã reconocer el Aribac me acompañaron el $Ten.^{te}$ Bolante D^{n} Pablo Romero, y dos vecinos de Tubac; encontré las ruinas de las Casas y el terreno tan enteramente falto de agua que me aseguraron los dichos vecinos no haverlo conocido jamás en iguales terminos; es un campo mui espacioso con abundantes pastos, y me aseguraron havia en este $R.^{l}$ muchos y buenas minas de Plata conocidas y algunos $Placer^{s}$ de oro.

Distra quatro leguas al SE 132.

el Puerto del Fresno, y once al NO. 4.ª O de tierra llana la sierra del Babuquiburi, hasta bolver ã unirme con la Gente en el nacimiento del Arroyo; hice......................... 3„ 132.

Este Pueblo de Tumacacori está casi cercado de pared en figura cuadrilatera, ā la que ban agregando varias Casitas para poder vivir con mas seguridad. Tiene mui buenas siembras pero se quejan en el dia de haverseles escaseado el Agua por la mucha seca, y así entretienen la que hay y no llega ā Tubac.

Dias 14. y 15.
Permanecimos en este Pueblo.

Dia 16.
Continuamos nra marcha una legua al N. hasta el antiguo Presidio de Tubac.......................... 1,,

136.

136. El referido Tubac se halla reducido á nueve vecinos que se han presentado al Sor Brigadier; manifestandole que no podian subsistir asi por la total falta de agua para sus labores, como por lo mucho que los hostilizaba el Enemigo; hay bastante numero de Casas pero estas mismas sirven de Trinchera ā los Apaches para ofenderlos.

Dia 17.
Caminamos cinco leguas por el N. 4.ª NO. hasta la Canoa, y otras quatro al N. NO. donde hicimos noche......... 9.

En la Canoa havia un pequeño ojito que no pudo dar abasto para la Gente, y en el parage que dormimos no havia ninguna agua..........

Dia 18.
Seguimos seis leguas al N. hasta el Pueblo de s^{n} Xavier del Bac.................6.

151.

151. Esta tarde ha llegado un correo con la noticia de que fueron atacados por los Apaches despues de nra salida y mataron dos vecinos.

Dias 19. H.^{ta} el 21.
No salimos de este Pueblo.

Dia 22.
Salimos por el S. SE. ā reconocer el nacimiento de esta aguas, distante una legua, reconocimos tanbien mucha parte de las siembras y nos retiramos haviendo caminado,,......... 3.

El expresado San xavier forma un quadro con sus mismas Casas, y soólo le faltan algunos pequeños Portillos para quedar enteramente cerrado, en los quatro extremos ban formando una especie de Torreónes atronerados en porcion circular; No obstante de estar en un espacioso valle, fueron 154.

precisamente ā situarlo entre unas lomas ō pequeños cerros llamados el mal Pais de san xavier, abrigados de los quales han solido presentarseles repentinam.^{te} los Apaches. Bá tomando mucho fomento esta mision en el cultivo de sus buenas tierras; tiene un competente num.^{o} de Yndios Pimas vecinos, con algunos de razon, y desde luego la juzgo de las más florecientes. Tiene una grande cienega inmediata por la parte del sur, y como este viento es el que mal reina discurro que las aguas detenidas en ella han de ser perjudiciales para la salud; en esta Cienega se mantiene regularmente la caballada del Presidio del Tucson, y los Ganados de la mision, y me aseguran que no faltaria en ella el Pasto 154. 154.

aunque permaneciese todo el año la caballada. 154.

Dia 23.
Permanecimos en este Pueblo.

Dia 24.
Seguimos nuestra marcha tres leguas al N. hasta el Presidio de s.^{n} Agustín del Tucson....................... 3.

Dia 25.
No salimos del Presidio.

Dia 26.

Fuimos al Pueblo del Tucson distante un quarto de legua por el SD. 4.ª al S. y al regresarnos me separé con el Capitan S.ⁿ Pedro Allande para reconocer la presa, y el parage donde se divide el agua en tres abundantes Azequias que sirven para el consumo y cultivo de las tierras del Pueblo, y del Presidio al que me restitui haviendo caminado una legua ....1.

158.

La fabrica de dho Pueblo (aunque no tan adelantada) sigue en los mis mos terminos que la de s.ⁿ Xavier del Bac. 158.

Dia 27.

Solicité el permiso del s.ᵒʳ Brigad.ʳ para hir á reconocer las maderas y en virtud de el, con la escolta que me señaló de doce hombres, y el Alferes D.ⁿ Cayetano Limon, y el Cap.ⁿ d.ⁿ Pedro Allande que se ofreció ã acompañarme; fui al Arroyo de S.ᵗᵃ Cathalina ã la falda de la sierra de su nombre distante del Presidio quatro leguas al Eeste, donde encontré con abundancia madera de Nogal, Alamo, y Fresno; este Arroyo trahia mui poco agua, y tambien suele faltarle; concluido este Reconocimiento me regresé haviendo caminado .... 9.

167.

Dia 28. 167.

Permanecimos en dho Presidio.

El capitan de él há tenido la curia de cercarlo provisionalmᵗᵉ con estacada, formando un cuadrado con una zanja por la parte exterior de quatro pies de ancho, y quatro de profundo; en los extremos há lebantado una especie de baterías ã barbeta sostenidos con palizada doble sus terraplenes que figuran unos pequeños Baluartes, donde ha colocado los quatro Cañoncitos de batallon; ha hecho un Almacen de Polvora, una troge, el Cuerpo de Guardia, y un genero de Capilla que suple por falta de Yglesia sin costo de la R.ˡ Haz.ᵈᵃ tambien me pidió le demarcase un Torreón para mantener una Centinela que descubriese el campo ã mayor distancia, y ya quedaban abriendole los cimientos. 167.

La

Situacion es bella, en terreno muy despejado con abundantes aguas, y tierras de labor, tiene la proporcion de un grande corral formado por dos Acequias entre el Pueblo y el Presidio donde resguardan su cavallada en caso de hallarse con limitada fuersa de Tropa; en sus inmediaciones es escaso de pastos en tpo de seca, pero los tiene con abundancia en la Cienega de s.ⁿ Xavier tres leguas al S. y en otros parages menˢ distantes. 167.

Dista de este Presidio el de Santa Cruz beinte y cinco leguas por el E. SE.; tres Alamos diez y siete al E., El Puerto de la Cebadilla nueve al E. ND. el de la Mololoa cuatro al N. 4.ª NO., el Aquitune diez y seis al ND., la sierra del Tucson tres al O. el Arroyo y Sierra de s.ᵗᵃ Catharina quatro al E., el ojo grande õ 167.

nacimiento de estas aguas una legua al S. y el Pueblo del Tucson un quarto de legua al SD. 4.ª S. 167.

Dia 29.

Seguimos nuestra derrota y caminamos siete leguas al N. 4.ª ND. sin encontrar agua alguna...................... 7.

Dia 30.

Hicimos quatro leguas al N. 4.ª ND. hasta la cañada del oro, y cinco mas al N. ND. donde hicimos noche............................. 9,,

En la Cañada del oro (que sesteamos) hay un pequeño aguage permanente; en el parage que hicimos noche no se encuentra agua.

Dia 31,,

Caminamos quatro leguas al N. ND. por la Cañada de la Virgen del Consuelo hasta salir al Rio de San Pedro (que lo pasamos seco) y otras cinco leguas por la margen 183.

de dicho Río hasta el vado del 183.
Alamo (que ya trahia agua) donde hicimos noche.............................. 9.

Dia 1.º de Junio.

Seguimos tres leguas por el NO. 4.ª N. hasta el vado del atascadero y otra hasta la junta de los Rios San Pedro y Gila; nos retiramos luego por la otra parte del Rio al vado del atascadero donde sesteamos, y continuamos otras tres leguas por el SE. 4.ª S. hasta el vado del Alamo.......................... 8.

Pareciendome indispensable para cumplir con las ordenes que tenia y reconocer con proligidad algunas leguas al E. y O. de la junta de los expresados Rios, el que nos mantuviesemos en ella uno ō dos diías, lo hice repetidas veces presente al s.^{or} Brigadier y no haviendolo juzgado conveniente dispuso que se 200.

quedara el campo con el Alferez 200.
Limon en el vado del atascadero pasando nosotros con treinta Hombres ā la precisa junta de los Rios y apenas tuve hecha la observaz.^{n} (aunque trabajosamente por el viento que lo impedia) nos restituimos al campo.

El parage de la Junta es un caxon que segun manifiesta se inundará en qualquier creciente del Gila, y sin ninguna proporcion; todas sus inmediaciones segun lo que alcanza la vista manifiestan ser terrenos muy quebrados.

Dia 2,,

Hicimos quatro leguas por el S. S.E. hasta el vado de la Xacaleria sesteamos y continuamos por las margenes de s.^{n} Pedro otras cinco leguas donde hicimos noche................. 9.

En toda esta Jornada que segui- 209.

mos la caja del Río de s.^{n} Pedro no 209.
encontramos Agua, en el parage que dormimos se hicieron unos Pozitos y pudo vever la Gente.

Dia 3,,

Caminamos seis leguas por el S. SD. hasta el vado de la cahida, sesteamos y continuamos otras tres p^{r} el mismo rumbo donde acampamos,,......... 9.

Dia 4.

Seguimos cinco leguas por el S. SE. hasta el vado del Peñasco, y otras tres por el mismo rumbo....................... 8.

Dia 5,,

Seguimos por el S. SE. una legua al vado de tres Alamos, ocho al Guiburi, y despues de sestear otras tres al S. 4.ª SE. hasta el Presidio de Santa Cruz..................... 12.

El Guiburi admite una pequeña poblacion por ser algo despejado, y con suficiente agua, tiene algunos 238.

veneros independientes del Río. 238.

La situacion de este Presidio me parece mui mala (segun los reconocimientos que hice para su traslacion al Campo de las Nutrias en mi anterior comision) carece de leña en quatro leguas de distancia, los pocos pastos que tiene llaman los inteligentes pajonales y tovosos que no sirven para la caballada, la que ā larga distancia no puede subsistir sin crecida Guarnicion por lo quebrado del terreno.

Dia 6.

Hicimos tres leguas S. al vado Pedregoso, otras tres ā los Nogales; sesteamos, y seguimos una legua al vado de las Tarabillas, y quatro por el S. 4.ª SE. al de las Palominas.................11.

Dia 7.

Caminamos dos leguas por el S.

4.a S.E. al vado del Fresno, tres por
el S. 4.a SD. al de la Tienda, tres por 249.

el S.SE. al de los Alamos, y otra p.^{r} 249.
el sur ã las labores de s.^{n} Pedro.............. 9.

El Rio de s.^{n} Pedro corre por un espacioso valle (sin cortarse mas q^{e} la porcion entre el vado de los Alamos, y el de la Tienda hasta pasar de Santa Cruz) y en el vado de las Tarabillas empieza ã ser el terreno mui quebrado. Desde s.^{ta} Cruz hasta el Río Gila sigue el de san Pedro formando Pielagos seco en muchas partes, y con pocas proporciones para establecimientos desde su nacim.^{to} hasta el vado de las Tarabillas, (aunque como llevo referido está en un espacioso valle), tiene el defecto de ser su caxa mui profunda, y carecer totalmente de leña.

Dia 8.

Seguimos por el SD. 4.ª O. tres leg.^{s}
hasta el campo de las Nutrias, y otras
quatro al S.D. hasta el ojo de Agua
permanente de Milpillas................. 7.
265.

Dia 9. 265.

Caminamos seis leguas por el SD.
4.a S. hasta el Pueblo de Cocospera........6.

Dia 10.

Nos mantubimos en este Pueblo, q^{e} tiene mui buenas siembras, y le destruyeron los enemigos todo su Ganado.

Dia 11.

Habiendome mandado el Sor Brigadier que fuese ã reconocer los valles del Rio de Sta María Suanca, y señaladome la escolta de cuarenta hombres y el Teniente volante Dn Pablo Romero, de la qual havian de restituirse diez al Presidio del Tucson con el cap^{n} agregado ã el Dn Juan de Oliva, sali esta tarde por el N. ND. y caminé seis leguas hasta el antiguo rancho
de San Lázaro............................... 6.

Dia 12.

Dejé el campo en este Parage, supli- 277.

candole al capitan Dn Juan de Oliva 277
dispusiera lo que juzgara conven.^{te} en qualquiera novedad que ocurriese, y con el Teniente D. Pablo Romero y quince hombres pasé ã reconocer el arruinado pueblo de s.^{ta} María Suanca tres leguas y media al N. 4.ª ND. segui otra legua y media al N. NO. hasta el ojo del Agua de san Antonio; nacimiento del Rio de s.^{ta} María (que es bastante caudaloso) y concluido este reconocimiento me regresé por el mismo camino al valle de San Lázaro donde me incorporé con mi Gente, y despues de sestear continué otras cinco leguas al S. SE. h.^{ta}
la Hacienda de Santa Bárbara.................15.

Una legua al SE. del ojo de s.^{n} Antonio estaba la grande Pastoria, õ Rancho del Torreón, tres leguas al S. SE. tiene el Puerto õ camino de Terrenate en la sierra de German.

Santa María Suanca fué Cabe- 292.

cera de mision, estaba situada en 292.
un hermoso valle con las mejores proporciones para Siembras, y cria de Ganados; tiene el Puerto de Santa Bárbara distante dos leguas y media al O. NO. el de s.^{n} Antonio quatro al NO. y las sierras de las Bolas una al SE.

El Rancho de s.^{n} Lázaro estava en un valle muy espacioso que antiguamente dicen no podia transitarse por los muchos Ganados que tenia, como igualmente en los pertenecientes á la Hacienda de s.^{ta} Barbara donde sus fertiles tierras manifiestan lo que puede haver sido.

Dia 13.

Segui por estos lindos valles una legua al NO. 4.ª N. hasta el Ranchito, media al Rancho de s.^{n} Luis tres y media ã la Hacienda de
Buenavista, una por el N. NO. 292.

á su estancia, y otras tres por el O. 292.
4.a NO. al pueblo arruinado de
Guevavi............................... 9,,

Todas los parages expresados son de la misma calidad que los de la Jornada antecedente; la Haz.^{da} de Buena-vista (que ha sido en ellos la mas afamada) tiene ã mas del Rio un ogito de agua permanente; su estancia es una grande mesa por cuyo pie pasa el Río; tiene unas lomas altas de las quales se descubren estos valles; dista del Presidio del Altar treinta y cinco leguas, de el de Tucson veinte y seis, y del parage señalado en el campo de las Untrias para el de Santa Cruz veinte y una; tiene la sierra de la Chihuahuilia abundante en maderas y ricos minerales quatro leguas al ND.

Guevavi proporciona mas las
distancias entre las Nutrias y el 301,,

Tucson, pero alarga la del Altar 301,,
y no es tan abundante de Pastos.

El Rio s.^{ta} María corre hacia el S. hasta San Lázaro q.^{e} cambiando su corriente hacia el N. sigue por los parages referidos pasando por este hasta los Pueblos de Calabazas, y Tumacacori; aunque no es muy caudaloso está siempre en corriente y solo un pedazo como mil varas (p.^{r} ser terreno arenoso) quedará cortado poco antes de llegar ã Guevavi, donde buelve ã brotar el agua con mas fuerza.

Luego que llegué á este parage despaché los diez hombres del Presidio del Tucson en cuya compañía marchó el capitán agregado Don Juan de Oliva.

Dia 14.

Me puse en marcha al romper 301.

el día por el S. SE. hice seis leguas 301,,
hasta el Agua Zarca; despues de sestear continué otras tres hasta el Ojo del Zibuta, y dos mas hasta
el de Cicurizuta donde hice noche............ 11.

En el Agua Zarca se cortó un rastro de bastante Yndiada que salia con robo por todo el camino R.^{l} y segun los practicos de la tierra habria como diez dias que pasaron; en dicho parage no tuvimos agua alguna; el ojo del Zibuta es permanente y con economia puede darse de verber ã alguna caballada; el de Cicurizuta es tambien permanente, y mas caudaloso, de él nace el Arroyo que pasa por Ymuris y San Ygnacio.

Dia 15.

Antes de amanecer sali por el cajon del Arroyo sumam.^{te} cerrado
de Bosque (en el que hay mucho 312.

Ganado meseño) caminé ocho leg.^{s} 312.
por el S.SE. hasta el Pueblo de Ymuris donde paré a sestear, y ã la cahida de la tarde continué otr.^{s}
tres h.^{ta} el Pueblo de s.^{n} Ignacio.............. 11.

En Ymuris me digeron los Yndios que el s.^{or} Brigadier havia salido de alli poco tiempo antes, dejandoles prevenido, me digesen quando llegara que sin detencion pasara ã San Ignacio donde me esperava; pero me fué forzoso detenerme por lo asoleada que venia de la Gente hasta el anochecer ã cuya hora lo egecuté y presentandome ã dho s.^{r} señor Brigadier le di cuenta de mi comision con el Diario correspond.^{te} entregandole mi Partida sin la menor novedad.

En el Pueblo de Ymuris se junta el Arroyo de Cocospera con el de Ci-
curizuta, y unidos pasan por este 323.

hacia el de la Magdalena. 323.

Dista de este Pueblo el Puerto del Zazava cinco leguas al S. SE. el de Dolores cinco al SE. y el de la Jojoba dos al O.

Dias 16. y 17.

Nos mantubimos en esta Mision que está en el dia de las mas abundantes en frutos y Ganados.

Dia 18.

Salimos esta tarde por el S. SD. y caminamos dos leguas hasta el Pue-
blo de la Magdalena.......................... 2.

Dia 19.

Caminamos seis leguas NO.4.ª O. hasta el Potrero y cinco al NO. ã las Pedradas............................. 11.

En el Puerto hay dos ojos de agua permanentes mui buenos, y en las Pedradas no hay ninguno.

Dia 20. 336.

Cuatro NO.4.ª O. al Pueblo de 236.
Tubutáma............................. 4.

Esta mision tiene algunas labores buenas, pero el cultivo de ellas, en este tiempo, es causa de que se les escasee el agua á los de s.ta Teresa, y el Ati.

Dia 21.

Hicimos ocho leguas ND. hasta el Pueblo del Saric, y dos mas ND. 4.ª N. al arruinado Pueblo del Busanic, regresamos por el mismo camino del Saric........................ 12.

En el Busanic no faltan tierras y agua para que pueda subsistir una Poblacion segun lo que me alcancé a ver desde el parage donde estava el Pueblo, proximo al qual nace el Arroyo que pasa por el Saric, Tubutama es que se corta en los intervalos de uno ã otro Pueblo. Dista de el 352.

el Arivac catorce leguas N.4 ND. 352
la sierra de la Arizona ocho al E. ND. Guevavi quince ND. 4.ª N. y el cerro del Chile una NO. 4.ª N.

Dia 22.

Hicimos ocho leguas SD. hasta Tubutáma, una y media SD. 4.ª O. al Pueblo de S.ta Teresa, y una y media al del Ati.......................... 11.

Este Pueblo del Ati carece en el dia total.te de agua, de modo que para el preciso consumo de la Gente, ban a buscarla cerca del de s.ta Teresa.

Dia 23.

Cinco leguas SD. al Pueblo de Oquitoa, y dos al O. SD. al Presidio de s.ta Gertrudis del Altar..................... 7.

La mision de Oquitoa se mantiene en un buen estado, y nada escasa de agua.

Dias 24 h.ta el 29. 370.

Nos mantubimos en este Presidio 370.
sin salir de su recinto.

Tiene el defecto de faltarle el agua para el cultivo de sus tierras en tiempo de seca (como en el dia sucede) que solo tiene la que necesita para su consumo lo que ha sido causa de secarse la mayor parte de sus Huertas, y las que subsisten manifiestan en la abundancia de sus frutos la fertilidad del Terreno.

Tiene ã distancia de doce leguas al ND. la sierra de s.ta Teresa una y media NO. 4.ª N. el Cerro del Bamuri una y media NO. 4.ª O. el Puerto del chanate, seis al O. SD. el Pueblo del Pitic, tres al S. SD. la sierra del Ojo de Agua, y una al E. SE. el puerto de Santa Ana.

Dia 30.

Hicimos catorce leguas al S. SD. hasta el llano verde sin encontrar agua ...... 14.
384.

Dia 1,,º de Julio 384.

Caminamos dos leguas al S. SD. hasta el R.l de la Cieneguilla...............2,,

Dias 3. y 4.

No salimos del Pueblo.

En este Real no carecen de agua por la cieneguita que siempre existe, y la facilidad con que la han encontraado en los diferentes Pozos que han hecho, por lo que discurro que valiendose de la industria podrían servirse de ella con mas utilidad.

En los Placeres de oro (que tanto han producido) suelen tener mucha escaces de agua, segun me han asegurado; los que en el dia se trabajan estan una legua al SD.

Dia 5.

Continuamos la marcha por el SE. 4.ª S. hicimos diez leguas hasta el ojo de agua permanente del Carricito..............10,,

Dia 6„ 396.

Tres leguas SE. al aguaje del Tecolote, y quatro por el ND. al de la Tortuga.. 7. 396.

Estos dos aguages dicen que no permanecen en tiempo de secas.

Dia 7„

Ocho leguas SE. 4.ª E. al Pozo de Chrisanto................................ 8.

Este Pozo es permanente pero se necesita sacar el agua con cubos.

Dia 8.

Hicimos quatro leguas SE. hasta la cobrisa, cinco al E. 4.ª SE. al zanjon, y seis SE 4.ª S. á la Hacienda del Torreón................................... 15.

En la Cobrisa y Zanjon hay agua en tiempo de lluvias.

Dias 9„ y 10„

Nos mantubimos en esta Haz.da del Torreón la que tiene abundantes siembras, Viñas, Caña y otros frutos 426.

tiene el Rancho de las Animas cinco leguas al SE. donde mantiene sus mandas. 426.

Dia 11.

Continuamos nuestra derrota por el S. cinco leguas hasta el Rancho de Alamillo.................................. 5.

Dia 12.

Caminamos seis leguas al S.SD. hasta el Presidio del Pitic.......................6.

Dia 13.

Salimos por el O. ã reconocer este terreno y caminamos dos leguas..............2.

Dia 14.

No salimos del Presidio.

Dia 15.

Salimos por el E. ã reconocer la entrada del Rio, y la toma õ saca de agua que se hace para el cultivo de las Tierras, caminamos............................ 1„

Dia 16. h.ta el 22.

Me mantuve en este Presidio, el 440.

qual tiene muchas tierras de labor abundancia de aguas, y facilidad p.a hacer de ellas las sacas que se quisieren, pero está el terreno expuesto ã la inundacion como se verificó en la mayor parte de él en el año de 70. al tiempo de la expedicion que tenian las Gentes que faborecerse del Cerro de la campana (segun me han informado) no tiene otra madera que de Mezquite, la qual es muy vidriosa y de corta magnitud, y siempre que se necesite de otra especie será forzoso traherla de la sierra de Sonibiate distante como treinta leguas al ND. y no juzgo muy fácil la conduccion. 440.

Dista el cerro del Tonuco quatro leguas al O. el cerro colorado dos al NO. 4.a N. el de los Pozos de s.n Jph diez al NO. el de Santa Teresa tres 440.

al E. 4.a SE. el de Palos blancos dos al S. SD. y el de la campana mui inmediato al Presidio ã la otra banda del Rio por el N. 440.

Dia 23.

Respecto de haver concluido mis comisiones, y no tener en este Presidio proporcion para trabajar los mapas y demás papeles correspondientes; ofreciendose al mismo tiempo el que en este dia saliese una Partida para traher el Situado de este Presidio de la capital de Arispe, determinó el s.or Brigadier que incorporado con ella me restituyese a dicha Capital, en virtud de lo qual salimos esta tarde por el N. ND. y caminamos seis leguas hasta el Rancho del Alamillo.......................... 6.

Dia 24.

Caminamos cinco leguas al N. 446.

hasta la Hacienda del Torreón, y quatro ND. hasta el Pueblo y Presidio reformado de s.n Miguel de Orcasitas......... 9„ 446.

Aunque el Presidio que se hallava en este Pueblo se transfirió al del Pitic, no ha desmerecido cosa mayor por ser su vecindario bastante crecido y tener un regular comercio. Su situacion es buena, tiene bastantes tierras de labor, agua suficiente, y en sus inmediaciones algunas minas conocidas de ambas especies. Se halla el cerro colorado dos leguas S. el Puerto de Antunes dos y media al E. ND. el de Nacameri quatro ND. 4.ª N. el R.l de s.n Joseph de Gracia siete al SE. el Pueblo del Populo (despoblado), una al ND. un ojo de agua permanente al NO. proximo al Pueblo.

Dia 25„

Nos mantuvimos en s.n Miguel 455.

por el mal tiempo. 455.

Dia 26.

Salimos ã la una de la noche, y ã corto rato nos empezó una fuerte tempestad y un continuo aguacero que nos duró quasi toda la Jornada; caminamos once leguas al S. hasta el Pueblo de Ures.............................. 11.

Esta mision está situada en un grande llano abundante de agua y Tierras de siembra.

Dia 27.

Estuvimos detenidos por no poderse badear el Rio en este Pueblo; dista de él, el Puerto y Rancho de Soniviate cinco leguas N. la sierra de Soniviate dos al ND. el Pueblo de los Alamos diez al SE. y su Puerto tres por el mismo rumbo; el Pueblo de s.ta Rosalia doce al S. SE. el R.l de Nacameri diez leguas al NO. 466.

Dias 28. y 29. 466.

Por la fuerte tempestad que hubo la noche del 27 nos dió estampida la Caballada, y haviendonos quedado sin ninguna, fue indispensable detenerse estos dos días mientras se logró el recogerla.

Dia 30.

Tomamos el escabroso camino q.e llaman de los altos, huyendo de los infinitos vados intransitables por las continuas abenidas que a la presente tiene este Rio, y caminamos catorce leguas por el ND. 4.a E. hasta el Real de la Concepcion.................. 14.

Dia 31„

Siguiendo el propio camino de los altos, caminamos dos leguas al N. hasta el Pueblo de Babiacora, tres ND. 4.ª N. al de Aconchi, quatro N. 4.a ND. al de Huepaca, tres 480.

ã Banamichi, y tres N. 4.ª NO. 480.
al Real de Motepore........................ 15.

Aunque pensabamos llegar esta noche ã Sinoquipe, fue preciso el detenernos por haver rodado una mula mía por una ladera õ despeñadero hasta el Rio, con lo que se me inutilizaron enteramente los Papeles, Libros, Yinstrumentos, Ropa, y demás que trahía.

Dia 1.º de Agosto.

Salimos de tardeada por el N. y caminamos dos leguas hasta el Pueblo de Sinoquipe........................ 2.

Dia 2.

Estubimos detenidos porque con la continuacion de las Aguas no podia vadearse el Rio, y los altos nos dijeron que heran intransitables.

Dia 3.

Seguimos por el N. NO. p.r todo 497.

el cajon del Rio (con bastante incomodidad por llegarnos el agua h.ta los borrenes de la Silla) quatro leg.s hasta Tetuachi, donde tomamos los altos por ser ya mas suaves, y continuamos otras tres leguas hasta la Capital de Arispe........................... 7.

Total de las leguas caminadas en este viaje...... 504.

Notas. [In the original document.]

1ª Asi de las distancias de las sierras, Puertos, ojos de agua, como de todo lo que pertenezca ã ynformes que haya recivido en este viage, tengo mui poca satisfaccion por la inconsequencia tan grande de los practicos de la tierra, pues me ha sucedido repetidas veces preguntar ã uno una cosa, repetirle la pregunta despues de pasado un rato y contradecirse regularmente en un todo; y en queriendoles reconvenir satisfacen con decir quien sabe? Es verdad que por lo que respecta á distancias no son culpables porque jamás han savido entenderse por el num.º de leguas.

2ª No se tengan tampoco por leguas legales las que yo expreso en mis jornadas, pues no ha sido otra cosa que un computo prudencial segun el tiempo que hemos empleado en ellas, y el paso que hemos llevado, pero en este ha havido tantas variaciones que no he podido asegurarme en la estimacion de dichas leguas, las que he considerado segun las establecidas en este Reyno.

3ª Gualquiera que haga el viage desde el Pueblo de ures hasta esta Capital por el camino regular del Rio, hallará precisamente alguna variaz.ⁿ en las distancias que Yo expreso por haverme obligado las crecientes á venir por los altos, en los quales los infinitos rodeos que causan sus quiebras hacen variar las distancias.

4ª En quanto á las Longitudes y latitudes demarcadas en mi Mapa, solo diré que he procurado hacer mis observaciones en los parages que he podido con la exactitud posible, pero no tengo total confianza de ellas por haver carecido de los justificados Ynstrumentos que requieren tan delicadas observaciones.

5ª Respecto de haver hecho estos viages en el tpo de la seca mas rigorosa que se ha experimentado en estas Provincias, la que ha ocasionado que infinitos aguages que nunca havian carecido de agua, los haya encontrado secos; me aseguro en que todos los que he visto existentes, serán permanentes, y son los que con esta expresion se encontrarán en mi diario.

6ª Lo expresado en la Nota antecedente no debe entenderse con la porcion de camino andado desde el R.ˡ de la Cieneguilla hasta la Hacienda del Torreón por havernos empezado las Aguas en dho R.ˡ y desde entonces raro ha sido el dia que ha dejado de llover, y asi aunque en todos los transitos encontramos agua (segun los yinformes que tengo) solo el carricito y el Pozo de Crisanto son los permanentes, y este ultimo con la incomodidad de necesitar sacar el agua con cubos, y valerse de unas pequeñas Canoas para hirla dando a las Vestias, de suerte que este camino en tpo de seca es penoso por falta de Aguages, y en tiempo de lluviás por los muchos Atascaderos que tiene.

7ª No dudo que si en el dia hiciere otro estos reconocimentos respecto ã lo mucho que ha llovido, tal vez encontraria algunos parages mui ã proposito para establecimientos que Yo no los he recivido por tales respecto de haverlos encontrado secos õ escasos de Agua= Arispe 5. de Agosto de 1780=Gerónimo de la Rocha y Figueroa.

Es copia de Su original de que Certifico. Arispe 31„ de Diz.ʳᵉ de 1781.
Antonio Bonilla

Map key

MAPA DE LA FRONTERA
De Sonora para el Establecim.ᵗᵒ de la Linea de Presidios

Explicacion

Capital de las Provincias Yn-
ternas de N.E.

Presidios de SM esistentes

Presidios propuestos para la
nueva Linea

Pueblos.

Haciendas.

Ranchos.

Reales de Minas

Placeres de oro conosidos.

Parages despoblados donde
se acampó.

Ojos de Agua caudalosos.

Y dm pequenos donde apenas puede vever La Jente.

Linea o cordon de Presidios.
Propuesto por el Teniente de
Yngenieros Comicionado.

Linea de Derrota que mani-
fiesta los reconocimientos-
hechos para los expresados establecimientos.

Lineas que dividen los terre-
nos pertenecientes a cada na-
cion, segun las mexores noti
cias que se han podido ad-
quirir.

<u>Notas.</u>

1ª. Los Pueblos, Haciendas, Ranchos, despoblados, Reales de minas
que no se trabajan. Y presidios reformados van indicados con las
mismas señales;, pero con la diferencia que en lugar de sus co-
lores se les ha dado de negro.

IIª. Las porsiones de Rios ó Arroyos que se encontraron secos en-
lugar del color de Agua tienen el de Tierra.

IIIª. De las demas circunstancias que no pueden expresarse en el Mapa se hallaran las correspondientes noticias en los Diarios del mismo Yngeniero. Arispe 4 de Septiembre de 1780.
Gerónimo de la Rocha y Figueroa

References Cited

Almada, Francisco R.

1952 *Diccionario De Historia, Geografía, y Biografía Sonorenses*. Ruiz Sandoval, Chihuahua.

Anderson, James M.

2002 *Daily Life During the Spanish Inquisition*. Greenwood Press, Westport, Connecticut and London.

Anza, Juan Bautista de

1977 Anza to Croix, Horcasitas, September 1, 1777, AGI, Guad., 516.

Baegert, Jacob

1952 Observations in Lower California. Translated by M. M. Brandenburg and Carl L. Baumann. University of California Press, Berkeley. https://books.google.com.mx/books?id=hb42i8cd-AMC&printsec=frontcover&source=gbs_ge_summary_r&cad=0#v=onepage&q&f=false

Bahre, Conrad J.

1991 *A Legacy of Change: Historic Human Impact on Vegetation in the Arizona Borderlands*. University of Arizona Press, Tucson.

Bahre, Conrad J. and Charles F. Hutchinson

1985 The Impact of Historic Fuelwood Cutting on the Semidesert Woodlands of Southeastern Arizona. *Journal of Forest History* 29(4): 175–186.

Baldonado, Louis

1959 Mission San Jose de Tumacacori in 1774. *Kiva* 24(4):21–24.

Ball, Eve

1970 *In the Days of Victorio: Recollections of a Warm Springs Apache*. University of Arizona Press, Tucson.

Bartlett, John Russell

1965 *The Mexican Boundary Commission papers of John Russell Bartlett, 1850–1853 Volume II*. The Rio Grande Press Inc., Chicago.

Barnes, Will C.

1935 *Arizona Place Names*. University of Arizona Bulletin, 6(1); General Bulletin No. 2. University of Arizona, Tucson.

1982 *Arizona Place Names*. University of Arizona Press, Tucson.

Batman, Richard

1988 *Personal Narrative of James O. Pattie*. Copper Mountain Books, Inc., Mountain Press Publishing Company, Missoula.

Bell, William Alexander

1869 *New Tracks in North America: A Journal of Travel and Adventure Whilst Engaged in the Survey for a Southern Railroad to the Pacific Ocean during 1867-8, Volume 2*. Virtue and Co, London.

Beltrán, José María

1796a Letter to Viceroy Branciforte, 25 September. México, Archivo General y Público de la Nación, México, Ramo de Provincias Internas, Tomo 216.

1796b Letter to the Viceroy Branciforte, 21 December. México, Archivo General y Público de la Nación, México, Ramo de Provincias Internas, Tomo 216.

Bolton, Herbert E.

1917 The Mission as a Frontier Institution in the Spanish-American Colonies. *American Historical Review* 23:42–61.

1930 *Anza's California Expeditions, Volume V, Correspondence*. University of California Press Berkeley.

1936 *Rim of Christendom: A Biography of Eusebio Francisco Kino Pacific Coast Pioneer*. Russell and Russell, New York.

1948 *Kino's Historical Memoir of Pimeria Alta*. University of California Press, Berkeley.

Bonilla, Antonio Bonilla

1774 Terrenate, "Revista pasada por el Capitan de Infanteria D. Antonio Bonilla Ayudante Inspector de los Presidios internos de esta Nueva Espana a la Compania de dotacion del expresado Presidio," AGI Audiencia de Guadalajara 2 72.

Bright, William

2004 *Native American Placenames of the United States*. University of Oklahoma Press, Norman.

2013 *Native American Placenames of the Southwest*. University of Oklahoma Press, Norman.

Brinckerhoff, Sidney B.
1967 The Last Years of Spanish Arizona 1786–1821. *Arizona and the West* 9(1):5–20.
Brinckerhoff, Sidney B. and Odie B. Faulk
1965 *Lancers for the King: A Study of the Frontier Military System of Northern New Spain, with a Translation of the Royal Regulations of 1772*. Arizona Historical Foundation, Phoenix.
Bryan, K.
1925 Date of Channel Trenching (Arroyo Cutting) in the Arid Southwest. *Science* 62:338–344.
1940 Erosion in the Valleys of the Southwest. *New Mexico Quarterly* 10:227–232.
Bucareli Y Ursua, Antonio Maria
1781 Document Relating the Events of the 1776 Las Mesitas Battle between Capitan of the Presidio of Santa Cruz de Terrenate Presidio, Don Francisco Tovar, and the Apache by Antonio Maria Bucareli y Ursua. Antonio Maria Bucarelli y Ursua to Jose de Galvez, September 24, 1776, AGI, Guad 515, Reel 3; Bancroft Library microfilm, Berkeley.
Burrus, Ernest J.
1965 *Kino and the Cartography of Northwestern New Spain*. Arizona Pioneers' Historical Society, Tucson.
1971 Kino and Manje: Explorers of Sonora and Arizona. In Sources and Studies for the History of the Americas, Vol. 10. Jesuit Historical Institute, Rome and St. Louis.
Cañete Paez, Francisco Angel
2009 El brigadier. Empleo atípico en el generalato español de los siglos XVIII Y XIX. http://www.belt.es/expertos/HOME2_experto.asp?id=4518
Canoa Community
2006 Canoa Ranch Master Plan. Available at: https://webcms.pima.gov/UserFiles/Servers/Server_6/File/Recreation/Canoa%20Ranch/Canoa_Master_Plan_Report_052407.pdf
Calderón Quijano, José Antonio
1984 Historia de las Fortificaciones en Nueva España, 2nd edition. Gobierno del Estado de Veracruz and the Escuela de Estudios Hispano-Americanos, Madrid.
Carlos III (Real Hacienda)
1768 Ordenanzas de su majestad para el régimen, disciplina, subordinación y servivio de sus ejércitos. n.p., Madrid.
1772 Reglamento e Instrucción para los Presidios que se han de formar en la linea de la Nueva España.Archivo Franciscano, Universidad Nacional Autónoma de México, Mexico City.
Castetter, Edward F. and Willis H. Bell
1942 Pima and Papago Indian Agriculture. INTER-AMERICANA SERIES. University of New Mexico Press, Albuquerque.
Chardon, Roland
1980 The Elusive Spanish League: A Problem of Measurement in Sixteenth-Century New Spain. *The Hispanic American Historical Review* 60(2):294–302.
Cobos, Rubén
2003 A Dictionary of New Mexico & Southern Colorado Spanish. University of New Mexico Press, Albuquerque.
Cook, Edward R.
2000 Southwestern USA Drought Index Reconstruction. International Tree-Ring Data Bank. IGBP PAGES/World Data Center-A for Paleoclimatology Data Contribution Series #2000-053. NOAA/NGDC Paleoclimatology Program, Boulder, Colorado. ftp://ftp.ncdc.noaa.gov/pub/data/paleo/treering/reconstructions/swd_recon.txt
Corbalan, Pedro
1778 Informe sobre Sonora (report concerning Sonora). September 30. Alamos. AGN. Historia, Tomo 16.
Coues, Elliot
1900 *On the Trail of a Spanish Pioneer, etc.* 2 vols. American Explorer Series, III. Francis P. Harper, New York.
Cox, Jerry R. and Gary Thacker
1996 Revegetation of Abandoned Agricultural Fields in the Sonoran Desert. In *The Future of Arid Grasslands: Identifying Issues, Seeking Solutions*, edited by Barbara Tellman, Deborah M. Finch, Carl Edminster, and Robert Hamre, pp. 306-311. Proceedings RMRS-P-3, United States Department of Agriculture, Forest Service, Fort Collins, CO.
Croix, Teodoro de
1781 Croix to Gálvez, Arizpe, October 30, 1781, General Report of 1781, Dice que el Ynforme general ofrecido con fecha de 30 de Abril lo hara por partes. AGI, Guad., 253.
1780a Caballero de Croix, Arizpe, announcing establishment of Arizpe as his residence and capital. Jan. 12, 1780, Reel-frame 11:2; No. 782. Spanish Archives of New Mexico II, 1621–1821, New Mexico State Records Center and Archives, Santa Fe, New Mexico.
1780b Jun. 23, 1780. Extracto de Novedades

Ocurridas en las Provincias Ynternas de N. E. en los tiempos que se expresan. Arispe. AGI, Guad. 271, Bancroft Library microfilm.

Davidson, M. Oliver

1865 Report of Special Agent for the Papago. In *Report of the Commissioner of Indian Affairs for 1865*, pp. 131–136. August 12, 1865 report addressed to William P. Dole, Commissioner of Indian Affairs. Government Printing Office, Washington D.C.

Deaver, William L.

2007 *Archaeological Resources of the San Xavier Sand and Gravel Property: A Class III Inventory.* United Metro Materials, Inc., Environmental Permitting Support. Westland Resources, Inc. Tucson.

Denevan, William M.

1992 The Pristine Myth: The Landscape of the Americas in 1492. *The Annals of the Association of American Geographers* 82:426–443.

Di Peso, Charles C.

1953 *The Sobaipuri Indians of the Upper San Pedro River Valley, Southwestern Arizona.* Amerind Foundation Publication No. 6. Dragoon, Arizona.

Dobyns, Henry F.

1959 *Tubac Through Four Centuries: A Historical Resume and Analysis.* Prepared for the Arizona State Parks Board, March 15; reformatted by Tubac Presidio State Historical Park and revised, August 1995. Electronic document, http://parentseyes.arizona.edu/tubac/ index.html.

1976 *Spanish Colonial Tucson: A Demographic History.* The University of Arizona Press, Tucson.

1980 The study of Spanish Colonial Frontier Institutions. In *Spanish Colonial Frontier Research*, edited by Henry F. Dobyns, pp. 5–25. Spanish Borderlands Research No. 1. Center for Anthropological Studies, Albuquerque.

1981 *From Fire to Flood: Historic Human Destruction of Sonoran Desert Riverine Oases.* Ballena Press, Socorro, NM.

Dunne, Peter Masten

1957 *Juan Antonio Balthasar: Padre Visitor to the Sonora Frontier, 1744–1745.* Arizona Pioneers' Historical Society, Tucson.

Emory, William H.

1957a General Geological Features of the Country. Geological Reports of Doctor C. C. Parry and Assistant Arthur Schott. Notes by W. H. Emory, p. 1–100, In Emory, W. H. 1857. Report on the United States and Mexican Boundary Survey, Made Under the Direction of the Secretary of the Interior, By William H. Emory, Major First Cavalry, and United States Commissioner. Vol. 1. Part II. A. O. P. Nicholson Printer, Washington. (PDF downloaded September 11, 2013 from http://openlibrary.org/books/OL6903367M/Report_on_the_United_States_and_Mexican_boundary_survey).

1957b Report on the United States and Mexican Boundary Survey, Made Under the Direction of the Secretary of the Interior, By William H. Emory, Major First Cavalry, and United States Commissioner. Vol. 1. Washington, D.C., C. Wendell. (PDF at http://www.archive.org/details/reportonuniteds01integoog).

1957c Mexican Boundary Survey Part II: Geology and Paleontology. General Geological Features of the Country. Report on the United States and Mexican Boundary Survey, Made Under the Direction of the Secretary of the Interior, By William H. Emory, Major First Cavalry, and United States Commissioner. Vol. 1. Part II. A. O. P. Nicholson Printer, Washington. (PDF downloaded September 11, 2013, from http://openlibrary.org/books/OL6903367M/Report_on_the_United_States_and_Mexican_boundary_survey).

Ezell, Paul H.

1955 De Anza Letter Reveals Various Indian Problems. *Arizona Daily Star (Tucson)* 114, 24 February:55.

1966 Fages, Noticia de los captivos y captivas. Ronald L. Ives, ed., "Retracing the Route of the Fages Expedition of 1781," AW, Vol. 8: 49–70, 157–170.

Fernald, Alexander, Vincent Tidwell, José Rivera, Sylvia Rodríguez, Steven Guldan, Caitriana Steele, Carlos Ochoa, Brian Hurd, Marquita Ortiz, Kenneth Boykin, and Andres Cibils

2012 Modeling Sustainability of Water, Environment, Livelihood, and Culture in Traditional Irrigation Communities and Their Linked Watersheds. *Sustainability* 4:2998–3022.

Fireman, Janet R.

1977 *The Spanish Royal Corps of Engineers in the Western Borderlands: Instrument of Bourbon Reform, 1764–1815.* Arthur H. Clark, Glendale.

Flint, Richard, and Shirley Cushing Flint

2005 *Documents of the Coronado Expedition, 1539–1541: They Were Not Familiar with His*

Majesty nor Did They Wish to Be His Subjects. Southern Methodist University Press, Dallas.

García, Luis Navarro
1964 Don José Gálvez y la Camandancia General de las Provincias Internas del Norte de Nueva España. Prólogo de José Antonio Calderón Quijano. Publicaciones Universidad de Sevilla. Escuela de Estudios Hispanoamericanso, 148. Consejo Superior de Investigaciones Científicas, Sevilla.

Garate, Donald T.
1999 Who Named Arizona? The Basque Connection. *Journal of Arizona History* 40(l):53–82.

Garcia, Jesús M.
2016 Cármenes of Mexico: Andalusian Influences and Garden Traditions in the Sonoran Desert. Desert Leaf , December 2016. http://trendmag2.trendoffset.com/article/Sonoran+Sage/2640257/358255/article.html

Gerald, Rex E.
1968 Spanish Presidios of the Late Eighteenth Century in Northern New Spain. University of New Mexico Press, Albuquerque.

Gonzales, Ygnacio Elias
1821 Plat map and land title for San Jose de Sonoita Land Grant. U S. Court of Private Land Claims-Records. Arizona State Department of Library and Archives, University of Arizona Special Collections Microfilm MS 312:11, San Jose de Sonoita. University of Arizona, Tucson.

Graybill, Donald A., David A. Gregory, Gary S. Funkhouser, and Fred L. Nials
2004 Long-Term Streamflow Reconstructions, River Channel Morphology, and Aboriginal Irrigation Systems along the Salt and Gila Rivers. In *Environmental Change and Human Adaptation in the Ancient Southwest*, edited by Jeffrey S. Dean and David E. Doyel. University of Utah Press, Salt Lake City.

Hadley, Diana
2000 San Ignacio de la Canoa Land Grant and Canoa Ranch History/Timeline. *SMRC-Newsletter* 34(123):11–15. Southwestern Mission Research Center, Tucson.

Hamilton, Leonidas
1882 Border States of Mexico: Sonora, Sinaloa, Chihuahua, and Durango, With a General Sketch of the Republic of Mexico, and Lower California, Coahuila, New Leon and Tamaulipas. Chicago.

Hammond, George P.
1929 Pimería Alta after Kino's Time. *New Mexico Historical Review* 4(3):220–238.
1931 The Zúñiga Journal: Tucson to Santa Fe, the Opening of a Spanish Trade Route 1788–1795. *New Mexico Historical Review* 6(1): 40–65.

Hardwick, Michael
2007 *Spanish and Mexican California Presidios of the Frontier Line*: The California State Military Museum, http://www.militarymuseum.org/PresidiosoftheLine.html (accessed July 31, 2007).

Hastings, James Rodney
1961 People of Reason and Others: The Colonization of Sonora to 1767. *Arizona and the West* 3(4):321–340.

Hastings, James Rodney and Raymond M. Turner
1965 *The Changing Mile: An Ecological Study of Vegetation Changes with Time in the Lower Mile of an Arid and Semiarid Region*. The University of Arizona Press, Tucson.

Heintzelman, Samuel Peter
1980 Samuel Peter Heintzelman and the Sonora Exploring and Mining Company, edited by Diane North. University of Arizona Press, Tucson.

Hendrickson, Dean A., and W. L. Minckley
1984 Cienegas—Vanishing Climax Communities of the American Southwest. *Desert Plants* 6(3):131–175.

Herford, Richard and Julio L. Betancourt
2009 Historic Geomorphology of the Lower San Pedro River: Archival and physical Evidence. In *Ecology and Conservation of the San Pedro River*, edited by Juliet C. Stromberg and Barbara Tellman, pp. 232–250. The University of Arizona Press, Tucson.

Hodge, Frederick Webb (editor)
1990 The Narrative of Alvar Nunez Cabeza de Vaca. In *Spanish Explorers in the Southern United States 1528–1543*, pp. 1–123. Texas State Historical Association, Austin.

Holterman, Jack Jose
1956 Zuniga, Commandant of Tucson. *Kiva* 22(1):1–4.

Howard, Janet G. and George Hearst
1881 Plat of the Preliminary Survey San Juan de las Boquillas y Nogales Private Land Claim papers, University of Arizona, Special Collections, AZ 232, Court of Private Land Claims, University of Arizona, Tucson.

Huckleberry, Gary, Sharon J. Lite, Gabrielle Katz, and Phillip Pearthree

2009 Fluvial Geomorphology. In *Ecology and Conservation of the San Pedro River*, edited by Juliet C. Stromberg and Barbara Tellman, pp. 251–267. The University of Arizona Press, Tucson.

Ilarione, da Bergamo, fra

2000 *Daily Life in Colonial Mexico: The Journey of Friar Ilarione de Bergamo, 1761–1768*. Translated and edited by Robert Ryal Miller, William J. Orr

Ives, Ronald L.

1966 Retracing the Route of the Fages Expedition of 1781. Arizona and the West 8:49–70, 157–70.

Jackson, Robert H.

1982 Demographic and Social Change in Northwestern New Spain: A Comparative Analysis of the Pimeria Alta and Baja California Missions. Unpublished Master's Thesis, University of Arizona, Tucson.

1999 *Race, Caste, and Status: Indians in Colonial Spanish America*. University of New Mexico Press, Albuquerque.

Karns, Harry J.

1954 *Luz de Tierra Incognita*. Arizona Silhouettes, Tucson.

Kessell, John L.

1965 Father Eixarch and the Visitation at Tumacácori, May 12, 1775. *Kiva* 30(3):77–81.

1966 The Puzzling Presidio San Phelipe de Guevavi, Alias Terrenate. *New Mexico Historical Review* 41(1):21–46.

1970 *Mission of Sorrow: Jesuit Guevavi and the Pimas, 1691–1767*. University of Arizona Press, Tucson.

1976 *Friars, Soldiers, and Reformers: Hispanic Arizona and the Sonora Mission Frontier 1767–1856*. The University of Arizona Press, Tucson. http://www.nps.gov/history/history/online_books/kessell2/

Kessell, John L., and Fray Bartholome Ximeno

1964 San José de Tumacácori—1773: A Franciscan Reports from Arizona. *Arizona and the West* 6(4):303–312.

Kinnaird, Lawrence

1958 *The Frontiers of New Spain: Nicolas de Lafora's Description*. California: Quivira Society, Berkeley.

Kino, Eusebio Francisco

1699 [This document is believed to have been written somewhere between 1699 and 1710. The Editor has cited 1699 throughout the text for ease of reference.] Favores Celestiales de Jesús y de María Santísima y del gloriosísimo apóstol de las Indias, San Francisco Xavier, experimentados en las nuevas conquistas y nuevas conversiones del nuevo reino de la Nueva Navarra de esta América septentrional incognita y paso por tierra a la California, en treinta y cinco grados de altura, con su nuevo mapa cosmográfico de estas nuevas y dilatadas tierras, que, hasta ahora habían sido incógnitas, dedicados a la Real Majestad de Felipo V, muy católico rey y gran monarca de las Españas y de las Indias. Microfilm of original, Office of Ethnohistorical Research, Arizona State Museum, Tucson.

Kiple, Kenneth F. and Kriemhild Con Ornelas

2000 *The Cambridge World History of Food*. Cambridge University Press, Cambridge.

Lamberton, Ken

2011 *Dry River: Stories of Life, Death, and Redemption on the Santa Cruz*. The University of Arizona Press, Tucson.

Logan, Michael F.

2002 *The Lessening Stream: An Environmental History of the Santa Cruz River*. The University of Arizona Press, Tucson.

Long, Keith R.

1991 A Partial Glossary of Spanish Geological Terms Exclusive of Most Cognates. Open-File Report 91-0579. U.S. Department of the Interior U.S. Geological Survey. https://pubs.usgs.gov/of/1991/0579/report.pdf

Lumholtz, Karl

1912 *New Trails in Mexico*. C. Scribner's Sons, New York.

2001 In 1780, Geronimo de la Rocha visited the Tucson Presidio. *Archaeology Southwest Newsletter* 15(2):14, Desert Archaeology, Tucson.

Machuca, Bernardo de Vargas

1892 [1599] *The Second Book of Milicia y Descripción de las Indias published in Madrid in 1599 by Bernardo de Vargas Machuca*, partial translation made by Richard Flint and Shirley Cushing Flint 1997, from the 1892 edition published in Madrid by Librería de Victoriano Suárez.

Madoz, Pascual

1847 Diccionario geográfico-estadístico-histórico de España y sus posesiones de Ultramar

Ultramar, Tomo IX. Tipográfico-Literario Universal, Madrid.

Mascaro, Manuel Agustín

1780 "Plano general de la mision y pueblo de Arispe, que S. M. en sus reales instrucciones destina para capital de las provincias internas de Nueva España, situado à los 30° y 30' de lat. y 260° y 10' de lon. boreal de la latitud de Tenerife." Dat. Arispe, 12 Sept., 1780; drawn by Manuel Agustin Mascaro, on a scale of 90 varas, or 40 toises, to an inch. 12 Sept., 1780.

McCarty, Kieran

1976 *Desert Documentary: The Spanish Years, 1767–1821*. Arizona Historical Society, Tucson.

Meyer, Michael

1984 *Water in the Hispanic Southwest*. University of Arizona Press, Tucson.

Moorhead, Max L.

1968 *The Apache Frontier: Jacobo Ugarte and Spanish-Indian Relations in Northern New Spain, 1769–1791*. University of Oklahoma Press, Norman.

1974 Rebuilding the Presidio of Santa Fe, 1789–1791. *New Mexico Historical Review* 49(2): 123–142.

1975 *The Presidio: Bastion of the Spanish Borderlands*. University of Oklahoma Press, Norman.

Nabhan, Gary Paul

1985 *Gathering the Desert*. The University of Arizona Press, Tucson.

Nassereddin, M. T.

1967 Hydrogeological Analysis of Groundwater Flow in Sonoita Creek Basin, Santa Cruz County, Arizona. Unpublished Master's Thesis, Department of Geology, University of Arizona, Tucson.

National Park Service

2007 Los Santos Ángeles de Guevavi. Electronic document, http://www.nps.gov/tuma/historyculture/guevavi.htm, accessed January 5, 2007.

Naylor, Thomas, and Charles Polzer

1986 The Presidio and Militia on the Northern Frontier of New Spain, 1570–1700, Volume 1. University of Arizona Press, Tucson.

1988 Pedro de Rivera and the Military Regulations of Northern New Spain 1724–1729. University of Arizona Press, Tucson.

Navarro García, Luis

1964 Don José de Gálvez y la Comandancia General de las Provincias Internas del Norte de Nueva España. Escuela de Estudios Hispano-Americanos de Sevilla, Sevilla.

Noonan, Gerald R.

2011 Fuelwood Cutting in the San Pedro River Valley. A stack of wood 119 miles long by 4 feet wide and 4 feet high. 4 p. Science Quest Technical Paper 3. (PDF at http://sciencequest.webplus.net/noonan%20san%20pedro%20river%20papers.html).

2012 Myth Busting along the Upper San Pedro River. Friends of the San Pedro River Roundup, pp. 9–15. Accessed electronically October 2, 2013, www.sanpedroriver.org/RiverRoundup_Feb_2012.pdf

Oblasser, Bonaventure

1931 Carnacion Tells Her Tale. *Arizona Historical Review* 3(4):97–98.

O'Conor, Hugo

1775 August 22, 1775, Certification of the site of the presidio of Santa Cruz, AGN, PI, 88.

O'Conor, Hugo, edited and translated by Donald C. Cutter

1994 *The Defenses of Northern New Spain: Hugo O'Conor's Report to Teodore de Croix, July 22, 1777*. Southern Methodist University Press, Dallas.

Parsons, James J.

1962 The acorn-hog economy of the oak woodlands of southwestern Spain. *Geographical Review* 52: 211–35.

Pennington, Campbell W.

1979 *Vocabulario en la Lengua Nevome, The Pima Bajo of Central Sonora, Mexico, Volume II*. University of Utah Press, Salt Lake City.

1980 *The Pima Bajo of Central Sonora, Mexico, Volume I*. University of Utah Press, Salt Lake City.

Polzer, Charles W. S. J. and Thomas E. Sheridan

1997 *The Presidio and Militia on the Northern Frontier of New Spain: A Documentary History, Volume Two, Part One*. University of Arizona Press, Tucson.

Powell, Philip Wayne

1952 Soldiers, Indians and Silver: North America's First Frontier War, 1559–1600. University of California Press, Berkeley.

1977 Mexico's Miguel Caldera: The Taming of America's first Frontier (1548–1597). University of Arizona Press, Tucson.

1982 Genesis of the Frontier Presidio in North America. Western Historical Quarterly, 13(2):125–142.

Pradeau, Alberto Francisco and Robert R. Rasmussen
1980 *Rudo Ensayo: A Description of Sonora and Arizona in 1764, by Juan Nentvig, S. J.*, University of Arizona Press, Tucson. Also available on line: http://www.library.arizona.edu/exhibits/swetc/rudo/front.1_div.1.html

Priestley, Herbert Ingram
1916 *José de Gálvez: Visitor General of New Spain (1765–1771)*. University of California Press, Berkeley.

Real Academia Española
1990 [1726–1739] Diccionario de Autoridades. Editorial Gredos, Madrid. (Facsimile reissue of 1726–1739 edition published by F. del Hierro, Madrid, under the title: Diccionario de la lengua castellana.)

Reff, Daniel T., Maureen Ahern, and Richard K. Danford (translators)
1999 *Perez de Ribas, History of the Triumphs of Our Holy Faith Amongst the Most Barbarous and Fierce Peoples of the New World*. University of Arizona Press, Tucson.

Reinhartz, Dennis, and Gerald D. Saxon
2005 *Mapping and Empire: Soldier-Engineers on the Southwestern Frontier*. The University of Texas Press, Austin. http://books.google.com/books?id=MRTUAAAAQBAJ&pg=PT115&lpg=PT115&dq=Ger%C3%B3nimo+de+la+Rocha+y+Figueroa&source=bl&ots=DTgrHZ-GDP&sig=uW8CmzpnBMwXLBtp2jFR7Qqh288&hl=en&sa=X&ei=kJE_Uv_3GPGEygGnx4HQBA&ved=0CEQQ6AEwAw#v=onepage&q=Ger%C3%B3nimo%20de%20la%20Rocha%20y%20Figueroa&f=false

Reyes, Antonio de los
1772 Del Estado Actual de las Missiones que en la Gubernacion de Sonora Administian los Padres del Colegio de Propaganda Fide de la Santa Cruz de Queretaro. The State of Sonora Provinces by the MRP Fr. Antonio Reyes, on April 20, 1772, Santa Cruz de Queretaro, letter K, leg. 14, no. 18.

Ríos, Mrs. Vincent
1959 Jan. 26, 1959. Interview. MS in files of Henry Dobyns.

Rivera, José A.
1999 "Water Democracies on the Upper Rio Grande, 1598–1998." In *Rio Grande Ecosystems: Linking Land, Water, and People*, edited by Deborah M.Finch, Jeffrey C. Whitney, Jeffrey F. Kelly, Samuel R Loftin, pp. 20–28. USDA Rocky Mountain Research Station, Ogden.

2006 "El Acceso Al Agua En La Historia De América" (Sevilla, España del 17 AL 21 DE JULIO DEL 2006). 52nd Congresa Internacional de Americanistas, Sevilla. Compilado por los organizadores del Simposio: Memorias *in extenso* del Simposio CIEN 06 Jacinta Palerm y Rolando García Blanco. Colegio de Postgraduados, México City. http://jacintapalerm.hostei.com/ICA_Sevilla_Rivera.pdf

Roca, Paul M.
1967 *Paths of the Padres through Sonora*. Arizona Pioneers' Historical Society. Tucson.

Rocha y Figueroa, Gerónimo de la
1780a *Mapa de la Frontera de Sonora para el establecimiento de la linea de presidios*. Woodbridge, CT: 2003. Microfilm, Reel 55 of 105. Manuscript No. Add. 17661a. Original in British Library, London.

1780b Diario de los reconocimientos hechos en la frontera de la provincia de Sonora en consecuencia de la superior orden del 19 de abril del presente año del señor comandante general de las provincias internas de Nueva España por el teniente de infantería e ingeniero extraordinario de los reales ejércitos Don Gerónimo de la Rocha y Figueroa. (Diary of the facts made in the frontier of the Sonoran province under the orders of the general commander of the Provincias Internas of New Spain... by the engineer of the royal armies Geronimo de la Rocha y Figueroa. Dated April 19th of 1780.) Manuscript obtained from Houghton Library, Harvard University, Cambridge, MA.

1780c Diario y Derrota de los reconocim.[tos] executados en las Frontera de la Provincia de Sonora para el Establecim.[to] del Presidio de Fronteras y translación del de Santa Cruz en virtud de la Orn. Superior de Sor Comand.[te] Gral de las Prov.[s] internas de N. E. el Mariscal de Campo cavallerro De Croix por el teniente de Ynfanteria e Yngeniero extradorinario de los R.[s] Exercitos d.[n] Geronimo de la Rocha y Figueroa. 69 page manuscript MS Sparks 98 Papeles varios de America vol. 7, no. 3, obtained from Houghton Library, Harvard University, Cambridge, MA.

1784 *Mapa del Terreno que ha de vatir la Expedición que deve executarse contra los Apaches Gileños, March 18, 1784*. AGI location: Gobierno, Audiencia de Guadalajara, 103-5-4. Newberry Library Map Photo Spain AGI 103-5-4.

Rodríguez, Sylvia
2006 *Acequia: Water Sharing, Sanctity, and Place.* School for Advanced Research Press, Santa Fe.

Roehner, Bertrand M.
1997 Jesuits and the State: A Comparative Study of their Expulsions (1590–1990). *Religion* 27:165–182.

Roskruge, George J.
1893 Official Map of Pima County, Arizona, 1893. Catalogue number: la000006. Library of Congress, Washington D.C. http://hdl.loc.gov/loc.gmd/g4333p.la000006.

Santiago, Mark
1994 *The Red Captain: The life of Hugo O'Conor, Commandant Inspector of the Interior Provinces of New Spain.* The Arizona Historical Society Museum Monograph No. 9. The Arizona Historical Society, Tucson.

Sanz-Sánchez, Israel
2016 Second person forms of address in New Mexican Spanish, 1687–1936. In *Forms of Address in the Spanish of the Americas,* edited by María Irene Moyna, and Susana Rivera-Mills, pp. 63–85. John Benjamins Publishing Company, Amsterdam and Philadelphia.

Seymour, Deni J.
1989 The Dynamics of Sobaipuri Settlement in the Eastern Pimeria Alta. *Journal of the Southwest* 31(2):205–222.

1990 Sobaipuri-Pima Settlement along the Upper San Pedro River: A Thematic Survey. Report submitted to the Bureau of Land Management. Sierra Vista Office. On file at the Arizona State Museum, Tucson.

1993 Piman Settlement Survey in the Middle Santa Cruz River Valley, Santa Cruz County, Arizona. Report submitted to Arizona State Parks in fulfillment of survey and planning grant contract requirements. On file at the Arizona State Museum, Tucson.

1997 Finding History in the Archaeological Record: The Upper Piman Settlement of Guevavi. *Kiva* 62(3):245–260.

2003 Sobaipuri-Pima Occupation in the Upper San Pedro Valley: San Pablo de Quiburi. *New Mexico Historical Review* 78(2):147–166.

2007 A Syndetic Approach to Identification of the Historic Mission Site of San Cayetano Del Tumacácori. *International Journal of Historical Archaeology 11(3):269–296.*

2008 Despoblado or Athapaskan Heartland: A Methodological Perspective on Ancestral Apache Landscape Use in the Safford Area. Chapter 5 in *Crossroads of the Southwest: Culture, Ethnicity, and Migration in Arizona's Safford Basin*, pp. 121–162, edited by David E. Purcell, Cambridge Scholars Press, New York.

2009a Evaluating Eyewitness Accounts of Native Peoples along the Coronado Trail from the International Border to Cibola. *New Mexico Historical Review* 84(3):399–435.

2009b Beyond Married, Buried, And Baptized: Exposing Historical Discontinuities in an Engendered Sobaípuri-O'odham Household. Chapter 12 *Engendering Households in the Prehistoric Southwest*, edited by Barbara Roth, pp. 229–259. University of Arizona Press, Tucson.

2009c Father Kino's 'Neat Little House and Church' at Guevavi. *Journal of the Southwest* 51(2):285–316.

2011a *Where the Earth and Sky Are Sewn Together: Sobaípuri-O'odham Contexts of Contact and Colonialism.* University of Utah Press, Salt Lake City.

2011b 1762 on the San Pedro: Reevaluating Sobaípuri-O'odham Abandonment and New Apache Raiding Corridors. *Journal of Arizona History* 52(2):169–188.

2011c Data Recovery on Sobaipuri and Spanish Colonial Sites Along the Middle and Lower San Pedro River on Bureau of Land Management Lands. Report submitted to the Bureau of Land Management in fulfillment of Permit No. AZ-000455. On file at the Bureau of Land Management and Arizona State Museum, Tucson.

2011d Dating the Sobaípuri: A Case Study in Chronology Building and Archaeological Interpretation. *Old Pueblo Archaeology Bulletin* 67:1–13.

2012a Introduction to "From the Land of Ever Winter to the American Southwest." In *From the Land of Ever Winter to the American Southwest: Athapaskan Migrations, Mobility, and Ethnogenesis*, edited by Deni J. Seymour, pp. 1–19. University of Utah Press, Salt Lake City.

2012b SANTA CRUZ RIVER: The Origin of a Place Name. *Journal of Arizona History* 53(1): 81–88.

2012c "Big Trips" and Historic Apache Movement and Interaction: Models for Early Athapaskan Migrations. Chapter 17 in *From the Land of Ever Winter to the American Southwest: Athapaskan Migrations, Mobility, and Ethnogenesis*, edited by Deni J. Seymour, pp. 377–409. University of Utah Press, Salt Lake City.

2012d Gateways for Athabascan Migration to the American Southwest. *Plains Anthropologist* 57(222):9–21.

2012e When Data Speak Back: Resolving Source Conflict in Apache Residential and Fire-Making Behavior. *International Journal of Historical Archaeology* 16(4):828–849.

2012f An Ethno-Geographic Evaluation of the Santa Cruz River Pima and Their Principle Great Settlement of San Xavier del Bac. Manuscript on file with the author.

2013a Platform Cave-Cache Encampments: Implications for Mobility Strategies and the Earliest Athabascans. *Journal of Field Archaeology* 38(2):161–172.

2013b The Sobaipuri-O'odham Presence at Guevavi Mission. *Arizona Archaeological Council Newsletter* 37(4):7–15.

2014 *A Fateful Day in 1698: The Remarkable Sobaípuri O'odham Victory over the Apaches and Their Allies*. University of Utah Press, Salt Lake City.

2015a Behavioral Assessment of a Pompeii-Like Event and Its Battlefield Signature. In *Explorations in Behavioral Archaeology*, edited by William H. Walker and James M. Skibo, pp.8–21. University of Utah Press, Salt Lake City.

2015b Sobaipuri-O'odham, Sonoita Creek Spanish Colonial Period Village Identified. *Arizona Archaeological Council Newsletter* 39(1):45-55

2017a (editor) *Fierce and Indomitable: The Protohistoric Non-Pueblo World*. University of Utah Press, Salt Lake City.

2017b Three Sisters Site: An Ancestral Chokonen Apache Encampment in the Dragoon Mountains. In *Fierce and Indomitable: The Protohistoric Non-Pueblo World*, edited by Deni J. Seymour, pp. 222–239. University of Utah Press, Salt Lake City.

2019a San Xavier del Wa:k's Late Eighteenth Century Fortified Village Revealed In Early Imagery and Texts. *Kiva* 85(2):161–165.

2019b Finding Father Eusebio Kino's San Xavier del Bac. Forthcoming in *International Journal of Historical Archaeology.*

Seymour, Deni J. and the Arizona Archaeological Society

2010 Tubac Presidio and The Poston-Territory Houses (AZ DD:8:252, ASM) On The Ellinor Parcel: Working Together To Preserve Tubac's Past. Report prepared to conclude excavations. On file at the Arizona State Museum, Tucson.

Seymour, Deni J. and Ron Stewart

2017 Naming Arizona's San Pedro River. *Journal of Arizona History*. 58(1):89–98.

Sheridan, Thomas E.

1999 *Empires of Sand: The Seri Indians and the Struggle for Spanish Sonora 1645–1803*. The University of Arizona Press, Tucson.

2004 Historic Resource Study, Tumacacori National Historical Park. https://www.nps.gov/parkhistory/online_books/tuma/hrs/index.htm

2006 *Landscapes of Fraud: Mission Tumacacori, the Baca Float, and the Betrayal of the O'odham*. University of Arizona Press, Tucson.

Silver Belt, A. P.

1931 Last of Indian Braves Tell Story Out of Rich Long Life. 1 April.

Smith, Fay Jackson, John L. Kessell, and Francis J. Fox, S. J.

1966 Father Kino in Arizona. Arizona Historical Foundation, Phoenix.

Socies, Bartolome

1797 Socies to Father Sebastián Ramis, San Xavier del Bac, March 20, 1797, Civezza Collection Miscellaneous. University of Arizona microfilm collection, Tucson.

Spicer, Edward H.

1981 [1962] *Cycles of Conquest: The Impact of Spain, Mexico, and the United States on the Indians of the Southwest, 1533–1960*. University of Arizona Press, Tucson.

Stern, Peter and Robert Jackson

1988 Vagabundaje and Settlement Patterns in Colonial Northern Sonora *The Americas* 44(4):461–481.

Stromberg, J. C.

1998 Dynamics of Fremont cottonwood (Populus fremontii) and saltcedar (Tamarix chinensis) populations along the San Pedro River, Arizona. *Journal of Arid Environments* 40: 133–155.

Stromberg, Juliet C. and Barbara Tellman
2009a Summary—Weaving the Threads Together. In *Ecology and Conservation of the San Pedro River*, edited by Juliet C. Stromberg and Barbara Tellman, pp. 419–428. The University of Arizona Press, Tucson.
2009b Introduction. In *Ecology and Conservation of the San Pedro River*, edited by Juliet C. Stromberg and Barbara Tellman, pp. 1–10. The University of Arizona Press, Tucson.
Studnicki-Gizbert, Daviken and David Schecter
2010 The Environmental Dynamics of a Colonial Fuel-Rush: Silver Mining and Deforestation in New Spain, 1522 to 1810. *Environmental History* 15(1):94–119.
Tellman, Barbara and Diana Hadley
2006 *Crossing Boundaries: An Environmental History of the Upper San Pedro River Watershed.* University of Arizona, Tucson.
Tellman, Barbara and Gary Huckleberry
2009 The Land and its People. In *Ecology and Conservation of the San Pedro River*, edited by Juliet C. Stromberg and Barbara Tellman, pp. 217–231. The University of Arizona Press, Tucson.
Thomas, Alfred Barnaby
1932 *Forgotten Frontiers: A Story of the Spanish Indian Policy of Don Juan Bautista de Anza, Governor of New Mexico, 1777–1787.* University of Oklahoma Press, Norman.
1941 *Teodoro de Croix and the Northern Frontier of New Spain, 1776–1783.* University of Oklahoma Press, Norman.
Thompson, Raymond H.
2014 *A Jesuit Missionary in Eighteenth-Century Sonora: The Family Correspondence.* University of New Mexico Press, Albuquerque.
Treutlein, T. E.
1945 The Relation of Philip Segesser. *Mid-America* 27(3), n.s. 16(3):139–187.
1949 *Pferfferkorn's Description of Sonora: A Description of the Province.* University of New Mexico Press, Albuquerque.
1965 *Missionary in Sonora. The Travel Reports of Joseph Och, S. J.* California Historical Society, San Francisco.
Tucson Citizen
1930 Last of Sobaipuri Tribe Passes with "Red Evening"; Words Left to White Man: Toibio Aragon, 85, Laid to Rest Last Night at San Xavier Mission Which His Forefathers Built—Service Is Simple. Tucson Citizen 14 March.
1931 Soba Puris Once Ruled Tucson Area: Encarnacion Mamake, Only Survivor, Taken by Death. Tucson Citizen, 21 December.
Turner, R. M., Webb, R. H., Bowers, J. E. and Hastings, J. R.
2003 The Changing Mile Revisited. An Ecological Study of Vegetation Change with Time in the Lower Mile of an Arid and Semiarid Region. The University of Arizona Press, Tucson.
Underhill, Ruth M.
1936 Autobiography of a Papago Woman. Memoirs of the American Anthropological Association, No. 46. American Anthropological Association, Menasha, Wisconsin; and Kraus Reprint Co., New York.
1939 *Social Organization of the Papago Indians.* AMS Press, New York.
1969 *The Autobiography of a Papago Woman.* Memoirs of the American Anthropological Association, No. 46. American Anthropological Association, Menasha, Wisconsin; and Kraus Reprint Co., New York.
Urrutia y de las Casas, Joseph Ramón de
1766a Plano del Presidio de Tubac en la provincia de Sonora, situado en 32º y 3' de latitud boreal;" drawn by Joseph de Urrutia, on a scale of 48 toises to an inch. Shelfmark: Cartographic Items Additional MS. 17,662.h.
1766b Plano del Presidio de Terrenate, dependiente de la governación de Sonora, y situado en 31º y 35' minutos de latitud boreal;" drawn by Joseph de Urrutia, on a scale of 50 toises to an inch. Shelfmark: Cartographic Items Additional MS. 17,662.g.
1766c Plano del Presidio de San Felipe y Santiago de Janos, dependiente de la governación de la Nueva Vizcaya, situado en 31º y 18' de latitud boreal;" drawn by Joseph de Urrutia, on a scale of 50 toises to an inch: with a profil on a scale of 32½ Paris feet to an inch. Shelfmark: Cartographic Items Additional MS. 17,662.l.
1767d Plano del Presidio del Altar, en la provincia de Sonora; drawn by Joseph de Urrutia, on a scale of 48 toises to an inch. Shelfmark: Cartographic Items Additional MS. 17,662.e.
1766e Plano del Presidio de Fronteras, dependiente de la governación de Sonora, situado en 31º y 17' de latitud boreal;" drawn by Joseph Urrutia, on a scale of 50 toises to an inch. Shelfmark: Cartographic Items Additional MS. 17,662.f.

1767b Plano della villa de S. Miguel de Horcasitas, residencia del governador de la provincia de Sonora;" drawn by Joseph de Urrutia, on a scale of 48 toises to an inch. Shelfmark: Cartographic Items Additional MS. 17,662.d.

1769 Mapa, que comprende la Frontera, de los Dominios del Rey, en la America Septentrional. Library of Congress, Washington D.C.

1771 Mapa, que comprende la Frontera, de los Dominios del Rey, en la America Septentrional. Library of Congress, Washington D.C.

Van Orden, Jay and Mary Ellen Barnes

2014 A Painting Worth a Thousand Words Edward Zinns's The Tully and Ochoa Wagon Train Fight. *Journal of Arizona History*

Waters, Michael R. and C. Vance Haynes

2001 Late Quaternary arroyo formation and climate change in the American Southwest. *Geol.* 29:399–402.

Webb, Robert H., Julio L. Betancourt, Raymond M. Turner, and R. Roy Johnson

2014 *Requiem for the Santa Cruz: An Environmental History of an Arizona River.* University of Arizona Press, Tucson.

Webb, Robert H., S. A. Leake, and Raymond M. Turner

2007 *The Ribbon of Green: Change in Riparian Vegetation in the Southwestern.* University of Arizona Press, Tucson.

Weber, David J.

1992 *The Spanish Frontier in North America.* Yale University Press, New Haven and London.

2005 *Bárbaros: Spaniards and Their Savages in the Age of Enlightenment.* Yale University Press, New Haven.

Whitmore, Thomas M. and B. L. Turner II

2001 *Cultivated Landscapes of Middle America on the Eve of the Conquest.* Oxford University Press, New York.

Willey, Richard R.

1979 La Canoa: A Spanish Land Grant Lost and Found. *The Smoke Signal* No. 38. Tucson Corral of Westerners, Tucson.

Williams, Jack S.

1986 The Presidio of Santa Cruz de Terrenate: A Forgotten Fortress of Southern Arizona. *The Smoke Signal.* 47 and 48(combined issues):129–148. The Tucson Corral of the Westerners, Tucson.

1991 Architecture and defense on the military frontier of Arizona, 1752–1856. Unpublished PhD Dissertation, Department of Anthropology, University of Arizona, Tucson.

2004 The Evolution of the Presidio in Northern New Spain. *Historical Archaeology* 38(3): 6–23.

Wilson, John P.

1999 *Peoples of the Middle Gila: A Documentary History of the Pimas and Maricopas, 1500's–1945.* Researched and written for the Gila River Indian Community, Sacaton, Arizona. Electronic document: http://www.griccrmp.com/PDF%20Files/Peoples%20of%20the%20Middle%20Gila.pdf.

Worchester, Donald E.

1951 *Instructions for Governing the Interior Provinces of New Spain, 1786, by Bernardo de Galvez.* The Quivira Society, Berkeley.

Wozniak, Frank E.

1998 *Irrigation in the Rio Grande Valley, New Mexico: A Study and Annotated Bibliography of the Development of Irrigation Systems.* Rocky Mountain Research Station, Fort Collins, Colorado.

Wyllys, R. K.

1931 Padre Luís Velarde's Relacíon of Pimería Alta, 1716. *New Mexico Historical Review* 6(2):111–157.

Ximeno, Bartolomé

1773 Ximeno to Guardian, Tumacácori, March 5, 1773. Ximeno's report in the Civezza Collection Miscellaneous. University of Arizona, Microfilm, Tucson.

Zuniga, José de

1795 Diario y estado de fuerza de la expedición. Tupson, Archivo General De Indias, Sevilla 103-5-11. Diario de José de Zúñiga. Bancroft Library, University of California, Berkeley.

Index